EXAMINING
HEISEI JAPAN

EXAMINING HEISEI JAPAN

DIPLOMACY AND SECURITY

Supervised by
KITAOKA Shinichi

KOKUBUN Ryosei

NAKANISHI Hiroshi

SHIRAISHI Takashi

TANAKA Akihiko

VOL. I

Japan Publishing Industry Foundation for Culture

Publisher's Note
This book follows the Hepburn system of romanization, with long vowels indicated by macrons. An exception has been made for the authors' names. The tradition of placing the family name first has been followed for Japanese, Chinese, and Korean names. All of the essays featured in this compilation are from academic sources and were written between the years 1992 and 2019. Each essay has been revised and updated to some degree for inclusion in this publication.

Examining Heisei Japan: Diplomacy and Security, Vol. I
Supervised by Kitaoka Shinichi.
Kokubun Ryosei, Nakanishi Hiroshi, Shiraishi Takashi, Tanaka Akihiko.

Published by
Japan Publishing Industry Foundation for Culture (JPIC)
2-2-30 Kanda-Jinbocho, Chiyoda-ku, Tokyo 101-0051, Japan

First edition: August 2021

This publication is the result of a collaborative effort between the Japan Institute of International Affairs (JIIA) and Japan Publishing Industry Foundation for Culture (JPIC).

Book design: Miki Kazuhiko, Ampersand Works

Printed in Japan
ISBN 978-4-86658-116-3
https://www.jpic.or.jp/

CONTENTS

Part II 11 September 2001, Ramifications   85

FOREWORD

This volume is based on a suggestion made by Dr. Kitaoka Shinichi, president of the Japan International Cooperation Agency (JICA) and a member of the steering committee for the territory, sovereignty, and history studies project that the Japan Institute of International Affairs (JIIA) undertook under a contract with the Japanese government. Compiled here under Dr. Kitaoka's direction and editing are English articles published during the Heisei years (1989–2019) by leading scholars engaged in research on Japan's foreign and security policies. This publication is intended, through these articles, to reexamine the features characterizing the Heisei era that extended over three decades of postwar Japanese history, and to make their insights more broadly available to the world.

The Heisei era, which started in 1989, was a period of turmoil both in Japan and internationally, contrary to the meaning of its name. Up until its end in 2019, the era was consistently characterized by unpredictability. By examining the writings of the leading scholars of the time, we can come to know how they regarded the era they lived through and, by sharing their thoughts in English with a global readership, we can provide important insights to better understand the Heisei era and to chart Japan's future path as we move forward in the Reiwa era.

While this volume's focus is on foreign and security policies, we also plan to produce subsequent volumes on the Heisei era focusing on other areas such as politics and economics.

In closing, I would like to express my profound gratitude to JICA president Dr. Kitaoka who suggested this program and guided it through to fruition; the outstanding scholars who supported the project's objective and so generously donated their time, insights, and writings; and all those who contributed so much to make this publication possible.

Sasae Kenichiro
President, JIIA
July 2021

Preface—General Remarks
The Heisei Era in Retrospect: Japan's Diplomacy and Security

Kitaoka Shinichi

The Japanese imperial era of Heisei began in January 1989—when Emperor Hirohito (posthumously Emperor Shōwa) passed away and Crown Prince Akihito ascended to the imperial throne—and ended in May 2019—when Emperor Akihito (now known as Emperor Heisei) abdicated and Crown Prince Naruhito ascended to the throne.

In the same year, 1989, Japan ushered in the Heisei era, the Cold War came to an end. The Berlin Wall fell in November 1989, and US president George H.W. Bush and Soviet general secretary Mikhail Gorbachev met off Malta in December of that year, declaring "the Cold War is over."

The Malta Summit was followed by a spate of events of global and historic magnitude: the reunification of East and West Germany in November 1990; the dissolution of the Soviet Union in December 1991; major changes in political systems in many Eastern European countries prior to, or in the wake of, the collapse of Soviet rule; and the emergence of all the former republics of the USSR as independent countries.

The end of the Heisei era coincided with the outbreak of the novel coronavirus disease, COVID-19. The epidemic developed into a pandemic, raging across the globe to the extent that the world began suffering from the worst economic crisis since the Great Depression of 1929. As a result, the global divide has widened further.

The world thus changed quite a lot during the 30-year-long Heisei era. In global terms, this era can be divided into two periods, which are defined by two major events.

One of them was the series of coordinated terrorist attacks against the United States on 11 September 2001. From then on, the United States got more deeply involved in Middle Eastern affairs. The other major event was the rise of China, which became notably apparent in and around 2008. Before long, its rise began provoking the antipathy of the United States. The US antagonism culminated with the beginning of a fierce US-China confrontation when Donald Trump won the US presidential election in 2016.

This book offers an opportunity to witness anew how Japan's foreign and security policy evolved during the Heisei era by giving a new focus on the era's relevant discourse. This preface is a new insertion at the outset of the book to provide an overview, in three timelines, of the aforementioned changes in the international community and Japan's responses to each of them.

I. The End of the Cold War

In the years following the end of the Cold War, there was a surge in regional conflicts. The Cold War, which was a confrontation between the US-led Western bloc and the USSR-led Eastern bloc, constituted a kind of international order where the two superpowers kept control over their respective allies. But the Cold War–era order maintained by superpower influence collapsed, only to be superseded by an increase in conflicts over regional order.

One such case was the series of ethnic conflicts seeking separation or independence from the multiethnic social republic of Yugoslavia. The Yugoslav Wars erupted in 1991, and some conflicts lasted until 2001.

What had a greater impact on the world, and on Japan in particular, was Iraq's annexation of Kuwait in August 1990. This was partially caused by the superpowers loosening control in this region. The world unanimously condemned Iraq's invasion of Kuwait. Then, a multinational coalition force was formed to liberate Kuwait.

Of all the world's leading countries, Japan was the most dependent on the Persian Gulf for oil imports. It made a massive donation of US$13 billion to the multinational coalition forces fighting to expel Iraqi troops from Kuwait. Nonetheless, it neither deployed Japan Self-Defense Forces (JSDF) troops to join combat operations against Iraq nor provided logistic support or medical cooperation to the coalition forces. After years of strictly rejecting the idea of dispatching JSDF members abroad, the Japanese government was unable to readily change this long-standing policy. Following Kuwait's liberation from Iraq, Japan was not one of the countries it named in a US newspaper advertisement thanking them for helping it. However, Japan was appreciated for dispatching minesweepers to the gulf after the Gulf War ended. Many Japanese learned from the war how important it is to confront a crisis by facing the danger together.

Until then, Japan benefited the most from the Cold War. The security of the country was ensured by the United States because Japan was geographically located to contain the Soviet Union. In those days, Japan continued to be thanked by the United States just for hosting US military bases on its soil. Against this background, Japan was able to concentrate on the acceleration of economic growth while remaining lightly armed.

However, the Gulf War brought a turning point for Japan, with voices growing at home and abroad for it to begin contributing to international missions. An increasing number of Japanese people, learning from Japan's failure to join forces with other countries during the Gulf War, argued that the country ought to at least participate in peacekeeping missions sanctioned by the United Nations. In 1992, Japan enacted the Law Concerning Cooperation for United Nations Peacekeeping Operations and Other Operations, also known as the UN Peace Cooperation Law. Later in the year, Japan dispatched JSDF personnel to Cambodia to serve as members of the United Nations Transitional Authority in Cambodia (UNTAC). Japan has since increased its participation in international peacekeeping activities little by little.

In the meantime, signs of democratization in parts of Asia had already emerged ahead of the end of the Cold War. But, in June 1989, China mobilized the Chinese People's Liberation Army to crack down on pro-democracy protests in the country. The scenes of protesters being crushed by troops were broadcast globally, shocking the rest of the world, triggering a salvo of denunciations, and prompting many countries to impose sanctions on China.

However, Japan, arguing that China's isolation would not be good for the international community, insisted on the importance of engagement with China. In 1992, the Japanese administration of then prime minister Miyazawa Kiichi even went ahead with plans for the emperor and empress to visit China.

China welcomed Japan's policies toward it—for tactical reasons. In 1992, months prior to the emperor's visit to China, it adopted the Law on the Territorial Sea and the Contiguous Zone, which stipulates that the Senkaku Islands are within its territory even though the East China Sea islands are an inherent part of Japan's territory. Likewise, China did not ease its criticism of Japan over historical issues, as in the cases of criticism of Japanese prime ministers for their visits to Tokyo's Yasukuni Shrine that is dedicated to the Japanese war dead.

North Korea (formally known as the Democratic People's Republic of Korea) was one of the countries that the Cold War's end affected in a different manner than it did China. North Korea decided to develop nuclear weapons in order to ensure its security now that it became impossible to receive the support of the Soviet Union. In 1993 North Korea's nuclear weapon development program became known to the rest of the world. Consequently, the Far East was in grave crisis. Then, former US president Jimmy Carter traveled to Pyongyang in June 1994, winning the North's promise to freeze its nuclear program in exchange for receiving shipments of fuel oil from the United States, Japan, South Korea, and other countries. The crisis in the Far East was thus averted—for now.

The end of the Cold War led some people in Japan to argue that the Japan-US Security Treaty was no longer necessary, as the pact had been signed to counter the Soviet Union. Nonetheless, this debate came to an end in the face of the emergence of the North Korean nuclear crisis.

In the summer of 1994, the Liberal Democratic Party and its archrival, the Socialist Democratic Party—previously known as the Japan Socialist Party in English—formed a coalition, with the socialist leader Murayama Tomiichi becoming prime minister. Soon after assuming the post, Murayama, citing changes in the international situation, declared his support for both the JSDF and the Japan-US Security Treaty, discarding the socialists' decades-long policy of negating the existence of the JSDF and the security pact.

However, three US servicemen abducted and raped a girl in Okinawa Prefecture in September 1995, fanning protests in Japan against the presence of US military bases in the prefecture. In April 1996, US president Bill Clinton visited Japan and held a summit with Hashimoto Ryūtarō, who had succeeded Murayama as prime minister. They reaffirmed the Japan-US Security Treaty, confirming its importance to Japan and the United States as well as the region and the world. The two leaders agreed that the issue of US military bases in Okinawa should be addressed and resolved in that context. Nevertheless, as of 2021, no solution to the issue of relocating the US Marine Corps Air Station Futenma in Okinawa is yet in sight.

Around the same time, there was a new and important development regarding the Japan-US relationship—the establishment of the World Trade Organization (WTO) in 1995. Since the 1980s, Japan had come under a barrage of criticism from the United States for its persistent trade surpluses with the world's largest economy. The establishment of the WTO made it possible for Japan to seek rule-based solutions to trade disputes. However, Japan's economic strength at that time no longer made the United States feel as uneasy as it once did.

Meanwhile, there were three noteworthy diplomatic approaches that also characterized Japan's foreign policy in the 1990s. In brief, they were as follows:

First, Japan continued to increase its official development assistance (ODA) against the background that other major donor countries remained involved in regional conflicts, among other reasons. Japan consequently became the world's largest ODA provider in 1989 and from 1991 until 1998. In 1993, Japan launched the Tokyo International Conference on African Development (TICAD), expanding its diplomatic outreach to Africa. TICAD summits were initially held once every five years. Since 2013, such summits have taken place once every three years.

Second, in 1991, a South Korean woman became the first woman to give public testimony of her experience as a wartime comfort woman and demand Japanese apologies and compensation. This immediately developed into a major diplomatic issue between Japan and South Korea. In 1995, the administration of Prime Minister Murayama set up the Asian Women's Fund, delivering compensation, together with a letter of apology, to many former comfort women. However, the Japanese effort has left many dissatisfied in South Korea, to the extent that their anti-Japanese campaign has become extreme—the campaign is still ongoing.[1]

Third, when the Russian economy was in tatters in the 1990s, Japan made various approaches to help Mikhail Gorbachev and then Boris Yeltsin, the first president of the Russian Federation, through economic cooperation. Japan's ultimate aim was to use economic support as a lever for facilitating a solution to the issue of the Northern Territories. However, the territorial dispute between Tokyo and Moscow over the Russian-occupied islands off Japan's northernmost main island of Hokkaido remains unresolved.

II. 11 September 2001, Ramifications

Throughout the 1990s, the United States emerged as the overwhelmingly predominant power in the world, leading many people to expect to live in a US-led unipolar world. However, the United States came under concerted terrorist attacks in September 2001. Worldwide, almost all countries supported the United States. Holding Al-Qaeda responsible for the 11 September attacks, the US government decided to launch attacks on both

Al-Qaeda and the Taliban regime in Afghanistan that harbored the terrorist organization. Japan, backing the US decision, decided to dispatch Maritime Self-Defense Force (MSDF) vessels to the Indian Ocean to provide fuel and supplies to coalition ships.

In March 2003, the United States began attacking Iraq while accusing it of possessing weapons of mass destruction (WMD). However, the United States was unable to win the backing of the UN Security Council. Pointing to the lack of evidence regarding Iraq's WMD possession, Russia and China as well as France and Germany, then participating in the council as a nonpermanent member, opposed the US-led military intervention in Iraq.

In response to the concerted terrorist attacks on the United States, US president George W. Bush said, "This is a war." Nevertheless, it was not a conventional war. Rather, it was an act of terror and international crime. In a conventional war, when a sovereign state chooses to surrender, it means a victory for the other warring side. But the terrorists would not surrender. As a result, the ongoing war in Afghanistan, in which coalition forces have been fighting religious fundamentalists and terrorists, has lasted longer than the Vietnam War.

On the other hand, in Iraq, the coalition forces managed to topple the regime of Saddam Hussein. However, no stable order exists yet. Although the United States officially declared the Iraq War over in 2010, the Middle East subsequently witnessed the outbreak of a civil war in Syria and the formation of a caliphate by the Islamic State of Iraq and Syria (ISIS)—which is now renamed the Islamic State. The fallout from these crises in the Middle East has continued to plague the world.

Japan took two remarkable diplomatic steps around this time. One of them resulted in Japanese prime minister Koizumi Junichirō's surprise visit to North Korea, with which Japan even now has no diplomatic ties. In September 2002, he flew into the capital Pyongyang and held talks with its leader, Kim Jong-il, leading the North to acknowledge that some of its "individuals" had abducted Japanese nationals. The Japanese leader promised that Japan would go ahead with the normalization of diplomatic relations with North Korea should Pyongyang return all of the Japanese abductees to Japan and stop developing nuclear weapons and missiles.

The Koizumi-Kim agreement was coupled with the homecoming of five of the Japanese abductees. But Pyongyang then insisted there were no other surviving Japanese abductees in North Korea. Japan, for its part, demanded that the North make further efforts to locate the remaining Japanese abductees. However, the issue of these abductees left behind in North Korea remains unresolved.

As for North Korea's nuclear and ballistic missile development programs, which are discussed later, Pyongyang, while carrying out a series of missile tests, conducted a nuclear test in October 2006. The UN Security Council adopted a series of sanction resolutions in response to the nuclear test. However, the efforts on the part of the concerned countries to dissuade North Korea from antagonizing the world have not produced any positive outcomes. The North even now continues to proceed with nuclear missile development.

The other remarkable diplomatic step taken by Japan under the Koizumi administration was an initiative for reforming the UN Security Council. In and around 1990 when the Persian Gulf crisis erupted, Japan began looking forward to increasing its say in the international community. Taking advantage of the 60th anniversary of the United Nations in 2005, Japan joined hands with Germany, India, and Brazil to form the so-called Group of Four (G4) in 2004, setting out in earnest to fulfill their aspirations to become permanent members of the Security Council. The group aimed to strengthen the Security Council with the permanent presence of two powerful democracies, Japan and Germany, as well as the emerging democratic powers of India and Brazil. The group's campaign achieved considerable success, as more than 60% of the United Nations' membership supported Security Council reform proposals, including one to boost the number of the council's permanent member countries.

However, Prime Minister Koizumi continued to be at odds with China over certain issues, such as his visits to Yasukuni Shrine. Despite China's repeated protests, he refused to change his policies. China consequently began expressing its vehement opposition to the G4's Security Council reform proposals. Also, because the prime minister placed greater importance on Japan-US relations than on the United Nations, he was not enthusiastic enough to persuade US president George W. Bush to support the G4 initiative. As such, although the G4 submitted a draft resolution for Security Council reforms, its campaign ended up going nowhere in August 2005.

China's opposition to Japan's efforts to facilitate UN Security Council reforms showed that it remained adamant in its position on the issues regarding wartime history. To prevent a confrontation between Japan and China over history issues from escalating, the two countries set up the Japan-China Joint History Research Committee in 2006. The joint panel held a series of meetings that lasted until 2009, helping close the gap in historical perceptions between Japan and China to some extent, but these joint efforts came to an end with little significant impact on bilateral relations.

III. China Rising

The rise of China became conspicuous in 2008 when Beijing hosted the Olympic Games and the major US investment bank, the Lehman Brothers, collapsed, with the latter sending a shock wave across the world. Around that time, China stopped referring to freedom and democracy as universal values. At the same time, China gained self-confidence after leading the world in economic recovery in the aftermath of the global financial crisis induced by the failure of the US investment bank.

As early as 2001, Brazil, Russia, India, China, and South Africa became known as emerging economic powerhouses, to the extent that they were collectively referred to as BRICS. In 2008, the Group of 20 (G20) was institutionalized as a forum bringing together the leaders of the Group of Seven (G7), major democracies, and BRICS countries, as well as Indonesia, Australia, Turkey, Saudi Arabia, South Korea, the European Union, Mexico, and Argentina.

Within the G20 universe, China has made

the most remarkable economic development. China surpassed Japan as the world's second largest economy in nominal gross domestic product terms as early as 2010. Xi Jinping, who assumed the post of general secretary of the Chinese Communist Party in 2012, promised in 2013 that he would pursue "a great renaissance of the Chinese nation" (*zhonghua minzu weida fuxing*). Xi's pledge meant that China would no longer act on the maxim of the late leader Deng Xiaoping: "Keep a low profile and bide your time" (*taoguang yanghui*). In the same year, the new Chinese leader unveiled a global infrastructure development strategy named the Belt and Road Initiative (initially known as the One Belt, One Road Initiative). Also in 2013, Xi proposed the establishment of an Asian Infrastructure Investment Bank (AIIB)—which was inaugurated in 2014.

In June 2013, Xi held a summit with US president Barack Obama in California and said he believed that "the vast Pacific Ocean has enough space for the two large countries of China and the United States." What Xi floated during the talks with Obama was tantamount to the idea of partitioning the Pacific Ocean into spheres of influence. Back in 2007, a high-ranking Chinese navy officer made a similar suggestion in a meeting in Beijing with Admiral Timothy Keating, then commander of the US Pacific Command. Though belatedly, the Chinese president made a similar suggestion to his US counterpart.

In the South China Sea, China has territorial disputes with several neighboring countries. Nonetheless, it has taken unilateral action to reclaim islands and shoals there and build military bases and other permanent facilities. In 2014, the Philippines initiated arbitration proceedings at the Tribunal at the Permanent Court of Arbitration in The Hague against China's "nine-dash line," arguing that the Chinese territorial claim was unlawful. The international tribunal awarded a complete victory to the Philippines, but China dismissed the international ruling as "just a sheet of paper." Ever since, China has been accelerating its push to turn the South China Sea into a vast maritime fortress.

With regard to its relations with Japan, in

2008, China had a government vessel intrude into Japanese territorial waters around the Senkaku Islands in Okinawa Prefecture for the first time. In 2010, when the Japan Coast Guard arrested a Chinese fishing boat skipper on suspicion of intruding into Japan's territorial waters around the Senkakus, Beijing staged strong anti-Japanese rallies, while, in 2012, when the Japanese government nationalized the ownership of the islands, Beijing carried out a series of furious demonstrations against Japan.

In Japan, Prime Minister Abe Shinzō came to power for the second time, immediately laying the groundwork for a robust national defense policy. In 2013, his administration mapped out a national security strategy and integrated national security and foreign policies through the launch of the National Security Council (NSC) and the National Security Secretariat (NSS) that supports the NSC. Moreover, in 2014, the Abe administration had the Diet (parliament) approve Legislation for Peace and Security, which led to a partial revision of the government's decades-long constitutional interpretation, permitting Japan to exercise the right of collective self-defense and enabling JSDF to act together with US armed forces in areas around Japan.

The Abe administration also successfully spearheaded Pacific Rim countries' efforts to sign the Trans-Pacific Partnership (TPP) free trade agreement. Prime Minister Abe bore in mind that the TPP could be a measure to encircle China. President Trump withdrew the United States from the TPP in pursuit of his "America First" foreign policy approach. However, Japan then managed to get the 11 remaining member countries of the TPP to agree to the Comprehensive and Progressive Agreement for Trans-Pacific Partnership (CPTPP), dubbed TPP11.

Furthermore, Prime Minister Abe advocated for a Free and Open Indo-Pacific (FOIP) in 2016. The new term was used initially with the word "strategy" and later with the word "vision." Whatever it is called, it means a new geopolitical initiative to counter the expansion of China's influence.

As mentioned above, the increased wariness of the fast rise of China was behind Trump's victory in the 2016 presidential election. In the final years of the Obama administration, although the United States became increasingly cautious about Chinese espionage and cyberattacks against the US government and business corporations, it took no sufficient countermeasures. Trump directly targeted China and, especially since 2018 when US vice president Mike Pence delivered a speech on the Trump administration's policy toward China, the United States began coming up with a spate of policies that were evidently hostile to China. Then, the Trump administration, working with Japan, endorsed the FOIP initiative and began strengthening "Quad" cooperation among the United States, Japan, Australia, and India. As such, around the time the Heisei era was almost over, the US-China confrontation emerged as the new key determinant influencing international politics.

Meanwhile, the last years of the Heisei era witnessed a couple of breakthroughs in international cooperation.

In September 2015, the United Nations General Assembly adopted a set of Sustainable Development Goals (SDGs). The SDGs, superseding the Millennium Development Goals (MDGs) that had aimed, among other things, at eradicating extreme poverty in developing countries, consists of 17 goals toward the realization of a sustainable Earth through joint efforts by both developed and developing countries. Further, in December 2015, the international community agreed on the Paris Agreement in order to jointly tackle global warming.

It is ironic that the world saw Donald Trump, chanting the slogan "America First," elected US president just a year after the world reached a consensus on the urgent need for international cooperation. By the way, Trump was not the first leader to prioritize the national interests of his or her country—there have been and still are like-minded people in many other countries. The rise of such people reflects an increase in the number of people in many countries who are afraid that international cooperation poses a threat to their respective countries.

Such a conflict between the necessity of international cooperation and the pursuit of a national-interest-first approach has become more apparent since the outbreak of the novel coronavirus pandemic at the end of 2019. Now that Trump has been defeated in the 2020 US presidential election, we need to wait and see what direction his successor, Joe Biden, is actually heading toward. For its part, Japan has to refine and define its foreign policy and national strategy against such a backdrop. To discern what will happen next, it is useful to look back at the proposals and insights of the Heisei era.

Notes

1. Among the 237 women who were recognized as former comfort women by the South Korean government, more than 60 received compensation with a letter of apology from the prime minister of Japan. However, more than 140 of the women rejected the offer. As of 2005, a total of 285 former comfort women in South Korea, Taiwan, and Indonesia have received compensation with a letter of apology.

Part
I

The End of the Cold War

I-(1) Opting for a Global Alliance

Kitaoka Shinichi

ABSTRACT Born in response to the Soviet threat, the Japan-US Security Treaty has endured despite voices arguing that the end of the Cold War has rendered it superfluous. The Security Treaty is important beyond its ability to meet external threats. In line with Article 2's commitment to contribute toward the further development of political and economic institutions grounded in freedom, the Treaty is a statement of the two countries' determination to work together for the maintenance and spread of their shared values and serves as a strong bond transcending the two countries' histories. As such, it is hoped the US-Japan alliance can be further strengthened and its values take root worldwide.

The last couple of years have seen a surge of interest in the basic orientation of Japan's foreign policy. One trigger for this interest was the end of the Cold War in the autumn of 1989. The winding down of the East-West conflict presented the Japanese with the question of whether their mutual security arrangements with the United States, which have set the course for Tokyo's diplomacy ever since World War II, are still needed now that the Soviet threat has greatly diminished. On the US side of this security system, many people are saying it is Japanese economic power, not the Soviet military machine, that now poses the greatest threat to the United States.

The second trigger for the interest was the crisis in the Persian Gulf. As the crisis escalated into war, the Japanese threw themselves into a raging debate over whether their country should—or indeed could—stick to its unilateral stance of noninvolvement in military affairs. Such fundamental questioning of foreign policy has not been seen here since at least 1960, when the Japan-US Security Treaty was revised in the midst of stormy protests; it may even qualify as the biggest debate since September 1951, when the Security Treaty came into being on the occasion of the signing of the San Francisco Peace Treaty.

Today, 40 years after the peace treaty restored Japan's independence, this country counts among the world's mightiest powers. One might ask, sarcastically of course, whether Japan really deserves to be rated as a great power, but one cannot deny that even slight tremors here can now sometimes rock the whole world. When the late Shōwa emperor became gravely ill in the autumn of 1988, for instance, it was reported that shrimp fishers in many countries fell on hard times because of a slump in exports to Japan, where the mood of national self restraint caused the cancelation of numerous fancy dinners and parties, which often feature shrimp. Whether we like it or not, this is the kind of country Japan has become. And it is a twisted country that has maintained silence on all international affairs except those affecting the region immediately around it and has placed a taboo on the discussion of military affairs, even though they are an integral element of foreign policy.

The time has come for Japan to make a new beginning and set out on a path to become a power that is aware of its influence and makes appropriate use of it. Without clinging to customs or succumbing to inertia, we must radically rethink the diplomatic posture suited to our country. Many momentous issues, each with its own complications, must be addressed. Here, I attempt only a rough sketch of some of the salient problems.

Misleading Talk about Contributions

For the past year or so it seems as if every talk on foreign affairs has included mentioning of Japan's "global contributions." The term *contribution*, it might be said, has emerged as the key word used to encapsulate the relationship between Japan and the world. Frankly, though, this makes me uncomfortable. While the term may not be entirely inappropriate, there are problems with thinking that equates the actions of one's own country with contributions.

For one thing, open references to contributions are best made by those on the receiving end, who are thankful for the help. And it seems rather audacious for a country to speak of "contributing" when all it is really doing is fulfilling its international obligations. Also, quite a few of the so-called contributions are more in the nature of exchanges for mutual benefit. Some people have been saying, for instance, that Japan is contributing to the United States by providing land for military bases and technology for weapons, but this can hardly be called a contribution, since Japan receives economic and security benefits in return.

A bigger problem with the word *contribution* arises from the connotations of altruism that go along with it. People make contributions without regard for their own interests, often at some personal cost. In diplomacy, however, there is little room for altruism. This is not just because nobody would believe that a policy packaged in altruistic wrapping was indeed altruistic; a more basic drawback is that altruism cannot generate sustained domestic support. People may be inclined to be generous in prosperous times, but at other times, it is hard to persuade them to support programs that are seen as only benefiting other countries, For the sake of constancy, which is essential in diplomacy, policy measures must not be portrayed as charitable acts.

It seems that the Japanese have the erroneous impression that diplomacy should be altruistic.

Without doubt there is a prevalent belief that global society is more civilized than Japanese society, that it operates on a higher plane of morality. In fact, however, the world has always been—and will probably always be—an arena where national interests compete. After all, the actors in the arena are governments, and the mission of each government is to promote the interests of the people it represents. A government that failed to put its citizens' interests first would be acting contrary to its duty.

Governments do not pursue national interests nakedly, however, since that would be counterproductive. A policy of milking another country for all it is worth would engender antipathy and eventually backfire. The best policies are those that bring benefit to other countries as well as one's own country. On occasion, moreover, the best policies put the interests of other countries first, causing short-term sacrifices at home in order to secure long-term domestic benefits. An interest is not a true national interest unless it has beneficial effects, from a broad perspective, over a long time span. Diplomacy, in other words, should be guided by enlightened self-interest.

To say that promoting national interests is the purpose of diplomacy is also to say that undue emphasis should not be placed on repaying old obligations. While it is true that the world has done much for Japan and that the United States in particular came to its rescue during the painful postwar years, this does not give us reason to think of contemporary diplomatic measures as return gifts. When we reach out to a country in friendship, we should not do this expecting that the country will do something for us at some future date. If our aid helps a country along the road to economic development, we should content ourselves with the success of our help without expecting anything more. In a similar vein, diplomatic decisions should not be based on personal friendships between the leaders of countries. Such friendships are welcomed, but they have little to do with the convergence or divergence of interests.

Changing the Rules of the Game

In the competition among states, the rules of

behavior and the meaning of victory vary from one age to the next. In the nineteenth century something approximating to the law of the jungle was applied, and the losers were turned into colonies or quasi-colonies. Such a situation is now nearly impossibile. If we fail to appreciate how much the times have changed in this respect, we will be unable to grasp contemporary international relations and may lose sight of our true national interests.

Take the case of Japan's defeat in World War II. Back in 1906, when Japan was beginning to build an empire, the government formulated a strategy for the empire's defense, and though the plan was later revised on three occasions, its basic thrust remained unchanged until the start of the war with the United States. Since neither airplanes nor submarines played a role in military power in 1906, the plan focused on warships, and it presumed that they would run on coal. By 1941 the advance of technology had totally changed the picture by adding planes, submarines, and oil to it, but the military strategists, hampered by a policy drafted in an earlier era, failed to keep up with the times. This lapse played a decisive part in the country's defeat four years later.

The Japanese also failed to anticipate the rise of nationalism. Though ideology is intangible, it can exert real power when people feel strongly about it, making it an integral part of international relations. In the years after World War I, the Chinese, the younger and better-informed people in particular, became ardent advocates of nationalism. The Japanese continued to disregard those aspirations, but they effectively blocked Japan's expansionism.

Most fundamental in my view, World War II signaled the demise of the period when a militaristic strategy could be used for national development. Both Japan and Germany sought, by means of military power, to create a sphere of influence containing all the resources and markets needed for their development, but other countries were no longer willing to condone such behavior. Failing to note this change in the rules of the game, Japan and Germany advanced toward goals that only brought about their destruction.

Much the same lesson can be drawn from the

Cold War. Hoping to guarantee its security and acquire control over resources, the Soviet Union implemented an expansionist policy that relied heavily on military might, but it wound up paying an enormous price for the upkeep of the occupied lands and the Soviet satellites. Moscow managed to secure a supply of fuel, material, and other products, but when they turned out to be poor in quality and high in price, it could not replace them with better purchases from the world's markets. In the end, it was the expansion of free trade and the upgrading of industrial capabilities that spelled the end of the militaristic development strategy.

The Forces of Fragmentation

In today's world, a nonmilitaristic development strategy seems to offer the most advantages. It is revealing that Japan and Germany, the two countries that have made the fastest progress in growth, are both lightly armed and have put economic considerations first. The world they are operating in has vastly changed during the largely peaceful decades of the postwar period. It has been turning into a single market, where goods and money flow easily over borders and where countries are widely and deeply dependent on each other. Tourists, workers, immigrants, and others are moving about far more freely than before, and cultural exchange is on the rise. Information now spreads everywhere with blinding speed, making the world smaller. The easy access to news from the outside played a key role in the collapse of the former Soviet empire and the failure of the August 1991 Soviet coup d'état.

At the same time, the actors strutting about on the global stage are states, and each houses a set of institutions and a culture that differs from those of other states. Even as global ties strengthen, counteracting movements gain power. John Gaddis, a noted scholar of the Cold War, has commented that the contemporary world is characterized by a confrontation between "forces of integration" and "forces of fragmentation" (Gaddis 1991).

Both forces can, of course, coexist within a single person. Executives whose companies do business around the world may at the same time espouse a nationalistic philosophy. Often, though, some people, organizations, and states can be identified as members of the integration camp while others align themselves with the fragmentation camp. The former argues that if we seek to solve problems by identifying and developing common interests, we can make the world a better place, while the latter see international relations as a "zero-sum game," one where the promotion of some interests necessarily causes a corresponding curtailment of other interests. A cooperative spirit guides the forces of integration, and a combative spirit drives the forces of fragmentation.

The defeat of Communism was a defeat for the combative spirit of class warfare, but many other combative forces remain to be dealt with. As the Iraqi invasion of Kuwait has demonstrated, it is possible for even a poor country to build a formidable military machine through the acquisition of relatively cheap weapons. The integrationists' dilemma is that they cannot suppress powerful combative forces without themselves bringing a certain amount of military might into play.

Within the integrationist camp, Japan occupies a place on the extreme right. By this I mean that it benefits greatly from the trends pulling the world closer together. In the game of economics, it has compiled a long string of victories. Elsewhere in the industrial world, though, the forces of protectionism and regionalism are on the rise. A country that scores too many victories arouses intense feelings of jealousy in other countries and there is no guarantee that those countries will not retaliate. They may erect protectionist barriers and form closed trading blocs even while recognizing that their actions are harmful to their own long-term interests and those of the world.

As a lightly armed trading state, Japan is in a vulnerable position. Its job as a champion of the integrationists will not be easy. Though the integrationist camp still has an edge over the forces of fragmentation, the positions may reverse in the future, a development that would threaten world peace and frustrate the progress toward global prosperity. If an integrated world is to be realized, we will have to make prudent and intelligent efforts.

Ideals and Values in Diplomacy

Another word people have been throwing around during the past year is *ideals*. The common refrain is that "Japanese diplomacy is bereft of *ideals*." More specifically, people are saying that Japan has a bad habit of following blindly in the wake of the United States and they are urging it to come up with "independent ideals."

We must note, however, that ideals are not something easily adopted, discarded, or replaced. The ideals of foreign policy reflect values that we hold so dear to our hearts that we will willingly make great sacrifices in their defense. To elucidate these ideals, we must pinpoint the values that we treasure the most.

The Japanese place great value on peace and affluence, but in this they are merely affirming things cherished everywhere. Peace and affluence have universal appeal; there is no reason to set them up as distinctive Japanese ideals. In addition, these two values are actually more in the nature of tools that are useful—and perhaps virtually indispensable—for attaining more fundamental values. A country that is at peace is not necessarily a good place if, for instance, it condones the practice of slavery. What peace and affluence make possible is the creation of a society that guarantees a wide range of political and economic freedoms and that treats all human beings with respect.

Where countries differ is not so much in their ultimate ideals as in the goals they set for moving closer to these ideals and the means they employ to achieve them. The immediate goals of a given country are determined to a large extent by its level of wealth. A country faced with famine will have different goals than a country that has a plentiful food supply. The means employed, meanwhile, vary from one country to the next under the influence of factors like tradition, culture, and religion.

In the practice of foreign policy, diplomats should first clarify their support for the ideals shared among countries; only then should they promote the independent means their country wishes to use to resolve a problem. However, Japan's diplomats sometimes put the means ahead of the ends, thereby damaging the country's interests. When China's democracy movement was crushed at Tiananmen Square, for example, Tokyo failed to make an immediate and vociferous protest, arguing that it did not want China to become isolated, and this drove a wedge between it and the other industrial democracies. What was crushed was an ideal that the Japanese, like people everywhere, hold aloft, one whose violation caused much sympathy here for the suppressed people in China. When something like that happens, diplomats should not remain silent on the grounds that other countries' internal affairs are none of their business. If Tokyo had expressed its outrage, confirming its solidarity with the West in this respect, and then stressed its desire to avert Chinese isolation, its arguments would have been more persuasive. As it was, Tokyo only gave the impression that it was reluctant to criticize a valuable customer.

Pinpointing Japan's Own Ideals

Ideals count among the weapons in the diplomatic arsenal. If the Japanese care deeply about some particular ideals, they should thrust them to the fore. But what specific ideals do the Japanese, by reason of their historical experience, have an unusually strong attachment to? Here I will mention just a few.

One is a peace-loving attitude that is coupled with great respect for human life. Japanese history is relatively free of the kinds of atrocities where thousands or tens of thousands of people are cruelly put to death. Especially after the establishment of the Tokugawa shogunate in the early seventeenth century, the Japanese managed to create peaceful conditions that lasted for centuries, and when they overthrew the Tokugawa regime and embarked on industrial development with the Meiji Restoration of 1868, they accomplished this revolutionary turnaround with little loss of life. People have been wont to criticize the restoration on the grounds that it did not go far enough, but at least it was not marred by the extensive spilling of blood that attended, for instance, the French and Russian Revolutions.

To this past can now be added the Japanese experience since World War II. People have grown so fond of the peaceful and orderly postwar society that they are highly unlikely to embrace different values in the years to come. I must admit, however, that this love of peace and respect for human life have sometimes been reserved for Japan alone. When the Japanese have advanced overseas, they have been quite warlike and cruel on several occasions. Henceforth, we must strive to eradicate any such tendencies, preserving and promoting our peaceful tradition.

It goes without saying that the Japanese also value hard work for the sake of economic growth. Among the miraculous events of the twentieth century, surely one has been Japan's rapid development under an ideology that placed business ahead of all else. The nation put top priority on making the economic pie bigger and bigger, not on channeling wealth from the rich to give to the poor, and yet the gap in the distribution of wealth remained comparatively small. As a result of this growth, moreover, the country was able to resolve a wide variety of social problems and create a society in which people have great freedom. I doubt there are many Japanese who would disagree with the proposition that the way to attain even more prosperity is to maintain the posture of a lightly armed, economy-minded nation. And certainly there are few Japanese who would willingly relinquish the freedoms they have gained.

Yet another Japanese value is the desire for a clean environment. This particular value rose to the fore in the 1970s, when pollution problems became critical, and it motivated a wide range of efforts that reduced pollution to more tolerable levels. Now that the destruction of the global environment has become a matter of concern, Japan has many of the necessary qualifications to lead an environmental cleanup.

In terms of diplomacy, values like these translate into such policy targets as peace, human rights, freedom, economic development, and environmental preservation. Japan is in a better position than many of the world's countries to give effective assistance for attaining these goals. Japan's problem-solving abilities can be put to good use by the country's diplomats. If they repeatedly declare their commitment to shared ideals and back up their declarations with concrete measures, they can augment the influence of the country's foreign policy. And the closer the world comes to realizing these ideals, the better a place it will be for Japan.

Defining a Military Role

Having clarified the kinds of targets Tokyo's diplomacy should be aimed at, let me comment on the nature of the role Tokyo should play. I will discuss this role in relation to three aspects of the world order: power, law, and economics.

Today, as in the past, power must be used to hold the world together. The country that can supply the most power is, of course, the United States. Its power is not just a function of the high level of US military technology; the United States is also unmatched in its modern military training and experience and its readiness to meet a challenge to fight. At least until a true United Nations army comes into being—and I am not convinced that such an army could ever fight effectively if it does not have a single commander in chief—the chances are that all attacks on the international order will be either ignored by the global community or turned back by the sort of US-led coalition that operated in the Persian Gulf.

Japan cannot expect to do much in order-preserving military endeavors. It has neither the training nor the experience for generating massive military clout, and no country can build a well-functioning army overnight. However, I am not saying that Japan should do nothing at all in this area. There is a fundamental flaw in the thinking of those who assert that, since Japan's forte is in the economic arena, it should stick to an economic role in global affairs, steering clear of any military involvement. This is equivalent to saying that, in times of war, nations without economic power must make the ultimate sacrifice—the lives of their soldiers—while an industrial nation like Japan needs only bear an economic cost. This is, to put it bluntly, a despicable argument.

Admittedly, Japan's financial aid in the gulf, which came to US$13 billion in total, represented a big expenditure, one amounting to roughly ¥10,000 from each Japanese citizen. But the pain of losing ¥10,000 in spending power is not all that great to the affluent Japanese. It would

be extremely unfair if wars were fought by having rich people like the Japanese cough up some money while poorer people put their lives on the line.

In my view, Japan's war-renouncing Constitution permits the overseas dispatch of the Self-Defense Forces, provided that their mission does not entail the direct use of military power. While Article 9 renounces the use of military force, the preamble stresses the even more important need to preserve peace. Because Japan should be doing everything in its power to promote the cause of global peace, it should resolve any contradictions in constitutional interpretations in favor of the spirit of the preamble. This means that, in cases like the Persian Gulf crisis, where the international community requested Japan support a plainly justified military operation, it should not hesitate to play an indirect, peripheral military role in such areas as minesweeping, medical services, transport, and refugee relief. The only actions it should avoid are those explicitly prohibited by Article 9.

Should Japan go even further than that, resorting to direct military action on occasion? The *New York Times* addressed this question in an editorial on 22 October 1990, titled "Bonn and Tokyo as Global Police." The position it adopted was that "genuine collective security has to mean that Tokyo and Bonn are prepared to fight as well as to finance." But it went on to note that both governments would upset their own citizens as well as their neighbors if they asserted the right to take unilateral action. Then again, they might limit themselves to deploying troops abroad only when authorized by the United Nations, but that, the editorial stated, would be too restrictive. "Perhaps the least troublesome approach," it said in conclusion, "would be constitutional changes permitting force deployments abroad only as a part of collective security and peacekeeping operations." I would not be surprised if the resolution of the issue comes in just such a fashion, though it will take much time to reach agreement on a constitutional amendment.

There is another side to the question of power. Through disarmament it is possible to reduce a country's power to invade other countries. Japan should be able to play a key role in this area. When it extends foreign aid, for instance, it should ascertain that the aid does not in effect pay for military spending. Thus far it has remained silent on how its money is being used, fearing criticism for interference in internal affairs, but the aid it was providing to Baghdad ended up assisting the Iraqi military buildup. When allocating its aid, Tokyo should not select recipients that are militarily powerful. Nor, for that matter, should it select countries that have a poor human rights record. As Japan's own example shows, a government that rides roughshod over its citizens' human rights is liable to turn into an aggressor. Tokyo may run into resistance when putting such an aid philosophy into practice, but if our diplomatic ideals cannot withstand attacks, they are not worth defending.

The proliferation of weapons should be curbed by imposing restrictions on the arms trade. As an initial measure, the monitoring of arms deals should be stepped up. This would permit warnings to be issued when a country goes on an arms-buying spree and seems likely to have aggressive intentions. I have long been in favor of a requirement that all arms deals be reported to international authorities, and now the Japanese government has proposed just such a system to the United Nations. Though the response has not been uniformly positive, I have high hopes for this proposal, especially since it represents a rare Japanese initiative. No country is in a better position than Japan, which has banned its own companies from joining in the arms trade, to champion an arms-monitoring system.

Legal and Economic Requirements

Power cannot in itself maintain order; law is also essential. People must perceive that the order is a just one, as prescribed by law. In this respect, it was gratifying that the Persian Gulf crisis was handled in strict accordance with resolutions by the UN Security Council. The use of force was initiated after a series of resolutions paved the way for it, and the fighting ended when Iraq withdrew from Kuwait, as the resolutions had demanded.

Some people faulted this handling of the war. One objection was that it left Iraqi president Saddam Hussein in power. This was in keeping with the law, however, since the UN resolutions did not require his ousting. As there was no clear and compelling reason to make Saddam's departure a precondition for peace, the war was brought to a stop at an appropriate juncture. The order within a country is best treated by its own people; no matter how powerful outsiders may be, they will have trouble imposing a new order on a nation that does not want it.

Another objection was that the resolutions, in the end, were a legal shield for American interests. One point to note here, however, is that the decision to seek legal authority had drawbacks as well as advantages for Washington. It gave Iraq time to consolidate its fortifications, and it may make it harder for the United States to embark on unilateral action, as it did when it invaded Panama to arrest its ruler, General Manuel Noriega. That the US government was willing to put the matter before the United Nations despite such considerations was, I believe, a noteworthy development.

In a sense, the second objection is on target. Washington did indeed have its own agenda when it asked the United Nations for authority. But that, after all, is how international society works. Each country pursues its own interests, using the law to justify its actions. Surely this is preferred over justifications based on the naked interests themselves or on claims of righteousness. The law, at least, places restraints on behavior.

Some people complained of a double standard when the United Nations, having taken a high-handed approach to Iraq, failed to condemn the Soviet Union for its military intervention in the Baltic republics, but they overlooked an elementary difference between the two cases. The Soviet action was within its borders, and international relations are premised on the sovereignty of the state in its own territory. Certainly, the intervention in the Baltics was regrettable, but it was on a far smaller scale than the Iraqi invasion, and it was not taken against a sovereign government. It was, we might say, a relatively minor legal infraction.

Another component of the international legal framework is provided by the General Agreement on Tariffs and Trade (GATT), which lays down rules for economic activity. Since a discussion of GATT could easily fill an entire essay, here I will make just one point. Without these rules, the relations among trading partners would tend to degenerate into endless squabbles over gains and losses and rights and wrongs. As a country that has reaped the maximum benefits from GATT, Japan should be striving to promote it. Though in doing so Japan may have to make some sacrifices, it will greatly benefit in the long run.

This brings us to the issue of economics, the third aspect of the world order. People support and defend the status quo when they sense that it offers them opportunities. When they despair of any improvement in their lot, however, they are apt to seek the order's overthrow. The opportunities most desperately needed now are for the third world's economic development. In the absence of such chances, less-developed countries may revolt.

There is much that Japan can do in this area, but there are also limits to what development assistance can accomplish. A nation can develop only through the efforts of its own people. Above all it needs an honest and efficient government, and only its own people can put such a government in place. The optimum development strategy is one that fosters export industries, and here there is room for outside assistance. The Japanese can give export-oriented growth a boost by forming joint ventures with and transferring technology to people in developing countries. They can also help out by opening the Japanese market wider and extending assistance for education and infrastructure. Judging from the successful growth of a number of Japan's Asian neighbors, I would say that the key lies in the advance of the industrial countries' companies into the developing economics.

By one means or another, the Japanese must devise schemes to facilitate the third world's development. If they fail in this endeavor, their own country, as a member of the integrationist camp that is heavily dependent on trade, will suffer as much as or more than other countries. Having noted this, though, I would repeat my warning against a Japanese role limited almost exclusively to the economic domain. Such an approach to Japan's global "contributions" overlooks the elements of power and law in the international order and underestimates the inherent difficulties in extending effective development assistance.

Working with the Appropriate Partners

What partners should Japan work with as it tackles the urgent tasks of global cooperation in a shrinking world? Upset by the behavior of the United States in the Persian Gulf crisis, some Japanese have been calling on Tokyo to chart an independent course, and others have been urging Tokyo to move closer to other Asian governments. The former suggestion, if it means parting ways with the rest of the world, deserves the strongest rebuttal. That style of independent national policy would present us with the need to look after our security all by ourselves, and this would entail Japan's transformation into a high-tech military power. There would be no advantage for us or for our neighbors from selecting such a course.

The latter suggestion must also be treated with caution. To be sure, Japan is part of East Asia, and when the Japanese come across Chinese or Koreans when visiting non-Asian countries, they feel as if they are among friends. But a foreign policy must not be based on things like similarities in facial features and physiques. Regionalism does not provide Japan with an adequate foundation for its international cooperation; far more important are shared ideals and similar political and economic systems.

The countries Japan has the most in common with are the industrial democracies of the West. Whether one considers political and economic institutions, living standards, value systems, or diplomatic goals, these countries and Japan are much alike. And, in many respects, they all have the same interests.

In my view the best framework for cooperation is provided by the annual summits of the seven largest industrial democracies. These summits were originally designed to grapple with economic problems, but in recent years, they have also been used for addressing problems in international politics. In an age when economic development is the overriding concern, it only makes sense to put the strongest industrial powers in charge of order-building work.

Viewed from another angle, my position is that we must not expect too much from the United Nations. While this world organization can perform a vital function in creating a legal order, it cannot do much to provide security in the region around Japan. Any major conflict in this region would draw in China or the Soviet Union, and their vetoes in the UN Security Council would prevent it from taking action. Insofar as regional security is concerned, we must look to the United States and to Japan's ability to provide the US armed forces with local bases and financial support. In this way, we arrive at the conclusion that Japan's single most important partner must continue to be the United States.

American Idealism

The question this raises involves relations across the Pacific. We must ask whether Japan and the United States can and should seek even closer ties. And if our answer is in the affirmative, we must ask what Japan should be doing.

Our first need in this inquiry is a proper understanding of the idealistic nature of US foreign policy. This can be illustrated by an episode involving US relations with China. Not long ago it came to light that China was making use of forced labor—of people in prison, in other words—to produce goods for export to the US market. In the eyes of Americans, this was a grave offense. It irritated the American sense of propriety so strongly, in fact, that people saw it as a sufficient reason for canceling China's status as a most favored nation. Reportedly, one American member of Congress went to China to investigate the situation, tried to smuggle out some socks from a prison, and was scolded by the prison authorities when the plan went awry.

Here we can appreciate the depths of American idealism. The United States, founded by people who sought to escape from oppression by moving to a free land, is held together more by ideals than by the natural bonds of history, culture, and language that unite other countries.

In such a country, foreign policy ideals tend

to be placed first, while rational calculations of long-term interests come after the fact. In the Spanish-American War of 1898, for instance, the United States set the objective of freeing Cuba before any realistic plans had been prepared for realizing that objective. In the two world wars, similarly, the decisions to join the fight were not based on national calculation of national interests or on assessments of how American participation could reduce the overall wartime suffering. In World War I it was Germany's indiscriminate submarine warfare that moved the Americans to enter the struggle, while in World War II it was Japan's attack on Pearl Harbor. The US chose to fight Germany and Japan, essentially because they saw them as moral enemies. They threw themselves wholeheartedly into both battles, demanding unconditional surrender, and once their enemies had surrendered, they executed a dramatic about-face and treated them with exceptional magnanimity.

Because of their intense belief in their own ideals, Americans sometimes fail to see that other countries also have good reasons for the positions they adopt. On occasion, moreover, they cast proper legal procedures aside in favor of the unilateral use of force. Even such a moral leader as President Woodrow Wilson approved a punitive expedition into Mexico in 1916. When people hold fast to lofty ideals, they become inclined to rationalize away small faults in the means used to reach them; when the cause is great, minor infractions of the rules are tolerated. No doubt an attitude of this type motivated the Congress member who sought to smuggle socks out of the Chinese prison.

Ingredients of an Exceptional Country

Formed on the basis of the ideal of freedom, the United States is not so much a country as it is a world. Most people see the modern sovereign state as an entity that, in form at least, is equal to all other states, but this is not the way the Americans feel about their own country. Because they opened up a "new world" to move beyond the old European world, they did not develop the habit of seeing their state as an entity strictly equivalent to European states. They came to perceive it as the leader of North and South America and as a teacher in Asia. Americans, in other words, have never had the experience of dealing with other countries on an equal footing.

A related point is that the Americans have never had to repel an invader. Protected from Europe by the Atlantic Ocean, they built a vast and wealthy nation that came to possess stupendous power after World War II. Whereas people elsewhere have grown accustomed to a world in which no country can by itself provide adequately for its own protection, Americans feel vulnerable if they cannot defend themselves without outside help (in this regard, see Chase and Carr 1988). Of all the world's peoples, they may be the least prepared for the emerging age of interdependence. When dealing with such people, for whom reliance on other countries produces feelings of anxiety, it is foolish to exacerbate their fears by boasting about how Japanese technology has become indispensable for US national security.

The independent role of Congress in US diplomacy also deserves attention. Under the US system of a clear separation of powers, Congress revels in its freedom to criticize and restrain the president's diplomatic decisions, and it often moves to reverse them. Though this congressional behavior may be par for the course in a system of checks and balances, it can be thoroughly upsetting to countries around the world. Many Congress members are rather insensitive to this global impact of their actions. A contributing factor is the declining influence of the senior party leaders; in order for the administration to gain congressional support, it must persuade far more people than before of the reasonableness of its legislation. The dissenters, meanwhile, are wont to adopt striking poses on camera. In an age when television determines the outcome of elections, politicians make a big show of tough talk to polish their electronic image. All in all, congressional criticism of the administration has become difficult to control.

The foregoing should help clarify why Americans, in their relations with other countries, tend to thrust forward their own concept of justice and apply high-pressure tactics. There can be no doubt that they believe fervently in ideals such as freedom. And only by holding these ideals aloft can they spur their immense country into action.

Naturally, the American style of behavior has various problematic aspects. The attitude that the US is an exceptional country hinders the treatment of other countries as equals. This mindset encourages isolationism of the sort common in the country's past, and it also encourages unilateralism, which can be seen as a variant of isolationism. Both are frustrating the construction of a cooperative framework for an interdependent world. Then again, the overdeveloped sense of vulnerability, coupled with a zero-sum outlook in which Japanese gains become American losses, is causing some Americans to treat Japan as their number-one enemy. (For a German evaluation of the concerns disturbing America in this respect, see Maull 1990/1.) However, hysterical talk about the Japanese threat is not widespread. There are not many enthusiastic Japan bashers in either the administration or at the local level. Outside of Congress, it seems, people are coming to terms with life in an interdependent world.

Some Japanese have been complaining that Americans are racists, but the problem with such talk—apart from its disregard of our own racism—is that it fails to take into account the great progress the Americans have made in overcoming racist thinking. One must always bear in mind the direction in which a country is moving. Back in the 1930s, when not a few Japanese were trying to justify their country's Asia policy on the grounds that it was a counterpart to the Monroe Doctrine, Kiyosawa Kiyoshi, a foreign policy analyst, observed that the United States under President Franklin Roosevelt had been, to a large extent, overcoming its habit of treating the Americas as its exclusive preserve. What the Japanese should be emulating, he said, was not the Monroe Doctrine but the American resolve to rectify outdated attitudes. In a similar vein, today we should be paying attention not to the lingering racism of some Americans but to the remarkable spread of positive attitudes toward the cultures of other countries.

By and large the people of the United States seem prepared to live cooperatively in a closely integrated world. Though the country has its isolationists as well as its advocates of unilateralism, they are being held down by the internationalist camp, which recognizes that American interests would be harmed by a failure to get along with other countries. We should not be complacent, however, because the United States is also a country that sometimes swings sharply in unexpected directions. And if the American giant begins thrashing about, the resulting havoc will hurt Japan far more than the United States. Japan may be superbly equipped for life in the world where international cooperation prevails, but it is not equipped at all for survival in a chaotic world. For our own good and for the good of countries everywhere, the world's two biggest economic powers must jointly tackle such problems as the destruction of the global environment and the gap between the industrial North and the developing South.

Strengthening the Integrationist Camp

Though Japan has not had a prominent global role thus far—it was not actively involved in the activities that terminated the Cold War, transformed Eastern Europe, and resolved the Persian Gulf crisis—the world is expecting much of it. And as Max Weber once noted, any major power has a duty as well as a right to take a hand in the shaping of world history.

Today, when the winds of economic and cultural nationalism are stirring, the postwar free trade system has reached a critical juncture. Japan and a handful of other countries have scored so many consecutive victories in the game of economics that Europe, to defend itself, is leaning toward a closed regionalism. If this tendency is to be checked, permitting the evolution of a more highly integrated and culturally diversified world, the United States will have to lead the way. And if the Americans are to exercise such leadership, they must have Japanese help. Among the allies of the United States, none has more responsibility than Japan to see that American internationalists retain the upper hand. We must strive to convince all Americans that it is in their own interest to seek greater integration and cooperate with Japan. Our external policy measures henceforth must center on efforts to achieve this end.

The Japan-US alliance is no longer needed to counter the Soviet threat, but it can still play a useful role in strengthening the integrationist camp. We should turn this bilateral partnership into a global alliance for dealing with environmental destruction, the North-South gap, the drug trade, and an assortment of other problems with global dimensions. With the arrival of the 40th anniversary of the formation of this alliance, the time has come to reconsider it, and our choice should be to make it even broader and stronger.

Japan's diplomats should put several specific tasks on their agenda. For one thing, they should get together with their American counterparts to reconfirm the essential sameness of our two countries with respect to ultimate goals and ideals. Miyazawa Kiichi, Japan's new prime minister, has just unveiled a proposal for creating something like a charter for the Pacific basin. This idea merits attention.

Another task is to further expand the bilateral consultations known as the Structural Impediments Initiative (SII). There are still many irrational barriers separating the two economies and they all deserve to be torn down. Some people may fear that the SII talks will turn Japan into a lackey of the United States, but at a time when economic activities have become global in scale, we should be seeking to at least standardize our economic systems to the greatest possible extent. Japanese culture is not so shallow, I am confident, that tinkering with institutions will cause it to degenerate.

One more task is to reinforce Japan's national power, which is based on strengths in a wide variety of fields. If Japan comes up short in this respect, the United States will not be interested in working with it. There is, moreover, little point in making a country rich unless its people become more powerful and appealing in the process. Japan's record in this regard has been far from satisfactory; much more emphasis must be placed on elevating the caliber of Japan's citizens. Now is not the time to rest on the laurels of our hard won wealth.

Courtesy of The Yomiuri Shimbun.

English version originally published by Japan Echo in a special issue of *Japan Echo* 19 (1992).

Translated from "Nichibei no chikyū teki dōmei wa kanō ka," in *THIS IS YOMIURI* (December 1991): 42–62; abridged by about one-third.

Bibliography

Chase, James, and Caleb Carr. *America Invulnerable: The Quest for Absolute Security from 1812 to Star Wars*. New York: Summit Books, 1988.

Gaddis, John Lewis. "Toward the Post–Cold War World." *Foreign Affairs* 70, no. 2 (Spring 1991): 102–122.

Maull, Hanns W. "Germany and Japan: The New Civilian Powers." *Foreign Affairs* 69, no. 5 (Winter 1990/1): 91–106.

I-(2) Putting Old Diplomatic Principles into New Bottles

Kitaoka Shinichi

ABSTRACT Japan's first *Diplomatic Bluebook*, issued by the Kishi administration in 1957, enumerated the three principles governing Japanese foreign policy: (1) centering policy on the United Nations, (2) acting as an Asian nation, and (3) cooperating internationally with other free countries. Japan subsequently emphasized the third of these and made relations with the United States so central to its policy development that there was some concern the other two bedrock principles might have been forgotten. They are, however, still crucial, and it is essential Japan rethink and renew all three principles within the current context.

It was in 1957 that the Ministry of Foreign Affairs published the first of its "bluebooks," annual reports on the state of Japan's foreign policy. Having restored diplomatic ties with the Soviet Union in October 1956 and joined the United Nations in December of that year, Japan had nearly completed its reintegration into the international community. The time had come for a comprehensive review of the diplomatic stance the country should assume, and the bluebook did just that. It set forth three basic principles for conducting diplomacy: focus on the United Nations, cooperate with liberal democracies, and strengthen Japan's status as a member of Asia. Great Britain and other concerned countries, which until then had harbored reservations regarding Tokyo's intentions, gave high marks to this statement of Japan's diplomatic principles.

Subsequently, however, Japan did not follow these principles very faithfully. Its foreign policy was shaped primarily with reference to relations with the United States. Whether one considers the revision of the Japan-US Security Treaty in 1960, the return of Okinawa to Japan in 1972, the oil crises that soon followed, or the later escalation and eventual termination of the Cold War, one can see that Japan neither pursued a diplomacy centered on the United Nations nor put much weight on its status as a member of Asia.

Perhaps this was inevitable. Since the possibility of an armed conflict between the United States and the Soviet Union posed the gravest threat to the world, a preoccupation with the relationship between Washington and Moscow characterized the foreign policies of most of the world's leading nations. However, this does not mean the three principles set forth 36 years ago (1957) were mistaken. Almost intuitively, the authors of the first diplomatic bluebook grasped those principles that Japan could not avoid heeding because of its historical, geographical, political, and economic situation. Now that the Cold War is over, the time has again come for a review of Japan's diplomatic stance. We must consider whether to reaffirm these principles or to reject them, and if we find them still basically sound, we must ask if they now require amplification.

The Significance of the Cold War's End

To set the stage for such an examination, I will first touch upon several of the fundamental changes in international relations that followed the defeat of socialism and the end of the Cold War. And the initial change I would like to call attention to is the passing of the age in which nations strove to expand their territories and spheres of influence. The belief that the road to security and prosperity runs through geographical expansion—whether in terms of territory or spheres of influence—is now outdated. It was this belief that led both Japan and Germany in the 1930s to define themselves as "have-nots" and to pressure the "haves," notably Great Britain, France, and the United States, to redistribute their colonies.

Even in those days there were some Japanese who saw the flaws in this expansionary policy. People such as Ishibashi Tanzan, who became a postwar prime minister, and the diplomatic expert Kiyosawa Kiyoshi asserted that even if Japan succeeded in drawing Manchuria, China, and Southeast Asia into its sphere, it would still be unable to procure all the materials it needed and sell all the products it manufactured. Such a policy might bring an Asian yen bloc into being, but trading with other countries in this bloc would not allow Japan to obtain the foreign currency needed to import high-level technology from the West. Worse than that, they said, Japan was likely to alienate Great Britain and the United States and lose them as trading partners. Their view was that Japan's national interests would be best served by trading with the whole world. But their numbers were too few to give them a loud voice.

The Soviet Union was the nation that clung to the territorial mode of thinking the longest. It attempted to maintain its sphere of influence in Eastern Europe and other regions of the world to the very end. As long as Moscow pursued this policy, however, the nations inside the Soviet bloc were forced to consume inferior, high-priced goods, and their economies stagnated.

After World War II, Japan headed in the opposite direction. It gave up all thought of securing a sphere of influence, opting instead to import high-quality, low-cost raw materials from around the globe and to target the entire world as its market. Japan's resulting economic development received a powerful boost from the epochal advances made in transport and telecommunications technologies in and after the 1970s. Thanks to these technologies and other factors, the world became a place where it was meaningless to raise borders between nations. These developments represented the triumph of economics over militarism, of trading nations over military powers.

Seen from a different perspective, the world ceased to be a place where nations could get ahead through confrontation and conflict. The most advantageous policy was not to usurp wealth from other countries but to cooperate with them, striving all the while to attain economic growth through self-help efforts. The historical record shows that the countries that devoted themselves to development through self-reliance (while receiving assistance from rich countries) were able to achieve growth, while the countries that relied heavily on their powerful friends and pursued a confrontational foreign policy failed to attain their goals. The willingness to strive to become richer through one's own power and to set aside any envy or resentment of other nations must be the starting point of national development.

Another fundamental change caused by the downfall of socialism is the ending of the politics of leaders and followers. Throughout history, thinkers and leaders ranging from Plato to Lenin to Pol Pot have maintained that welfare can be maximized when power is in the hands of an elite corps of superior leaders. Against this, the philosophy of liberal democracy maintains that power inevitably corrupts, and even the most intelligent leaders make mistakes. It is now manifestly evident that the elitists are wrong and the democrats are right.

All attempts to shape society with extreme ideologies have ended in failure. At times, people have made great sacrifices for the sake of exalted ideals, and at other times, they have committed extreme atrocities in the name of the same ideals. By and large, though, people are motivated by small doses of self-interest (greed and fear) and good intentions. Today there can be no doubt that the easiest way to mobilize people is by appealing not to their ideals but to their self-interest, particularly their greed.

Such is not to say that we no longer need to fear a resurgence of expansionism, militarism, or dictatorship. Such tendencies are still present throughout the world, as the events currently unfolding in Bosnia demonstrate. My point is simply that such ideas and policies do not offer a future for humankind. Global stability and progress depend on whether nations everywhere follow policies that stress economic achievement, international cooperation, and liberal democracy.

Eurasian Empires and Trading States

Now I would like to consider the three basic principles of a UN-centered diplomacy, cooperative relations with democratic countries, particularly the United States, and a special emphasis on Japan's status as an Asian country. I will address these principles in reverse order and focus primarily on relations with Asia.

Over the past two or three years, Japanese interest in Asia has grown remarkably. Throughout modern Japanese history, interest in Asia has usually increased when Japan's relations with Europe and the United States have arrived at an impasse. This time as well, the interest in Asia has been motivated in part by a surge in anti-US sentiments, which became conspicuous around the time of the war in the Persian Gulf, but many other factors are also involved. One is the fact that Japan is now in a position to formulate its own Asian policy, unlike before, when Tokyo had to match its policy to the stance adopted by Washington in consideration of Cold War imperatives.

The question now before us is one concerning which principles we should apply to which parts of Asia in a bid to strengthen Japan's Asian ties. Asia is a diverse place, but perhaps we can get a handle on it by using the theory formulated by the acclaimed scholar Umesao Tadao (1920–2010) in his 1956 essay "Bunmei no seitai shikan josetsu" (*An Ecological View of History: Japanese Civilization in the World Context*). To sum up his theory in my own terms, the main dividing line in civilization is not between East and West, as is often assumed, but between the interior and the coastal areas of the Eurasian landmass. Whereas huge despotic empires evolved in the continental interior, trading nations generally developed in the coastal regions, which Umesao saw as including Japan and much of Europe. In the coastal areas, trade has worked to limit the authority of the state and make society multidimensional, with the result that relatively weak states and free societies have come into being. Moreover, trade brings states together by fostering mutual interests, and nationality loses some of its importance. Among trading nations, accordingly, cooperation is stressed over confrontation.

Japan and the members of the Association of Southeast Asian Nations (ASEAN) count among the Asian countries that exhibit characteristics typically associated with the trading state. Japan and ASEAN members have all been developing with an emphasis on economics and trade and without relying on military power, and they have forged ties with each other through trade and investment. Critics have claimed that Japan is practicing a new form of colonialism in Southeast Asia, but in fact, both sides have profited from their exchanges and have developed a cooperative relationship. Actually, Umesao's view was that Southeast Asian countries should be categorized culturally as a cross between the coastal and interior state types, but in recent years, Southeast Asia has clearly been moving closer to the Japanese model.

By contrast, Japan, even today, is having difficulty getting along with the continental empires. China, for example, is still clinging to a territorial-based policy, as indicated by its claims to the Spratly Islands in the South China Sea. Furthermore, Chinese diplomacy has traditionally been characterized by a unilateralism that downplays international cooperation. When Japan was preparing to dispatch minesweepers to the Persian Gulf, China at first objected to the deployment of Japanese military units overseas, but then it changed its mind, stating that it could understand why Japan would want to cooperate militarily with a region so important to it. The implication here is a dangerous one: big countries are justified in sending military forces abroad whenever their national interests are at stake. In fact, Tokyo dispatched minesweepers for the purpose of promoting international cooperation and maintaining peace, but this was a point Beijing was unable to grasp.

Beijing's Outlook on the World

An immense country like China can handle its defense all by itself. Self-defense is much harder in a relatively small, highly developed country like Japan. The only way for Japan to defend itself on its own would be to transform itself into a high-tech military power, but that would pose dangers to both Japan and the world. The massive destructive power of contemporary military technology makes it important that peace be achieved through international cooperation. The fact that Beijing seems unable to comprehend this need for cooperation is probably related to its long tradition of Sino-centric thinking, its self-reliant reconstruction after the attacks on it by imperial powers, and its continuing insistence that outsiders should not interfere in its internal affairs.

China has long sought to protect itself by pitting barbarians against barbarians. In the contemporary world, this translates into a policy of joining hands with the United States when Japan needs curbing and joining hands with Japan when the United States becomes too pushy. As the Chinese see it, international politics is a zero-sum game. I might also note that Beijing has long had the habit of playing up foreign threats when its domestic politics reach an impasse. China is a very political country in which the state has assumed a large role.

Granted, China's economic development has been spectacular in recent years, but we should not read too much into that. The development has been concentrated mainly in the coastal regions, and this has created huge gaps with China's interior. Bridging these gaps will not be easy. The Chinese have been recognized over the ages for their business abilities, but political problems have prevented the use of these skills to develop the entire nation. The political system needs to provide a stable order so that excessive economic competition does not become disruptive, but China's system has failed to do that. Politicians in the country have tended to become parasites who feed off the economy and undermine it.

Above all, the Chinese leadership unrealistically assumes that people will be forever willing to put up with a lack of political freedom, even after the country has acquired a certain level of affluence. It seems more likely that the yearning for political freedom will increase, and this will make it difficult for the giant Chinese state to continue to develop in a stable fashion without at least the rudiments of a system that reflects the will and desires of its people. Perhaps the best way to sum up such features of the Chinese state is to say that the government's presence has grown too large. This is a problem that can also be seen in Russia and India to a certain degree and has plagued the continental empires throughout history.

I am not saying here that we should treat China as a country that will be a more dangerous threat to Japan the further it develops. On the contrary, an affluent China will probably become an important customer for Japan, and no doubt its diplomacy will be modified as it matures. My point is simply that we should not be unguardedly optimistic about this process.

Law and Order in East Asia

One weakness of East Asia, a region I see as including Southeast Asia, is its lack of an adequate legal and security system to guarantee regional law and order. In a study of Japanese-South Korean relations since World War II, Lee Chong-sik observes that the two countries took contrasting approaches to reconciliation. South Korean president Syngman Rhee adopted an Oriental approach, demanding a comprehensive and spiritual reconciliation and apology, to which the Japanese responded in a business-like and legalistic manner. It is interesting that President Rhee opted for this approach despite having spent much of his life in the United States.

As I see it, we cannot expect two countries to reach a complete reconciliation backed up by full mutual understanding in today's world with its diversity of interests. A foreign policy that seeks mainly to appeal to people's emotions will probably not serve as a vehicle for long-term stability. In the past, the Japanese government, relying on the available principles of international law, concluded reparations agreements and other treaties with the countries it had injured, seeking thereby to smooth over many virtually irreconcilable clashes of interests. It should not be necessary to renegotiate these treaties now. At the state level, we should assume, the problem of postwar reparations has already been settled. To be sure, recently many people injured by Japan's past actions have been asking for compensation, but they really should be petitioning their own governments instead of Tokyo. If their governments determine that they deserve compensation and proceed to aid them, then Tokyo should respond with assistance to the governments. I am arguing, in other words, that Japan's Asian diplomacy should transcend emotionalism; it should be based on objective, realistic, and practical considerations. South Korea's policy in this respect has recently been admirable. Seoul is asking the Japanese to look squarely at what their country did in the past, but it is not asking for more money.

East Asia also suffers from a lack of security arrangements to form the basis of a regional order. The region's countries have never tried to create a security framework of their own initiative. Prior to World War II, most of Southeast Asia was under colonial rule, and after the war, the region came largely under the influence of the United States. Until recently the military capabilities of the ASEAN group amounted to little more than the level of power needed for maintaining public order at home. Now that these countries have become more economically advanced, though, they are buying a considerable quantity of the arms that are being sold cheaply around the world. These arms purchases have been prompted by the US's receding influence and China's expansionist maneuvering. Building a security framework in East Asia has become an urgent task.

The time has come to give serious consideration to convening an Asian version of the Conference on Security and Cooperation in Europe (CSCE). In this regard, the linchpin of the CSCE is the agreement by all participants to respect the status quo regarding national borders and to reject changes in national borders brought about through the use of military force. This will be a hard principle for China to stomach, since it refuses to recognize Taiwan's independence. But China's refusal to participate should not cause us to give up on forming a security framework. It

should still be possible to develop an organization centered on Asia's coastal states, such as Japan and the ASEAN members, with Australia, Canada, and of course the United States also participating. North Korea and Russia will probably hold back, but we should simply wait patiently for their eventual participation after they have seen the benefits that accrue from membership.

The members of this organization should adopt a ban on the export of arms to dangerous countries. Japan is already observing such a ban, and it has also been cooperating with the international groups seeking to block arms exports to places like Communist countries. But these days it is difficult to determine what constitutes a weapon and which products can be used in the manufacture of arms. To make matters worse, confirming the final user of a product is often hard, since the country it is exported to may ship it to a third country. Such problems aside, the members should pledge to at least not provide nuclear weapons or the technology for delivering them to Iran, Iraq, Libya, North Korea, or Syria, or to regions with high levels of political tension.

A regional security framework will force Japan to alter its defense policy. Regional security is based on providing assistance to a regional ally if it is attacked without provocation. What is involved here is the right of collective self-defense. In interpreting the war-renouncing Constitution, the government has ruled that while Japan possesses the right of collective self-defense, it cannot exercise this right. In view of the high level of today's military technology, however, I would say that international cooperation is absolutely indispensable for peace, and the right of collective self-defense is essential for this cooperation. What this means is that the government will have to change its constitutional interpretation.

Turning America into a Normal Country

In light of this Asian setting, the crucial importance of the US military presence is apparent. The United States can provide the glue to cement a union in the Western Pacific region, which is faced with such countries as China, North Korea, and Russia. Let us consider where Washington is heading while bearing this point in mind.

I believe that the 1993 inauguration of President Bill Clinton was an extremely important event in American history. The significance l have in mind here is not the elimination of the gridlock produced by having the White House and Congress controlled by different parties. As I see it, the birth of the Clinton administration may mark a shift to a new political style, one whose advent may, in the long run, be even more important than the ending of the Cold War.

In the past, the United States constituted not just a single nation with independent national interests but something like a separate world. It was a country that refused to become a regular member of the international community. Until the end of the nineteenth century, the United States turned its back on the Old World and devoted itself to a westward expansion it saw as its manifest destiny. Even as late as the early twentieth century, the US Department of State was no match for the diplomatic teams of Great Britain and other powers. Indeed, it divided the world's countries alphabetically, which meant that the officials responsible for Costa Rica and Cuba were also placed in charge of China policy. Not until a 1908 reform was a Far Eastern section created, and it was given only a tiny staff. This illustrates the degree to which the United States, a world of its own, took foreign policy lightly.

Subsequently, Americans began to participate in international affairs. But while they played a major role in World War I, they turned isolationist again after that. The real turning point, when the United States made a full-fledged commitment to international issues, came during World War II. And ever since then, its involvement in world affairs has been extreme. Never before in history has a single country wielded so much power and been involved in so many regions around the world. The fact that the United Nations is located in New York is symbolic of the predominant status the United States has achieved.

Thus far, the United States has never had the experience of cooperating with other countries on an equal footing. With the advent of the Clinton administration, however, this is finally beginning to change. In contrast to President George H.W. Bush, who was a war hero in World War II, President Clinton is not a hero of the Vietnam War. He knows that the US is capable of making mistakes and that there are limits to its power. Clinton's experience as the governor of Arkansas has taught him that when late developers seek to catch up with early developers, they make earnest efforts in many areas. With Clinton in charge, a government that has consistently refused to formulate an industrial policy will be seeing for the first time what the state can do to influence the direction of economic activity. Simply stated, the US is finally becoming a normal state.

In the past, the idea of placing American troops under a commander from another nation was unthinkable, but Clinton's America has shown a willingness to do this. Washington's proposal to give Japan and Germany permanent seats on the United Nations Security Council is also motivated by an internationalist spirit. While some people say that the United States will not be able to rid itself of its superpower mentality, the same charge in reverse might be leveled at Japan. That is, Japan might be accused of conducting a foreign policy that places excessive weight on superpowers. Of course, it will not be easy for the United States to shed its long-ingrained habits. Traces of its unilateralism are likely to surface from time to time. The recent statements of the 1992 presidential candidate Ross Perot are indicative of this tendency. All in all though, there seems no doubt that the US is heading in the direction I have indicated.

Is the US likely to pull out of Asia? At present, having a US military presence in Asia is in line with American interests. Since the United States receives host-nation support from Japan, the cost of stationing its forces here is not very high. But it is a fact that Japan reaps even greater benefits from this arrangement, and we should not assume blithely that the US will never pull out simply because it obtains benefits from staying. For states, as for people, a gain from an arrangement that is relatively smaller than the gains of others is apt to be perceived as a loss.

It would be wrong to assume that the United States would be unable to exercise political influence in Asia without maintaining a major military presence there. And it would also be wrong to assume that the United States will be able to exercise commanding influence as long as its troops do not pull out. After all, the US military presence has not helped to promote American interests in such areas as trade disputes with Japan. But in any event, it is extremely desirable for Japan and the rest of East Asia to have American armed forces around. There seems little reason to doubt that this military presence will remain for the immediate future, but we should not take this for granted.

A Political Power Needing No Military Clout

It should be evident from the above that Japan needs to play a larger political role. But critics have been saying recently that surely efforts by Japan to transform itself from an economic power into a political power will lead to moves to make the country a military power as well. And, they add, since Japan needs to establish a track record of international contributions in order to increase its voice in the international community, surely it will be going all-out to lend support to peace-keeping operations and UN peace initiatives, aiming to secure a permanent seat on the Security Council. As they see it, this would amount to a reassertion of the old nationalism in a new guise. In my view, though, this line of thinking is anachronistic. It fails to take into account the changes that have occurred in the international community.

For one thing, it is nearly impossible for an economic power not to be a political power. In an age of global economic interdependence, economic powers wield strong clout around the world. Japan's official development assistance has the ability to turn a country into a military power capable of threatening its neighbors, and it might also be used to reinforce an authoritarian regime, causing hardships to the people of that nation. Were Japan to cut off its aid to a recipient, its people would suffer. In the field of trade, moreover, other countries feel profound repercussions from developments in Japan, such as decisions to open markets or leave them closed. Even a slight shift in the preferences of Japanese consumers may help or hurt Japan's trading partners. This massive economic influence is exercised primarily through companies, and what the government can do to control it is limited. One could even say that the government does not really comprehend where and in what ways Japan's influence is being exerted. In this way, Japan does not have a choice between becoming or not becoming a political power. It already is a political power, and all it can do is decide how it wants to use this power for the stability and prosperity of the world.

Actually, the very people who assert that Japan should not become a political power want it to exercise active leadership on behalf of the cause of global arms reduction. But what is a leader in such a field if not a political power? Here as well we can see that the only question is about the kind of political power Japan should wield.

If Japan became a military power, however, its interests would be harmed more than helped. There is no need for Japan to acquire military might. To put it somewhat crassly, Japan can afford to buy almost anything it wants. Were the country to start displaying military power and even using it, the days of prosperity would quickly come to an end. But actually, there is almost no possibility that Japan will try to force its will on other countries, much less to subjugate or control them, and this will hold true even if it builds up its military a step or two further.

Should Japan aspire to permanent membership on the Security Council? To answer this question, I would pose another question. If the council arrives at an important decision without Japan's participation and then asks Tokyo to help pay for the decision's implementation, will Tokyo be able to turn down the request? It will probably be difficult to do so. Japan has essentially two choices: refuse to participate in decision making but bear a financial burden or participate in decision making and bear a financial burden. By participating, we will at least be able to register our objections to decisions we disagree with. If we choose not to participate and the council continues to ask us to cough up money, the public will eventually become fed up. Already earlier this year the Japanese people reacted quite frostily when Tokyo was asked by other countries to lend assistance to Russia. Herein we can see the limits of the international cooperation our country can offer.

Suppose a conflict breaks out somewhere and a debate begins over whether to dispatch a UN military force to resolve it. And suppose further that Japan objects to the dispatch of the force. Will this objection carry more weight if Japan says it opposes the deployment of troops in this case but will extend its full cooperation when necessary in other cases? Or will it be more persuasive if Japan refuses to ever participate in such operations because of constitutional constraints? Obviously, the correct answer is the former. It is participation in the decision-making process, not the sharing of costs, that will be important for Japan.

There can be no doubt that the United Nations should play a greater role in resolving conflicts around the world, that preventing conflicts before they get serious is best, that economic and civil stability is needed for this purpose, and that peaceful rather than coercive or military means should be used. Japan's participation in the Security Council should help push the United Nations in this direction. It serves no purpose for a country that has not participated in a decision to complain loudly about it and trot forth fine-sounding objections. It may seem paradoxical at first glance, but some toning down of Japan's resolute anti-military attitudes is needed if the country, while maintaining confidence in its economy-first approach, is to assist the resolution of conflicts in a more peaceful fashion on a broader global scale. If we really wish to do more for peace, then it is only natural that we lend a hand in campaigns like the one in the Persian Gulf and cooperate in other ways with peacekeeping missions.

From Consensus to Competition in Politics

Needless to say, the fall from power of the Liberal Democratic Party (LDP) and the inauguration of an "anti-LDP" coalition government mark an important turning point in the foundation of Japanese diplomacy.

Prior to the July general election for the House of Representatives, critics of the Social Democratic Party of Japan voiced concern about what its participation in a coalition government might mean to the Japan-US Security Treaty, the Self-Defense Forces (SDF), and Japan's South Korean policy. Actually, however, the Socialists could not possibly govern if, as they did in the past, they insisted on abolishing the Security Treaty, disbanding the SDF, and spurning South Korea. In fact, they had been looking for an opportunity to distance themselves decisively from unrealistic policies like these. Unlike in the old days, the party's left wing does not have much influence. In this light, we should welcome the inauguration of the new administration for demonstrating that all political parties, with the exception of the Japanese Communist Party, have accepted the basic tenets of Japanese diplomacy, such as the need to cooperate with the United States and preserve the mutual security arrangements.

We should also welcome the advent of a competitive political system, one in which a number of parties that all endorse international cooperation are vying to lead the country. Over the past several years, particularly during times of rapid changes in international circumstances, the LDP's capacity to make political decisions has eroded considerably. During the many years of LDP rule, personnel decisions, legislative procedures, budget appropriations, and other matters all became institutionalized, and politics came to be carried out on the basis of consensus among the LDP's factions and the ministries (see Kitaoka 1993). The problem here is that consensus politics is not suited to an age of internationalization. It takes time to build a consensus, and once it is formed, it hardly ever changes. As a result, Japan has been extremely slow in announcing its positions on issues to the international community, and once they are announced, they hardly ever change. As I have argued elsewhere, such a setup makes it difficult to formulate blueprints that transcend the narrow concerns of the respective ministries. Consensus politics does not lend itself to the kind of flexibility where people speak their minds but also lend an ear to the views of others, modifying their positions as appropriate. We should therefore be pleased that a more competitive style of politics is taking shape.

As I have argued in this essay, the three basic principles of Japanese diplomacy enunciated in 1957 can be reaffirmed today and given some new content. Japan's responsibilities today are incomparably larger than they used to be. And with the disappearance of the Soviet threat, getting countries to cooperate is in some respects harder than in the past. If Japan sticks to the passive stance it has resorted to up until now, simply responding to the demands of other countries, international cooperation will not go smoothly.

In shifting to a new diplomatic style, we must steer clear of the habit of pandering to public opinion. Prime Minister Hosokawa Morihiro's grandfather, wartime Prime Minister Konoe Fumimaro, and LDP president Kōno Yōhei's father, the influential politician Kōno Ichirō, both had an unprincipled tendency to let the public decide their policies for them. I can only hope that neither the prime minister nor the LDP president follows in the footsteps of his forebear, that instead they compete with each other based on forward-looking visions of the ways in which Japan can cooperate with the rest of the world.

Courtesy of Sekai-no-Ugoki-sha.

English version originally published by Japan Echo in *Japan Echo* 21, no. 1 (1994).

Translated from "Furuku katsu atarashii gensoku," in *Gaikō Forum* (October 1993): 22–30.

Bibliography

Kitaoka Shinichi. "Bureaucratization of Japanese Politics." *Japan Echo* 20, no. 2 (Summer 1993).

Hegemony, Chaos, Interdependence
Three Scenarios for China

Tanaka Akihiko

ABSTRACT This essay posits three different scenarios for China—the pursuit of hegemony, internal chaos, and global interdependence—and analyzes the likelihood and ramifications of each scenario taking the actions of the two external superpowers (the United States and Russia) into consideration. Based upon this review, it argues the need for Japan to respond appropriately as the situation unfolds (a) creating conditions conducive to enhancing China's economic interdependence and social openness, (b) devising policies that will work against China's either seeking hegemony or descending into chaos, and (c) being prepared to cope with whatever scenario plays out.

The international political situation in East Asia can best be described in two contradictory words: peaceful and unstable. There are various ways to define the extent of this region, but if we take it to include the member states of the Association of Southeast Asian Nations (Brunei, Indonesia, Malaysia, the Philippines, Singapore, and Thailand), the Indochinese Peninsula, China, the Korean Peninsula, the Russian Far East, and the Japanese archipelago, the region is at peace insofar as no armed conflict is underway at present.

We can see what an achievement this represents if we review the last 100 years of East Asian history. The date 1 August 1994, marks the 100th anniversary of the outbreak of the First Sino-Japanese War. This was followed by the Russo-Japanese War, World War I, fighting among rival warlords in China, Japan's Siberian Intervention, armed conflict between the Kuomintang and the Communist Party of China, the Second Sino-Japanese War and the Pacific War, the Franco-Vietnamese War, the Korean War, uprisings and rebellions in various Southeast Asian countries, civil war in Laos, the Vietnam War, border clashes between China and the Soviet Union, civil war in Cambodia, and border clashes between China and Vietnam. There was incessant strife well into the 1980s. In view of the past war-ridden century, the present peace is precious indeed. Moreover, East Asia is not only peaceful but also prosperous. No other region is experiencing such dynamic economic growth.

This does not mean we can allow ourselves unalloyed optimism. The present tension over suspicions about North Korea's nuclear ambitions is enough to show the basic instability of the Korean Peninsula. We cannot assume that US negotiations with North Korea will proceed smoothly. Depending on how the talks go, economic sanctions against Pyongyang are a definite possibility, and we cannot rule out the danger that such a step could lead to armed conflict. Given North Korea's domestic problems, even resolving the nuclear problem will not eliminate the peninsula's instability. If economic difficulties cause political instability in North Korea, the present regime could collapse, plunging the entire peninsula into chaos.

At this time the most pressing danger is on the Korean Peninsula, but other parts of the region are also plagued by potentially destabilizing problems. In regard to China, for example, it is impossible to predict how smoothly the 1997 reversion of Hong Kong will proceed. And despite the dramatic increase in economic exchange between China and Taiwan in recent years, Beijing's attitude toward the island still gives cause for concern. China has not yet repudiated the possibility of attempting forcible reunification. No one can tell how it would react if Taiwan began exhibiting a stronger resolve toward independence. China is also contesting sovereignty over certain islands, and thus the extent of territorial waters in the South China Sea, with Vietnam and other Southeast Asian countries. Nor is it clear what shape relations with Russia will take.

In Indochina, meanwhile, the prospects for stability in Cambodia remain uncertain. Moreover, in many East Asian countries we are seeing, along with economic growth, increasing arms procurements. Although there is not actually an arms race, the level of armament is definitely rising yearly. An emergency, such as firm evidence that North Korea possessed nuclear capabilities, could set off an arms race—including nuclear weapons—in the region.

Thus, even aside from the Korean Peninsula, East Asia includes a variety of factors militating against stability. This means that when evaluating the region we must take into account not only its present peace and prosperity but also its potential instability. To put it simply, East Asia is now at a crossroads. Having finally hauled itself out of the abyss of incessant warfare, it has climbed to a sunny pass. If it chooses its route skillfully, it will progress along a sunlit ridge. But if it takes a wrong turn, it could descend again into a foggy ravine.

Perhaps the most important country poised at this crossroads is China, for it embodies all the characteristics of East Asia. How many of the region's wars during the last century have involved this country! That it is not currently embroiled in any military conflict is an extremely significant development in its modern history. Moreover, East Asia's affluence in the 1990s would not have been possible without China's recent economic growth. Thus, China is emblematic of the region's peace and prosperity.

At the same time, most of the destabilizing factors in East Asia are linked to China: Hong Kong, relations with Taiwan, territorial disputes in the South China Sea, fears of an arms race, and China's own domestic problems. In short, China also poses the greatest long-term threat to the region's stability.

What are the prospects for this nation that is both a symbol of peace and prosperity and a source of instability? I believe we can envision three major scenarios: China will become a hegemonistic power, it will collapse into chaos, or it will be integrated into the international community's network of interdependence.

The Hegemony Scenario

Needless to say, the hegemony scenario is premised upon China's amazing economic growth over the past dozen or so years. To be sure, in 1981 and 1982, and again in 1989, the year of the crackdown on dissidents in Tiananmen Square, growth dipped between 4% and 5%, but otherwise it has been in the neighborhood of 10%. The World Bank estimates that in terms of purchasing power parity, China already has the world's third-highest gross national product. If growth continues at the present tempo, there is no doubt that China will be the biggest or second-biggest economic power in the world early in the twenty-first century.

The question is, what kind of economic power will it become. There are some who see Japan's evolution from an economic to a political power and then to a military power as inevitable. If the same reasoning is applied to China, it is destined to become a military superpower by the beginning of the next century. But just as this reasoning is not necessarily on target with regard to Japan, it need not be accepted uncritically in China's case. Nevertheless, recent trends in China appear to justify the hegemonic power scenario.

First, in the five years since 1989 military spending has risen more than 10% annually. Second, China has taken a fairly hard-line attitude over territorial claims. In 1992 it enacted a territorial waters law, officially declaring that the Senkaku Islands, as well as the Spratlys in the South China Sea, are part of China's territory. Third, high-level naval officers and other leaders have made it clear that China intends to undertake a concentrated buildup of sea power. And at the 14th National Congress of the Communist Party of China, convened in October 1992, Admiral Liu Huaqing was made a member of the Standing Committee of the Politburo. Fourth, China has been eagerly procuring weapons from the former Soviet Union, purchasing 26 Sukhoi-27s from Russia in 1992 and ordering another 24 in 1993 (apparently, however, it has not yet been agreed whether China will manufacture these under license). And fifth, in 1993 China conducted an underground nuclear test in the face of international expressions of concern.

Of course we cannot conclude from these trends that China is bound to become a military superpower. In the report on the work of the government that he delivered at this year's National People's Congress, Premier Li Peng sought to allay such fears by stating, "China opposes hegemony in any form. It does not seek hegemony now, nor will it ever do so when it is fully developed. China does not pose a threat to any country or region in the world. On the contrary, it has always been a reliable force for the preservation of regional and world peace" (*Beijing Review*, 4–10 April 1994, xvi).

Nevertheless, this scenario cannot be dismissed out of hand. Even if we can be certain that China's per capita GNP will not rise much even after the year 2000, a nation's military strength rests on the total human and material resources it can mobilize; per capita wealth is irrelevant. In fact, countries with high per capita GNP also have high personnel costs, which limits their ability to mobilize human resources. Therefore, if China continues to modernize its armed forces, it is reasonable to project that the nation will boast substantial military strength early in the next decade.

How will a China possessing such military power behave? If the nation reverts to its traditional pattern (that of imperial China), we could see a revival of "tribute diplomacy"—China will refrain from bullying other nations as long as they pay it due respect and accede to its demands. But countries that have undergone the baptism of nationalism, based on the concept of sovereignty that originated in early modern Europe, will not be able to accept the status of "tributary states" or a "China versus the barbarians" order. We could see a return to constant conflict between China and surrounding countries, or China might resort to force to get its way.

Even if China became the predominant power in Asia, it would be extremely difficult for it to dominate the entire world. Strong though China might be, it would probably find itself vying for supremacy with the United States, the European Union, Russia, India, and Japan. In other words, if China seized hegemony in Asia, this would generate a global power-balance game. The power politics of the eighteenth and nineteenth centuries would be reenacted in Asia with twenty-first-century weaponry.

The Chaos Scenario

Diametrically opposed to the scenario of a hegemonistic China is that of a China in chaos. The former is premised on continued economic expansion, the latter on the failure of growth policies.

Speaking in July 1990, Deng Xiaoping presented the following classic formulation of the chaos scenario:

[During the Great Cultural Revolution] aged leaders like Chairman Mao Zedong and Premier Zhou Enlai had prestige. Though it may have seemed like "total civil war," there were no major battles; civil war in the true sense of the term did not break out. Now, however, things are different. If disorder occurs again, the party will be of no use and the state power will be of no use. One faction will take control of one part of the military; another faction will take control of another part. In short, there will be civil war. Even if a few "champions of democracy" seize power, they will end up fighting one another. If civil war breaks out, rivers of blood will flow. There will be no room for talk of "human rights" and such. If civil war occurs, each side will claim supremacy, production will fall, transport will be cut off, and a million or even 10 million refugees will flee to other countries. The greatest impact will be on the Asia-Pacific region, the region the world expects the most of. It will be a global disaster.

Naturally, the point Deng was making was that the way to prevent chaos is to perpetuate Communist Party rule. But by his logic, sustained economic growth is an indispensable condition of continued party rule. *The Selected Works of Deng Xiaoping* contains the following passage: "It is most essential to strengthen ideological and political work and stress the spirit of hard struggle, but counting just on these will not suffice. The most fundamental factor is the rate of economic growth which, moreover, should be manifested in a gradual improvement of the people's living standards. Only when the populace comes to see the real benefits that stability brings and the advantages of current systems and policies can we have genuine stability" (*Beijing Review*, 3–9 January 1994, 9).

According to Deng's thinking, if China fails to achieve economic growth, it will be unable to improve the people's standard of living and the chaos outlined above will occur. If the possibility of failure cannot be ruled out, and if we accept Deng's reading of the consequences, we cannot ignore the plausibility of the chaos scenario. Deng is not the only one who has painted such a picture. Many observers outside China have done the same. The Sinologist Nakajima Mineo, for example, has warned, "China today is a pressure cooker. If we draw near, thinking delicious rice is being cooked, it could blow up in our faces" (1994, 107).

Moreover, chaos could occur even if things went well according to Deng's criteria. He assumes that as long as satisfactory economic growth continues, Communist Party rule and national stability will persist. But economic success could lead to increased pressure for political liberalization, threatening the party system and leading to political unrest.

If the chaos scenario became a reality, the impact on surrounding countries would be enormous. The situation during the second and third decades of this century, following the collapse of the Qing dynasty in 1911, may provide a historical precedent. Civil strife continued as contending warlords defended their turf; no group could establish a unified government. To understand the deleterious effect this had on the security of East Asia as a whole, we have only to look at the Sino-Japanese War that broke out in 1937 and led to the Pacific War.

The Interdependence Scenario

There is a third scenario, however, that is more promising, both for the international community and for China. This one posits increased prosperity leading to stronger ties of interdependence with the international community and open, restrained behavior.

To be sure, economic expansion increases the possibility of a strong, hegemonistic China. But we must note that, at present, growth is occurring in the context of extremely close ties of interdependence with the international community. China would not be enjoying its present extraordinary development without an increasing flow of direct investment from overseas and rapidly rising exports to the United States and Japan. A continued influx of funds and technology, as well as expanding markets, is indispensable to future growth. If China indulged in big-power arrogance or militaristic behavior toward other countries, it would jeopardize the funds, technology, and markets it needs. It is becoming increasingly difficult for China to act without taking this fact into account.

Even the present degree of economic interdependence is having a deterrent effect on adventurism. In the 1980s something happened to cause tension between China and Japan every two or three years. In 1982 Beijing protested against Ministry of Education-mandated revisions in a Japanese history textbook that minimized Japan's aggression in World War II. In 1985 there was a fuss when Prime Minister Nakasone Yasuhiro visited Yasukuni Shrine, a shrine dedicated to Japan's war dead, in his official capacity on the anniversary of the end of World War II—the first postwar prime minister to do so. In 1987 there was a diplomatic flap when the Osaka High Court ruled that the Kōkaryō, a dormitory for Chinese students since prewar times, was the property of Taiwan rather than China. The main reason none of these incidents escalated into a major confrontation was China's wish to maintain good relations with Japan in order to pursue its open-door economic policy, though of course Japan's conciliatory approach was also a factor.

Sino-American relations have been highly awkward since 1989. It is easy to see that one reason China has not reacted in an extreme manner is the importance of the US market. In 1992, the US sold Taiwan 150 F-16 jet fighters, but China took no retaliatory measures. By contrast, when the Netherlands sold Taiwan two submarines in the early 1980s, the Chinese government expressed its displeasure by recalling its ambassador from The Hague and requesting that the Dutch ambassador in Beijing leave.

In addition to increasing its ties of economic interdependence, involving China deeply in the activities of international organizations could help restrain its behavior abroad. The basic raison d'être of such organizations is, after all, to impose certain restraints on nations' actions. Moreover, the multilateral conferences and negotiations of these bodies tend to generate a kind of international consensus. It is not unreasonable to conjecture that participation in the Asia-Pacific Economic Cooperation Forum and in the ASEAN Regional Forum is constraining China's actions in the South China Sea.

It is also quite possible that China will become more open internally. At this stage it is hard to imagine the nation shifting from Communist Party rule to a stable system of liberal democracy. Despite human rights violations and political repression, however, Chinese society is definitely opening up. With economic growth, more information is circulating. Interchange with the external world is also expanding. Open societies find it harder than closed societies to engage in extreme actions outside their borders, since people can learn what the government is doing from unofficial information sources.

Of course, there is no guarantee that China will always put economic considerations first, nor can we conclude that membership in international organizations will deter it from bringing military power to bear if it judges that life-and-death interests are at stake. An open society does not mean a government that always respects public opinion, and nationalistic public opinion could incite a hard-line stance toward the external world. My point here, however, is that the interdependence scenario is neither impossible nor unrealistic.

Still, the future being uncertain, both the hegemony and the chaos scenarios are also within the bounds of possibility. What is important is to consider the policies we want to adopt toward China in light of these three scenarios. If, as I wrote above, East Asia's security is at a crossroads, and if trends in China have a decisive impact on regional security, without question the most desirable scenario for neighboring nations, including Japan, is that of an interdependent China. The major issues for anyone concerned over regional security are two: first, what to do to encourage greater economic interdependence, more active involvement in international organizations, and the development of a more open society; and second, how to minimize the danger if the first or second scenario unfolds.

Relations with America and Russia

Even if we know what kind of China we would like to see, the way to make this a reality is not self-evident, since a variety of factors are involved. When we consider East Asia's international political picture, it is not enough to examine trends in the region's nations; trends in certain extra-regional powers, namely the United States and Russia, are also important—so much so, in fact, that these nations could almost be called regional powers.

Most important are trends in the United States. Frankly, the Clinton administration's Asia policy is not very well coordinated. On the one hand, the present policy evinces an interest in the Asia-Pacific region that is unusual for a US administration. Behind this, needless to say, is the region's economic growth and the administration's recognition that developing markets there is in America's long-term interest. On the other hand, policies toward the individual countries of the region are being handled rather clumsily. There is tension with China over human rights, and economic friction with Japan is not being dealt with smoothly. It is also difficult, at this point, to think highly of US policy toward North Korea.

Despite this lack of coordination and finesse,

however, the fact that the administration is taking the Asia-Pacific region seriously is a welcome development. This is clear in light of the three scenarios for China discussed above. If China were to show hegemonistic tendencies, the United States is the only country that could impose military restraints on its behavior. If China fell into chaos, US involvement would be needed to minimize the regional effects and to coordinate the response among the countries of the region. And if we want the third scenario, in order to show China the advantages of economic interdependence it is necessary that the US market be closely linked to the Asian economy.

Russia is also a key player in East Asia, and its instability has important ramifications for regional security. Its relations with China are also extremely important. In Japan, we tend to think of Russia exclusively in relation to the bilateral dispute over the so-called Northern Territories, a handful of small islands off Hokkaido. And because, naturally enough, most of our attention during the Cold War was focused on dealing with the Soviet threat, we seldom thought of our relationship with the giant to the north in the context of multilateral relations. Now that the Cold War is over, however, it is becoming increasingly inappropriate to perceive Russia in terms of bilateral relations alone.

If we add Russia to the multinational framework of East Asia, bearing in mind the three scenarios for China, we will see that this country occupies a position very like that of the United States. Should China turn hegemonic, Russia could also act as a restraining force, even if not to the same extent as the US. As for the chaos scenario, the harmful effects on surrounding nations can not be minimized without Russia's cooperation. If Russia did not share in the coordinated action, we could see a return to the kind of lawlessness that characterized China in the 1920s. Finally, Russia might not be able to play as large a role as the United States or Japan in making the interdependence scenario a reality, but greater economic interdependence between northeastern China and the Russian Far East would be helpful. In short, Russia has a key part to play as a restraining force in the event of the first scenario,

as a cooperative force in the case of the second, and as an economic partner to help avert the first two and bring about the third.

Japan's Policy Options

What policies should Japan adopt to improve East Asian security, especially from the perspective of China's future? Given the scenarios outlined above, the principles are clear. First, we should create the conditions for strengthening China's economic interdependence, increasing its participation in international organizations, and encouraging a more open society. Second, we should consider measures to ensure that China does not become hegemonistic or fall into chaos. And third, we should prepare to deal with these unfavorable developments in case they come to pass.

In real politics, principles often contradict one another. Encouraging interdependence would lead to greater economic growth, thus laying the groundwork for hegemony. Alternatively, growth could invite social unrest, thus paving the way for chaos. In short, the first and second principles are potentially contradictory. As for the third principle, preparing for a hegemonistic China could be perceived by the Chinese as hostile behavior, which might encourage them to opt for hegemonistic rather than cooperative behavior.

Therefore, as we formulate our plans we must be aware that there is no such thing as a single perfect policy. We also need to consider what specific measures have the highest probability of bringing all three principles to fruition at once. I cannot enumerate all the possible measures here, but I will suggest a few things Japan can do.

First, Japan, along with the United States, Taiwan, and as many other countries as possible, should make direct investments in China and should welcome the global expansion of Chinese exports. We should also actively promote China's membership in international organizations. Membership in the General Agreement on Tariffs and Trade (GATT) should be accomplished as quickly as possible, for the sake of GATT as well as China. This means doing our best to persuade the United States, which is cool to the idea. We should welcome US pressure on China in regard to human rights, but we should also quietly make the point to Washington that it is unwise to link human rights to most-favored-nation status. In addition, we should cooperate as far as possible in improving China's communications network.

We should constantly demand greater transparency with regard to China's military capability and press China to exercise restraint in weapons trade. We should ask the same of Russia in regard to arms sales to China, using economic aid as leverage. Japan's official development assistance guidelines, which call for caution in providing aid to countries that sell weaponry, will probably not be applied strictly to Russia, but we should at least adhere to their spirit.

It is not advisable at this time for Japan to build up its own military strength in readiness for hegemony or chaos, since there is a high probability that this would be counterproductive. Instead, we should concentrate on maintaining our basic defense capability and seek America's continued military presence in the Pacific. We also need to begin building long-term friendly relations with Russia.

In any case, specific measures should be implemented on the basis of judicious evaluation of their suitability to a given situation; they should not be applied inflexibly. Diplomacy always requires subtlety. What is most important is to constantly bear in mind the principle of promoting China's interdependence and preventing both hegemony and chaos. Concrete measures should be weighed against this principle and applied as appropriate.

Courtesy of TBS-Britannica.

English version originally published by Japan Echo in *Japan Echo* 22, no. 3 (1994).

Translated from "'Haken, konran, sōgo izon' mittsu no shinario," in *Asteion* (Summer 1994): 76–83.

Bibliography

Li Peng. "Report on the Work of the Government." Speech delivered 10 March 1994. *Beijing Review* 37, no. 14 (4–10 April 1994): i–xvi.

Deng Xiaoping. "China Will Never Allow Other Countries to Interfere in Its Internal Affairs." Remarks made 11 July 1990. In *The Selected Works of Deng Xiaoping, 1982–1992*, Vol. 3. Beijing: Foreign Languages Press, 1994.

———. "The International Situation and Economic Issues." Comments made 3 March 1990. *Beijing Review*, no. 1 (3–9 January 1994). Also published in *The Selected Works of Deng Xiaoping, 1982–1992*, Vol. 3 (Beijing: Foreign Languages Press, 1994).

Nakajima Mineo. "Shin Ajia shugi ni mirai wa aruka" [Does the New Asianism Have a Future?]. *Shokun!* (January 1994).

I-(4) The Emerging Political and Security Order in the Asia-Pacific

A Japanese Perspective

Nakanishi Hiroshi

ABSTRACT There were no multilateral frameworks in the Asia-Pacific region on security and politics in the early Heisei years. As of 1994, when this paper was written, Northeast Asia and Southeast Asia were the two most important geopolitical security areas for Japan. In Northeast Asia, attention centered primarily on North Korea's drive to become a nuclear state, yet the reality of different interests and different goals meant that a multilateral framework was impractical even though all of the countries in the region were concerned. In Southeast Asia, there are two core frameworks that, it is hoped, can complement each other in the search for solutions. One is APEC, which is primarily economic with the potential for political influence, and the other is ASEAN with its openness to extra-regional players.

Japanese political and security concerns in the Asia-Pacific region can be subdivided into two subregional and one region-wide categories: (1) the concern for the Northeast Asian subregion, in which Japanese territorial security is directly affected, (2) the concern for the Southeast Asian subregion, through which vital Japanese sea lines of communication pass, and (3) the concern for the mode of institutionalizing political and security dialogues in the Asia-Pacific region for the purpose of, among other things, cultivating an environment amenable to regional stability and economic development. The first two subregional categories each include one potential flashpoint, the North Korean nuclear doubt issue and the South China Sea territorial dispute respectively. Though both issues require crises prevention and preparation for possible crisis management, their handling must also be considered with a long-term perspective for the subregional and regional peace and stability in mind. In general, when it comes to political and security matters in the region, Japan prefers an evolutionary approach to a hasty, mechanistic system-building one.

Security in the Northeast Asian Subregion

In spite of the drastic ups and downs in Japan's fate since the opening of the country in the 1850s, the geopolitical conditions that affect Japanese territorial security have been relatively constant. Theoretically, the potential threat could come from the north from Russia, later the Soviet Union and now again Russia, or from the south from sea powers, especially Great Britain or the United States. But the direction that has worried Japanese leaders since the Meiji era is the northwest, the Korean Peninsula. The peninsula in the hands of an antagonistic power was thought to pose the most imminent threat to the Japanese territory. Whatever motivated Japanese imperial expansion until its defeat in the Pacific War, the instability of the Korean regime and the fear of the penetration of a great power influence on the peninsula gave Japan an excuse to annex Korea in 1910. After the collapse of the Japanese Empire, the Korean War and the ensuing American presence in South Korea saved Japan from the potentially most serious security concern. Now that the Cold War is over, the Korean problem looms large among Japanese security concerns again.

The current concern over the Korean Peninsula has two aspects: short-term and long-term. The current crises as to North Korean nuclear proliferation is the short-term concern. The issue of stability on the Korean Peninsula and unification is the long-term one. Even though the former constitutes a very serious security concern, the geographical proximity of the peninsula makes it imperative Japan put the problem into the perspective of long-term stability in Northeast Asia. The ideal scenario for Japan is that North Korea succumbs to the relatively moderate international pressure and quits its attempts to own nuclear weapons, if it really is conspiring to do so. In due course, the scenario continues, North Korea opens up its society slowly and makes a gradual and peaceful transition toward coexistence with or absorption by South Korea.

If things do not go as ideally as just described, Japan will be forced to make a difficult choice. UN economic sanctions against North Korea, if carried out, might raise the question of the remittance of Koreans in Japan to North Korea or the debate on the legality of the Maritime Self-Defense Force engaging in an economic blockade, both of which could become not only very divisive issues within Japanese society but could also have a negative influence on the long-term stability in the region, because mishandling these issues may result in ill-feelings between the Japanese and the Koreans, in the North and in the South. Military sanctions against North Korea can cause even greater trouble, ranging from a direct military attack on Japanese territory to the problem of massive refugees from the peninsula.

The long-term problem of the peninsula is no less a headache for Japan. If the North Korean regime collapses, the possible arrival of refugees from the peninsula would surely cause a strenuous political problem. Even if the collapse takes place without shots fired, the Japanese government will be asked to help the South Korean government, which will have to bear a heavy cost for absorbing the collapsed society. Japan will help the Korean government, but underdoing it may cause Korean resentment and overdoing it may draw Japan into Korean politics.

The current Japanese government does not seem able to come up with a solution to avoid these gloomy prospects. In this sense, Japan is counting on crisis prevention rather than crisis management. Still, it is possible to point to the basic policy stance of Japan. Firstly, it regards the continued US engagement in the security of the Korean Peninsula as extremely significant. Different from other powers in the region, such as Korea, Russia, China, and Japan, who have too large security stakes on the peninsula, the US is the only country who has the capability and reasonable detachedness to play the role of an "honest broker" on the peninsula. Secondly, Japan is more willing than before to have closer contact on security matters with the South Korean government. It seems that both the Japanese government and the South Korean government recognize the importance of policy coordination in preparation for a possible crisis. The three-party discussion among the United States, South Korea, and Japan is also thinkable. Thirdly, Japan has started bilateral talks with China and Russia respectively. Japan wants these two countries to wield influence over North Korea so that they will take an open, reasonable stance.

Is there a possibility for creating a Northeast Asian multilateral security regime? Given the current situation in the region, the prospect does not look favorable. There are too many bilateral problems among the countries in the region. Japan has territorial problems with Russia regarding the Northern Territories, with China on the Senkaku (Diaoyutai) Islands, and with South Korea on Takeshima (Dokdo) Island. The differences of regime and ideology among the states in the region will also be an obstacle against the formal discussion. Still, some problems may be better handled in a multilateral setting. For example, the issue of security in the Okhotsk Sea may be discussed trilaterally by the US, Russia, and Japan. The problem of security in Mongolia can also be a matter for multilateral discussion.

In short, the Northeast Asian security scene, which has significant relevance for Japanese territorial security, looks more like a place for a balance of power and the tactful diplomacy of a few independent actors than a place for collective problem-solving. The possibility of some matters being taken up by a multilateral framework is not excluded, but in general, multilateral dialogues seem better left to a wider regional setting, which the paper will discuss below.

Security in the Southeast Asian Subregion

Since Japan is heavily dependent on foreign countries for raw materials, markets, and investments, Japan's security interest in maintaining a stable environment for the flow of goods, money, and human beings is almost as strong as the one regarding its territorial security. In particular, Japan holds the safety of sea communication to the American continent and to the Middle East as vital for its economic security. Since the former is thought to be relatively secure in the hands of the US navy and the Japan Self-Defense Force, the discussion of nonterritorial security has focused on the line linking Japan and the Middle East.

During the Cold War, the major threat to the Japanese sea lines of communication (SLOC) was thought to be the Soviet Far Eastern Fleet stationed at Vladivostok. Now the focus of our attention seems to be moving to the South China Sea, stretching from the Straits of Malacca to the Bashi Strait between Taiwan and the Philippines. The South China Sea has islands and reefs on which several countries have rival claims, most notably the Spratlys and the Paracels.

In spite of the interest Japan feels in the security of the South China Sea, Japan recognizes that the direct presence of the Japanese maritime forces there is likely to do more harm than good for stability in the area. Therefore, the American commitment to the protection of the safety of SLOC, backed by the appropriate military presence, is viewed as a significant factor for Japanese security, and Japan, for its part, will assist the US to fulfill this commitment as long as Japanese political consensus, including constitutional interpretation, allows.

Historically, the existence of a predominant sea power, such as the present US navy, is the most important factor for the security of the SLOC. Still, new types of threats to the SLOC in the form of piracy or terrorism may need a different approach for security at sea, for which purpose the US navy may be too large an axe. In addition, it is desirable the interested countries reach a consensus as to the safety of the SLOC. Thus, a multilateral framework for discussion and possibly confidence-building measures or naval cooperation among the interested parties, including the US, the ASEAN member states, Indochinese states, China, Taiwan, South Korea, Japan, and possibly Russia and India, seems worth considering.

One of the keynotes of Japanese policy toward Southeast Asia from the late 1970s on has been the economic cooperation of the Indochinese states with the ASEAN countries. One of the first articulations of this policy was the so-called Fukuda doctrine expressed in 1977. The recent Japanese involvement in the Cambodian peace process and its later participation in the UN peacekeeping operations there under the UNTAC prove that the policy line since the Fukuda doctrine still continues. Japan will continue to use its, mainly but not exclusively, economic influence so that political stability based on an open economy will be maintained in the region.

As to the territorial disputes in the South China Sea, in the San Francisco Peace Treaty, Japan "renounces all right, title and claim to the Spratly Islands and to the Paracel Islands" [Article 2 (f) of the Treaty of Peace with Japan]. Given this historical background, Japanese direct involvement in the dispute will confuse, rather than contribute to, its peaceful resolution. Still, Japan's own territorial disputes, especially with China over the Senkaku (Diaoyutai) Islands makes Japan a keen observer of the way the territorial disputes in the South China Sea are handled. Therefore, while the informal workshops held under the auspices of Indonesia are looked on favorably, the creeping unilateral occupation by one or more claimants, if it acquires tacit international recognition, will be seen as setting a bad precedent for the peaceful resolution of territorial conflicts in the region. The American stance on this problem is of great interest to Japan.

Political and Security Dialogues in the Region

In addition to the questions at the subregional level, there is an upsurge of interest in the institutionalization of the regional political and security dialogues covering the whole Asia-Pacific region. Currently, there are two burgeoning institutions that may deal with political and security matters. First the APEC, which was initiated by Australia more as a process for economic dialogue in the Asia-Pacific in 1989, is increasingly becoming an institution for regional dialogues, though its scope is still predominantly limited to economic matters. (APEC, which stands for Asia-Pacific Economic Cooperation, currently consists of 17 members: the United States, Japan, Australia, Canada, New Zealand, South Korea, and the six ASEAN countries, China, Taiwan, Hong Kong, Mexico, and Papua New Guinea.) Second, there are various fora linked to ASEAN, such as the Post-Ministerial Conference (PMC) and the proposed regional forum, which is to meet for the first time this summer. (ASEAN consists of six members: the Philippines, Indonesia, Malaysia, Singapore, Brunei, and Thailand. Seven dialogue partners joined the PMC: the United States, Japan, South Korea, Australia, New Zealand, the EU, and Canada. The regional forum is expected to invite China, Laos, Vietnam, Papua New Guinea, and Russia in addition to the PMC members.) Japan has been positive in promoting political and security dialogues, whose expression can be seen in Foreign Minister Nakayama Tarō's proposal at the ASEAN PMC in 1991 and the Bangkok address by Prime Minister Miyazawa in January 1993.

The Japanese attitude to the regional dialogue can be termed "gradualism." Japan favors increased chances for regional discussion, but only to the extent it does not throw the baby out with the bathwater. Given the diversity of the Asian countries, too hurried an approach calling for a universal stance on such issues as human rights or the environment can disturb the emergence of the sense of community in the region. Therefore, current Japanese policy puts priority on cultivating the atmosphere conducive to discussion through the promotion of economic growth and maintenance of political stability within the region. It does not mean that Japan ignores the human rights infringement in some of the states in the region, but postwar Japanese diplomacy has regarded "carrots" such as economic assistance as more important tools than "sticks." In addition, the Asian way of social communication, which puts importance on "keeping face," tends to make open denunciation at a formal place counterproductive.

Based on this recognition, Japan finds the functional division of labor between APEC and ASEAN fora reasonable for the moment. While the legitimacy and prestige of ASEAN as a group of Asian countries makes political and security discussions in ASEAN-related fora less objectionable in the eyes of the Asian people, APEC can call for the wider participation of the countries in the region, including such "entities" as Taiwan and Hong Kong. And the limited focus of APEC on economic issues can be easily overruled from time to time, if the matter is recognized as a common concern for all the participants, as the reference to the importance of US-China-Japan cooperation at the Seattle informal summit last November suggests. After all, economic growth through an open economy is the most common thread that unites the countries in the region together. In a sense, APEC can function as a safety net, supporting the political and security dialogue in ASEAN-linked fora from below.

Among other things, the major objective for regional political and security dialogue from the Japanese perspective is to involve China in the multilateral framework. Intermeshing China with various networks linked to the outer world will hopefully strengthen the position of those in China who think that cooperation with neighbors is truly advantageous to the country's national interest. Japan does not favor a militarily powerful and expansionist China, but nor does it want to have a politically divided China in turmoil. The latter, which we experienced in the first half of this century, was the largest element of uncertainty in the region, and given the current size of the Chinese population, its political paralysis can be a serious security threat to its neighbors. The soft landing of the Communist regime, gradually transforming itself to a more open, democratic, and decentralized governing system, is the best imaginable scenario at this moment.

In the region, there was never a system consisting of multiple modern states. Actually, the region has never seen an autonomous international system among equal actors, though we had the tribute system centered around China. Therefore, creating a regional political and security system is an ambitious challenge for the countries in the region, including the United States and Japan. But Japan is willing to take on this challenge, based on cooperation with the United States.

Originally published by the University of California Institute on Global Conflict and Cooperation in *Policy Paper 10: The United States and Japan in Asia Conference Papers* (1994).

I-(5) China's Place in the International Community

Kokubun Ryosei

ABSTRACT The "China threat" has been part of the international discourse since the 1990s. It was triggered by the end of the Cold War and the loss of the Soviet Union as the common hypothetical enemy, yet it was also fueled by the fact that China is both strongly Sino-centric and exceedingly opaque politically and militarily. Externally, China's policies may be characterized as neo-realistic in seeking to benefit from economic interdependence and to co-structure an international order led by the great powers, including China. We are now at a crossroads. Will China become a constructive member of the international community or will it be a disruptor? Security dialogue and more among Japan, the US, and China are clearly imperative.

Across the globe, much of the current discussion on China has focused on it as a threat. Recent opinion polls in Japan, too, indicate a worsening of China's image. Why is this so? Behind this heightened mistrust lies China's increased defense spending, continued nuclear weapons tests, arms exports, military exercises during the Taiwanese presidential election, and moves to press its claim to the Spratly Islands. The fast growth of China's economy at a time when many economies are slumping is adding to the concern. The gigantic scale of China's population of 1.2 billion is also rather overwhelming. It creates the impression of a country that is liable to demand huge volumes of food, consume great quantities of energy, and severely pollute the environment as it rapidly industrializes.

The international community has begun to grow impatient with China. Whenever Beijing is called upon to explain Chinese behavior with respect to one problem or another, its responses come across as insufficient and doctrinaire. And at times, they show evidence of the old Sino centric thinking. Proud of their glorious history and tired of the humiliation they have endured in recent times, the Chinese people must feel that they are at last coming into their own. But if they become too stridently assertive, they will only alarm people in other nations. Asked about the rise in military spending, they say the extra money is merely a response to inflation and is mainly going into pay. Asked about nuclear tests, they explain that China conducts few of them, adheres to a peaceful nuclear policy, and would never be the first to use nuclear weapons. Concerning the Spratly Islands, they say what they really want is to cooperate in multilateral development of oil resources.

The China-as-Threat Camp

What does it mean when a country is seen as a threat? The term has a range of definitions, but military and security issues should be considered first and foremost. Assessments of the validity of a Chinese threat should be based, in this case, on the purposes and potential of China's armed forces. Here is how the "China-as-threat" camp sees it: Chinese military ability is currently quite low. But the nation clearly aspires to future status as a superpower in all respects, including military clout, and this is very worrisome. China's moves must therefore be observed closely.

It is hard to get a grip on what China's true objectives may be. It is said that military personnel are moving into key political positions, but how much power they may have cannot be ascertained because of the extreme opacity of Beijing's policymaking process—an opacity that only amplifies the view that China is a menace. China appears to have begun to recognize this and is trying to avoid projecting its military might. But if it resumes nuclear weapons testing, international opinion, particularly in Japan and Southeast Asia, will shift suddenly and markedly toward seeing China as a threat.

Viewed objectively, China's current internal problems are such that it has little leeway to concern itself with its threatening image abroad. These include the gradual fragmentation of the country brought on by the weakening of the central government, widening economic differentials between fast-growing and slow-growing regions, accumulating debts in state-owned enterprises, deteriorating conditions in impoverished farming communities, and unrest in minority regions. Lengthening this list is the instability of Chinese leadership on the eve of the post–Deng Xiaoping era.

In this situation, Beijing has been seeking to make domestic use of the China-as-threat argument. The leadership of the Chinese Communist Party (CCP) wants to divert the people's attention from internal problems by shifting their focus to the world's supposed attempt to "contain" China. The CCP is trying to whip up patriotic indignation at this containment ploy. The upshot of this preoccupation with internal affairs and insensitivity to external appearances is that alarmist views of China are spreading internationally.

It is not only Chinese factors that have contributed to China's menacing image. Conditions in other nations and international factors have done their part. In this respect, the ramifications of the end of the Cold War deserve comment. Under the conditions of this conflict, Japan, the United States, and China maintained a strategic alliance in the face of a common antagonist, the Soviet Union. But now the enemy has disappeared, and a new one is needed. In this context, "irrepressible Chinese behavior" offers a convenient target.

A certain sense of superiority, held perhaps unconsciously by Japanese and Americans, based on China's status as a developing country has also been involved. Today, the United States and Japan both have slow-moving economies, while China's economy is zipping along. Many Japanese and Americans are having difficulty coming to terms with this. Even as China seems unable to grasp how to function as a member of international society, the global community, confronted with China's huge presence, is equally unable to decide how to deal with it.

We must not forget the lessons of history. If we treat China as a threat, it will come to see us similarly and take action to defend itself. Mutual distrust may escalate into an inability to talk together, and a new Cold War may begin. We have reached a truly critical juncture in our relationship with China. We must work wisely and ceaselessly to avoid another Cold War.

Political Science with Chinese Characteristics

What is China's diplomatic strategy for the post–Cold War era? An examination of recent trends in Chinese political science is informative when considering this.

The study of international politics was an undeveloped science in Mao Zedong's China. Not until the 1980s, when Beijing had begun to pursue its open-door policy, did international political science become an independent discipline. Under Mao, China made changing the world order the focus of its existence, but under Deng Xiaoping, it switched to a global strategic outlook premised on the existing order. The times called for a more realistic policy, which could only be fashioned through the study of international politics.

Chinese political science is highly critical of its American counterpart. It rejects both the idealism of American political science, which raises the banner of humanism rooted in democracy and human rights, and its realism, which endorses the use of state-centered power politics. The Chinese claim their country could never come to appreciate such a value system fostered by the American political climate. As an alternative, they have patched together a theory of international politics "with Chinese characteristics." This is a study that uses the conditions of China as its starting point and seeks to safeguard Chinese sovereignty and promote its national interests. Here, the salient Chinese characteristics are the fact of being a socialist country, the fact of being a developing nation, and the Chinese people's traditional love of peace.

Frankly speaking, these do not appear to be uniquely Chinese traits. It may further be observed that the central place given to China's sovereignty and interests makes this a highly "realistic" approach to international politics. But in a China that has been complaining about US "hegemony" in the post–Cold War world, a realism that reduces foreign affairs to power politics is not to be welcomed.

In this respect, the thinking of the "neorealists" seems better suited to the Chinese situation. Neorealism takes the economic interdependence of states as the starting point for studies of the significance of sovereignty and national interests, and it favors the use of collective-security arrangements backed by major powers to preserve peace. And in fact, criticism of this neorealism has been muted in China's political science community. This is because this theory provides the best description of the actual course of China's socialist market economy. This course was reaffirmed by Deng in 1992, when he realized that China could avoid going the way of the Soviet Union only by actively increasing its participation in the world's interdependent economic framework.

China's goal since then has been to acquire "comprehensive national power." During the Cold War, countries competed to build up military power, but now they are also competing on many other fronts. Apart from military strength, the ingredients of power include economic strength, technological capabilities, natural resource endowments, academic excellence, political skills, and diplomatic influence. Anticipating further globalization of the world market, among these, Deng accorded economic power primary importance.

An "economy first" thesis underlies Deng's thinking. The idea is that if and only if a country makes economic progress can it also make progress in democracy, human rights, and other areas. Certainly, no country adhering to this thinking would allow the "clash of civilizations" Samuel

Huntington has prophesied as getting in the way of economic progress. But in recent days, China's advocates of this approach have been stifled by the rise of a harsher, nationalistic realism. Though China's continued progress along the route made official in 1992 depends on harmonious relations with the West, primarily with the United States, this path has been rocky ever since Washington allowed Taiwanese president Lee Teng-hui to visit the United States in June 1995. And now Sino-American relations have been further strained by the spread of China-as-threat thinking and the ascent of China's military faction.

Chinese nationalists are turning away from Asia-Pacific cooperation inclusive of the United States and loudly proclaiming "Asianism" in its place. Here, Confucianism takes the role of the unifying value system. But Asianism's intellectual paucity becomes readily apparent when we understand that Confucianism is the sole tool available for the attempt to bring all of Asia under a single roof. The nationalists know the dangers of reviving Sino-centric rhetoric, and they have cloaked their ideas in Asian garb to conceal their true intents. They are, essentially, narrow-minded cultural relativists aspiring to recreate a Chinese empire.

There is thus an intellectual struggle going on over China's international strategy. Pitted against a neorealism based on an internationalistic approach to economic development is a realism predicated on a chauvinistic cultural relativism. The evolution of China's market economy and the permeation of Western culture should boost the neorealists, while deteriorating Sino-American relations and spreading talk of a Chinese threat would give momentum to the nationalists. To return China to the stability of the course enunciated in 1992, we must apply a policy that will support the persuasiveness of the internationalists.

Wary of Japan—and of the United States

Relations between Japan, the United States, and China were relatively clear and free of contradictions during the Cold War. Whenever Japan-US, Japan-China, or US-China ties grew stronger, the other two bilateral relationships also improved.

Two conditions ensured this. First, the common antagonist they had in the Soviet Union served to solidify the trilateral relationship. Second, Japan and the United States agreed that China's efforts to modernize and participate in international society worked to their own benefit, and China itself was enthusiastic about progressing in this direction. Today, however, the Soviet Union has broken up, leaving a Russia that does not present a threat, and Japan and the United States have become unsure about how to deal with China's huge presence. Managing foreign relations is proving perplexing for China as well.

When Beijing made friends with Washington and opened ties with Tokyo in the early 1970s, it voiced its basic approval of the Japan-US Security Treaty. This was partly because the treaty served as a check on Moscow, but it was also a result of Chinese wariness toward Japan. Accounts now public of the talks at that time between Richard Nixon, Henry Kissinger, Mao Zedong, and Zhou Enlai make it clear that both Washington and Beijing saw the Japan-US security setup as an effective means of preventing Japan's remilitarization. The first reason for China's accepting attitude dissipated along with the Soviet Union, but the second reason, China's desire to restrain Japan, remains intact.

This has been reconfirmed by a series of visits to China since the autumn of 1995 by such American officials as Assistant Secretary of Defense Joseph Nye. But while continuing to approve of the treaty, China has expressed considerable misgivings at the way it has recently been reinterpreted to broaden the arena for Japan-US security cooperation from Japan's shores to the surrounding region. Reportedly, Chinese officials told their American counterparts that the expansion of Japan's security responsibilities would encourage it to become militarily independent and could eventually give the United States problems in relation to controlling Japan. To be sure, the potential for a remilitarized Japan may not be all that China finds troubling about the treaty's reinterpretation. They may be even more disturbed by the possibility that concealed in the Japan-US agreement is a scheme to contain their country.

East Asian aftereffects of the Cold War include the problems of unifying the Korean Peninsula and straightening out the relations between Taiwan and mainland China. Previously, only the situation on the Korean Peninsula was considered a security issue. But the Taiwanese situation has also been recognized as a problem since President Lee's visit to the United States last year, and especially since China's missile rattling during the campaign for the island's presidential election this March. China, insisting that the Taiwan issue is a domestic matter, is fiercely resisting all attempts to internationalize it. But in truth, this has already become an international problem. The Chinese military exercises showcased Taiwan's perilous situation to the entire world, ironically promoting the very internationalization of the problem Beijing wishes to avoid.

Weighed down by these concerns, China is growing ever more suspicious of the United States' presence in East Asia, and these doubts can only have been deepened by the menacing presence of the American aircraft carrier group that patrolled the seas around Taiwan during its election campaign. But at least for now, China is adopting a calmly observant attitude toward the revised security ties between Japan and the United States. Actually, it is probably quite nervous about the change but fears an increase in ill will if it makes too much of a fuss.

As I have repeatedly argued, China stands at a critical juncture. Will it join international society as a mature member, or will it behave like a rebellious child? Our own course is quite clear: We must welcome China to the community of nations as a full, cooperative, key member. Japan and the United States confirmed this necessity at their summit last April. We need to make real efforts to draw China in. We could involve it in future discussions of the division of roles in the Japan-US security setup, and we could launch a trilateral security forum that meets regularly. South Korea and Southeast Asian nations are growing in importance to China, and their participation in such discussions is worth considering.

Courtesy of The Yomiuri Shimbun.

English version originally published by Japan Echo in *Japan Echo* 23, no. 3 (1996).

Translated from "Chūgoku no yukue," in the *Yomiuri Shimbun*, 8, 9, and 10 May 1996, evening editions; slightly abridged.

I-(6) The Currency Crisis and the End of Asia's Old Politico-Economic Setup

Shiraishi Takashi

ABSTRACT The currency crisis started in Thailand in early July 1997, spread to South Korea toward the end of 1997, led the collapse of Suharto's "New Order" regime in Indonesia in May 1998, and brought about serious power struggle in Malaysia in September 1998. This essay was written in March 1998 (and published in April). It anticipated the fall of Suharto in the near future, but did not see the serious rift developing between Prime Minister Mahathir and Deputy Prime Minister Anwar Ibrahim.[1]

Economists have already had much to say about the Asian currency crisis that began with the devaluation of the Thai baht in July 1997, and I have no wish to wade into this particular debate. My concern is instead with the political implications of the currency turmoil.

Two broad issues stand out. The first concerns the meaning of the crisis for international politics. In structural terms, we have been presented with a question of hegemony. In terms of systems, this is a question of whether to continue to make use of the International Monetary Fund (IMF) or to rely instead on an Asian monetary fund, a concept that has been proposed as a regional mechanism for maintaining financial stability.

The crisis occurred in the context of a major current in history featuring financial liberalization and globalization and causing Asian-style politico-economic systems to be reshaped in line with the American-style capitalist system. In the process of resolving the crisis, elements of the Asian systems that do not fit with American-style capitalism are, in accordance with neoclassical economic thinking, being weeded out. Just as the fall of the Berlin Wall spelled the demise of the Soviet empire, the currency crisis may herald the end of the Cold War in East Asia. But the result is not likely to be a restructuring of the East Asian order in perfect conformity with neoclassical economics. Herein lies the significance of regional efforts to build a mechanism for currency stability, perhaps by creating an Asian monetary fund.

The other issue raised by the currency crisis falls in the domain of comparative political science. In Southeast Asia the crisis revealed that the politico-economic setups in a number of countries had reached an impasse. This was particularly true of Thailand and Indonesia, which were forced to ask the IMF for help. But the way to meet this challenge is not, as the Western media have argued, to dismantle authoritarian regimes and establish democratic systems. To be sure, the question of whether to employ authoritarian or democratic means is important. But the crisis struck with just as much intensity at democratic Thailand as it did at authoritarian Indonesia.

On closer examination, we find that the causes of the impasses in Asia's politico-economic systems differ from country to country. How did the differences arise? Let us see what the currency crisis can tell us about this, with our focus on Southeast Asia.

Party Politics and Technocracy in Thailand

Looking first at Thailand, we find that the administration of Field Marshal Sarit Thanarat, who came to power in 1957, established a "developmentalist regime" featuring conservative fiscal policy and freedom of private enterprise. A development planning and implementation organ was set up within the Finance Ministry, and the central bank achieved considerable independence from the government. I call this developmentalist regime stage one in Thailand's modern political history. It was a time of alliance between the military and technocrats, and it continued under Sarit's successor, Field Marshal Thanom Kittikachorn.

The second stage began when the student demonstrations of 1973 toppled the Thanom administration, and it lasted until 1988. This was an era marked by "power sharing." That is, the military and the technocrats worked together in coalition governments with entrepreneurs and leaders of business groups, people who had risen to the fore in the 1950s and 1960s, mainly in Bangkok.

Stage three, which is an era of "party politics," began in 1988 and is still continuing. During the previous stage, regional bosses had built up power through the management of construction firms, hotels, bus companies, and other such businesses, and by the middle of the 1980s they had gained enough clout to wrest control over political parties from the hands of the Bangkok elite. There were, to be sure, many twists and turns in this tale, but from roughly 1988 on, Thailand reached the stage of party politics—and also of "money politics."

Over this 40-year period there were two major currents in Thailand's political situation. One was progress toward democracy in the form of an increase in the number of participants in the political system. The other was the opening of fissures in the domestic political structure. A variety of clashing interests can be found in any society. In Thailand's case there were conflicts: between Bangkok and the regions; among the military, the technocrats, and Bangkok's big industrialists; and between regional bosses and Bangkok's middle class. Complicating the situation was the fact that

no "catch-all" party that could have brokered among the competing interests came into being. The era of party politics has for this reason been an era of coalition governments, and they have lacked stability because the departure of just one of the coalition partners has had the potential to bring the whole government down.

It was during the era of party politics that Thailand liberalized its financial sector and deregulated foreign-exchange controls and capital transactions. A major turning point came in 1993 when Bangkok set up an offshore financial center. This enabled an inflow of dollar-denominated funds for loans to Thai residents and caused the money supply to swell, the upshot of which was the formation of a speculative bubble. The bubble popped in 1996, and many real estate and consumer loans turned sour. Financial institutions experienced sudden deterioration in their balance sheets, and a number of them became insolvent.

With the Mexican currency crisis in the background, the Thai baht came under attack from sporadic speculation starting from January 1995, and in June 1996, the IMF was already advising the Thai monetary authorities to take a more flexible approach toward pegging their currency to the dollar. But Bangkok delayed action for a year. In June 1997 it decided to suspend the operations of 16 insolvent financial institutions, on 2 July it allowed the baht to float, and on 19 July it determined to ask the IMF for financial aid.

It cannot be said that the Thai authorities adopted the right policies at the right times with respect to either foreign-exchange controls or failing financial institutions. As this is a country that had built up a reputation for superior macroeconomic management, what could have gone wrong? No doubt many factors were involved, but from the viewpoint of the Thai politico-economic system, two factors stand out.

One was a failure of party politics. During the period of coalition governments, the available cabinet posts came to be parceled out in proportion to the number of legislative seats held by each of the parties in the coalition. The development planning and implementation organ that was created in the Finance Ministry during the Sarit administration degenerated into a center for parceling out pork among politicians, and the voice of the technocrats in determining policy grew much smaller. To put this another way, "veto groups" established bases throughout the administration. Their members, intent on protecting their own interests, would threaten to bolt the ruling coalition and cause it to collapse unless measures they viewed as unfavorable were scrapped. This undercut the government's ability to dispose of issues and resolve crises.

The other factor was an impasse reached by Thailand's technocracy. In its macroeconomic management, the Thai government had sought to maintain a sound fiscal stance, a disciplined financial policy, a stable exchange rate, and an open door to the world. The idea was that this would hold down prices and encourage confidence in the economy's management, thereby enhancing the economy's stability. In the 1990s, though, the government's concern came to focus on just fiscal soundness and exchange rate stability, particularly on the latter. Then the dollar began to soar, and the baht went up with it. This put a dent in Thailand's international competitive power, caused its balance-of-payments position to worsen, and triggered a rapid rise in short-term foreign debts.

Thailand essentially came under the control of the IMF in August last year. To the groups that had been threatening to disrupt the administration's stability unless their interests were protected, this raised the political cost of their veto power. In October 1997 Prime Minister Chaovalit Yongchaiyut lifted the taxes on gasoline and diesel oil under an economic reconstruction agreement worked out with the IMF. When one of the ruling parties protested loudly, he retracted the measure four days later, but then his finance minister resigned and his government collapsed. With the IMF's backing, the next administration, of Chuan Leekpai, was able to shut down 56 failed financial institutions. Favorable conditions will probably prevail in Thailand as long as the IMF is overseeing it. But with a regime under a new Constitution in the offing, the future is unsure. The key question is how to secure the existence of a technocracy requiring sophisticated specialists under a democratic system.

Multiracial Malaysia Wants No Aid

In the case of Malaysia, one of the key issues is its multiracial society. At the time of the census of 1970, about 56% of the population consisted of Malay (or *bumiputra*), 34% of Chinese, and 9% of Indians. The question of how to maintain harmony among these ethnic groups and prevent the kind of situation that has developed in Bosnia has been the foremost issue in Malaysian politics.

What has been done to preserve peace among these ethnic groups? During the 1950s, before the country became independent, the United Malays National Organization (UMNO), and the Malaysian Chinese Association (MCA), which represents Chinese business interests, made what is called the "bargain." Both sides agreed that once independence was attained, the Malays would be allowed a dominant position in government while the Chinese would enjoy freedom in economic activities. This pact led to the creation of the Alliance Party, which also had the support of the Indians in the Malaysian Indian Congress. Under the Alliance Party, the newly independent Malaysia got its start.

But the alliance broke apart in the wake of racial rioting in Kuala Lumpur following the general election of May 1969. The disturbance presented evidence that in the late 1960s neither the Malays nor the Chinese were still entirely pleased with the bargain they had reached. The Malays in particular were disturbed by the gap between them and the local Chinese in terms of economic status. It was around this time that Mahathir bin Mohamad, who is now Malaysia's prime minister, emerged as an advocate of rethinking the bargain to give priority to native Malays. The results of the election were another major factor. The MCA, representing the Chinese community, saw the number of its legislators fall from 27 to 13, while Muslim forces picked up seats at the expense of UMNO, which was under attack for taking a line of appeasement toward the local Chinese. The Alliance Party failed to secure two-thirds of the seats, the number needed for a constitutional amendment.

To get around this problem, the National Front, or Barisan Nasional (BN), was formed early in the 1970s, and practically all the parties, with some Muslim and Chinese exceptions, joined it. The BN gained enough seats to amend the Constitution. And with its establishment, UMNO being the major force within it, the bargain was revised. Measures favoring the *bumiputra* were pushed to the fore, including a "new economic policy" and a decision to make Bahasa Malaysia the country's official language. Needless to say, the Chinese and Indian residents were not pleased. But the government was intent on preserving racial harmony even as it sought to iron out economic imbalances, and it strove to cool down any dissatisfaction before it boiled over. Also helping to calm down emotions around this time was economic growth, which was moving at an annual pace of some 3%–4%.

With the National Front in command, the government pursued a dual policy of import substitution and export promotion, enabling the economy to build up momentum in the second half of the 1980s. The export-oriented development drew in foreign capital, while the import substitution helped to enrich Malay-operated firms that had been set up as public enterprises. The combination of these moves drove the economy forward. A multitrack approach was applied not just to industrial development but also to financing. The use of dollar-denominated funds was approved for export-oriented development aided by foreign capital in special export zones, and the funds were drawn from an offshore market. In the case of import substitution, though, the state and other public firms relied on domestic sources for their capital and loans. Then, in the 1990s, the state began selling off public enterprises at prices below market values. This privatization move was designed both to bolster the Malay middle class and to generate public support for the UMNO.

It should be clear from this brief review that Malaysia under Prime Minister Mahathir had no desire to ask the IMF for help. The currency crisis represented a danger to the multitrack approach the government had adopted for industrial development. And if growth dropped below the 3%–4% line, maintaining peace among the country's ethnic groups would have been difficult. In this light, the crisis was undoubtedly a

real threat. But if Malaysia was forced to ask the IMF for funding to get out of its difficulties, it would surely have been required to make basic changes in the economic measures it had in place. This was not an option that was desirable from the standpoints of preserving the BN coalition, retaining the UMNO's political edge, and keeping the Mahathir administration in power.

In the end, Malaysia was saved by the fact that it had adopted a multitrack policy toward raising funds in addition to its multitrack development strategy. Thus, when the value of the ringgit dropped, this did not pose a systemic risk to Malaysia's domestic financial system. But if the country's growth rate slows in the future, discontent among the Malays may turn into criticism of Mahathir from within the UMNO, which itself could come under attack in election campaigns. And the relations between the Malays and the Chinese are liable to get tense. As I said earlier, the key issue in Malaysia is maintaining harmony among racial groups. The response to the currency crisis will depend on the decisions reached about preserving the peace.

The Impasse of the Suharto Family's Business

After Suharto came to power in 1966 he proclaimed a "New Order," and it has now lasted for 32 years. The two basic tasks in this order are maintaining stability and achieving development, and the success achieved on both fronts has given legitimacy to the Suharto regime. Participation in government by the people has remained limited, but standards of living have steadily improved with the help of the implementation of development projects. Indonesia practices, we might say, "developmentalist politics."

From the beginning there were two ways of thinking about development strategy. One is the doctrine of the free trade camp, which seeks to hold government interference in the market economy to the minimum. The idea is that economic development is best accomplished by making maximum use of comparative advantage in trade. As there is not much that a government can do to alter the conditions that determine comparative advantage, the private sector should be given freedom to make its own decisions on business activities. The other strategy is state-led development, a form of economic nationalism. The idea here is that the government should take the initiative in fostering domestic industries, acting to shelter them from competitors in the world market until they reach a level of development where they can stand on their own.

During the 1970s and 1980s Indonesia wavered between these two courses, and its economy went back and forth from boom to bust as a result. On the political stage there were battles among technocrats, military officers, engineers, and politicians. The technocrats, citing the need for liberalization, took charge of macroeconomic management and supervision of the country's external debts. Under their direction, the Ministry of Finance, the central bank, and the National Development Planning Agency managed the debts, with monitoring and support from a consortium of creditor nations.

By the mid-1980s, though, developmentalist politics was being transformed. There were several reasons for this. One was that Suharto's children had grown up and moved into the business world. Another was that, with the passing of the period of high oil prices, state-led development was giving way to development led by the private sector. In addition, measures instituted to liberalize finances during the decade enabled many private-sector groups to set up their own banks, which brought in dollar-denominated loans. The moves in this direction gained full momentum in the 1990s.

Two problems then emerged. First, whereas Indonesia's external debts in the 1980s had been public debts with the government backing them, many of those in the 1990s were debts in the private sector. The established system of macroeconomic management was meant to deal with public debts only, and it did not function well in overseeing the private-sector red ink that built up in the 1990s. In the case of public-sector debts as well, the technocrats found themselves unable to slow down big government-backed projects associated with Suharto's children.

The second problem involved the raising of dollar-denominated funds by public and private

banks. Management of the state-run banks is overseen by the Finance Ministry, which means that the banks were vulnerable to political pressure. When politicians, members of the president's family, or Finance Ministry officials came calling, bankers felt compelled to extend loans, even for projects they figured would be unprofitable, and when repayment of the loans became doubtful, they concealed the problem. The nonperforming loans of public banks swelled in the 1990s for this reason. Private-sector banks were also accumulating bad debts. Their function was to serve the business groups that had set them up, and when a member of the group ran into trouble, they would lend it additional funds brought in from foreign sources at high interest rates.

The family businesses of Suharto's children were at the center of the troubles. Though initially the president had advocated state-led development, over time this degenerated into fostering the Suharto family's businesses. Such nepotism cannot be corrected merely by having some of the businesses shut down, as the IMF has demanded as part of its economic reform plan. In the twilight of the Suharto regime, the dividing line between the nation of the Indonesians and the nation of the Suharto family has become blurred. Family-centered politics is a system that relies on connections. Seen from the market perspective of neoclassical economics, it is a very degenerate system indeed. And yet this has become, for Suharto, the key to running the New Order he has ushered in.

It was in this context that Indonesia's currency crisis began, and the development of the crisis has been quite different from the Thai case as a result. Thailand's political parties may have been able to hold the government captive, but they were in no position to threaten the stability of the whole politico-economic system. Thus, when the IMF stepped in and the political costs of vetoes issued by parties rose higher, reform of the economic structure under the IMF's guidance moved forward. In Indonesia, by contrast, rumors about whether Suharto's health was deteriorating triggered worries about who might replace him early in December 1997, and Chinese Indonesians began converting assets into dollars in anticipation of social and political instability. Around the same time some government projects associated with Suharto's children that had been canceled in November were brought back to life, and the whole world began wondering whether the president would abide by his agreement with the IMF.

Such concerns grew greater early in January this year with the unveiling of Indonesia's plans for its budget. The Indonesian currency fell in value to 10,000 rupiahs to the dollar, and in the middle of the month a new agreement with the IMF was worked out. Even so, the crisis continued to worsen.

The only way to end the crisis is to restore domestic and international confidence in Indonesia's politico-economic system. This cannot be accomplished as long as the operating principle of the system is the running of the Suharto family's businesses. Thus, we find that at the root of the Indonesian crisis is an impasse reached by the Suharto regime. The crisis may have been touched off by Thailand's currency troubles, but it developed its own momentum after that.

Toward a New Politico-Economic Order

It should be apparent from what I have said that there are clear differences in the politico-economic systems of Thailand, Malaysia, and Indonesia. And yet all reached an impasse as a result of the currency crisis. In each country the way to assess the nature and seriousness of the impasse is to examine the vested interests within the politico-economic system and see how they are distributed, and also to consider how close reform measures can get to the system's core.

In Thailand's case, the impasse resulted basically from a cabinet system that parceled out both posts and pork to all the coalition partners. The currency crisis in Malaysia posed a threat to the parties in power, principally the UMNO, to the economic policies they had adopted, and most notably to the preservation of peace among ethnic groups, the key Malaysian concern. The impasse in Thailand has now been cleared away, at least for the time being, under the guidance of the IMF, and the question for the future is how to establish a solid technocracy under a democratic system. In Malaysia's case the question is how to keep the ethnic coalition of the National Front intact over the long term while also maintaining economic momentum; toward this end, economic policies are being adjusted, and political maneuvering is in progress. In short, in Thailand the IMF provided a management mechanism for overcoming the crisis, while in Malaysia a homemade mechanism was constructed to preserve racial harmony.

The Indonesian crisis is of yet a different type. The basic problem is not the failure of some mechanism to overcome the crisis but the absence of any such mechanism at all. More than that, Indonesia does not want to accept the IMF's advice. The politics centered on Suharto's family within the New Order he established has created a huge structure of vested interests, and dismantling it will mean putting an end to the Suharto regime.

The prospects for the future are still in doubt. But if, as I have argued, the Asian currency crisis was caused by the failure of the Asian politico-economic setup at a time of financial liberalization and globalization, it is clear how the problems can be solved. Even as the countries concerned seek to renew their systems, efforts should go forward to create a new politico-economic order for the Asian region. The biggest question is what Indonesia will do about its own crisis. The answer has significance not just for Indonesia but also for the overall Asian politico-economic setup. (Courtesy of Iwanami Shoten)

English version originally published by Japan Echo in *Japan Echo* 25, no. 4 (1998).

Translated from "Ajia-gata seiji keisei taisei no owari to tsūka kiki," in *Sekai* (May 1998): 44–53; slightly abridged.

Notes

1. (Ed.) This essay was written in March 1998, two months before Suharto's resignation in May.

Dynamic Stability
Cooperative Strategies for Averting Crisis in East Asia

Tanaka Akihiko

ABSTRACT Given that change is the one inevitability in the East Asian situation, efforts to develop effective security policies must be formulated recognizing that stability is dynamic, not static, and oriented not toward maintaining this or that status quo but toward ensuring change happens peacefully. This essay thus advocates (a) maintaining and strengthening the US network of alliances with Japan, Korea, and other allies, (b) strengthening the dialogue among the leading countries with interests in East Asia (particularly Japan, the US, and China), and (c) working to rebuild Asian economies.

The status quo is not sustainable in East Asia. North Korea will not stay the same in the decades to come. It may not launch a war against South Korea, and its regime may not collapse, but it seems almost certain that radical changes will eventually take place in Pyongyang or in its relations with the South. China, too, will experience significant change economically, socially, and politically. Beijing's relations with Taipei will never be static. Russia's approach to East Asia, and even its relevance to the region, will depend on its entirely unpredictable domestic politics and the viability of its economy. The democracies in the region—Japan, South Korea, and Taiwan— will have new leaders, leaders not necessarily of the post–World War II, Cold War mold. And the United States' approach to the region may vary as well. In sum, changes are inevitable in East Asia.

Any attempt to achieve international security in the region in the first few decades of the coming century should take as a basic premise the inevitability of significant change. Peace and stability are, in general, what most nations seek in their security policy. However, "stability" in any viable security policy should be understood as "dynamic stability," not "static stability." Rigid attempts to preserve the East Asian status quo will prove unworkable and may do more harm than good. The goal of a security policy in East Asia is peaceful change, not the indefinite preservation of the status quo.

Hard Landing, Soft Landing

The most obvious place where the preservation of the status quo is impossible is North Korea. Many predictions of imminent collapse of the Kim Jong-il regime have proven wrong. Five years have already passed since the death of North Korea's "Great Leader," Kim Il-sung. The successor government of Kim Jong-il has survived large-scale floods, drought, and horrendous famines. It has shown tremendous resilience to internal economic and social dislocations, as well as adroitness in bargaining with the United States, South Korea, and other countries. North Korea's record, then, might seem to suggest that collapse is not inevitable. But a "soft landing," or the gradual change of the North Korean regime so that it can coexist peacefully with South Korea and its other neighbors, is possible only if the North Korean government changes its policies substantially. As long as North Korea maintains its extreme isolation from the world community while pursuing what some observers have called "militant mendicancy," a "hard landing" or "crash landing" seems always around the corner. The neighboring countries cannot tolerate North Korea's militant mendicancy forever.

To the extent that a hard landing is undesirable on the Korean Peninsula, the policy of the United States, Japan, and South Korea should be targeted to entice changes in North Korea that are consistent with peaceful resolution of tensions. In fact, it is unrealistic to believe that we can somehow freeze the conditions in North Korea. Catastrophic famines have already loosened the regimented social fabric in North Korea; the traditional mechanism of totalitarian distribution has been shattered and replaced by emerging informal market systems. Contacts with foreigners have increased as humanitarian aid workers flow into the country. Furthermore, the site of nuclear power plants now being built by the Korean Peninsula Energy Development Organization (KEDO) could become a significant window to the outside world that cannot easily be controlled by Pyongyang. Some 150 foreigners (most of them South Koreans) have already been working together with 100 North Korean workers to build the site. As full-fledged construction starts, several thousand workers from both North and South Korea will work together there.

Soft landing will only be possible if the opening of North Korean society is promoted. But opening North Korea does not guarantee a soft landing. It could unleash social forces that would topple the North Korean regime, effectively bringing on the conditions of a hard landing. Furthermore, faced with the loosening of totalitarian control and increasing contact with outsiders, the North Korean government could re-intensify internal regimentation in the belief that opening up its society would surely lead to the demise of the current regime. The North Korean leadership quite understandably believes that it is faced with a catch-22 and that the only way out is to entreat the world community for economic support while simultaneously making militant threats. But this brings back the disastrous possibility of a crash landing, in which the North Korean government would collapse suddenly and create turmoil on the Korean Peninsula. In other words, any policy aimed at a soft landing should include provisions to cope with a hard landing. The encouragement and inducement of internal change in North Korea should be accompanied by measures both to deter Pyongyang's adventurous activities and to handle the sudden collapse of its regime, taking into consideration the host of destabilizing possibilities this would engender (including massive outflows of refugees and the spillover of internal strife).

Shifting Dragon

Conditions surrounding China are anything but static. As democratization takes root in Taiwan, more Taiwanese are losing their ties of identity with the mainland. They may choose a Nationalist candidate in the March 2000 presidential election, but even under a new Nationalist administration, the current international understanding that Taiwan is part of China will appear increasingly fictitious. If a Democratic Progressive Party candidate wins, he or she may be tempted to make the current de facto independent status of Taiwan more formal. Beijing, seeing these developments in Taiwan, could be tempted to influence them by flexing its military muscles again as it did in 1996, when it menacingly fired missiles into waters off the Taiwanese coast. Although outright military confrontation is unlikely at the moment, the situation could degenerate quickly should the wrong combination of accidental international developments arise. A war across the Taiwan Strait, in other words, cannot be ruled out.

On the other hand, it is impossible to rule out a radical compromise between Beijing and Taipei. Under current circumstances, direct contact between Beijing and Taipei is moving very slowly. As long as Beijing adheres to its current formula of "one country, two systems," Taipei is unlikely to agree to unification with the mainland. Furthermore, President Jiang Zemin, who is too deeply committed to the current formula, may not be able to come up with a new compromise. No dramatic breakthroughs are in sight at the moment. Nevertheless, the current standstill does not mean that nobody in Beijing could revise China's position. A successor to Jiang may feel compelled to strike a deal with Taipei and stabilize China's relations with the island province, as well as with the United States and Japan, who have a great stake in the safety of Taiwan.

Over the long run, China itself may undergo significant changes. If China successfully manages current difficulties with its state-owned enterprises and other problems, and continues its economic growth well into the first decade of the twenty-first century, it could become a sizable economic power. With such an achievement, it could become a force of stability, responsible for the management of international order; it could even transform itself into a democracy with widely guaranteed political liberties. However, economic growth does not in itself guarantee democratization. Growth may even reinforce the authoritarian nature of the Communist government and its highly nationalistic and assertive foreign policy.

Furthermore, it is not certain whether China can manage its current economic difficulties. If these problems overwhelm the management capability of the Communist government, they may lead to domestic instability, as has been the case most recently in Russia. The future could also see a weak, internally unstable, and possibly more nationalistic China. As elsewhere in the region, changes in China seem inevitable, while their direction is highly uncertain.

Whimpering Bear

Russia is almost irrelevant in East Asia at the moment. When Prime Minister Hashimoto Ryūtarō of Japan and President Boris Yeltsin announced in November 1997 that they hoped to sign a "peace treaty" by 2000 resolving lingering World War II-era territorial disputes between Japan and Russia, it appeared that Russia had finally emerged out of internal chaos and begun reorienting its foreign policy in East Asia. But Russia's recent economic problems, as well as the confused state of its domestic politics, deprives Yeltsin's government of the ability to take foreign-policy initiatives in East Asia. Internal political and economic realities have made it almost impossible for Russia to make compromises on the territorial issue with Japan, ruling out an avenue for radically improving its relations with Tokyo. However, in the longer run, it is impossible to exclude the possibility of a reactivated Russia once new leaders are in place. Changes in Russia may not be as radical as in North Korea or China, but some changes are still quite likely after Yeltsin's departure.

South Korea and Japan are undergoing continual transformation, although future change will be more incremental than in North Korea or China. In South Korea, radical reform already took place in the late 1980s and early 1990s. The consolidation of democracy has been a real achievement that South Koreans should be proud of. But the Kim Dae-jung government remains dominated by politicians of the Cold War generation. The post–Kim Dae-jung era will usher in a new generation of politicians in South Korea. Japan, too, is witnessing the transition out of its Cold War generation of leadership. Obuchi Keizō, if he serves as prime minister for longer than the few more years expected, may be succeeded by a politician who does not remember when Japan was impoverished after defeat in World War II.

The Keys to Success

What are the keys to maintaining "dynamic stability" in a region full of possible changes? What are the conditions for peaceful, and not violent, change?

The first is the effectiveness of the alliances of the United States—namely, the US-Japan alliance and the US-South Korean alliance. There are no alternatives to these alliances to deter North Korea's adventurous and bizarre flouting of international norms (i.e., recent covert commando intrusions into the South) and to cope with the possible chaos that might arise out of the collapse of the North Korean regime. Current trends are positive. The Japanese Diet is expected, as this magazine goes to press, to pass legislation to implement the Guidelines for Japan-US Defense Cooperation, ascertaining smooth joint cooperation between the two countries in a contingency occurring in "areas surrounding Japan." Another positive development in support of the US alliance system in East Asia was the real improvement of relations between Seoul and Tokyo following Kim Dae-jung's visit to Tokyo in October 1998. President Kim agreed with Prime Minister Obuchi on a "future-oriented" partnership between the two countries in exchange for Obuchi's "apology" for Japan's colonization of Korea in the past. The degree of improvement between the two countries has been truly unprecedented. Many Japanese were impressed by Kim's leadership, and public opinion polls showed significant improvement of South Korea's image among Japanese. Korean prime minister Kim Jong-pil made a moving speech to Japanese college students in flawless Japanese in November 1998, while Obuchi started his speech at Korea University in March 1999 with a few sentences in (albeit clumsy) Korean.

The second key to peaceful change in East Asia is enhanced dialogue among the major powers, most critically the United States, China, and Japan. If only to encourage North Korea to take the high road of reforms and greater openness, Chinese collaboration is essential. The minimum necessary condition for a successful soft landing is close cooperation between the major countries, including China. In case a hard landing or crash landing becomes likely, close cooperation among the major countries is not only necessary but essential. Without close coordination between South Korea, the United States, Japan, China, and Russia, a crash landing could be a disaster not only between North Korea and other countries involved but also among those other countries themselves. The temptation to intervene unilaterally in the event of a catastrophe in North Korea could trigger a dangerous chain reaction among neighboring countries. East Asia cannot afford to repeat the folly of the Sino-Japanese War of 1894–95, which was triggered when both China and Japan intervened to suppress the Tonghak Rebellion in Korea. In this sense, current four-party talks between North Korea, South Korea, the United States, and China are key. But this framework should be augmented by further deepening of dialogue among relevant countries, including Japan and Russia. Prime Minister Obuchi's proposal of six-party talks about the Korean Peninsula is a logical next step.

Increasing dialogue between the major countries involved is not only needed for peaceful change on the Korean Peninsula, it is needed to ensure peace in the Taiwan Strait as well as to increase understanding among new leaders coming onto the scene in the twenty-first century. Several "Track II" dialogues, which pursue less formal diplomatic channels, are being organized between the United States, China, and Japan. These activities should be further promoted, and in due course, a more official meeting between defense ministers of the three countries should be established. Much larger multilateral frameworks, like the ASEAN Regional Forum (ARF) and Asia-Pacific Economic Cooperation (APEC), should also be utilized. Particular importance should be attached to the APEC Economic Leaders' Meeting, the only occasion where the leaders of the United States, Japan, South Korea, China, and Russia all convene, together with other leaders from the Asia-Pacific region.

The third key to peaceful change in East Asia is resolution of the Asian economic crisis. Though international management of the Asian financial crisis since the summer of 1997 was less than satisfactory, it has at least prevented the financial and economic crisis from becoming an international political and military crisis. In Indonesia, the economic crisis triggered internal political upheaval, but foreign relations were not strongly affected. But if economic conditions across Asia do not take a turn for the better, the political conditions for peaceful change will grow distant. To the extent that international economics is perceived as a positive-sum game, peaceful change is likely. Nothing contributes to the popular perception that international economics is a zero-sum game more than prolonged economic recession. In this sense, coordinated economic policy is also sound security policy. The recovery of the Japanese economy and the continuation of the US boom are both critical for the future international security of East Asia.

Changes are inevitable in East Asia, and the direction they will take is uncertain. But with three key efforts—the continued viability of US alliances, deepened dialogue among major countries with a stake in East Asian affairs, and efforts toward economic recovery—peaceful change is possible.

Originally published by the Harvard International Relations Council in *Harvard International Review* 21, no. 3 (1999): 72–75.

I-(8) Japan-China Relations after the Cold War
Switching from the "1972 System"

Kokubun Ryosei

ABSTRACT Sino-Japanese relations have deteriorated steadily since the end of the Cold War. While this is in part attributable to events such as Tiananmen, the changes in the four structural elements underlying Sino-Japanese friendship since the 1972 normalization of relations are more important factors. These four are (1) the changes in the international order commensurate upon the collapse of the Cold War order, (2) the increased friction inherent in the broader contacts accompanying closer interdependence, (3) the passing of the generation that originally promoted bilateral friendship, and (4) the existential change in Taiwan's status as a result of democratization. These sources of stress highlight the need to restructure the 1972 system for the future.

It will soon be 30 years since the normalization of diplomatic relations between Japan and China in 1972. At that time, China fever raged throughout Japan. "Japan-China friendship (*yūkō=youhao*)" was a slogan heard everywhere. When one thinks about it, China was then in the throes of the Cultural Revolution—a closed country with its internal politics characterized by constant power struggles to a much greater extent than they are today. In spite of this, the two countries suddenly entered a honeymoon period. The direct trigger for this was the rapprochement between Washington and Beijing highlighted by President Richard Nixon's visit to China.

It struck me that this "Japan-China friendship" was a product of commercial-oriented media coverage and advertising, built up by exploiting images like pandas and the Silk Road. Up to the first half of the 1980s, numerous Japanese "friendship delegations" visited China and were taken to model people's communes, state-run enterprises, and schools. These visits heightened the mood of "friendship," producing all sorts of glowing comments that ran like this: "The eyes of the Chinese people are sparkling, and they are advancing in solidarity toward modernization."

In the second half of the 1980s it became possible for ordinary Japanese to travel in China relatively freely as individuals. It was also at this time that Chinese started coming to Japan in large numbers as students. In other words, Japanese and Chinese could at last come into direct contact with each other from this time on.

According to a public opinion poll conducted by the Prime Minister's Office in 1980, the proportion of respondents who "felt close" to China was 78.6%, while only 14.7% replied that they "did not feel close." The figures vis-à-vis the United States that same year were 77.2% and 17.7%, respectively. Thus, in statistical terms, the degree of friendship felt toward China was higher than that toward the United States. In subsequent years during the 1980s, the affinity ratings toward China ran in the upper 60% or lower 70% range, roughly comparable to the figures for the United States.

The Tiananmen incident in 1989, however, produced a sharp change in the favorable image of China. According to the same questionnaire survey, while 68.5% of correspondents felt an affinity with China in 1988, this dropped to 51.6% after the incident, and the proportion of respondents who "did not feel close" to China leaped from 26.4% to 43.1%. There was no

71

improvement in the image of China after this time, and indeed, in the second half of the 1990s the nonaffinity rating topped 50% in some years, reflecting such developments as the Taiwan Strait crisis.

A similar lack of warm feelings can also be observed on the Chinese side. A frequently cited survey by the *Zhongguo qingnian bao* (*China Youth Daily*) shows deeply ingrained mistrust of Japan among Chinese young people. Among the respondents to this survey, the results of which were published in the paper's 15 February 1997 edition, only 14.5% had a good impression of Japan, 43.9% had an "average" impression, and 41.5% had a bad impression. Asked which famous person first came to mind when Japan was mentioned, the most frequent. reply was Tōjō Hideki (Japan's wartime prime minister) at 28.7%. And the most frequent reply to "What do you associate with Japan?" was "the Nanking massacre" (83.9% of multiple replies); in second place were "Japanese devils" (*Riben guizi*: the wartime Chinese term for the Japanese invaders) and "the war of resistance against Japan" (*Kangri zhanzheng*) at 81.3% each.

Matters have not been exactly rosy in the area of bilateral government relations since the early l990s either. For Japan, the visit of Emperor Akihito and Empress Michiko to China in 1992 was intended to mark the end of the "history problem" and the start of a new relationship. But, from about 1995, 50 years after the end of World War II, the Chinese Communist Party embarked on repeated drives to drum up patriotism as if in response to the mounting regional self-assertiveness accompanying the shift within China toward a market economy and decentralization and the weakening of central authority. And these drives were accompanied by increased stridence in reminders of Japan's invasion of China in the 1930s. On top of this, the visit to the United States in 1995 of Taiwan's President Lee Teng-hui, followed by his reelection in 1996 in direct elections for the presidency, led to China holding military exercises involving the launching of missiles into the waters off Taiwan. By this action China provided the material for talk of the "China threat."

President Jiang Zemin's official visit to Japan in November 1998, the first by a Chinese head of state, also ended in discord. Under the new slogan of a "partnership of friendship and cooperation for peace and development," the visit was to mark a new phase in Japan-China relations with a joint declaration providing for, inter alia, setting up a hot line, encouraging youth exchanges, relaxing restrictions on Chinese tourists entering Japan, and promoting cooperation on environmental conservation. All this was accomplished, but nobody focused on these positive results. Jiang was furious because, in the drafting of the joint declaration, the Japanese side would not agree to include even a single word of apology concerning the past, and he took every opportunity to bring up the history problem during this stay, even at the palace banquet. This attitude created powerful resentment within Japan.

In July 1999 Prime Minister Obuchi Keizō visited China. The visit was concluded uneventfully, with no reference to the history issue. In October 2000, Premier Zhu Rongji of China visited Japan and undertook various activities aimed at improving bilateral relations. A highlight was when he took part in a televised dialogue with a group of ordinary Japanese citizens, turning in a fine performance with skillful answers to questions put to him. The visit was a success, in sharp contrast to Jiang's.

And yet, somehow official relations between Japan and China are still less than smooth. One aspect that is noticeable is that, while Japan is being relatively severe toward China, the Chinese are taking a soft line toward Japan, as seen, for example, in their restraint from reference to the history issue and in the arrangements made for visiting dignitaries from Japan to meet with officials more senior than themselves. This is probably a manifestation of their wish for foreign countries, especially Japan, to renew the involvement of their economic strength in the Chinese market to help China revitalize its domestic economy, which continues to be plagued by such problems as inefficient state-owned enterprises and rural poverty. China's intention is probably to slow down the trend of rapidly shrinking Japanese direct investment in China and the heavy criticism within Japan of the official development assistance (ODA) that Tokyo has been providing. If Japanese interest in China continues to plummet in spite of this, however, Beijing may run out of patience before much longer. In fact, criticisms of the country's soft policy toward Japan are already appearing on Chinese websites and elsewhere.

Why have we fallen into this vicious circle? In the remainder of this essay I will examine the background to the deterioration of relations by comparing the structure of the Japan-China relationship before and after the cessation of the Cold War and analyzing the structural change. What I refer to as "structural change" here is the fact that the stable structure formed after the normalization of diplomatic relations in 1972 has been undergoing a process of transformation since the end of the 1980s. In this essay, I construe this as a switch from the "1972 system (*taisei=tizhi*)" of Japan-China relations and will examine it from four angles: (1) the changing international order and China, (2) growing mutual dependence, (3) the changeover of generations, and (4) developments in Taiwan.

The Changing International Order and China

The 1972 system of Japan-China relations was defined by other sets of international relations. Tokyo's normalization of diplomatic ties with Beijing would have been impossible without Washington's approval. It would also not have been possible without China's acceptance of the Japan-US Security Treaty. What made it effectively possible to fulfill these conditions was the rapprochement between the United States and China in 1971–72. The sudden reconciliation between these two countries was in opposition to their common "virtual enemy," the Soviet Union. The Cold War structure in Asia, which had up to then been based on the antagonism between the United States and China, here saw a major turnaround.

After this, the United States approved the normalization of diplomatic relations between Japan and China, and China for its part tolerated the existence of the Japan-US Security Treaty, judging that the treaty was useful as part of its anti-Soviet strategy. Immediately after the normalization of Japan's relations with China, in February 1973, Mao Zedong told US presidential aide Henry Kissinger that China would prefer Japan to have improved relations with the United States rather than closer relations with the Soviet Union (Burr, ed., 1999). Another frequently cited explanation for China's acceptance of the treaty is that the Chinese saw it as effective in keeping Japan from becoming a military power.

In this way, the United States, China, and Japan came to form what was in effect a strategic relationship, having the Soviet Union as a common target of opposition. This is the most important reason why relations among the three countries were stable from that time until the end of the Cold War. In the 1980s, the United States supplied arms and provided military cooperation to China in opposition to the Soviet Union. It barely made an issue of the nuclear tests that China was carrying out at that time or its defense expenditures. Japan's attitude was essentially the same. But when the Soviet Union disappeared from the scene, the three lost the glue that bound them together.

After Tiananmen and the end of the Cold War, Washington and Beijing clashed frequently over such issues as Taiwan, human rights, most-favored-nation (MFN) status, membership in the World Trade Organization (WTO), and arms exports. In certain quarters of the United States the "China threat" theory even began to gain influence. Meanwhile the Chinese became increasingly exasperated with the repeated diplomatic pressure coming from Washington. This sentiment came to a head in May 1999 when the Chinese embassy in Belgrade was mistakenly bombed by North Atlantic Treaty Organization (NATO) forces.

During the 1990s, Washington and Tokyo undertook a tentative exploration of the possibility of expanding Japan's contributions to the international community, including in the area of security, and against this background they moved to redefine the Japan-US Security Treaty. In reality, inasmuch as the treaty was originally directed at the Soviet Union, this exercise was undertaken because of the need to give the treaty a new significance in order to preserve the two countries' relationship as allies now that the Soviet Union no longer existed. The result was the Japan-US Joint Declaration on Security issued at the bilateral summit in April 1996 and the subsequent revision of the Guidelines for Japan-US Defense Cooperation, implemented with a series of new laws passed by Japan's National Diet in May 1999. Meanwhile, in response to North Korea's missile development program, Japan began to show interest in working with the United States on the joint development of a theater missile defense (TMD) system.

China reacted strongly against these moves, since the redefinition of the Japan-US treaty seemed like part of a containment strategy directed against China now that the Soviet Union no longer existed. Moreover, the timing was bad. Originally the redefinition of the treaty had been undertaken at an unhurried pace following the end of the Cold War. But it became a major item on the agenda of the Japan-US summit meeting held just after the Taiwanese presidential election in March 1996, which had been preceded by Chinese military exercises intended to intimidate voters. From China's point of view, it appeared as though Tokyo and Washington were taking preliminary steps toward joint action in relation to the Taiwan issue. And regarding the missile defense concept, Beijing suspected—and continues to suspect—that the North Korean missile program is just a pretext and that the TMD system will be directed against China in the future.

On the economic front, there has been no change in the basic Japanese and American position of supporting China's program of reform and opening and encouraging its integration into the international economic system. And though the issue of China's accession to the WTO raised some complex issues, Japan gave its approval in July 1999, and the United States did so in November of the same year. In spite of considerable domestic opposition, the Chinese government in recent years has been pushing hard to get into the WTO and has made some major concessions, perhaps reflecting the country's serious economic recession.

At the same time, it is a fact that, as the scale of China's socialist market economy increases, Japan and the United States harbor some concerns about its future course. The biggest among these are the country's military buildup, appropriations for which have been swelling at a rate of over 10% a year, and the apparent rise in the military's clout within the government, as exemplified in the provocative exercises carried out in the Taiwan Strait in 1995 and 1996. Both Japanese and US policy makers feel some bewilderment and concern at these trends. A report on Chinese military power released by the Pentagon in June 2000 concluded that China will seek great power status as its economy grows, that the China-Taiwan military balance will begin to shift in China's favor from 2005 onward, and that China will, in the course of time, strengthen its nuclear deterrence policy and compete with the United States. And Japan's 2000 defense white paper referred, in connection with intermediate-range ballistic missiles, to the issue of China's missile development program in more detailed terms than before.

The orderly relationship among the United States, China, and Japan, which was the prop of the "1972 system" until the end of the Cold War, has begun to wobble.

Growing Mutual Dependence

After the normalization of diplomatic relations between Tokyo and Beijing in 1972, various practical agreements were concluded between the Japanese and Chinese governments, including the Japan-China Trade Agreement (January 1974) and the Japan-China Air Transport Agreement (April 1974). Only in 1978 was a peace treaty between the two countries signed. Up to this point, Japan-China relations were almost entirely government-initiated.

The role of the private sector became important after the outlines of the two countries' policies on trade with each other were set out in the Japan-China long-term trade agreement of February 1978, signed a short while before the conclusion of the peace treaty. This agreement had a bearing on China's across-the-board switch to a policy of economic modernization, symbolized by the decision of the Third Plenary Session of the 11th Central Committee of the Communist Party of China (December 1978).

A major change in the structure of the economic relationship between Japan and China took place starting in the latter half of the 1980s as the yen rose sharply and Japanese manufacturers turned toward China in search of cheap labor. Japanese businesses moved to set up production facilities in China, and this accelerated in the 1990s, notably after Deng Xiaoping's "southern tour" in 1992, during which he affirmed Beijing's commitment to reform and opening, and again after the "socialist market economy" line was put forward.

According to Chinese statistics, during the five years from 1979 through 1983, there were 27 cases of direct investment by Japanese companies, amounting to US$950 million (contract base), while in 1995 alone there were 2,946 cases totaling US$7.59 billion. The character of bilateral trade also changed. Up until 1987 China had a deficit in its trade with Japan, but in 1988 the deficit shifted to Japan's side, and it has continued to grow ever since. This may be seen as a result of China having improved its competitiveness and promoted the development of its export industries by such means as direct investment from overseas. And it led to a deepening of the mutual dependence between the two countries.

This mutual dependence can be easily understood by looking at the movements of people between the two countries. In 1979, seven years after the normalization of diplomatic relations, when China's modernization line had just been adopted, about 54,000 Japanese entered China. Ten years later the number was some 395,000 people, and by 1999 the figure had exploded to about 1.2 million. However, there is also a negative side. Although these figures do not appear in the official statistics, the number of illegal entrants from China into Japan grew rapidly from the beginning of the 1990s. This situation has created fertile ground for crime, and incidents involving Chinese illegal residents are reported in the media almost daily, contributing to the negative image of China among the Japanese.

Japan-China relations started under the banner of "friendship," and because mutual dependence progressed on this premise, the differences and incompatibilities between the two sides were kept under wraps as their exchanges expanded and deepened. In today's Japan-China relations, however, awareness of these differences and incompatibilities has become widespread.

Changeover of Generations

The joint communiqué of 1972 makes clear the Japanese position vis-à-vis its invasion of China in the past, stating: "The Japanese side is keenly conscious of the responsibility for the serious damage that Japan caused in the past to the Chinese people through war, and deeply reproaches itself." The document goes on: "The Government of the People's Republic of China declares that in the interest of the friendship between the Chinese and the Japanese peoples, it renounces its demand for war reparation from Japan." The document further declares the termination of the state of war between the countries, and the two sides reconfirm their intention to develop good-neighborly and friendly relations, overcoming differences of social systems. What was common to the generation that experienced the Sino-Japanese War of 1937–45 was a determination not to get involved in war again, and this was symbolized by the slogan "friendship between Japan and China," premised on setting aside minor differences and focusing on major areas of agreement.

The people who were involved throughout the whole process of normalization of diplomatic relations—Japan's Prime Ministers Tanaka Kakuei and Ōhira Masayoshi and China's Mao Zedong and Zhou Enlai—are long gone. Those who came after them on the Japanese side—figures like Fukuda Takeo and Sonoda Sunao, prime minister and foreign minister, respectively—at the time of the Japan-China Treaty of Peace and Friendship, have also died, while Deng Xiaoping, the political giant who dominated China as a leader from the late 1970s, entered a process of gradual retirement during the 1990s and passed away in 1997.

Although China's renunciation of its demand for war reparations was one of Japan's conditions for the normalization of diplomatic relations,

I think it cannot altogether be denied that this renunciation implanted a certain subconscious sense of moral responsibility and duty to atone among Japanese leaders in all fields, which subsequently acted as a hidden catalyst for Japan's economic cooperation with China. Of course, inasmuch as the waiving of reparations was an official decision of the Chinese government, no public mention was made of a connection between it and Japan's provision of yen loans or other forms of economic cooperation, nor is there mention of such a connection in any official document. We can only surmise that it was a connection rooted in the psychology of the generation that had experienced the war.

Once the Japan-China long-term trade agreement was signed, Japanese companies rushed into the Chinese market. At the time the Baoshan (Jp: Hōzan) steel factory, set up in Shanghai with Nippon Steel Corporation's across-the-board cooperation, was considered a symbol of "Japan-China friendship." Among those who were very active in preparing public opinion for economic cooperation with China were Inayama Yoshihiro, who was chairman of the Nippon Steel Corporation, vice-chairman of Keidanren (Japan Federation of Economic Organizations), and chairman of the Japan-China Long-Term Trade Committee; Dokō Toshio, who served as chairman of Keidanren and chairman of the Japan-China Economic Association; Kawai Ryōichi, president of the Japan-China Economic Association; and Okazaki Kaheita, advisor to the Japan-China Economic Association.

Okazaki once said: "Zhou Enlai was emphatic: 'Let us improve Asia through cooperation between China and Japan. Let us make it stronger.' He said, 'To achieve this, let's forget our grudge against Japan.' That would be very desirable. From this point of view, I think we have to change our way of thinking and doing things quite a lot in relation to cooperation on China's 'four modernizations' and Japan's stance on the Korean Peninsula as a whole." Okazaki's words encapsulate a line of thought that was common among his generation.

However, with the advent of the 1990s, the members of the wartime generation who had been the mainstay of relations between the two countries began to make way for their successors, and by 1995, 50 years after the end of the war, the makeup of the network of people responsible for Japan-China relations was beginning to change considerably. Of course, the changeover of generations did not mean that the historical fact of Japan's invasion of China disappeared. Nevertheless, however much emphasis may be placed on historical awareness and education, the fact that the new generation did not directly experience the war is bound to produce a difference between them and their seniors in the sensitivity of their perception. This is essentially true for both Japan and China. There is, however, an asymmetry in education between the two countries. Whereas in China modern and contemporary history is taught exhaustively at the primary and middle school level in connection with the history of the Chinese Communist Party, it does not receive particular emphasis in Japan.

Eventually, the Chinese side's repeated references to the history issue during Jiang Zemin's autumn 1998 visit to Japan led even many of those Japanese people who recognized the wrongness of Japan's past actions to feel somewhat weary of the matter. A group centered on the Japanese Society for History Textbook Reform is currently working on preparing a history textbook for middle schools. As this is considered to have quite a nationalistic flavor, it may trigger a new textbook flap.

With the changeover of generations, such slogans as "Japan-China friendship" are now heard less frequently.

Developments in Taiwan

The normalization of diplomatic relations between Japan and China became possible because Japan severed diplomatic relations with Taiwan and recognized the government of the People's Republic of China as the sole legitimate government representing China. From 1952 to 1972 Japan recognized the government of Taiwan (Republic of China) as the legitimate government representing China. However, with the rapprochement between the United States and China and the increasingly favorable public feeling within Japan toward the mainland, normalization of diplomatic relations with Beijing was realized. Japan declared diplomatic relations with Taiwan severed and the old bilateral peace treaty terminated. Private-sector relations between the two continued, mainly in the economic sphere, even after the cessation of diplomatic relations, and despite various complications, airlines continued their direct flights between the island and Japan. Overall, however, from this point on Taiwan's existence was much less noticeable to ordinary Japanese, apart from the areas of business and tourism.

I need not dwell long on the introduction of bold democratization policies and the consequent rapid progress in the "Taiwanization" of the Republic of China following the inauguration of Lee Teng-hui as president in 1988.

At about the same time as Taiwan was carrying out its democratization, China embarked on its own political reforms process. In January 1987 Hu Yaobang, the CCP general secretary who had taken a soft line toward the student movement, fell from power, but the reforms continued under his successor, Zhao Ziyang. It almost seemed as if the mainland was vying with Taiwan, but the entire process finally ended in tragedy with the Tiananmen incident on 4 June 1989. Taiwan's democratization resulted in success without loss of life, while the Chinese attempt at democratization, which did cost lives, failed.

This set of developments attracted the attention of the whole world. In Japan too, goodwill toward China sank rapidly from this point and at the same time, a well-disposed interest in Taiwan grew rapidly. Lee Teng-hui, who had grown up in Taiwan while it was under Japanese rule and had a particular attachment for Japan, charmed a succession of Japanese dignitaries visiting Taiwan with his perfect Japanese, contributing tremendously to the promotion of warm feelings toward the island.

Of course, both Japan and the United States still consider the People's Republic of China the sole legitimate government representing China. There is no possibility of their switching their recognition back to the government in Taipei. Nor will they readily support Taiwanese independence, an issue over which there is a good

likelihood China will resort to military force. In this respect, there is no change in the "1972 system" as far as the Taiwan issue is concerned. However, regarding the question of how to evaluate Taiwan's independent economic and political development, there has been a great change not only in Japan and the United States but in countries around the world, In short, it would be no exaggeration to say that a positive evaluation of the newly democratic Taiwan and a kind of sympathy for it have spread on a global scale.

Conclusion: The Road to Harmony

The present phase of Japan-China relations is a transitional one—a new structure is not yet apparent. I want to conclude this essay with a few proposals regarding what should be done in order to construct a new framework for a new century.

In regard to the changing international order, it is not conceivable that, at this stage, a target for opposition common to the United States, China, and Japan, such as the Soviet Union was during the Cold War, will appear again. Moreover, building an order on such a basis is unhealthy. A key factor in determining the shape of the future order in this region will be the path that China follows, both domestically and internationally. In the past, external variables, such as US-China relations and China-Soviet relations, exerted a strong influence on the direction of Japan-China relations. It seems, however, that in the twenty-first century it is Japan-China relations that will be an important influence on the regional order. Many aspects of the agenda for Japan-China relations must of course be dealt with between the two countries themselves. But at the same time, it should be possible to consolidate the foundations of bilateral relations indirectly through involvement by both Japan and China in regional cooperative frameworks such as the "10+3" (the 10 members of the Association for Southeast Asian Nations plus China, Japan, and South Korea), which has finally started to take on a concrete form over the past few years following the experience of the Asian currency crisis.

In regard to growing mutual dependence, this is not in itself a minus from the point of view of the formation of cooperative relations. However, depending on how the frictions that arise are dealt with, it may be a source of further confrontation. What is required is to construct a mechanism that will prevent friction or at least minimize it. Particularly important is the prevention of friction in economic relations. It is essential each side have a correct understanding of the rights, customs, and ways of thinking with respect to contracts and management arrangements, as well as the realities of the economic, legal, and political institutions underlying these, in the other country.

As regards the changeover of generations, the way to cope with this is logical and simple—build up personal networks at all levels. For a start, we can consider exchanges at three levels. The first is at the government level—contacts between political leaders, including summit meetings. I think it is necessary to beef up the channels of communication between senior-level counterparts, particularly those responsible for security and economic issues, on which further friction can be expected. The second is at the grassroots level. Such contacts— exchanges at the level of private citizens, regional exchanges, business contacts, student exchanges, and so forth—form a broad base for Japan-China relations. The third is at the level of experts in various fields who are in a position to influence policy decisions. Today, the usefulness of so-called "track two" contacts between experts at a level somewhere between government and grassroots who are capable of exerting influence in both directions is attracting attention. I believe there is a need to further increase such channels of communication between Japanese and Chinese experts.

In relation to developments in Taiwan, it is certainly true that Taiwan's image in Japan has changed greatly with its democratization. Nevertheless, sympathy and other emotions do not by themselves move international politics. A realistic sense of balance is needed. It is quite inconceivable that Japan would move to reestablish official relations with Taiwan at the cost of its relations with China. The fundamental point is a peaceful resolution of the China-Taiwan problem. There is a need to keep the channel of communication between China and Taiwan open, even if only slightly, so as to avoid the heightening of the tension between them. Japan

should provide some help from the side in creating a suitable climate for this. It should not be forgotten, however, that a forced unification of states without the agreement of their peoples eventually leads to failure, as has been proved by the experience of the twentieth century. Was it not the historical wisdom of Deng Xiaoping that said the problems we cannot solve should be left to the next generation?

The gates to the twenty-first century are open. Japan and China—two neighbors who are eternally unable to move house—have boosted their sense of incompatibility vis-à-vis each other, and this remains unchanged. Japan-China relations in the twentieth century ultimately were unable to mature sufficiently, and the road to harmony remains unfinished. I believe that in the first decade of the twenty-first century, Japan and China will face a tremendous test on their internal political and economic fronts and will enter a period of major change. It is better for neighbors who are both in difficulty to cooperate rather than be constantly quarreling. This is surely a matter of the most basic common sense. We must spare no effort in applying our collective wisdom toward the achievement of harmony.

Courtesy of the Japan Institute of International Affairs.

English version originally published by Japan Echo in *Japan Echo* 28, no. 2 (2001).

Translated from "Reisen shūketsugo no Nitchū kankei: 'Nanajūnnen taisei' no tenkan," in *Kokusai Mondai* (January 2001): 42–56; abridged by about one-fourth.

Bibliography

Burr, William, ed. *The Kissinger Transcripts: The Top-Secret Talks with Beijing and Moscow.* New York: The New Press, 1999.

Itō Takeo, Okazaki Kaheita, and Matsumoto Shigeharu. *Warera no shōgai no naka no Chūgoku: Rokujūnen no kaiko* [China in Our Lives: Reviewing the Past Sixty Years]. Tokyo: Misuzu Shobō, 1983.

Ministry of Foreign Affairs of Japan. "Joint Communiqué of the Government of Japan and the Government of the People's Republic of China." 29 September 1972. https://www.mofa.go.jp/region/asia-paci/china/joint72.html.

The Gulf War and Japanese Diplomacy

Nakanishi Hiroshi

ABSTRACT The start of the Heisei era roughly coincided with the end of the Cold War. Even so, it was the Gulf War which conspicuously affected Japan's foreign policy to mark the line dividing Shōwa from Heisei. Unlike the efforts to shake off Communism in Eastern Europe and the events following the protests in Tiananmen Square, none of which seemed to be of immediate concern to Japan, the crisis in the Persian Gulf in August 1990 drew intense discussion on Japanese foreign policy ends and means. After receiving international criticism for having done "too little, too late" to help with the crisis, Japan made huge financial contributions. However, Japan could only show a very meager presence in the battle and its aftermath. This essay reviews that traumatic experience and argues that it has been central to subsequent discussions on foreign policy in Japan.

More than 20 years have passed since the Gulf War, set off by the Iraqi invasion of Kuwait in August 1990. The first international crisis since the end of the Cold War rocked the Japanese government and brought the shortcomings of Japanese diplomacy painfully into the open. We look back on the "Gulf shock" and its lasting consequences for Japan's foreign policy.

The Gulf War, which began with Iraq's invasion of Kuwait on 2 August 1990, was the first major international crisis in the waning days of the Cold War. For Japan, the war represented a rude awakening to the realities of the post–Cold War world and resulted in what some Japanese commentators have referred to as Japan's Gulf War "shock" or "trauma." Twenty years on, it is worth taking a fresh look at the Gulf War and what it meant for Japan. Why was Japan so slow to react to events? And what lasting impact did the war have on Japanese foreign policy in the years that followed?

Japan's initial response to the crisis was actually quite speedy and clear: Prime Minister Kaifu Toshiki's government imposed economic sanctions against Iraq on 5 August—a day before the UN Security Council moved to do so. In retrospect, however, this early response already

showed one of the weaknesses of Japanese diplomacy. Although the Japanese government is quick to respond in cases where there is a historical precedent, unexpected situations tend to plunge it into a state of confusion over basic policy from which it finds it difficult to extricate itself. The Kaifu government's response to the Persian Gulf crisis leaned heavily on Japan's experiences during the Soviet Invasion of Afghanistan in 1979 and the lessons drawn from those events. Essentially, the Japanese government interpreted what was happening in the Persian Gulf as a situation similar to the Soviet invasion of Afghanistan and, without deep thought, figured that it would follow the same sort of pattern—that the major Western powers would extend support to local resistance forces without becoming directly embroiled in a regional conflict in the Middle East.

Tough Choice: Should Japan Support Military Action?

In fact, the international situation and Japan's position had changed considerably during the 1980s. The Cold War had moved swiftly to a conclusion. The Berlin Wall had come down in November 1989, the year before Iraq invaded Kuwait, and in Malta that December US president

George H.W. Bush and his Soviet counterpart Mikhail Gorbachev had declared the Cold War over. Despite the Tiananmen Square protests that had rocked China in June 1989, Deng Xiaoping was insisting that his reform and opening movement would continue, and China adopted an increasingly cooperative stance toward the West in the early 1990s. US secretary of state James Baker was on a visit to the Soviet Union when the invasion took place. The United States and the Soviet Union immediately issued a joint declaration condemning Iraq. The Persian Gulf crisis was seen as a test case for improving US-Soviet relations—and the UN Security Council, so often paralyzed by superpower rivalry during the Cold War, played a leading role in the international response to the crisis. With the Security Council legitimizing the use of military force, and the United States contributing its formidable military power, Japan was expected to provide clear support for military action, in light both of its stated commitment to a "UN-centered" foreign policy and the reality of its military alliance with the United States.

At the same time, international suspicion of Japan had been mounting since the second half of the 1980s, including in the United States, following Japan's rise to economic superpower status through its expansionary financial policies. Theories of Japanese exceptionalism were rife, and there was a widespread feeling that Japan, interested only in its own interests, was out to dominate other countries economically. Such views had gained a certain currency in the United States, both in Congress and among the general public. The discovery that a subsidiary of the Toshiba Corporation had exported machine tools to the Soviet Union in 1987, in violation of the COCOM (Coordinating Committee for Export Control) rules limiting technology exports to the Communist bloc, unleashed a major political backlash in the United States. Congress canceled preexisting agreements between the Japanese and US governments and amended plans for the joint development of the FSX, a planned new support fighter for Japan's Air Self-Defense Force. And the insensitive behavior of Japanese corporations, as seen in the purchases of such American cultural landmarks as the Rockefeller Center (Mitsubishi Estate) and Colombia Pictures (Sony) in 1989, left Japan open to accusations of arrogance.

Japan's Refusal to Contribute Personnel

Another factor was the revelation of the Recruit Scandal in 1989, just as Japan was at the height of its economic success. The scandal seriously shook the political system led by the Liberal Democratic Party (LDP), and by the time the Persian Gulf crisis struck the following year, the opposition parties had won a majority in the upper house of the National Diet. Within the LDP itself, Prime Minister Kaifu had only a relatively weak political base of his own and was dependent on support from the members of the powerful Takeshita faction, particularly Ozawa Ichirō, who held the key post of party secretary-general. In these circumstances, the need to respond promptly to the situation in the Gulf forced Japan into an extremely tight corner.

It was clear that Japan had very little leeway in terms of making a military contribution. No Self-Defense Forces (SDF) unit had ever been sent on a mission outside the country, and both the legal provisions and the training required for such action were lacking. It was clear that the biggest contribution Japan could make was in financial and material aid. But a purely economic contribution was fated to come in for strong criticism from countries that were supplying troops, particularly the United States. Japan's failure to dispatch personnel strengthened the impression of Japan as a self-centered mercantilist state. Not only did this increase anti-Japanese sentiment, it also threatened to become a factor in the debate within the United States, where opposition to the use of force was mounting. This was enough to make Washington push Tokyo hard to make something more than a merely monetary contribution. Michael Armacost, the US ambassador to Japan at the time, got the nickname "Mister Gaiatsu" (Mr. External Pressure).

In reality, Japan had not always shown unquestioning support for US policy in the Middle East. Japan continued to maintain diplomatic relations with Iran, for example, even after the Islamic Revolution. Confronted with the crisis in the gulf, some people in Japan suggested that the time had come for Japan to distance itself from the United States and use its own methods to persuade Iraq to withdraw from Kuwait. In reality, Japan's policy options were limited—but with Japanese citizens being held hostage alongside Westerners in Iraq, the argument that Japan should minimize its support for the coalition was one that appealed to the national mood.

In these conditions, the Japanese government's response can only be described as confused. President Bush requested Japanese support in the areas of transport and supply, where the United States' own resources were stretched to their limits for a time in the midst of logistical planning for sending large numbers of troops to the gulf. Because of the lack of a framework that would allow Japan to dispatch the SDF to the gulf, the government considered the possibility of chartering commercial ships and aircraft instead. But private-sector firms were reluctant to undertake missions to a war zone. When senior Japanese diplomat Tanba Minoru informed the United States that Japan could do virtually nothing to help in this respect, the Americans responded by noting that many of the ships then in the Persian Gulf were bound for Japan. The implicit suggestion was that Japanese shippers were willing to take risks when it was for the economic benefit of their own country.

Japan Donates $13 Billion in Support

After the Americans made their displeasure clear to Tanba, Japan announced on 29 August that it would contribute funding to the coalition against Iraq. But the initial announcement referred to a figure of only US$10 million. The next day, following an extremely frosty American response, the Ministry of Finance came out with an amended figure of US$1 billion. In fact, this was the amount that had been on the table in internal government discussions from the outset, but the ineptness of the announcement only served to strengthen the impression of Japan as a self-centered country that would not contribute to international efforts without external pressure. Anxious to not alienate the Americans any further, the Japanese government later supplemented

this amount with further funding, ultimately bringing the total to some US$13 billion. But a dispute arose between Tokyo and Washington regarding the US$9 billion of support that Japan announced after the opening of hostilities by the coalition. Was this amount denominated in yen or dollars? US treasury secretary Nicholas Brady and Japanese finance minister Hashimoto Ryūtarō came to a speedy agreement on the extent of Japanese support, but no clear announcement was made on the currency question. Following exchange rate fluctuations, Japan announced that the contribution would be denominated in yen, only for the United States to demand payment in dollars. In the end, Japan yielded—but squabbles of this kind over technical details did not make a good impression.

While this was going on, the Kaifu government submitted a "United Nations Peace Cooperation Bill" to the Diet in October in an attempt to provide the legal framework for Japan to contribute personnel. But there was no consensus even within the LDP leadership over the status of the personnel to be dispatched. Prime Minister Kaifu was leery of sending SDF units to the gulf; even if members of the SDF were dispatched, he thought they should go under the auspices of a different organization. LDP secretary-general Ozawa Ichirō, by contrast, insisted that even under the existing Constitution it was permissible for Japanese soldiers to take part in UN-organized operations for collective security and argued for Japanese forces to be sent to the gulf under the SDF banner. Opinion was similarly divided within the Ministry of Foreign Affairs. This split dimmed the prospects for passage of the legislation. And with the opposition holding a majority in the upper house of the Diet, it was unlikely that any sort of bill authorizing the dispatch of the SDF would pass. In addition, only around 20% of the population was in favor of such a move. There was an impassioned debate within the government, but in the end, the bill was shelved on 8 November.

The government also failed to take any noteworthy action to secure the release of the Japanese citizens being held, effectively as hostages, in Iraq. Japan had little leeway for negotiations with Iraq—and even if it had dealt directly with Baghdad and secured the release of Japanese citizens, there was a concern that this might lead to increased criticism of Japan for acting in its own interests. With military action imminent, the Japanese hostages were eventually released in late November, after various efforts, including a visit to Iraq by former prime minister Nakasone Yasuhiro as a special emissary. But given that the remaining Western hostages were released the following day, it seems likely that this decision represented a last-ditch Iraqi attempt to influence international opinion rather than the result of successful Japanese diplomacy.

A Lingering Sense of Failure

The international coalition began its attack on Iraq at 3 AM local time on 17 January 1991. Official notification was given by Secretary of State James Baker to Murata Ryōhei, the Japanese ambassador in Washington, and to Foreign Minister Nakayama Tarō 30 minutes before the attack began. The war turned out to be a demonstration of the overwhelming superiority of US military power. In addition to devastating air raids, American Patriot missiles were credited with amazing successes in shooting down Iraqi Scud missiles (though it later emerged that their strike rate was rather lower than originally believed). The live coverage of events provided by the new American news channel CNN astonished the world. In Japan as elsewhere, people sat transfixed in front of their televisions and watched the war unfold in real time.

Of course, it was not the case that Japan did nothing. Our country in fact made considerable efforts on the ground. Materiel contributions, from four-wheel drive vehicles to Walkmans, were gratefully received by troops. Japanese civilians and diplomats who remained behind in Iraq persevered despite harsh conditions. Japanese funding went through smoothly, and coalition commander General Norman Schwarzkopf expressed his deep gratitude to Japan. After the war ended in April 1991, a mine-clearing unit from the Maritime Self-Defense Force was dispatched to work on minefields in the Persian Gulf, following a decision that minesweeping

operations were permissible under the existing legislation governing SDF activities. But despite these efforts on the ground, the overall experience of the Gulf War left Japanese diplomats with a deep sense of failure. Whether the omission of Japan's name from Kuwait's official expression of thanks was deliberate or accidental is not known.[1]

But it is undeniable that Japan got poor marks from the international community for its contribution to the Gulf War, and the prestige of Japanese diplomacy suffered as a result.

The Lessons Drawn from Japan's Gulf War Experiences

What lessons did Japan learn from its experiences in the Gulf War? First of all, the fact that our country had been all but impotent in the face of an international conflict, even at a time when its postwar economic prosperity was at its apogee, brought an awareness of Japan's weakness in terms of supporting and maintaining the postwar international order. The "Gulf shock" made Japan aware of the need to contribute personnel to international efforts, and in 1992 the International Peace Cooperation Law was passed in the face of strong political opposition. This allowed limited participation by Japan's SDF in United Nations peacekeeping operations, and the following year the SDF were dispatched on their first such mission, joining the United Nations Transitional Authority in Cambodia following the end of the civil war in that country.

The Gulf War also deepened the debate on Japan's alliances and national security policy. Politicians began to talk explicitly about the importance of the Japan-US Security Alliance, and in 1997, Tokyo and Washington formulated a set of "Guidelines for Japan-US Defense Cooperation" with an eye to a possible emergency contingency on the Korean Peninsula. The two countries subsequently introduced a joint missile defense system following North Korean missile launches.

Considering the chaos and confusion of the Gulf War period, these changes might seem to have taken place surprisingly smoothly. To a certain extent, it is fair to say that the Japanese once again showed their ability to learn from past mistakes. But this was not all—during the 1990s and into the first years of the twenty-first century, Japan used this framework to pursue reform of the UN Security Council and strengthen the Japan-US alliance.

Weakness in Strategic Decision Making

This approach was based on the assumption that the system of international cooperation in which the United States had taken the lead throughout the Gulf War, backed up by its overwhelming military and technological supremacy, would continue. Japan sought to build its own diplomacy and national security policy around the alliance with the United States and within the context of an international order founded on cooperation. This basic thinking has not changed substantially ever since the Gulf War, despite the waning of the international consensus over the past two decades, along with the increased American inclination toward unilateral action. But with the United States' pursuit of two asymmetrical wars in Central Asia and the Middle East, it has become clear that there are limits even to America's much vaunted military might. American hegemony no longer looks quite so secure. The rise of the newly emerging economies has brought additional complications to international cooperation between the world's leading powers. There is a risk that the weaknesses of Japanese diplomacy laid bare by the Gulf War might come to the fore again.

The first weakness concerns Japan's diplomatic identity: What kind of role should Japan play in international politics? Since the end of World War II, Japan has renounced military force as an instrument of foreign policy and relied exclusively on peaceful economic means. Questions of military legitimacy continue to be hot issues today. Is it legitimate for SDF members participating in peacekeeping operations to use armed force? Does the right of collective defense extend to Japanese soldiers defending US forces when they come under enemy fire? Such questions are highly significant, and not just for the technical reason that interpretations happen to be shifting. The continuing debate over these issues reflects the lack of a clear consensus within Japan about

the identity that the country has maintained since the war: How much of it should be retained, and how much of it needs to be reassessed?

The second weakness concerns the government's strategic decision making in the face of a major crisis that cannot be resolved within existing frameworks. There are many aspects to this problem, from intelligence gathering to sectionalism among bureaucrats and the uneasy relationship between politicians and the bureaucracy. These continue to be major issues today. In recent years, the government's handling of the territorial dispute with China over the Senkaku Islands and its bumbling response to the earthquake disaster of 11 March 2011 and the nuclear crisis that followed have made it clear that its ability to respond to unexpected events still leaves much to be desired.

It cannot be said that Japan has overcome the experiences of the Gulf War. The crisis and its effects continue to cast a shadow over Japanese diplomacy to this day.

Originally published by Nippon Communications Foundation online at *Nippon.com* (2011).

Notes

1. (Ed.) In March 1991, after the war ended, the government of Kuwait published a full-page advertisement in the *New York Times* and other major newspapers thanking the UN coalition for liberating its country. The ad listed dozens of countries that had assisted, but Japan was not among them.

11 September 2001, Ramifications

Beyond Normalization
Thirty Years of Sino-Japanese Diplomacy

Kokubun Ryosei

ABSTRACT It is once more Sinophilia season in Japan. These bouts of Sinophilia seem to occur at regular intervals: 1972 with the normalization of relations, 1978 with the signing of the Treaty of Peace and Friendship Between Japan and the People's Republic of China, 1984 with China's broader opening, 1992 with Deng Xiaoping's southern tour speeches and his socialist market economy proclamation, 2001 with China's joining the WTO, and so on. Yet these optimistic bouts of Sinophilia are typically followed by periods of pessimism and distrust that leave mutual understandings in doubt. We clearly need to move away from emotion-based friendly relations, rethink the old 1972 system, and structure a reality-based cooperative relationship.

The days when "Sino-Japanese friendship" was a slogan that exerted overwhelming influence upon the China-Japan bilateral relationship are over. The two countries share a common destiny—a situation they seem not to recognize. The time has come for Sino-Japanese diplomatic relations to take on a new maturity.

China and Japan marked the 30th anniversary of normalization of diplomatic relations on 29 September 2002. In Japan, 2002 was proclaimed "China Year," and the anniversary was celebrated with ceremonies, events, and an unprecedented number of official visits between the two nations. The investment in time and money was considerable, yet media coverage was minimal, reflecting the degree of general interest. What the media did cover widely were events that posed problems for Sino-Japanese relations: Chinese People's Armed Police Force storming the Japanese consulate in Shenyang, Japan salvaging a suspected spy boat in the East China Sea, and the ever-controversial prime ministerial visits to Yasukuni Shrine, where Japan's war dead, including Class-A war criminals, are enshrined. Every press article about China, or Japan's stance on China, began with a combative headline. After 30 years of normalization, one would hope for better.

The years marking the 10th and 20th anniversaries of normalization were similarly rife with difficulties between the two countries. In the summer of 1982, the 10th anniversary, the history textbook issue emerged, with Japan accused of inaccurately portraying the role Japan had played in Asia in the first half of the twentieth century. This brought a quick end to the friendly mood that had prevailed since Chinese prime minister Zhao Ziyang visited Japan some months earlier. Relations picked up in autumn, when Japanese prime minister Suzuki Zenkō visited China.

The 20th anniversary, in 1992, came in the wake of the Tiananmen Square protests, and passions were running high. A state visit to China by the Japanese emperor, planned as the main anniversary event, was the subject of heated debate in Japan. The visit did eventually take place—evidence that anniversary events can be helpful in improving relations.

Unfortunately, the same cannot be said of the 30th anniversary in 2002. Yes, the usual ceremonies have gobbled up the usual large budgets. But there has been nothing to suggest progress toward resolving tensions, nor have there been ideas or initiatives for moving forward. The only thing certain is that a planned visit to China by Prime

Minister Koizumi Junichirō has been postponed indefinitely.

Even with these problems, the overall tenor of Sino-Japanese relations since 1972 has been characterized by a sense of good neighbors separated only by a narrow strip of water. There has always been a commitment to the preservation of "Sino-Japanese friendship" born, perhaps, of a tacit agreement that the misery of war should never be repeated, and no problem has been allowed to fester beyond the necessary minimum. However, the days when professions of friendship were enough to sustain the relationship are now over. The relationship must move on from a state of affairs where, time and time again, glasses are raised to an "unconditional friendship" and mutual dissatisfactions are washed down with wine. The 30th anniversary is an important milestone, but future years are of no less importance. Relations between the two countries need to mature.

The years since normalization have been a succession of booms and busts in Japan's affection for China. Tracing the history of these peaks and troughs highlights the chronic problem in the Sino-Japanese relationship: the feebleness of a relationship built on sentiment.

The "China Boom" Trap

In recent years, the rate of Japanese investment into China has been frenzied. There has been huge growth in the number of businesses contemplating relocation to China, particularly in the manufacturing sector. There are also increasing instances of factories moving to China from Southeast Asia and other regions. The current boom in investment in China is, in fact, the fifth in a series since the normalization of Sino-Japanese relations in 1972.

The first China boom took place during the year diplomatic relations were normalized. After the visit to China of US president Richard Nixon in February 1972, Japan experienced a surge of interest in restoring diplomatic relations with China. The issue was key to the election of the president of the ruling Liberal Democratic Party after the resignation of Satō Eisaku. Tanaka Kakuei campaigned on the promise of normalization of relations with China, and as a result, he

was elected party president, defeating Fukuda Takeo, whose approach to China was more cautious. On 25 September, soon after taking office, Tanaka made an official visit to China and, with full public support, normalized relations and broke off diplomatic ties with Taiwan. Numerous manifestations of public interest in China followed, including a "panda boom," focused on two pandas sent as a gift to Japan. The boom continued for some time, eventually declining in 1974, at the same time that Tanaka was forced to resign in the face of the financial scandal.

The second China boom occurred in 1978, following the signing of the Japan-China Treaty of Peace and Friendship. This had been preceded by a long-term trade agreement, signed in February of that year, promoting economic ties between the two countries. The trade agreement led to China exporting oil to Japan for hard currency and Japan exporting modern industrial plants to China. That was also the year when China launched itself on a path of economic modernization and Japanese firms began to move to China. Government intervention on both sides led to the Nippon Steel Corporation financing Baoshan Iron and Steel—the flagship symbol of friendship between the two countries. By the end of 1980, however, China was suffering from a decrease in oil production along with inflation and a financial deficit, and Japan and other trading nations were notified that the plant shipment contracts would be rescinded. The second China boom thus turned into a bust, and views about China once again turned pessimistic. Japan began to offer large-scale yen loans and official development assistance to China in order to reinstate the contracts that had been annulled.

The third boom was in 1984 when China embarked on rapid economic reform. Coastal cities were given freedom to open their ports to foreign trade, and consumer durables, such as television sets, refrigerators, and washing machines, streamed in from overseas. Japanese goods began selling well among the Chinese public. In 1985, with the Chinese market flooded with Japanese goods, Prime Minister Nakasone Yasuhiro made his controversial visit to Yasukuni Shrine. The Chinese boycotted Japanese goods, and the boom fizzled out.

The fourth boom occurred in 1992, following Deng Xiaoping's "southern talks" to promote economic growth during his tour to major cities in the south, as well as his declaration of China as a socialist market economy. His statement was calculated to open China's doors fully to the market economy, while reasserting the continuation of the Chinese state in the face of Tiananmen Square and the breakup of the Soviet Union. The effect was enormous, and the whole world flocked to China to trade. Japan, in particular, was spurred by the strength of the yen. In China the result was an average annual economic growth of over 10% during the first half of the 1990s. The International Monetary Fund (IMF) and the World Bank issued reports suggesting that China could become the leading economic force in the twenty-first century. Once again, however, optimism turned into pessimism. In the second half of the 1990s, problems emerged concerning the investment environment in China. In addition, there were the Asian financial and the Taiwan Strait crises. Japanese and other international companies began to withdraw, and the fourth China boom came to an end.

Japan is now experiencing its fifth China boom. Numerous Japanese companies are considering moving to China, and the rate at which moves are actually occurring is accelerating. Behind the current boom, however, is partly a deep-seated fear of China. The fear is not so much of the military as the economic threat. It is the fear that cheap Chinese goods will flood the Japanese market, dealing a fatal blow to domestic production. There is increasing concern that relocation of Japanese factories to China, along with the import of Chinese goods into Japan, will eventually result in the hollowing out of Japanese industry.

The reason for the present China boom is thus different. Previous booms occurred when expectations about the Chinese market were high. Many attribute the current rush into China by Japanese companies to the fact that China has now become a member of the World Trade Organization (WTO). But this explanation needs careful study. This author's view is that the rush is not about China's membership in the WTO; it is a result of the serious recession in Japan.

Between 1999 and 2000, the rate of Japanese business investment in China, which had been declining considerably, increased by 42%, with contracts totaling US$3.68 billion. There was a further 47% increase in 2000–02, with the total reaching US$5.42 billion. By contrast, US investment in China in 2000 rose 33% compared with the previous year, with contracts worth US$8 billion, but in 2001 fell 6% to US$7.51 billion (Mitsubishi Research Institute 2001). The pattern was similar with European countries. Germany's investments in China rose a dramatic 209% in 2000, with contracts amounting to US$2.9 billion, but the following year showed a 60% decrease. France's investment rate for 2000 showed an increase of 35% (US$630 million) compared to the previous year, but a decrease of around 11% for 2001 (US$570 million). Thus, while Japan's rate of investment continued to increase dramatically in 2000–01, the levels of investment from Europe and the United States were showing caution about over-investment.

Reviewing the trends of industries investing in China, we can observe other differences. Until 2000, a wide variety of US and European businesses were moving to China, but these were predominantly advanced industries such as information technology (IT), automobiles, finance, insurance, and services. In other words, these industries were making investments aimed at tapping into the Chinese economy following China's accession to the WTO. By the end of 2000, the necessary investments had essentially been put in place, so the overall rate of investment declined in 2001. Japanese investment, on the other hand, only very recently began to focus on advanced industries. Investment in the finance industry has been especially slow—perhaps an aftereffect of the Guangdong International Trust and Investment Company (GITIC) incident, in which Japanese banks suffered losses due to bad loans. Consequently, Japanese investment has been primarily in the manufacturing industries, in particular in small and medium-sized businesses.

In short, Japan's move into China, which has focused overwhelmingly on manufacturing industries, is not based on any careful strategy tied to China's membership in the WTO. Rather, the move of Japanese manufacturing industries into China has been the result of firms suffering through Japan's structural recession and in search of a cheaper labor force. The majority of these small- and medium-sized businesses are faced with downsizing or bankruptcy if they remain in Japan, and so they are trying their luck in China. Thus, the situation occurs where US and European investment is going into the sophisticated white-collar industries filling the high-rises in Shanghai and other cities, while investment from Japan, as well as Korea and Taiwan, concentrates on manufacturing industries. Since the latter creates more employment opportunities for the Chinese, it is helping to stabilize the foundation of the Chinese economy and also to facilitate the transfer of technology.

Let us briefly consider the concern of the hollowing out of Japanese industry. In 2001, there was contention between Japan and China over agricultural products. Cheap Chinese imports of green onions, shiitake mushrooms, and rushes used for the coverings of tatami mats were threatening the livelihood of domestic producers of these goods, so politicians sought to introduce measures to safeguard domestic agriculture. This became an issue in the House of Councillors elections in July 2001, and before the elections in April the government invoked temporary safeguard measures with respect to the three products in question. In June, however, China countered by imposing retaliatory tariffs of 100% on imports of Japanese cars, mobile telephones, and air conditioners. In the end, the Japanese government did not make the temporary safeguards permanent, China rescinded its tariffs, and the crisis subsided.

At first glance, this incident was clearly a matter of Sino-Japanese relations. On the other hand, it also bears considerably on relations among different sectors within Japan. In many cases, Chinese goods are sold in Japan because Japanese trading and distribution companies have availed themselves of cheap Chinese production, which has been aided by Japanese technology, and imported the goods to Japan themselves. The question thus is one of domestic politics: which

industries should be nurtured in Japan and which should be weeded out. Once again, the problem boils down to the recession in Japan.

The Subtleties of Mutual Dependence

How can the state of Sino-Japanese relations be best understood? Obviously, the elements for full confrontation are not present in the relationship as it now stands. Indeed, if friction did arise, it seems that both countries would have effective crisis management measures to bring relations quickly back to where they were. The greatest problem, then, is one of image: growing anti-Japan sentiment among the Chinese and growing anti-China sentiment among the Japanese. The level of antipathy seems to serve as a barometer of the quality of future relations. Chinese cities are overflowing with all manner of Japanese cultural products: cartoons and game software, cars and consumer durables, everyday goods and luxury items, rotating sushi bars, and fashion goods. In Chinese magazines and Internet chat rooms, however, anti-Japanese comment is rife. The diffusion of Japanese goods and culture has not seemed to improve the average Chinese opinion of Japan one iota, or prevent the periodic flare-up of strong anti-Japan feelings.

The Japanese image of China is no better. Government opinion polls show that ever since the low point of the Tiananmen Square incident in 1989, the proportion of respondents claiming affection for China has been approximately equal to the proportion claiming no affection. In autumn 2001, for example, 47.5% claimed affection while 48.1% claimed none (*Gaikō ni kansuru yoron chōsa* [Public Opinion Polls on Foreign Policy], October 2001). These figures stand in contrast with figures from earlier years. The peak of affection for China, at 78.6%, was in 1980, when 14.7% felt no affection. This was a time when contact between the two countries was minimal. The number of Japanese visiting China in 1980 was only around 70,000, with Chinese visitors to Japan fewer than 20,000. Compare that with recent years, when Japanese visitors to China have numbered around 1.5 million and Chinese visitors to Japan have exceeded 400,000. A comparison of the figures for investment is similarly dramatic. Between 1979 and 1983, Japanese investment into China amounted to a mere 27 contracts with a total value of US$950 million, whereas in 2001 alone, there were 2,000 contracts worth a total of more than US$5.4 billion (*Chugoku jōhō handobukku*, 2002). The rapid increase in mutual dependence seems to have complicated the image of China held by the Japanese. The cynical conclusion is, the lower the level of contact, the greater the level of Sino-Japanese friendship.

A positive side to international exchange with China is that a large proportion of the research on China in Japan is now conducted by Chinese researchers, and the number of Chinese academic research and teaching staff in Japan in all fields, but particularly in science and technology, has also grown dramatically. There is also a negative side. Of the 16,000 foreign criminals convicted in Japan every year, over 40% are Chinese. When such figures are reported in the daily news, they are bound to affect the average Japanese opinion of China.

One would imagine that, as mutual dependence increases, relations would become more cooperative. In the case of Sino-Japanese relations, however, it is the opposite, with friction more prominent. Why should that be? In my view, the lack of cooperation lies in a number of structural problems. Many changes have taken place since the so-called "1972 system" of diplomatic relations was set up at the time of normalization. No new structure has been established to incorporate changes since then, making the bilateral system unstable.

Structural Changes since the "1972 System"

First, there has been a change in the world order. The backdrop to the 1972 normalization of Sino-Japanese diplomatic relations was the reconciliation of China and the United States earlier in the same year. Détente between these two powers was also seen as an act of opposition to the Soviet Union, and the establishment of diplomatic relations between China and Japan signified that Japan allied itself with China and the United States. In other words, Japan, China, and the United States had formed an alliance in opposition to the Soviet Union. However, with the events of 1989—the end of the Cold War and the Tiananmen Square incident—the alliance became meaningless, since the common focus of opposition has disappeared. The effects of this change can be felt to the very foundations of Sino-Japanese relations.

The second change is a related issue: China's position within the global society. Until the end of the Cold War, the United States and Japan shared a consensus that the modernization of China was essential for peace and prosperity in the Asia-Pacific region and that they should actively support integration of China into global society. This policy was adopted as a response to the key external and internal issues shaping China's position in the world. Externally, there was the Soviet Union as the main enemy; internally, there was the lack of certainty regarding the future of China. Japan's yen loans to China were made in this context. However, with China now a member of WTO and becoming more confident in global politics, Japan's interests have begun to waver. China used to be considered a developing country, but Shanghai and other Chinese coastal cities are, increasingly, no longer "developing" but "developed." Japan urgently needs to revise its view of China in light of these changes.

A third change is generational. While the reconciliation of China and the United States formed the external background of the normalization of Sino-Japanese relations, there was also a strong movement within Japan calling for the restoration of Sino-Japanese diplomacy. Even within the Liberal Democratic Party itself, there were many who were deeply involved in this movement. The majority were motivated by a desire to atone for Japan's invasion of China and the subsequent war and regretted the loss of Chinese relations after the founding of the People's Republic of China. Even after normalization in 1972, these politicians, through the mediation of their various networks, strove to maintain relations whenever problems arose. In China, too, there were Japan experts with links to members of the Japanese government who were sympathetic to China. Now, however, most of these politicians have retired or passed on. The new generation is not motivated by the same feelings about China. Few will dedicate themselves tirelessly to maintaining relations; nor do they have the necessary robust networks of human relations.

A fourth change has to do with domestic policies in both countries. In Japan, it was the Tanaka Kakuei faction that consistently worked to maintain Sino-Japanese relations. After Tanaka's resignation, Takeshita Noboru, who came out of the Tanaka faction, carried on this tradition. Thereafter, maintenance of Sino-Japanese relations has been supported predominantly by politicians like Nonaka Hiromu, leader of the former Tanaka faction with links to the Hashimoto Ryūtarō faction. Gradually, however, a strong political group that will bend over backward for the sake of Sino-Japanese friendship is becoming a thing of the past.

The situation is similar in China. Problems between China and Japan arose during the eras of Mao Zedong, Zhou Enlai, and Deng Xiaoping, but these leaders ultimately made decisions to prevent the situation from worsening. Under the leadership of Jiang Zemin in the 1990s, this is no longer the case. Chinese society has become increasingly pluralistic and the authority of the Communist Party less absolute. Along with these changes, the issue of Japanese history textbooks has been used to stimulate patriotism. Indeed, Jiang appears to have very harsh views about Japan. When he visited Japan in 1998, he brandished the history issue (past Japanese militarism) like a sword. This did not win friends for China in Japan, and since that visit, Chinese authorities have begun to take a softer attitude as they review their relationship with Japan. Nonetheless, it is clear that a pro-Japan stance is not ascendant within the Chinese government and its policy-making process. In this regard, China's treatment of Japan differs completely from its treatment of the United States. Jiang is manifestly pro-US.

A fifth change is the status of Taiwan. When Japan broke off diplomatic ties with Taiwan in 1972, the only people in Japan who strongly opposed this were a number of conservative groups. The majority of Japanese strongly supported normalization of relations with China, and Taiwan was placed in the back of the public mind. Now, however, the situation has changed dramatically. Although there is currently no likelihood of Japan reinstating diplomatic ties with Taiwan, the Japanese feeling of friendship toward Taiwan is growing rapidly, and in Taiwan, evidence of friendship for Japan can be seen everywhere. This is the result not only of the fiercely pro-Japanese former president, Lee Teng-hui but also of the development of democracy in Taiwan under his leadership. Consequently, there is now exchange between Japan and Taiwan on all levels, with both mainstream and subcultural information flowing freely. For China, this growing friendship between Japan and Taiwan can only be viewed as a threat given their historical ties. Thus this too represents a structural change in Sino-Japanese relations.

Re-Rooting the Relationship in the Present

"The rise of China and the fall of Japan." This is the leitmotif cropping up again and again at international conferences on Asia. The eyes and ears of the world are moving from Japan to China, and, undeniably, the process is gathering speed. Perhaps in response to this mood, Japan now abounds in masochistic ideas about loss of confidence or Japan-centric notions lacking international perspective. In addition, China's emergence onto the world stage is being hyped by the media with stories of "China the superpower" and the "deindustrialization of Japan." These stories touch a raw nerve in Japan's psychology and bring on feelings of resentment toward China.

The general Chinese view of Japan is distorted as well. It is stuck with the image of Japanese militarism prior to 15 August 1945. Although the Chinese praise Japan's postwar economic growth, they ignore the fact that this growth was one of the fruits of a democratic system. Nor does there seem to be much recognition of the fact that, for over half a century, Japan has not engaged in any military activity whatsoever. For the general public in Japan, Chinese accusations of history-related Japanese militarism seem so divorced from reality that they have come to doubt China's comprehension of any issue.

The conclusion that China and Japan lack

mutual understanding is obvious. Mutual understanding does not simply entail understanding the other party; it must also include some understanding of oneself. Japan and China are two very different countries. Japan has achieved democracy and, through its economic growth, a significant degree of prosperity for its people; for China, these are long-term goals. It is meaningless to try to compare two such opposites with the same measure. At the same time, both countries are full of people with a burning sense of victimization at the hands of the other. In China, people fear Japan's economic recovery, it becoming a political giant, and its attempts to suppress the rise of China. In Japan, people fear China developing into an economic and political power and its attempts to put Japan in its place.

The fact is, arguments on both sides are governed predominantly by emotion. Neither has advanced to a coolheaded analysis of the relationship. To state the case plainly, China and Japan should not be wasting time with petty jealousies or smoldering with feelings of victimization. Domestic problems in both countries are too serious for such indulgences. The reality is that, in Japan, prospects for economic recovery are still cloudy, while in China, although the benefits and pitfalls of economic growth are all too evident, there are no effective policies in place. Economic recovery in Japan would actually be a boon to China, and healthy growth in China would be a tonic for Japan's economic recovery. That is the reality of mutual dependence, and if Japan and China do not move in a direction of accepting it, they will both be left with a zero-sum society. The two countries share a common destiny, yet, at present, awareness and appreciation of this truth are fundamentally lacking.

What Japan and China need now is to move from emotion-based relations to cooperative working relations based on the premise of mutual benefit. In other words, it is time to move on from 1972 and create a new structure for this important relationship.

English version originally published by Toshi Shuppan in *Gaikō Forum* 2, no. 4 (2003): 31–39.

Translated by Heather Marsden from the original Japanese, "Senkyūhyaku-nana-jū-ni-nen taisei o koeta Nitchū kankei o motomete," published in *Gaikō Forum* 15, no. 10 (2002): 16–23.

Bibliography

Mitsubishi Research Institute. *Chūgoku jōhō hando-bukku 2002* [Handbook of Information on China 2002]. Tokyo: Sōsōsha, 2002.

II-(2) Globalizing China
The Challenges and the Opportunities

Kokubun Ryosei

ABSTRACT Signifying its desire to link its economic structure with the international market economy, China joined the WTO in 2001. It was assumed at the time that the Chinese political system would also change as it increasingly became a market economy. Confounding these expectations, Jiang Zemin proclaimed the "Three Represents" and condoned a shift in the nature of the Communist Party to co-opt the emerging wealthy class. At the same time, this shift facilitated political involvement in the market economy by Party officials and fostered corruption. If China is to achieve stable development going forward, it is essential the Party democratize and implement other reforms.

Globalization and System Transformation

Globalization (*Qianqiuhua*) has been greatly debated in China in recent years, particularly since China became interested in joining the World Trade Organization (WTO), and then started preparing for entry to the world trading body. Cadres of all ranks, farmers, laborers, intellectuals, and students—all segments of society have become interested in the phenomenon of globalization, and the international organization called the WTO. This interest stems from the possibilities they represent of reconstructing China's very foundation.

The WTO is distinctly different from the multilateral trading body, the General Agreement on Tariff and Trade, which it succeeded in 1995. Once a country becomes a WTO member, it has no choice but to change its domestic economic system in accordance with WTO rules. In other words, once it is admitted as a member of the WTO, a country is obliged to reform its economy to conform with market mechanisms. All features of an economic system, such as taxation, business practices, and property and intellectual property rights, have to be addressed. It is for this reason—that there are so many aspects and instruments of the Chinese economic system that will have to

be reformed, and China will not be able to avoid reforming them—that interest in globalization and the WTO in China is so high.

As a result of it formally becoming a WTO member in December 2001, China has particular obligations that it must meet. For example, average tariffs for mining and manufacturing products must be lowered to 9.4% by 2005, from their current rate of 24.6%; major agricultural products must be reduced to 14.5%, from their present 31.5%; and tariffs on automobiles must drop to 25% by 2006, from the current 80%–100%. Also, two years after China joined the WTO, foreign-affiliated banks and securities companies must be able to do business in renminbi with Chinese companies, and five years after WTO accession, they must be able to do business with individuals. As a WTO member, and by opening its markets to the world, China will increasingly be directly affected by the international economic system. Yet WTO accession also means that inexpensive but relatively high-quality Chinese products can be easily marketed, and that production of Chinese textile products—which already dominate world markets—can be accelerated. Exports of more technology-intensive tools, machinery, household appliances, and other basic industrial products are also expanding. Overall, increased interdependence between the Chinese market and world markets, and closer economic cooperation also mean increased potential for economic conflict of various types.

The essential reason that China wanted to become a WTO member lies in the hard reality of its economic situation. China kicked off the next phase of economic reform in 1992 with Deng Xiaoping's tour through southern China and the subsequent declaration of the "socialist market economy." China's economy grew 14.2% in 1992 and 10.5% in 1995, and the driving force behind this remarkable economic growth was increased trade and foreign direct investment (FDI). China's economic growth then slowed—to 9.6% in 1996 and 7.1% in 1999—due to the 1997 Asian financial crisis and a resulting decline in FDI. In terms of contracts, there were 7,273 cases of FDI in 1990, amounting to approximately US$6.6 billion; 8,347 cases in 1993, amounting to roughly US$111.4 billion; and 16,918 cases in 1999, totaling roughly US$41.2 billion (Mitsubishi Research Institute 2000, 343 and 506).

In 1990, 29.8% of China's gross domestic product was dependent on trade; in 2000, this trade dependence was 43.9%. Half of China's economic growth depends on trade, foreign corporations contribute 50% to exports, and close to 18% of state tax revenue is from foreign corporations (Hosokawa 2002, 68–69). In short, China's economic growth depends greatly on foreign capital, specifically on FDI. So, the Chinese government pushed for WTO membership in order to accelerate the marketization of China's economy through "forceful" opening.

In its history, China has always been very "Sino-centric" and very cautious about the penetration of external influences. Late Qing dynasty reformists tried to introduce science and technology from the West as a means to modernize the nation (*zhongti xiyong*) without really changing the system. However, through exposure to scientific and technological principles, people became interested in Western values, so, sensing danger, the government suspended the reforms.

Since 1978, socialist China has pursued modernization under the slogan of "reform and opening," with the idea being to use Western science and technology to complement and complete socialist rule. In the 1980s, when "planning" was regarded as primary and "the market" as secondary, China was considering internal reform premised on the maintenance of socialism. After the Tiananmen Square incident and the collapse of the Soviet Union, China recognized the limits of "planning" and decided to introduce a "socialist market economy." Although many aspects of a market economy were to be implemented, the point was definitely the maintenance of socialism, the principles of public ownership, and the leadership of the Chinese Communist Party (CCP).

Some actions that the Chinese have taken in order to join the WTO have, however, caused contradictions in the basic principles of public ownership and CCP leadership. Indeed, the very act of reforming its domestic system using external sources—an unusual phenomenon in China's history—may be considered an encroachment on China's spirit and Chinese values.

The economic substructure alters the superstructure of politics and other arenas according to the proposition of Karl Marx. In China, too, many considered that basing economic reorganization on collectivization would transform politics and the social superstructure into socialism. The "uninterrupted revolution" of Mao Zedong's Cultural Revolution is a powerful example of attempts to radically transform politics and society. In the end, however, the superstructure could not change the substructure. Only later, with the economic reforms introduced by Deng, did transformations of the economic substructure start to affect the superstructure. In this regard, Marx's view appears to have been correct.

So the issue arises of state power and the political regime that supports it, and, more specifically, the type of political regime that accords with a market-based system. The market mechanism definitely functions best with a small government that supports the principles of competitiveness, liberalization, and freedom of information. In the case of China, the CCP is unable to really implement these principles, as it cannot allow changes that threaten its control and create pressures for a multiple-party system. CCP leaders have, however, been attracted by the principle of corporatism. By co-opting actors to give the suggestion of pluralizing, the CCP might be able to maintain its power. Jiang Zemin's theory of the "Three Represents" is an attempt to provide the theoretical underpinning of the CCP's new corporatist strategy.

By joining the WTO, China has chosen to proceed with marketization. Various government departments are attempting to reduce their size in the interests of "small government," and market forces will become more determining. Yet conflicts will arise, especially if the CCP intervenes too much. Given the experience of the collapse of the Soviet Union and the fact that the CCP is the core of the Chinese political regime, discussing the direction of the CCP is urgent (Dickson 2000–01).

The "Three Represents": A Theoretical Breakthrough?

In parallel with Deng's 1992 visit to southern China that reinvigorated China's reform drive, Jiang first mentioned the "Three Represents (*Sange daibiao*)" early in 2000 during a visit to Guangzhou. He declared that, "The practices of our 70 some years tell us that one very important factor is the cause of overwhelming support of people at different stages of the revolution, construction, and reform. It is the fact that our Party has represented a need for the development of advanced productive forces of China; it has represented the direction for China's advanced culture; and it has represented the fundamental interests of the masses of the people. Furthermore, the Party is constantly fighting for the fundamental interests of the state and people through the establishment of correct lines, directions, and policies" (Jiang 2001, 2).

In other words, the CCP was seen as representing three factors: advanced productive forces, advanced culture, and the people. The seemingly simple reference to "the people" is very revealing. According to Marxist-Leninist principles, the CCP is supposed to represent a certain class of people, namely, the "proletariat." The nonchalant switching to "the people" could be perceived as suggesting the CCP was moving away from being a class-based party. At the same time,

numerous cases of political corruption within the CCP were exposed and, given the reference to the CCP representing "the people," harsh criticisms were directed against it.

"Since China adopted the reform and opening policy, the composition of China's social strata has changed to some extent. There are, among others, entrepreneurs and engineers employed by scientific and technological enterprises of the nonpublic sector, managers and technocrats employed by foreign-funded enterprises, self-employed, private entrepreneurs, employees in intermediaries, and freelance professionals. Moreover, many people frequently move from one ownership, sector, or place to another, changing their jobs or capacity from time to time. This trend of developments will continue. Under the leadership of the Party line, principles, and policies, most of these people in the new social strata have contributed to the development of productive forces and other undertakings in a socialist society through honest labor and work or lawful business operations. They work, together with workers, farmers, intellectuals, cadres, and the officers and men of the People's Liberation Army. They are also working for building socialism with Chinese characteristics" (Jiang 2001, 169).

With these words at celebrations for the 80th anniversary of the founding of the CCP, Jiang reemphasized his earlier suggestion that the CCP should admit private entrepreneurs into its ranks to reflect the rapid expansion of the private sector and the scaled back state sector. The reality is that many CCP members became entrepreneurs while maintaining their CCP membership, and many private entrepreneurs were CCP members. Jiang also proposed admitting "newly emerging private entrepreneurs" into the CCP.

As private ownership has not been approved, private entrepreneurs are only responsible for management, thus they are not "capitalists" who own "private property." Yet the concept of "private property rights" was officially acknowledged at the Third Plenum of the 16th CCP Central Committee in October 2003, and it is to be included in the newly revised Constitution to be adopted by the National People's Congress in the spring of 2004. The CCP will then no longer be a

"Communist party" in the Marxian sense. Chinese intellectuals have, in fact, already been discussing changing the CCP's name. The "People's Party of China," the "Social Democratic Party of China," and the "Liberal Democratic Party of China" are some of the suggestions. Introducing a change of such magnitude will, however, take time.

The "Three Represents" can also be interpreted as part of the theoretical preparations for China shifting toward a market economy before entering the WTO. Taken as a cornerstone for the regime shift to allow the markets greater market leeway, it aroused harsh criticism from conservatives. According to *Zhenli de zhuiqiu* (The Pursuit of Truth), published by the Chinese Academy of Social Sciences, conservatives worried that, if private entrepreneurs were admitted to the CCP based on the "Three Represents," the CCP would then become a bourgeois party. In a July 2001 editorial in *Zhongliu* (Middle) magazine, a group connected with *Guangming ribao* (Guangming Daily) suggested that entrepreneurs were not a class that formed the base support of the party. Subsequently, in the buildup to the Sixth Plenum of the 15th CCP Central Committee meeting in the summer of 2001, both publications were ordered to stop publishing (Ohe 2002, 16).

On 31 May 2002, in a graduation speech for provincial-level cadres at the Central Party School, Jiang stated, "The 'Three Represents' is the underlying spirit of the formation of the Chinese Communist Party, the foundation of the administration, and the source of energy. And it is the greatest theoretical weapon to reinforce and advance Party building and to enhance self-reforms and the development of our socialism" (*Renmin Ribao* [*People's Daily*] 6 June 2002). The concept of the "Three Represents" was formally included in the newly adopted CCP charter at the CCP's 16th National Party Congress in November 2002. The new leadership of Hu Jintao and Wen Jiabao has inherited this official guiding theory, the theoretical preparation for corporatism with Chinese characteristics.

The Issue of Politics: Corporatism with Chinese Characteristics

After the 1989 experience in Tiananmen Square and the collapse of the Soviet Union, China is extremely cautious about political reform. Political reform in recent years has encompassed allowing villagers to elect mayors directly, while the CCP has concentrated on justifying its political control by enhancing economic growth. In the late 1980s, reforms were going to be introduced to separate the functioning of the CCP and the government. But the Tiananmen Square incident and the implosion of the Soviet Union intervened, and any reforms that could potentially dilute the CCP's leadership were avoided. In particular, any thoughts about separating the CCP and the government were set aside. Indeed, the socialist market economy is premised on the CCP's leadership.

Yet China must address the need for political reform. Serious corruption is one of the reasons. Thousands of corruption cases are exposed annually, which are, in a way, the unwanted product and unavoidable consequence of the socialist market economy being under CCP leadership. The political mechanisms necessary to expose corruption need to be examined. Under a political regime that does not sanction freedom of speech and expression, there are no other means but to expect the CCP to purge corrupt officials. The Commission for Inspecting Discipline is in place at every level. But, without outside supervision, it is difficult to determine how this self-cleansing mechanism is really functioning. It may be able to eliminate small evils successfully, but it is failing to eliminate heinous evils.

Then there are questions relating to the widening economic disparities in China and the ironic issue of whose interests the CCP represents. Does it represent the interests of the newly co-opted private entrepreneurs, or does it represent those of the workers and peasants who used to be the CCP's core, many of whom may now be slighted by globalization?

The fundamental principle of socialism is the fair distribution of wealth. However, inequality is spreading rapidly in China: affluent coastal regions and lagging inland regions, especially poverty-ridden farming villages spread out in rural areas; the super-wealthy urban elite in their new homes; and the so-called *waidiren* (outsiders) in the urban metropoles, barely surviving in overfilled collective living quarters—these are some of the diverging contrasts. Addressing the uneven distribution of wealth is a definite political issue. In the past, the CCP tried to reach a balance by transferring surpluses from the wealthy regions to the poorer regions. However, the wealthy regions are solely concerned with their own prosperity and they demand that the central government aid the poor regions. In terms of the loyal competition principle, they feel they cannot afford the luxury of caring for others. The CCP is positioned to show political leadership, but it does not have sufficient financial resources. Thus, it is seeking foreign capital to help bolster China's economic growth. If its efforts are not successful, those now on the margins will remain on the periphery.

Attention is being devoted these days to peasants and rural villages. Agricultural issues were extensively mentioned in government work reports by Prime Minister Zhu Rongji at the Fifth Meeting of the Ninth National People's Congress in 2002 and at the First Meeting of the 10th National People's Congress in 2003. In the revolutionary period, most top CCP leaders came from farming villages, and, given their direct connections with farming society, they made sure the rural regions benefited. Yet, nowadays, most pivotal CCP leaders and their families are urban. They may hear and speak of rural poverty, but they have little direct experience of it. Their promotion is mainly related to the strength of their ties to top leaders. Although village level elections exist, these elections do not seem to influence the central government directly, and they are unable to produce politicians who can represent the interests of peasants at the central level.

In Japanese national elections, votes from farming villages play a very important role, and politicians who ignore them cannot win. In Japan, in contrast to China, farmers are a minority interest group, yet their interests are reflected in the national government—to an exaggerated degree, in fact. China and Japan have something in common in this regard, namely, that the interests of the majority of the people are not necessarily reflected in national politics.

At this stage in China, progressive democ-ratization may not be possible. The focus of political reform in China should then be reforming the CCP. And this will not be an easy task, as the vested interests of close to 70 million people are at stake. An important element could be democratizing the CCP internally. The CCP should clarify and systematize the process whereby it selects leaders so that this occurs in accordance with well-defined and established rules. Also, systemized rules and instituting a supervisory agency outside the CCP would help expose and control political corruption. Some Chinese researchers have begun to address this point, although it is not a position on which there is consensus (see, for example, Lin 2002).

State or authoritarian corporatism was one of the transitional stages in Taiwan's democratization process. China seems to be groping for a similar course. As seen in the "Three Represents" theory, the CCP seems to be trying to stabilize its governing ability by co-opting private entrepreneurs, a particular group with vested interests, as part of the newly emerging elite. The major pitfall for state or authoritarian corporatism to work in China is how to co-opt or involve workers and peasants, who are the vast majority of people. The premise of homogenous development for the unity of a huge nation like China is absent.

A Chinese Academy of Social Sciences survey on China's divergent social strata highlighted the extent of the challenge (Lu 2002). It showed the upper social strata, consisting of party and state administrative personnel, managers, private entrepreneurs, experts, and technocrats, and the lower social strata, comprising industrial workers, peasants, and the unemployed. This view of China's social reality shows that the road to corporatism with Chinese characteristics has not been leveled. In order to minimize this contradiction, and to help pave the way for a successful corporatist strategy, the CCP's response is maintaining its focus on attaining rapid economic growth.

China and Japan in the Global Contexts

News on China appears frequently under sensational headlines, with readers' images of China never settling but constantly shifting. This has been true for much of its recent history. Sometimes, a discussion on China has been filled with romantic descriptions of its grand history or culture. At other times, China has been discussed in idealistic tones, with a focus perhaps on its utopian socialist goals. It has also been examined through pessimistic lenses, as perhaps when its harsh political power struggles have been noted. Whether glorifying China at the birth of the People's Republic, agonizing over the Cultural Revolution, or simplistically suggesting China's breakup at the time of the 1989 Tiananmen incident, rarely have views on China been presented logically or objectively, allowing more realistic images of China to be formed. Debate about China has often been tinged with emotion and subjective value judgments.

These days, much discussion in Japan is about the rise of China. Even this topic seems to reflect more Japan's self-awareness about its recent dismal economic performance than objective analysis of the real situation.

The circumstances of Japan and China are incomparable. Japan is suffering now from problems stemming from years of successful high economic growth, while China is trying to remain on a growth track. In 1964, Tokyo hosted the Summer Olympic Games after years of high Japanese economic growth; in 2008, China is going to host the Olympic Games in Beijing. Incidentally, Seoul hosted the Olympics in 1988, after South Korea successfully accomplished economic growth and democratization. It will be very difficult for China to accomplish both by 2008. Comparisons are also misleading, because China is 25–26 times larger in area than Japan, and it has 10 times Japan's population. Also, China's "rise" is particularly evident in the eastern and southern coastal cities and provinces, but much of the rest of China's vast interior is relatively untouched by the coast's successes.

Even in China, many experts are convinced that Japan will emerge from its present economic recession and will, one day, be a politically and militarily significant nation. Yet, in many cases, Chinese views of Japan remain stuck in the late 1930s or early 1940s, not reflecting at all the changes in Japan's politics and social status.

Objectively speaking, both countries have many problems and issues to deal with, and neither party can afford to be envious of the other.

At this point, China has no choice but to concentrate on economic growth. Ongoing growth gives the CCP its political legitimacy, and, for this growth, China relies heavily on foreign trade and foreign direct investment as mentioned. Due to this economic logic and its domestic needs, China can no longer function without fully participating in and cooperating with the world market (see Medeiros and Fravel 2003).

In this regard, China's relations with the United States are crucial. It must have smooth, cooperative relations with the United States in order to survive and thrive. China's leaders were remarkably silent regarding the US war in Iraq, with their criticisms being very vague and low key. China has also been very active as a host of, and an intermediary in, the six-party talks process on the North Korean nuclear problem. This is an area where the United States has been greatly appreciative of Chinese help. Yet stable US-China relations are not a given. There are apprehensions in the United States about China, specifically about China's military profile and its posture toward Taiwan. Indeed, despite increasing economic integration between China and Taiwan, the Taiwan issue is the most serious problem in the US-China relationship.

China has also maintained a low-key attitude toward Japan. The Japanese media widely reported on the May 2002 incident involving North Korean refugees at the Japanese Consulate-General in Shenyang; this was not at all the case in China. When Japan insisted on salvaging a sunken North Korean ship suspected of having been on a spy mission, China agreed. News coverage in China remained relatively muted on Lee Teng-hui's visit to Japan in 2001, a series of problems related to Japanese history textbooks, and Prime Minister Koizumi Junichirō's visits to Yasukuni Shrine. China's calm reaction to these types of issues has continued under the leadership of Hu and Wen.

Japan is economically quite important to China, particularly for its generous official development assistance (ODA). China is well aware that "anti-China" sentiment is deep-rooted in Japan and that it would strengthen if China over-reacted to historical issues. Moreover, China is very aware of the present close relations between Japan and the United States, and it is keen to avoid unnecessary conflict. As Deng stated, it is essential China secure a peaceful and stable international environment for the sake of economic growth.

In recent years, China has also shown a positive interest in Asian regional cooperation. Perhaps its aim is to help China's economy by integrating it with East Asia to secure economic growth. In so doing, China would establish a vast economic bloc centered on the Chinese market, with Taiwan presumably being part of it too. Its decision to pursue a free trade area (FTA) with the Association of Southeast Asian Nations (ASEAN) also reflects its interest in allaying ASEAN fears about its increasing economic muscle.

For China, the Korean Peninsula is a sensitive area. China would certainly like to strengthen its relationship with South Korea, given deepening economic ties between the two, yet it cannot neglect relations with North Korea. North Korea's participation in the ASEAN Regional Forum (ARF) has facilitated China's involvement in multinational conferences and frameworks. China would undoubtedly support North Korea's "reform and opening" policy, especially if it would improve their relations with the United States. Problems in North Korea impact China very negatively, as evidenced by the North Korean refugee flows into China because of the north's dire economic circumstances. And any tension between the United States and North Korea—such as the crisis over North Korea's development of nuclear weapons—has a huge effect on China too. Although China feels the implications of any North Korean action more directly than the United States, it is a mistake to overestimate China's influence on North Korea.

Concerning Japan, after it entered into an FTA with Singapore, FTAs with South Korea and ASEAN may be next. Yet in order to pursue these arrangements, various complex national issues will have to be confronted, starting with domestic agricultural issues. Globalizing pressures and its

serious economic slump may force Japan to open its markets, while manufacturers simultaneously move increasingly overseas, especially to China, in their quest for cheap labor. Specialization and division of labor are making headway in securing less expensive but skilled labor and efficient production. Supporting such private enterprise activities could lead to the revitalization of Japan and could benefit not only Japan but, ultimately, Asia and the rest of the world. Japan cannot remain internationally competitive by protecting its domestic market; indeed, such an attitude hinders Japan's revitalization in the long run. Compared to the relative openness of the Chinese market, the Japanese market and society continue to be somewhat closed, with a "quasi-socialist" system. Although Japan should adopt and execute reform and opening policies immediately, Japan's political leadership is fragile. Yet if nothing is done, Japan will remain debilitated and not competitive.

At this point, Japan must think seriously about proposing the establishment of an FTA in East Asia. Discussions on FTAs between Japan and South Korea, Japan and ASEAN, China and ASEAN, and so forth should be geared to cover all of East Asia. An East Asia-wide FTA should be viewed not as being a zero-sum exercise but instead as being plus-sum, and as bringing mutual benefits for all. Including Taiwan in an East Asian FTA would presumably benefit China's economy based on the current expansive economic relations between the two.

Gradually relieving the tension among East Asian nations through regional economic integration is the way forward. As Japan has to play an important role in such cooperation, given its overwhelming economic power, an economic recovery in Japan is absolutely essential at this time. China's ongoing economic growth and its success in further opening are equally important. As interdependence between Japan and China is actually increasing, it is desirable to build up a relationship of mutual trust between the governments and leaders of both nations in order to avoid or minimize possible friction. All in East Asia are in the same boat, and the fate of the Titanic should be avoided at all costs.

Originally published by the Japan Center for International Exchange in *The Rise of China and Changing Asian Order*, edited by Kokubun Ryosei and Wang Jisi (2004).

Bibliography

Dickson, Bruce J. "Co-optation and Corporatism in China: The Logic of Party Adaptation." *Political Science Quarterly* 115, no. 4 (2000–2001): 517–540.

Hosokawa Mihoko. "WTO ni kameishita Chūgoku keizai no genjō" [The Current Situation of the Chinese Economy since Joining the WTO]. *Kokusaikinyū* [International Finance] 1078 (January 2002): 66–72.

Jiang Zemin. *Lun "Sange Daibiao"* [Discussion of the "Three Represents"]. Beijing: Zhongyang Wenxian Chubanshe [Central Documents Publishing House], 2001.

Lin Shangli. *Dangnei minzhu: Zhongguo gongchangdangde lilun yu shijian* [Party Democracy: The Chinese Communist Party's Theory and Practice]. Shanghai: Shanghai Shehuikexue Chubanshe [Shanghai Social Sciences Publishing House], 2002.

Lu Xueyi, ed. *Dangdai Zhongguo shehuijiecheng yanjiubaogao* [A Research Report on Contemporary China's Social Strata]. Beijing: Shehuikexue Wenjian Chubanshe [Social Sciences Documents Publishing House], 2002.

Medeiros, Evan S., and M. Taylor Fravel. "China's New Diplomacy." *Foreign Affairs* 82, no. 6 (November–December, 2003): 22–35.

Mitsubishi Research Institute. *Chūgoku jōhō handobukku 2000* [Handbook of Information on China 2000]. Tokyo: Sōsōsha, 2000.

Ōe Shinobu, and The Yomiuri Shimbun Research Department. "Kō Takumin sōshoki saigono tōsō: 'Mittsu no daihyō' ron to Chūgoku kyōsantōtaikai" [A Final Battle for General Secretary Jiang Zemin: The "Three Represents" and the Party Congress of the CCP]. *Chōken Quarterly* 3 (March 2002).

Hostage Crisis
A Matter of Reconciling Two Norms

Shiraishi Takashi

ABSTRACT Iraqi armed groups took Japanese as hostages and demanded the Japanese government withdraw its Self-Defense Force troops from Iraq. The Japanese government argued that they were there on their own volition despite the warning by the Japanese government, while some of the media called for the withdrawal of Japanese troops. This essay calls on the public and the government to handle the two issues separately.

On 8 April, an armed group calling itself Saraya al-Mujahideen announced through a Qatari satellite television station that it had captured three Japanese in Iraq. It threatened to kill the hostages within three days unless the Japanese government withdrew Self-Defense Forces (SDF) personnel from Iraq.

In response, the government reiterated its basic policy of not yielding to terrorist threats and said there was no reason to pull the SDF out of Iraq.

Fortunately, the three Japanese were released on Thursday. On Saturday, two other Japanese who had been taken captive in Iraq were released unhurt.

Nonetheless, the Japanese public was divided during this period over how to deal with the hostage case, with differing news media reactions being good examples. Without exception, the press agreed that the government must not give in to the threat and that no effort should be spared to save the three Japanese, but differences arose over the hostage-takers' demand for the withdrawal of the SDF. Some newspapers maintained that Japan should stand up to terrorist threats while others argued that the prevailing situation in Iraq was making it increasingly difficult for the SDF contingent to concentrate on reconstruction efforts.

In other words, the latest debates have linked the hostage situation to the advisability of sending the SDF to Iraq.

But the hostage case is not necessarily tied to the issue of dispatching the SDF to Iraq. The latest incident actually poses a deeper question: how can we reconcile the international norm of refusing to yield to terrorism with Japan's domestic social contract that obliges the government to ensure the safety of the Japanese people?

There is good reason to refrain from linking the hostage case to the issue of dispatching the SDF to Iraq. Consider the following scenarios.

First, Japan, complying with a UN request, has stationed SDF personnel in East Timor to engage in an international peacekeeping operation and offer nonmilitary assistance to the populace there. What would Japan have done if the remnants of a pro-Jakarta militia, seeking to maintain the integration of East Timor with Indonesia, abducted Japanese aid workers and threatened to kill them unless Japan withdrew the SDF peacekeepers?

Second, many Japanese are involved in medical support activities elsewhere in the world. What should Japan do if an Islamic fundamentalist group kidnapped Japanese medical workers in Egypt, for example, and demanded that Japan halt all medical support efforts in Egypt and withdraw Japanese medical specialists?

Common to both scenarios is the seizure of Japanese by political groups who push their political demands by issuing threats to the Japanese government, demanding that it change specific policies in exchange for the lives of the Japanese hostages. This could happen elsewhere and is not unique to the situation in Iraq. Arguing that the presence of the SDF contingent in Iraq triggered the hostage crisis is tantamount to accepting the kidnappers' justification for taking hostages.

What is the real issue then? The policy of not yielding to terrorist demands is an international norm that exists alongside an equally powerful social contract within Japan that makes it the state's obligation to protect its people. Each norm constrains the other. As a result, neither the government nor the people can expect an easy solution to the problem by simply choosing one norm over the other. At best it can attempt to reconcile these norms, though whether reconciliation is at all possible remains in question.

People agree on two points—"Do not yield to terrorism" and "Do the utmost to save the hostages"—but they clearly disagree over their order of priority. The government's position reflects this dilemma.

What is happening to Japan can happen to any country—not even a superpower can guarantee the safety of its people all over the world. But approaches to the issue of reconciling the international norm with the domestic social contract vary from one country to another. For its part, Japan is unlikely to resort to military force to rescue hostages.

What happened during the 1996–97 hostage standoff at the Japanese ambassador's official residence in Peru is a case in point. At the time, police in Japan already had formed a special unit trained to deal with terrorists. But there is no indication that the government seriously considered dispatching the unit to Lima, an option the public would have strongly opposed.

Former prime minister Fukuda Takeo declared that "one person's life is more precious than the Earth" to explain his government's decision to give in to the demands of the Japanese Red Army

hijackers in 1977. Indeed, the cost in political terms would have been too high for the government if a hijacking or hostage crisis resulted in the death of any Japanese involved.

Therefore, the Japanese government has routinely sought to negotiate with the kidnappers. For instance, the government successfully negotiated the release of four Japanese mining engineers in the central Asian country of Kyrgyzstan from an armed Islamic fundamentalist group in 1999. It remains unknown whether the government paid a ransom or not.

To put it simply, the Japanese government has tried to maintain a balance between the international norm (do not yield to terrorists) and the domestic social contract (save Japanese lives) by negotiating with kidnappers.

Such an approach is, of course, not the only option. Imagine what the US government would do in similar circumstances. The lives of Americans are precious to the US government.

What would the US government have done if it were involved in crises such as the standoff at the Japanese Embassy in Lima or the abduction of the four mining engineers? It would immediately have dispatched an interagency special task force to the scene and worked out countermeasures, including the use of military force. It would probably rule out negotiating with the kidnappers.

Why are Japan's approaches so different from those of the United States? The main reason is that, unlike the United States, Japan lacks military capabilities and the only viable option is to negotiate.

As long as the Japanese government remains bound by the two norms, it has no choice but to find the best possible compromise between the two positions. This is why it said it would not give in to terrorists but at the same time it would make every effort to save the three hostages in Iraq.

It is fortunate that the hostages were eventually released. But similar hostage situations can happen any time, and should the crisis result in tragedy, the government should turn to the Japanese people and accept their verdict concerning the decisions it made.

It must be emphasized that what is at issue is

not which norm takes precedence but the best way to reconcile the two norms. The issue should therefore not be framed as a question of choosing between the rescue of the three hostages and the withdrawal of the SDF contingent from Iraq.

Obviously, Japan is incapable of protecting its citizens all over the world. Similar hostage crises have happened in the past and will take place in the future. When such cases occur, the government should seek the best possible reconciliation between the international norm and the domestic social contract and, above all, should assume responsibility for the outcome.

Originally published by The Yomiuri Shimbun in *THE DAILY YOMIURI* "INSIGHTS into the WORLD" (18 April 2004).

Time for a Permanent Seat on the Security Council

Kitaoka Shinichi

ABSTRACT Even though Japan's financial contribution is the second largest of all members—its 19.5% second only to the United States' 22%—and dwarfs the combined contributions of the other four permanent members of the Security Council (China, France, Russia, and the UK), Japan does not have a standing voice in SC deliberations. Seeking to rectify this anomaly, Japan joined with Germany, Brazil, and India (in what was called the G4) and started a full-scale movement to drastically reform the Security Council in 2004 and 2005. This was arguably the most ambitious postwar foreign policy campaign ever mounted by Japan. In this essay, the author, on the front lines as deputy permanent representative of Japan to the United Nations at the time, argues the justice of Japan's quest for a permanent seat.

Seven months have passed since I took up my position as Japan's deputy permanent representative to the United Nations. During this period, partly by chance, the issue of Security Council reform has been the focus of my work. Japan, which is now seeking a permanent seat on the Security Council, pays 19.5% of the UN general budget, second only to the 22% funded by the United States. Great Britain and France provide around 6% each. China is treated as a developing nation and pays 2%, and Russia accounts for 1%. In other words, aside from the United States, Japan contributes more to the UN budget than all of the permanent members of the Security Council combined. Though the permanent members pay a larger share of the budget for peacekeeping operations than they do for the general budget, as such operations directly relate to international peace and security, and it is the council that approves them, Japan pays for 19.5% of these operations as well, and here too its share is greater than the combined amount provided by the four non-US permanent members.

Why does Japan pay so much? While the United States accounts for about one-third of the world's gross domestic product, its assertion that no single country should have too much influence in the UN has resulted in the imposition of a 22% ceiling on contributions. Developing nations, meanwhile, get a discount. The difference is made up by Japan, along with some other countries, such as Germany, France, and Great Britain, which make contributions larger than their respective shares of global GDP. I am of the opinion that permanent members of the Security Council should pay extra when it comes to assessing their portions of the UN budget, but aside from the limited increase in what they pay for peacekeeping operations, no such arrangement exists. If we consider that the Soviet Union once bore 18% of the burden and the Republic of China (Taiwan) 6%, it seems hard to deny that some of the current permanent members are getting a free ride.

The upshot is that Japan is paying for 19.5% of the budget, and while that may be unfair, there is little prospect of changing the situation. The UN would collapse if the United States were to completely turn its back on the organization, so it has no choice but to accept America's wishes to a certain extent. (If Japan were to withdraw, the UN would be in deep trouble, but it would not collapse.) Also, developing countries comprise a majority of the UN's membership, so eliminating their discount would be extremely difficult. And considering that the permanent members of the Security Council each hold a veto, it is difficult to imagine them accepting an increased burden for themselves. The next reassessment of UN dues will take place in 2006. It will not be easy for Japan to get its share reduced by even 1 percentage point; achieving a large reduction would be impossible unless it were backed up by a firm resolve on Japan's part to quit the UN otherwise.

Given that Japan cannot have its share of the UN budget significantly reduced and is not going to quit the organization, it is left with two options: continue to pay the money while remaining silent or continue to pay the money while making its voice heard. When I hear the arguments of those who take a "cautious" stance on the idea of Japan gaining a permanent seat on the Security Council (such people are essentially opposed), it comes across as nothing more than advocacy of "checkbook diplomacy." More importantly, gaining such a seat will greatly expand Japan's diplomatic options in dealing with future developments, such as China's further rise.

Some of those taking a "cautious" stance ask whether Japan would be able to say no to the United States after taking a permanent seat on the council. The fundamental interests of Japan and the United States are much the same, so there would likely be many occasions when the two countries would synchronize their positions. But when it comes to saying no to the United States, would that be easier for a Japan without a permanent seat or a Japan with a permanent seat? The answer should be obvious. In this light, it seems to me that those in the "cautious" camp are actually advocating a diplomacy of toeing the American line.

Japan's Ample Qualifications

The next question to be addressed is whether Japan is qualified to hold a permanent seat on the Security Council. I think it obviously has the qualifications, beginning with its considerable financial contributions. On this point there is surely no need for further explanation. When it comes to military affairs, however, some have suggested that Japan's contributions are inadequate.

In terms of dispatching the personnel required for peacekeeping operations, the countries of South Asia are in the lead, and Japan lags far behind. The countries that dispatch troops, however, receive about US$1,000 a month in compensation for each person sent, a stipend that amounts to a large sum of money for developing countries. The countries' governments keep some of the money, and some of it goes to the troops—the result being there are a number of countries where people are queuing up to become peacekeepers. Peacekeeping operations also provide countries with the chance to upgrade armaments and train troops, and they facilitate the maintenance of a large military force for national defense.

Another point is that the dispatch of peacekeeping troops is optional. If a country does not wish to send peacekeepers, it has no obligation to do so. Financial contributions, however, are fixed at a certain rate and are thus mandatory. While I of course have no intention of denigrating the efforts and sacrifices of the countries that send large numbers of peacekeepers, I would just like to note that there is a reason for the high regard in which financial contributions are held.

We have also heard suggestions that Japan's military contributions are inadequate in respects that cannot be quantified numerically. In July and August of 2004, it was reported that Deputy Secretary of State Richard Armitage and Secretary of State Colin Powell had suggested that Japan might need to consider amending its Constitution if it were to gain a permanent seat on the Security Council. There were voices of agreement within Japan. Conversely, there are also those who oppose Japan's quest for a permanent seat on the grounds that it would entail playing a military role. A few comments might be made in response to this point. First, formally speaking, when it comes to military obligations there is no distinction between permanent members of the Security Council, nonpermanent members, and UN members that are not on the council at all. Second, while it is of course necessary to be prepared to confront danger on behalf of the world's common goals, Japan has become capable of doing so and has taken part in a number of peacekeeping operations since its first such action in Cambodia in 1992. Third, peripheral activities outside of purely military roles are becoming increasingly important in the activities of the Security Council. For example, the resolution on Iraq passed by the council in June 2003 included a call for multinational forces to provide reconstruction assistance, to which Japan has responded, Fourth, it is not as though all of the permanent members are adequately fulfilling their roles at present.

Under the Constitution as currently interpreted by the government, Japan cannot even exercise the right of collective self-defense. Some commentators have asserted that it is hypocritical for Japan to seek to become a permanent member of the Security Council as long as this constitutional constraint remains in force. The conduct of diplomacy, however, is something that involves hypocrisy to one degree or another. Or to put it more nicely, when countries interact with each other, they take into account their respective domestic circumstances. If Japan becomes a permanent member of the Security Council, there may be occasions when it votes in favor of an action in which Japan itself is unable to participate, and this could put the nation in an awkward position. It would be unrealistic to demand the perfection of Japan from the start, though. The Constitution can be reexamined later. As I will explain below, reform of the Security Council will reach a pivotal stage in 2005, and the argument that we need to revise the Constitution before seeking a permanent seat on the council ignores this issue of timing.

Perceptions of History

There are also those who voice the opinion that it is important for Japan to gain the understanding of neighboring countries before becoming a permanent member of the council. Some claim that Japan is unqualified because of shortcomings in its interpretation of history and acceptance of responsibility for its wartime acts.

The understanding of neighboring countries is important, but neighboring countries do not always enjoy friendly relations. Italy, for example, is strongly opposed to the idea of Germany gaining a permanent seat on the council, and Pakistan is completely against the

same for India. By comparison, opposition from Japan's neighbors is not so fierce. South Korea is a member of the "Coffee Club" that opposes the enlargement of the Security Council. The reason for this, however, is that Seoul believes it will be difficult to create a consensus on the enlargement of permanent membership and that the goal for the time being should be to boost the number of nonpermanent members. South Korea opposes a permanent seat for Germany on the grounds that the difference between that country and Italy is relatively slight in terms of their financial contributions. While it may in reality be opposed to a seat for Japan, it has not said so explicitly. And if one is going to consider the differences between countries' UN dues payments in this connection, I might point out that while Germany's dues are less than twice Italy's, Japan's dues are about 10 times South Korea's.

As for the perception of history, though it is true that this is a significant issue among the people of China and South Korea, arguments that Japan is unqualified for a permanent Security Council seat because of its shortcomings in this respect will lack cogency at the UN. Many of the nations in that body have experienced war and internal strife quite recently, and so it is rather unnatural to single out Japan for criticism about its interpretation of events that happened more than 60 years ago.

The usual outcome of a war is that the responsible party is punished, borders are redrawn, reparations are paid, and the matter is then closed. Japan has gone through this entire process, which is standard practice within the international community. It did not pay reparations to China, but that is because China abandoned its claims. Both the Republic of China and the People's Republic of China waived reparations for reasons of their own, though I will not go into the details here. By way of comparison, let me ask, has the United States ever apologized to Vietnam or paid that country an indemnity? Has China apologized or given compensation to Vietnam for invading that country in 1979? There is also the issue of Japan's past colonial rule, which still rankles many Koreans. But what is the international standard in regard to such cases? What apologies have

Great Britain, France, and the Netherlands made to their former colonies? What sorts of assistance have they offered them, and what results has this assistance produced? On these points the record leaves room for doubt.

It is of course important to make every effort to gain the understanding of China and South Korea. War and colonial rule are legitimate targets of criticism. Also, in these countries, as in many others, public opinion has an effect on foreign policy, meaning that it is not enough just to settle matters at the government level. I would like to point out, though, that arguments relating to these issues cannot be theoretical grounds for blocking Japan from becoming a permanent member of the Security Council.

The Process Ahead

I would now like to examine the path that must be taken to become a permanent member of the Security Council. Article 23 of the UN Charter defines the makeup of the council, specifying the 5 permanent members and providing for the election of 10 nonpermanent members. Therefore, increasing the ranks of either the permanent or nonpermanent members will require revising the charter.

Changing the UN Charter requires that amendments be approved by two-thirds of the members of the General Assembly (meaning 128 of the 191 current members) and then ratified by two-thirds of the UN membership, including all the permanent members of the Security Council. It does not matter if the permanent members initially voted against adopting an amendment, abstained, or were absent; it is enough if they subsequently ratify the amendment. In fact, when the charter was revised in 1963, only one of the permanent members initially voted in favor of the amendment—two were opposed, and two abstained. So the process is to first get the approval of two-thirds of the General Assembly and then win the agreement of the permanent members of the Security Council.

The High-Level Panel on Threats, Challenges, and Change, appointed by Secretary-General Kofi Annan in November 2003, has played a major role in advancing the debate over Security Council reform. The panel is expected to release its report

on 2 December 2004; it should be out before this essay appears in print.[1] On 1 November the secretary-general sent a letter to UN members stating that he would promptly distribute the report to them after adding a few brief comments. He will then await their deliberations on the report and will follow up with some sort of report of his own in March 2005. His plan is to submit a set of proposals relating to the panel's report and to the Millennium Development Goals, which I will touch on later, as a package for approval by participants at the UN summit scheduled for September 2005.

If a set of decisions are made at the September summit, it will be because most of the work on reaching an agreement has been done beforehand. A summit of heads of government is not the occasion to hammer out agreements, especially on a matter as weighty and complicated as Security Council reform. A basic understanding must be reached in advance. There are some who hold that a consensus is necessary when undertaking major reforms. Complete agreement, however, is not possible, and one wonders whether there has ever been an example in history of a profound change being adopted by consensus. Change only comes when people have the courage to press forward. It can be expected that Japan will put forward a proposal at some point between March and September. If this proposal appears likely to win the support of a two-thirds majority, there is a chance that countries that have been sitting on the fence will decide to back the winning horse, leading to much larger than two-thirds majority in the end.

Veto Power Not Absolutely Necessary

Getting an amendment adopted will not be easy. More than 110 countries are in favor of adding both permanent and nonpermanent members to the Security Council, but few of them have a major stake in this matter. There are a few countries, like Japan and Germany, that are seeking seats and a few other countries, like Italy and Pakistan, that are opposed to the additions; the vast majority of UN members, however, lack strong feelings. Many of them would probably be inclined to support increased membership on the council and a permanent seat for Japan, but they would most likely not be particularly bothered if such changes do not come to pass. Even so, the prospects for Security Council reform are better than they have been in the past. The proponents of expansion are in a better position than they were in 1997–98, when a proposal to add five permanent seats and four nonpermanent seats to the council failed. The governments of Japan and Germany are taking the matter seriously now, and the opposing camp has weakened, with some countries dropping out of the Coffee Club.

There are two basic approaches to the handling of the amendment process. The first involves seeking a revision of Article 23 of the UN Charter in a single stage. This would require a proposal that includes the names of the countries to be given permanent seats: Japan, Germany, India, Brazil, and one or two countries from Africa (the likely candidates being South Africa, Egypt, and Nigeria). The second approach would be to undertake the process in two steps, first submitting a proposal to add two permanent members from Asia, one from Europe, one from Latin America, and one or two from Africa and then holding an election to choose the specific countries afterward.

Each of these approaches has merits and demerits. Carrying out reform in one step would be simpler, but it also has the potential to draw more opposition. For example, a country that supports a permanent seat for Japan but opposes one for Germany, or vice versa, might oppose the entire plan or abstain from voting. On the other hand, though the two-stage approach may lessen opposition, it will require greater time and effort, and it presents potential pitfalls.

How to deal with the veto power that comes with a permanent seat is another issue that must be addressed. Japan has taken the position that it is opposed to an unequal setup in which new permanent members lack the veto power held by existing permanent members. At the same time, the government is of the opinion that there are a number of problems with the way veto power is exercised at present and that measures are needed to prevent its abuse.

In reality, the veto is not a matter of decisive importance to Japan. Veto power represents the ability to block the international community from taking some particular action. The United States, for example, needs its veto to protect Israel. Japan, however, stands with the majority of the international community on most issues. And as long as the Japan-US alliance remains firm, Japan does not necessarily need a veto of its own. Perhaps we can watch how the debate on Security Council reform unfolds and at some point make it clear that our country is flexible on the issue of a veto for new permanent members.

If an amendment for Security Council reform gets the approval of two-thirds of the General Assembly, how will the existing permanent members react? France has actively supported reform of the Security Council. There are various reasons for this, but essentially France's position is the same as Japan's, which is that it is necessary to bring in countries that can make significant contributions, as well as promising developing nations. Also, it is in France's national interest for Germany to get a permanent seat on the council, and this entails giving one to Japan as well. Great Britain is not backing the idea of reforming the Security Council as actively as France, but it is in favor of the addition of Japan, Germany, India, Brazil, and a country in Africa. Russia has not taken a clear position, but it is not opposed to reform.

The two permanent members that pose difficulties are the United States and China. The US would support expanding the Security Council if Japan were the only new member, but that approach will not lead to any type of solution. The United States used to be in favor of a permanent seat for Germany as well, but it has recently stopped voicing such support. Washington is also opposed to a large increase in the number of nations on the Security Council from the standpoint of efficiency.

It is critical to get the US to move forward from support for Japan alone to support for a package that includes Japan, and though this will be extremely difficult, it is not impossible. I had thought that if Democratic candidate John Kerry were elected president in November, with the Republicans maintaining control of the Senate, getting the United States to change its position over the coming four years would be impossible. The Republican Senate would have opposed everything having to do with the internationalist approach of a newly elected President Kerry. But with President Bush reelected and both houses of Congress remaining under Republican control, a decision by the president should be all it takes in order for the United States to make bold policy moves.

If the United States comes around to support enlarging the Security Council roster, that will leave only China. It would probably be difficult for the Chinese to scuttle a decision that required more than 10 years to reach. There are many issues on which they require Japanese cooperation, and so it is hard to imagine them doing anything that would deal a major blow to Sino-Japanese relations. In any event, it is far from unusual for the ratification of a major treaty to take several years; I am sure there would be a chance to get the UN Charter amendment ratified by China sometime prior to the 2008 Olympics in Beijing.

A Just Cause

I would now like to address two other important issues. The Millennium Development Goals that the members of the UN adopted in 2000 include provisions for greatly increasing aid to developing countries. The majority of UN members are developing nations and are thus keenly interested in this issue. Japan's official development assistance, however, is on a downward trend. Once the world's largest provider of ODA, Japan has recently fallen to second place behind the United States. Furthermore, other developed countries are increasing their own outlays of aid. If present trends continue, Japan will find itself being passed by Great Britain, France, and Germany and dropping to fifth place. It could even end up being outdone by the Netherlands and Italy. And Japan's present outlays for ODA amount to only 0.2% of its per capita GDP, ranking alongside the figure for the United States as the lowest among the developed countries. Additionally, much of Japan's aid consists of loans, meaning that if a project succeeds, the money gets repaid. While

this in itself is a good thing, since the global statistics on development assistance are based on net outlays, the repayments are subtracted from the amounts of new assistance provided, and this further accentuates the downward trend in Japan's position as a donor.

I think that assistance in the form of loans is meaningful and has led to significant achievements, notably in the development of East Asia. However, it is unclear if success can be attained in South Asia or Africa using the same methods. In short, the time has arrived for Japan to begin searching for a new ODA strategy. With the rest of the world shifting to increased aid, Japan will have to return its own ODA to a growth track in order to deepen the level of trust that other countries place in it.

The second key issue is the need for the government to marshal all its resources on a limited basis in pursuit of the goal of a permanent Security Council seat. This is one of Japan's biggest diplomatic undertakings since the end of World War II, ranking alongside such historic events as the conclusion of the San Francisco Peace Treaty in 1951, the revision of the Japan-US Security Treaty in 1960, and the return of Okinawa in 1972. An extraordinary situation like this calls for an extraordinary response. Whether it is personnel for the Ministry of Foreign Affairs or appropriations in the budget, the government needs to be ready to devote whatever resources may be necessary to achieve this objective.

In the past, reorganizations of the international order were the results of wars and revolutions. The UN itself was born in the aftermath of World War II. War among the world's major powers is highly unlikely anytime soon, however, and while that is of course a good thing, it means that the needed adjustments must be achieved in peace. The ability to adapt to new circumstances is of decisive importance for every organization; without it, an organization cannot maintain its vitality. In a system like the UN, it is essential that powerful countries occupy key positions. Otherwise it may be difficult for the UN to continue to exist as an influential organization in the twenty-first century. We can see this from the example of the post–World War I League of

Nations, which was dramatically weakened by the nonparticipation of the United States. In this respect, the admission of the People's Republic of China to the UN as a permanent member of the Security Council in 1971 was a positive development, inasmuch as it reflected the power of that country.

It is important that a country like Japan—a nonnuclear civilian power, Asian, and with memories of its experience as a developing nation—become a permanent member of the UN Security Council. One could even say that this is Japan's duty. It is a matter of our country's responsibility with respect to the international order, transcending parochial national interests. This is the nature of the cause, and Japan must as a matter of course do its utmost in pursuing it.

English version originally published by Japan Echo in *Japan Echo* 32, no. 2 (2005).

Translated from "Jōnin rijikoku iri wa Nihon ga hatasu beki sekinin de aru," in *Chūō Kōron* (January 2005): 126–45; shortened by about one-half.

Notes

1. The 2 December 2004 report can be viewed at https://www.un.org/en/ga/search/view_doc. asp?symbol=A/59/565.

Cool Heads Needed to Solve Japan-China Problems

II-(5)

Shiraishi Takashi

ABSTRACT Anti-Japanese protest movements mounted in China in 2004–05 to denounce Japan's history textbooks, to oppose Japan joining the United Nations Security Council, and to condemn Prime Minister Koizumi Junichirō's visit to Yasukuni Shrine. This essay calls on Prime Minister Koizumi (and his future successors) not to visit Yasukuni Shrine.

After the 23 April 2005 meeting in Jakarta between Prime Minister Koizumi Junichirō and Chinese president Hu Jintao, the storm of anti-Japanese demonstrations that had taken place in many urban centers in China last month appear to have passed. But the abrupt departure of Chinese vice-premier Wu Yi before her scheduled meeting with Koizumi and the heated reaction on the part of some Japanese have further mired Sino-Japanese relations in the emotional quicksands of "saving face."

The political cost of the entire episode is very high. On 12 April, when asked about the demonstrations at a press conference during his visit to India, Chinese premier Wen Jiabao stated, "Only the country respecting the history, with the courage to take responsibility for the history and obtaining the trust of the people in Asia and the world could play greater role in international affairs." In effect, Wen expressed China's opposition to Japan becoming a permanent member of the UN Security Council.

I do not believe that the anti-Japanese demonstrations in April were all stage-managed by the Chinese government. There is no question that anti-Japanese sentiment exists among young Chinese, but the Chinese government undoubtedly mobilized these sentiments to achieve its political purposes. Over the last three years, the Japanese government has been trying to deal separately with important diplomatic issues, such as UN reform and becoming a permanent member of the Security Council, Sino-Japanese relations and Koizumi's visits to Yasukuni Shrine, the East Asian economic partnership, and US military realignment and Japan's adjustment to it.

But this time the Chinese government made it clear, in a way that could no longer be ignored, that some of these issues are connected. There is no point in getting angry at the way the Chinese went about making their point. The legitimacy of the current regime in China is dependent on nationalism and the performance of its socialist market economy. Besides, the Chinese government is confronted with the daunting challenge of overcoming a serious internal social crisis, manifested in regional imbalances and class tensions. The Chinese government can be expected to use patriotism to shore up its regime and achieve its political objectives. No diplomacy worth its name can afford to ignore this reality. It is useless to harp on the "discourtesy" of the Chinese government. Both countries now need to address the problems in a coolheaded way.

What are the problems? The bottom line is: How do we deal with the mutual distrust between Japan and China? Seen from the Japanese perspective, the anti-Japanese demonstrations at the Asia Cup soccer matches last year, China's exploration of natural gas resources in the East China Sea, the incursion of a Chinese nuclear submarine into Japanese territorial waters, the recent nationwide anti-Japanese demonstrations, and China's opposition to Japan's aspirations to become a permanent member of the UN Security Council all appear to signify China's hostility toward Japan. Seen from the Chinese perspective, Koizumi's visits to Yasukuni, references to Taiwan in the Japan-US strategic dialogue, discussions in Japan about ending Japanese official development assistance to China, and the history textbook controversy all appear to signify Japan's hostility toward China. Dissolving this mutual distrust, however slowly, is the primary task.

What to do then? Strategic decisions on the history question must be made by both sides.

It is a mistake to say that Japan has never apologized for its colonial and wartime past. The Japanese government, for instance, expressed its "deep regret" in the 1972 Sino-Japanese Joint Statement, the 1978 Sino-Japanese Peace and Friendship Treaty, and the 1995 Sino-Japanese Joint Declaration. The Chinese government accepted these statements. At the recent Jakarta summit meeting, Hu proposed that the principle and spirit of these three documents be upheld. In 1995, then prime minister Murayama Tomiichi declared that "Japan, following a mistaken national policy, advanced along the road to war, only to ensnare the Japanese people in a fateful crisis, and, through its colonial rule and aggression, caused tremendous damage and suffering to the people of many countries, particularly to those of Asian nations. In the hope that no such mistake be made in the future, I regard, in a spirit of humility, these irrefutable facts of history, and express here once again my feelings of deep remorse and state my heartfelt apology. Allow me also to express my feelings of profound mourning for all victims, both at home and abroad, of that history."

This Japanese official policy was decided on by the Cabinet and has since been reaffirmed, most recently by Koizumi in his speech at the Asia-Africa Conference in Bandung this April. And yet Japan continues to be criticized for not confronting its wartime past. This criticism is shared not only by Chinese and Koreans but also by the world, as evident in Southeast Asian, American, and European reports on the demonstrations.

There are two reasons for this. The first is Koizumi's visits to Yasukuni Shrine. The prime minister's visits to the shrine where Class-A war criminals are enshrined have created the impression that the Koizumi administration has quietly undermined the government policy formulated by Murayama. But the policy committee headed by then cabinet secretary Fukuda Yasuo had already recommended in 2002 the building of a new national war memorial. What the prime minister should do now is stop visiting the shrine and decide on the establishment of a new war memorial to back up his speech at the Asia-Africa Conference.

The second reason is the history textbook controversy. The Japanese government has proposed undertaking collaborative research on history with the Chinese. This is welcome but takes time. Besides, only one out of eight middle school history textbooks argues that the "Greater East Asia War" was a war of liberation, and this textbook is used by less than 0.1% of high schools (or fewer than 10 schools). But it is useless to argue this point. As long as the current national textbook authorization system exists, whatever it authorizes will be viewed as state-sanctioned by people in China and South Korea, countries that use state-sanctioned textbooks. A third-party inspection system similar to that used in Germany should replace the current national authorization system.

I do not propose this because of external pressure. Japan's freedom of action has been constrained by its colonial and wartime past. This is undesirable. The Chinese premier opposed Japan's aspiration to become a permanent member of the UN Security Council by stating that "Only the country respecting the history, with the courage to take responsibility for the history . . . could play greater role in international affairs."

What the Japanese government should do is to deal with this question in a way that cannot be misunderstood by anyone so that no one can criticize the Japanese government for its failure to deal with the past.

But, at the same time, restoring the friendship between Japan and China is not solely Japan's responsibility. What the Chinese government must do is up to the Chinese themselves, of course. However, I urge the Chinese government to consider two points. First of all, the Chinese government should punish those who damaged Japanese property and injured Japanese citizens during the demonstrations, as well as provide compensation for the damage and the injured. Second, the Chinese government should stop disseminating misinformation concerning Japan's "failure" to apologize for its colonial and wartime history. As long as the Chinese government relies on anti-Japanese patriotism and tries to occupy the moral high ground in relation to Japan, there can be no Sino-Japanese friendship built on equality. The Chinese government should educate its citizens about postwar Sino-Japanese efforts to promote amity and economic cooperation between the two countries.

Stabilizing and strengthening Sino-Japanese relations is crucial for Japan and China as well as for Asia and the world. Sino-Japanese rapprochement is indispensable for building an East Asia community. What is needed is to transform the current relationship of mutual distrust into a relationship of mutual trust. It is natural for people to love their country, but the kind of nationalism that seeks its enemies outside the nation is dangerous in this age of growing interdependence. Containing such nationalism and channeling its energies into forging mutual trust and cooperation between these neighboring countries is the task of political leaders.

Originally published by The Yomiuri Shimbun in *THE DAILY YOMIURI* "INSIGHTS into the WORLD" (29 May 2005).

Bibliography

Ministry of Foreign Affairs of Japan. "Statement by Prime Minister Tomiichi Murayama 'On the occasion of the 50th anniversary of the war's end'." 15 August 1995. https://www.mofa.go.jp/announce/press/pm/murayama/9508.html.

Ministry of Foreign Affairs of the People's Republic of China. "Premier Wen Jiabao Meets with Journalists, Talking about 3 Achievements of His Visit to India." 12 April 2005. https://www.fmprc.gov.cn/mfa_eng/topics_665678/wzlcfly_665842/t191621.shtml

Introduction to *An East Asian Community and the United States*

Tanaka Akihiko

ABSTRACT Coming off the 1997 Asian currency crisis, there have been increasing calls for regionalism and community-building, and the bonds among the East Asian nations have been strengthened in a number of ways. Complementing this, there have been developments in such multilateral regional frameworks as APEC, ARF, ASEAN+3, and the East Asia Summit. Even so, a number of issues remain to be resolved in creating an East Asian cooperative structure. This essay looks at the factors accounting for the increasing East Asian unity, highlights the distinctive features of East Asia's multilateral political frameworks, and illuminates the issues involved in East Asian community-building.

Ten years after the Asian financial crisis of 1997, East Asia is now a region of dynamic growth and the East Asian economies are striding again. However, no one calls the dynamic growth of East Asia a miracle anymore; it is a fact of economic life in today's world. Uncertainty obviously abounds around the future of the East Asian economies, especially China's, but it has become an assumption of many businesspeople and politicians that the economies of East Asia will continue to be one of the centers of the world economy.

Along with the recovery of the East Asian economies from the 1997 crisis, voices of regionalism and efforts of community building in the region have grown. The year 2007 marks the 10th anniversary of the first Association of Southeast Asian Nations plus Three (ASEAN+3) Summit—the gathering of the leaders of the 10 ASEAN countries, along with China, Japan, and South Korea. When the ASEAN+3 Summit took place in the midst of the Asian financial crisis, it was an ad hoc meeting where three Northeast Asian leaders happened to be invited to join the ASEAN leaders who gathered together at the ASEAN Summit.[1] In the following years, however, ASEAN+3 has developed to be one of the pillars of East Asian regionalism. It released the "Joint Statement on East Asian Cooperation" in November 1999, which identified the vision and comprehensive areas of cooperation among member states. It is now expected to agree on the "Second Joint Statement on East Asian Cooperation" when it meets in November 2007.

These developments, the reestablishment of East Asia as a center of global economic growth, and the emergence of regionalism, are important not only for East Asia but also for the entire world, including the United States. The purpose of this volume (*An East Asian Community and the United States*) is to demonstrate how phenomenal East Asian regionalization is and how wide-ranging changes are taking place in various sectors of international relations. By examining these changes, the volume is also intended to explore how these East Asian developments affect relations between East Asia and the United States. In fact, it is impossible to understand East Asian developments without examining the role of the United States. The alliance systems of the United States have set the political parameters in East Asia. The US market is the most important destination of manufactured goods that East Asian economies produce. In addition to these obvious facts about the important roles played by the United States, the volume intends to demonstrate the importance of the process of international relations between East Asia and the United States.

As is well known, the direction of East Asian regionalism has always been closely related to the American views of regional order in East Asia. In the early 1990s, when Mahathir bin Mohammad, the Malaysian prime minister, proposed forming an East Asian Economic Group (EAEG, later renamed the East Asian Economic Caucus, EAEC), US secretary of state James A. Baker strongly denounced it, and the idea was virtually shelved. In 1998, when the Japanese government explored the possibility of establishing an Asian Monetary Fund to cope with the Asian financial crisis, the United States' objection to the idea was the critical factor in its withdrawal.[2]

ASEAN+3 is not as same as Mahathir's EAEC. However, its members are virtually the same as the countries that Mahathir had in mind when he proposed his EAEC. The United States under the Bill Clinton and George W. Bush administrations has made no critical comments about this framework. In 2005, an additional framework of East Asian regionalism was created: the East Asian Summit, in which India, Australia, and New Zealand participate, in addition to the original ASEAN+3 countries. Some comments, including critical ones, have been voiced in the United States about the East Asian Summit. But generally, Washington does not seem to care much.[3] Has Washington fundamentally changed its attitude toward East Asian regionalism? Has the United States decided to embrace East Asian regionalism as such? Or is it simply an indication that the United States has lost interest in developments in East Asia?

Many things have happened during the past 10 years. China firmly established its image as a global manufacturing center. After a decade-long stagnation, Japan reemerged as an economic power with sophisticated technological bases. South Korea and many Southeast Asian countries also demonstrated their viability as promising global economies. The potential of India as a future economic giant now looms large. Politically, North Korea became the center

of focus in late 2002, when its compliance with the Geneva Agreement to not produce nuclear materials came to be seriously doubted. North Korea then declared its possession of nuclear weapons in 2004 and conducted a nuclear test in 2006.[4] Mainland China's relations with Taiwan went through various stages, from a more confrontational attitude to a recent, more measured approach to maintain the status quo. The long-term political and strategic implications of China's continuing growth are still uncertain.[5] Politically and economically, East Asia is a promising region, but its promising future is colored by the continuing fragility of its politics and security problems.

Obviously, the terrorist attacks on the United States on 11 September 2001 ushered in a new era of global insecurity and shifted the attention of the US leadership to focus on the war on terror. The overwhelming amount of US decisionmakers' energy has been devoted to the policies to cope with Afghanistan, Iraq, and the Middle East in general. Partly because of this understandable shift of attention of the leaders, East Asia may appear secondary in the minds of the critical decisionmakers of the United States. Yet as this entire volume demonstrates, East Asian developments are phenomenal and deserve continuing and sustained American attention; it is in the United States' interest to engage with East Asian affairs. Likewise, the volume intends to demonstrate that the continuing and sustained attention of the United States to, and engagement with, East Asian affairs is critical for East Asia.

A Background of Rapid Regionalization

To gauge the current characteristics of East Asian community building, it is necessary to recognize how recently rapid regionalization started in East Asia. The concept of East Asia itself is still in flux. Traditionally, "East Asia" was long regarded as an area centered on China—that is, China, the Korean Peninsula, Japan, and Vietnam. It was only in the 1990s that the term East Asia began to be used for an area consisting of both Northeast Asia and Southeast Asia. In the 1950s and 1960s, under the shadow of the Cold War and various regional hot wars, no meaningful regions existed in what we now call East Asia. Instead of creating a region, countries on the eastern edge of the Eurasian continent were fighting each other or fighting civil wars. The Indochina Peninsula was in constant military turmoil, and an East Asia comprised of Northeast and Southeast Asia was impossible because of the big war zone between the north and south.

New developments occurred in the 1970s, gradually proceeded in the 1980s, and expanded in the 1990s. The Sino-American rapprochement in 1971 and Deng Xiaoping's initiation of the "reform and opening" (*gaige kaifang*) policy in 1978 began to connect China with the rest of the world. The Cambodian Civil War was the most difficult and complex remnant of the final phase of the Cold War in Asia. But no new interstate wars have occurred in East Asia since the Sino-Vietnamese war of 1979, and no new large-scale civil wars have been fought in East Asia since the 1991 Paris Peace Agreement on Cambodian peace. This quarter century-long interstate peace is unprecedented in East Asia in the 150 years since the Opium War of the 1840s. The 14-year peace without civil war is further unprecedented. This breakout of peace and the process of ending the Cold War in East Asia created a denser political network that was hitherto nonexistent in the region and became the basis for the region's tremendous economic progress. One should recall that, as recently as 1990, Indonesia and Singapore normalized their relations with China, and in 1992, South Korea did the same. Until the end of the Cambodian Civil War, it was impossible to think of a contiguous East Asia consisting of both Northeast Asia and Southeast Asia because Indochina was the battleground and Vietnam was regarded as the number-one source of concern for the then members of ASEAN. Peace and normalization of political relations, at least in the southern part of East Asia, was the political basis for the East Asia-wide economic miracle.

Coinciding with the gradual emergence of peace, the impact of economic globalization has spread throughout East Asia. As a result, from 1980 to 2003, the total nominal GDP of East Asian economies grew 4.7 times, exports grew 6.9 times, and investment inflows grew 16.3

times. Now the economic size of East Asia is comparable to that of Western Europe and North America. Economic interdependence within the region has also grown. Intraregional imports have grown from 34.8% of all imports in 1980 to 58.6% in 2003. As economic development continues in East Asia, international financial capital, short term as well as long term, has flowed into East Asia. The Asian financial crisis of 1997 demonstrated the importance, and the fragility, of the East Asian economies in a world of globalized financial interaction.[6]

Social interaction within East Asia has also grown rapidly in the late 1990s and early 2000s. In the past, the "ugly tourist" behavior was dominated by Japanese because they were the only Asians who traveled abroad in groups. Now, many other Asians are traveling all around the world, especially in neighboring countries. Many items of popular culture—such as comic books (*manga*), karaoke, popular songs, movies, television dramas, and video games—are being widely shared, especially in the urban centers of East Asia.[7] Some scholars have begun to argue that there is emerging of what might be referred to as the East Asian way of life among the new middle classes.[8] Environmentally, too, a consciousness of regional unity has emerged. Acid rain and haze are not the concerns of a single country, and thus they should be tackled multilaterally.

What one should remember about East Asian regionalization, then, are its recentness, its rapidity, and its comprehensiveness. East Asian integration is not limited to economic areas; it has social, cultural, and environmental implications. Comprehensive integration requires comprehensive expertise in various functional areas, which necessitates regional cooperation but may also require global cooperation. The rapidity of regional integration is another challenge; this implies that along with the rapid transfer of desirable things, there can also be a rapid transfer of undesirable things, as was seen in the rapid contagion of the economic crisis. Again, this requires more regional cooperation but may also require global cooperation. The recentness of the regional integration implies its fragility. Although the very long-term influence of traditional culture may have a positive impact on East Asian regional community building, the short-term history of actual regional political contacts implies that there will be problems in settling difficult issues, let alone in achieving convergence in political values and political systems. Close regional dialogue is essential, but systems for maintaining political stability as well as mechanisms to encourage progress in universal values are also needed.

The Emergence of Regional Frameworks

Along with the regionalization of economic and social dimensions, regional multilateral political frameworks have also developed: the Asia-Pacific Economic Cooperation forum (APEC), the ASEAN Regional Forum (ARF), the Asia-Europe Meeting (ASEM), ASEAN+3, and the East Asia Summit. There are several characteristics of the development of regional political frameworks in East Asia.

First, many political frameworks are organized with ASEAN as the hub; the ASEAN Post-Ministerial Conference (ASEAN PMC), ARF, and ASEAN+3 are obvious examples. One of the worries of ASEAN countries in establishing the East Asia Summit was that the centrality of ASEAN might be reduced by dropping "ASEAN" from the name of the summit. In fact, however, the pivotal role of ASEAN was again reconfirmed through the process of discussing the participants in the East Asia Summit. As is known, some ASEAN+3 members, such as Malaysia and China, did not want to add new members to the summit; whereas others, such as Japan, Indonesia, and Singapore, wanted to add Australia, New Zealand, and India. In the end, the ASEAN foreign ministers meeting at Cebu in April 2005 and, following the ASEAN+3 foreign ministers' meeting at Kyoto in May 2005, resolved this issue by creating a set of criteria for participation. East Asian Summit members should: (1) have close relations with ASEAN, (2) be a full-dialogue partner with ASEAN, and (3) be a signatory to the Treaty of Amity and Cooperation. The three Northeast Asian countries gave consent to these criteria set by ASEAN, thus reconfirming that ASEAN continues to occupy the driver's seat in regional cooperation in East Asia.

Second, on the other side of the centrality of ASEAN in East Asian regional frameworks is the open-ended nature of overlapping frameworks. APEC is a framework that encompasses countries and economies in East Asia and many countries on the rim of the Pacific, including Russia, the United States, Canada, Australia, New Zealand, Peru, Chile, and Mexico. ARF involves the United States, the European Union, India, and Russia in addition to many East Asian countries. ASEM is a framework to connect East Asia with European countries. The newly created East Asia Summit is a halfway point between ASEAN+3 and ARF; it has India, Australia, and New Zealand in addition to ASEAN+3. The leaders of Japan, China, and South Korea regularly meet on the margins of the ASEAN+3 meetings. In addition to these, there are many ASEAN+1 meetings: ASEAN+Japan, ASEAN+South Korea, ASEAN+China, ASEAN+the United States, and so on.

The outer boundary of East Asian regional frameworks is not rigidly determined. If the boundary definition of many European institutions is characterized as a membership rule of a clublike organization, the boundary definition of East Asian institutions is quite open-ended and pragmatic; one can create any number of ASEAN+X formulas. There are a few non-ASEAN-based institutions in East Asia. One is the six-party talks on the North Korean nuclear issues, and another is the Shanghai Cooperation Organization (SCO). The six-party talks is a conference specifically tasked to deal with North Korea's nuclear issues, but it can be transformed to become a more regular regional security forum once some kind of solution is reached on the North Korean nuclear issue. The SCO focuses mostly on Central Asia, but—being an international institution in whose creation China played an important part and in whose maintenance it continues to play a part—it can have a long-term impact on any regional arrangements involving China. This multiplicity and open-ended nature of the regional frameworks of East Asia seem to indicate the continuing fluidity of the concept of East Asia. The formation of an East Asian community is only possible through the continuing interaction of many major powers of the world: the United States, the European Union, and Russia.

Third, as a result of the centrality of ASEAN in East Asian regionalism, the "ASEAN way" tends to prevail as a modality of most political frameworks. In the ASEAN way, it is desired that all issues should be managed by consensus. Open confrontations in open forums are the least desired political situation. Everyone has to be sensitive to everyone else's "comfort" level; one should not raise an issue that can embarrass others. As a result of these tendencies, the ASEAN way also implies a strong attachment to the principle of noninterference in the domestic affairs of other countries and a resistance to hard institutionalization. Partly as a result of the ASEAN way of refraining from interfering in other countries' domestic affairs, and partly as a result of fundamental differences in the political systems of the region's countries, regional cooperation has long centered on "functional" areas, such as finance, trade, energy, the environment, science, technology, culture, and education. Political and security issues are also discussed, but emphasis is placed on nontraditional security issues such as anti-terrorism and anti-piracy cooperation.

However, for ASEAN to maintain its leading role as a driver of regionalism in East Asia, it has also recognized the need to reform itself. There have been more efforts of dynamic interaction beyond the traditional ASEAN way, such as mutual economic surveillance and the politics of Myanmar under the concept of "constructive engagement." Whether ASEAN could address the compatibility of these issues with global values and norms while maintaining the region's resilience as a unit would be the important benchmark. ASEAN's effort to create the ASEAN charter as a constitutional document is an important juncture for its own reform.

Fourth, discussion of "visions," "ideals," and "norms" for regional integration came very slowly. If regionalism is defined as an articulated idea for creating a region with specific goals in mind, East Asian regional integration could, until very recently, have been characterized as regionalization without regionalism. The facts show

that regionalization preceded ideas and visions of regionalism. As mentioned above, the first ASEAN+3 Summit of 1997 was planned as an ad hoc gathering without any "vision statements." However, as political leaders gather together, it seems inevitable for them to attach some meaning to their gatherings. The emergence of regionalism thus seemed inevitable as the degree of regionalization proceeded to a certain degree. Therefore, in 1999, at the third ASEAN+3 meeting, the leaders issued a "Joint Statement on East Asian Cooperation" as the first official statement of their cooperative activities. President Kim Dae-jung proposed establishing an East Asia Vision Group as an advisory panel to the ASEAN+3 Summit, and this was tasked with presenting a report to the 2001 summit. The idealistic and universalistic tone of the East Asia Vision Group report was expressed very well by its first sentence: "We, the people of East Asia, aspire to create an East Asian community of peace, prosperity, and progress based on the full development of all peoples in the region."[9] However, there are tensions in the East Asian discussion of regionalism between those emphasizing universal values and those emphasizing specific local conditions. The report used concepts such as "progress," "human security," and "good governance" but not "democracy" or "human rights."

The Challenges of Community Building in East Asia

The characteristics of the political process already allude to some of the challenges facing the people of East Asia in proceeding with East Asian regional integration. First, one major challenge involves visions of regionalism and how to reconcile the tension between the principle of noninterference and the emphasis on universal human values. The current way to reconcile this tension seems to be to accept both principles and regard the entire process of regional integration as an evolutionary process of realizing universal values without making apparent attempts to interfere in other countries' domestic affairs. Setting up norms of universal values as clearly as possible but not hastily pressuring those not willing to follow these norms seems the current formula for an "evolutionary strategy" of regional integration. Obviously, this strategy does not resolve the problems that countries like Myanmar pose. In the end, this strategy cannot but depend on the hope that the process of regionalization eventually fosters the process of democratization in currently nondemocratic countries.

Second, there are problems of political reconciliation among important countries and other political entities in the region. The recent political tension between Japan and its Northeast Asian neighbors was a case in point. Since Prime Minister Koizumi Junichirō declared his intention to make annual visits to the Yasukuni Shrine, where the Japanese war dead and controversial generals and politicians categorized by the Tokyo War Crimes Tribunal as "Class-A War Criminals" are enshrined, political relations between Tokyo and Beijing have been strained. The Yasukuni Shrine issue is also a source of tension between Tokyo and Seoul, but the territorial issue over Takeshima/Dokdo has also become very thorny since 2004.

Although Koizumi asserted that Japan's relations with China and South Korea were good enough, it was abnormal that the leaders of Japan, China, and South Korea did not agree to have mutual visits or meetings. It was a welcome change that Japan's new prime minister, Abe Shinzō, decided to shelve the controversial "history" issues and chose China and South Korea as the destinations of his first foreign visits in October 2006. Japan and China agreed to "build a mutually beneficial relationship based on common strategic interests."[10] On the occasion of the APEC meeting in Hanoi in November 2006, Abe had a meeting with Chinese president Hu Jintao, and on the occasion of the ASEAN+3 Summit and the East Asian Summit, Abe had a meeting with Chinese premier Wen Jiabao. On the margin of the ASEAN+3 Summit, the leaders of Japan, China, and South Korea had their trilateral meeting and issued a joint press statement stressing their determination to promote East Asian community building as well as promoting their trilateral cooperation.[11] As Tokyo's relations with Beijing and Seoul improve, chances for more constructive East Asian cooperation will increase.

There are also other political divisions in East Asia that hinder further regionalization. North Korea is one, and the Taiwan Strait is another. Unless these two persisting political divisions are resolved, true regionalization in East Asia will not be complete.

The third challenge of East Asian regionalism involves its boundaries and its external relations. If political divisions on the Korean Peninsula and over the Taiwan Strait are resolved, it seems natural to give proper places to North Korea and Taiwan in East Asian cooperation. The roles of Australia, New Zealand, and India could also be rather controversial in future discussions of East Asian regional integration. However, to the extent that the current process of regional integration is a long-term process of evolution, this controversy may not need to be settled immediately. As in the past, the concept of "East Asia" may evolve as the process of regionalization further progresses.

East Asia's relations with North America and Europe are also important. As pointed out earlier, multiplicity and an open-ended nature characterize the development of East Asian regional frameworks. Many countries normally regarded as non-Asian countries have long been involved in many regional institutions in East Asia. APEC is the most important framework to connect the countries of East Asia with the countries on the Pacific Rim. ASEM is the key forum where Europeans and Asians get together. There are many more, such as ARF and ASEAN PMC, that involve both Americans and Europeans. To the extent that the future of East Asian economies depends on good relations with North American and European markets, continuing dialogue with Europeans and Americans is essential in promoting East Asian regionalism. The functional cooperation that East Asians are currently promoting requires expertise from all over the world, most notably from Europe and North America.

Good relations with the United States are critical for East Asian regionalism for the reasons just mentioned. But good relations and close coordination with the United States are required for more fundamental security reasons for East Asia. Given the short and rapid history of regionalization in East Asia, preservation of peace is the most crucial factor for the future success of community building. One can expect the growth of "liberal forces" to bring about a zone of peace in East Asia: the further deepening of economic interdependence, the spreading of functional cooperation in many areas with their "spillover" effects on international relations, the transformation of authoritarian governments, the improvement of good governance, and the eventual democratization of many countries. But there are continuing and complex geostrategic realities in East Asia that do not allow the "liberal" tendencies to guarantee peace. For the victory of these liberal tendencies, realistic support of peace is needed. And the United States is the only country that plays a constructive role both to promote "liberal" tendencies as well as to provide "realistic" support for peace in East Asia. In this sense, community building in East Asia cannot be separated from a healthy US alliance system, the US strategic engagement with China, and the parallel promotion of Asian-Pacific community building.

The fourth and final challenge may be the most difficult for the countries of East Asia as well as the United States: the task of realizing concrete and substantive achievement in many functional areas. If functional cooperation only means holding meetings and conferences, it is easy. And if functional cooperation only means the participants join activities on which they can easily agree, again it is easy. Further still, if functional cooperation means that countries contribute to activities that do not cost much, it is easy. But if functional cooperation is limited to these easy activities, it does not achieve much, let alone produce spillover effects into other, more politically charged areas.

Free trade agreements and financial cooperation are the two most important areas of functional cooperation that East Asian countries now face. If East Asian countries can agree only on a "dirty free trade agreement" and cannot agree on truly effective financial surveillance systems, a strong impetus toward more substantive regional cooperation may be lost. East Asia may have to suffer another round of unexpected crises.

In the late 1990s, APEC lost momentum partly because it did not produce concrete results.

The current process of ASEAN+3 and the East Asia Summit should not repeat APEC's mistakes. The ASEAN+3 Summit and the East Asia Summit held in the Philippines in January 2007 achieved more than the previous meetings. It was significant that Japan and China made concrete proposals with some financial backing. Japan's proposal for energy security is a positive proposal to meet the region's necessities. But to proceed further, leaders and diplomats should talk with substance in preparation for future meetings rather than about such formalistic subjects as which countries should participate in the meetings.

Originally published by the Center for Strategic and International Studies in *An East Asian Community and the United States*, edited by Ralph A. Cossa and Tanaka Akihiko (2007).

Notes

1. For the development of ASEAN+3, see Jimbo 2007 and Tanaka 2006.

2. Ibid.

3. For a detailed analysis, see Cossa 2007.

4. For the renewed crisis over North Korea, see Funabashi 2007.

5. Tanaka 2006.

6. For economic regionalization of East Asia, see Urata 2007; Shirai 2007.

7. For an empirical survey of people's attitudes toward life, society, politics, and values, see Inoguchi, Sonoda, Tanaka, and Dadabaev 2006.

8. Shiraishi 2006.

9. East Asia Vision Group 2001.

10. Ministry of Foreign Affairs of Japan 2006.

11. Ministry of Foreign Affairs of Japan 2007. On East Asian community building, the joint press statement states: "The leaders agreed that trilateral cooperation among China, Japan, and ROK [South Korea] is an important part of East Asian cooperation. Such trilateral cooperation enriches East Asian cooperation, enhances institutional building in this regard, and plays an active role in promoting the ASEAN Plus One (10+1), the ASEAN Plus Three (10+3), the East Asia Summit (EAS), and the building of an East Asian community. The leaders reaffirmed their commitment to the enhancement of cooperation with ASEAN, the promotion of East Asia cooperation and their respect to the leading role of ASEAN in East Asian cooperation. They shared the view to realize an East Asian community as a long-term goal with

ASEAN Plus Three (10+3) process as the main vehicle. They reaffirmed that the East Asian Summit (EAS) could play a significant role in community building in this region. They also pledged to continue their work toward a dynamic and harmonious Asia-Pacific community in the APEC."

Bibliography

Cossa, Ralph A. "An East Asian Community and the United States: An American Perspective." In *An East Asian Community and the United States*, edited by Ralph A. Cossa and Tanaka Akihiko. Washington, DC: CSIS Press, 2007.

East Asia Vision Group. *Towards an East Asian Community: Region of Peace, Prosperity and Progress.* Bandar Seri Begawan: East Asia Vision Group, 2001. https://www.asean.org/wp-content/uploads/images/archive/pdf/east_asia_vision.

Funabashi Yōichi. *The Peninsula Question: A Chronicle of the Second Korean Nuclear Crisis.* Washington, DC: Brookings Institution Press, 2007.

Inoguchi Takashi, Sonoda Shigeto, Tanaka Akihiko, and Timur Dadabaev, eds. *Human Beliefs and Values in Striding Asia: East Asia in Focus— Country Profiles, Thematic Analyses, and Sourcebook Based on the AsiaBarometer Survey of 2004.* Tokyo: Akashi Shoten, 2006.

Jimbo Ken. "An Emerging East Asian Community?: The Political Process of Regionalism in East Asia." In *An East Asian Community and the United States*, edited by Ralph A. Cossa and Tanaka Akihiko. Washington, DC: CSIS Press, 2007.

Ministry of Foreign Affairs of Japan. "Japan-China Joint Press Statement." 8 October 2006. https://www.mofa.go.jp/region/asia-paci/china/joint0610.html.

———. "Joint Press Statement of the Seventh Summit Meeting among the People's Republic of China, Japan and the Republic of Korea." 14 January 2007. https://www.mofa.go.jp/region/asia-paci/pmv0701/joint070114.pdf.

Shirai Sayuri. "Economic Integration in East Asia: A Financial and Monetary Perspective." In *An East Asian Community and the United States*, edited by Ralph A. Cossa and Tanaka Akihiko. Washington, DC: CSIS Press, 2007.

Shiraishi Takashi. "The Third Wave: Southeast Asia and Middle-Class Formation in the Making of a Region." In *Beyond Japan: The Dynamics of East Asian Regionalism*, edited by Peter J. Katzenstein and Shiraishi Takashi. New York: Cornell University Press, 2006.

Tanaka Akihiko. "The Development of the ASEAN+3 Framework." In *Advancing East Asian Regionalism*, edited by Melissa G. Curley and Nicholas Thomas, 52–73. London: Routledge, 2006.

———. "Global and Regional Geo-Strategic Implications of China's Emergence." *Asian Economic Policy Review* 1, no. 1 (June 2006): 180–196.

Urata Shūjirō. "Trade, FDI-Driven Economic Growth, and Regional Economic Integration in East Asia." In *An East Asian Community and the United States*, edited by Ralph A. Cossa and Tanaka Akihiko, 42–68. Washington, DC: CSIS Press, 2007.

Trilateral Strategic Dialogue
A Japanese Perspective

Tanaka Akihiko

ABSTRACT While working steadily since the end of the Cold War to normalize its security policy, Japan has yet to formulate a stable, comprehensive international strategy integrating the many relevant policy elements. Similarly, while Japan's approach to the trilateral strategic dialogue (TSD) with the US and Australia reflects the fact that the TSD is an element in normalizing Japan's security policy, the quest for a stable, comprehensive national security policy complicates Japan's role within the TSD. This essay thus looks first at the four elements: (1) whether or not the normalization of the legal framework will continue; (2) whether or not strengthening the prime minister's powers will result in the formulation and execution of a more integrated foreign policy and national security policy; (3) whether or not China will sustain its moderate foreign policy line; and (4) how the new administration in Washington will approach security in the Asia-Pacific and considers how different answers to these different questions might impact the TSD scope and structure. This essay was originally featured in NBR Special Report no.16 *Assessing the Trilateral Dialogue* (© The National Bureau of Asian Research).

Main Argument

Although Japan has undergone a fairly steady process of normalization in its security policy since the end of the Cold War, the country has failed to devise an enduring and comprehensive international strategy to integrate various policy elements. Japan's approach to the TSD has also reflected these two trends: on the one hand, the TSD is an element of the "normalization" of Japan's security policy; on the other hand, the lack of a stable comprehensive national security strategy has complicated Japan's role in the dialogue.

The three prime ministers who succeeded Koizumi—Abe, Fukuda, and Asō—all tried to reestablish Japan's international policy in their respective ways. Although the general election that should be held by September 2009 may affect Japan's international and security policy, the basics of this policy are not likely to change regardless of who wins. The TSD is expected to continue, but the scope and concrete modes of operation remain to be clarified.

Policy Implications

The critical variables in Japan's international and security policy may include: whether or not further normalization of the legal framework continues; whether or not the Japanese government increases the power of the prime minister to formulate and implement international and security policy in a more integrated fashion; whether or not China continues to take a moderate foreign and international policy; and what kind of approach the new US administration takes toward international security in the Asia-Pacific. As these variables change, the scope and modes of operation of the TSD may vary.

Although Japan has undergone a fairly steady process of normalization in its security policy since the end of the Cold War, the country has failed to devise an enduring and comprehensive international strategy to integrate various policy elements. On the one hand, Japan has steadily normalized the legal framework for its security policy. Legislation has been enacted in the last 15 years both to deploy the Self-Defense Forces for limited UN peacekeeping operations and to facilitate better coordination with the United States in case of East Asian contingencies other than a direct attack on Japan. The Defense Agency was also promoted to the level of a full-fledged ministry in 2007. Though still limited, Japan has been acting more and more like a normal US ally. Japan sent the Maritime Self-Defense Force to the Indian Ocean to supply fuel to allied ships participating in the operation in Afghanistan. Japan has also sent the Ground Self-Defense Force for humanitarian and reconstruction missions in the southern part of Iraq and the Air Self-Defense Force for transport cooperation in Iraq.

On the other hand, Japan has failed to integrate this evolution of its security policy into a coherent and comprehensive international strategy. Sino-Japanese relations were nearly hijacked by the controversy over Prime Minister Koizumi Junichirō's visits to Yasukuni Shrine. Whatever the merit of Koizumi's view of his visit to the shrine (he believed that China was wrong to interpret his visit as glorifying Japanese militarism in the past), Japan lost maneuverability in policy toward China. Domestic instability after Koizumi's departure from office has not helped Japan formulate an enduring security strategy. Both Abe Shinzō, Koizumi's successor, and Fukuda Yasuo, Abe's successor, were more conscious of Japan's regional strategy than Koizumi; however, because they pursued two different approaches, the rapid succession from Abe to Fukuda brought about a rather abrupt change in Japan's regional policy (at least rhetorically). The fact that the ruling coalition of the Liberal Democratic Party (LDP) and New Kōmeitō Party, which controls a two-thirds majority in the lower house, lost the majority in the upper house in July 2007 further complicates the government's efforts to pursue a consistent international policy—especially where new legislation is needed.

The TSD under Koizumi

Japan's approach to TSD has reflected these two trends: on the one hand, TSD is an element of the "normalization" of Japan's security policy; on the other hand, the lack of a stable, comprehensive national security strategy has complicated Japan's role in the dialogue. The inauguration of the TSD was a natural step in normalizing Japan's security policy. Given the similarities between Japan and Australia—both are mature democracies with economies that are naturally complementary—and given that both countries

are allies of the United States and have been working closely together as diplomatic friends, there is nothing stopping the expansion of a bilateral strategic dialogue between Washington and Tokyo to include Canberra. With Koizumi's attention to security affairs focused almost exclusively on relations with President Bush, however, this opportunity for expanding the TSD escaped the prime minister's attention.

The process of upgrading the TSD from the vice-ministerial level to the ministerial level in May 2005 coincided with other developments in Japan-US security relations. Japan and the United States upgraded their alliance through 2+2 meetings (the Japan-US Security Consultative Committee involving the US secretaries of state and defense and the Japanese ministers of foreign affairs and defense). In February 2005 the committee announced the "common strategic objectives" and agreed in October 2005 on the roles and missions that the two allies will pursue in the coming years.

These developments also coincided, however, with a rapid downturn in Sino-Japanese political relations. China criticized Japan for including Taiwan in the list of the alliance's common strategic objectives mentioned above. Although the 2+2 document simply encouraged "the peaceful resolution of issues concerning the Taiwan Strait through dialogue" and proposed to develop "a cooperative relationship with China, welcoming the country to play a responsible and constructive role regionally as well as globally," China regarded this as an anti-Chinese posture. Sino-Japanese relations were further strained by the violent outbursts of anti-Japanese nationalism in various parts of China, including Shanghai and Beijing, in April 2005.[1] Following these protests, Tokyo and Beijing were not able to engage in meaningful diplomatic activities until the departure of Koizumi in September 2006. Koizumi's intention was certainly not to antagonize China either by visiting the Yasukuni Shrine or by agreeing to the 2+2 documents; rather, he wholeheartedly endorsed the concept of helping China become a constructive member of the international community. Nonetheless, whatever his motive for visiting the shrine and whoever is to blame, as a result of the Yasukuni controversy, constructive engagement with China became almost impossible.

Abe's Value-Oriented Diplomacy

Abe, who succeeded Koizumi in September 2006, understood the futility of sticking to the controversial issues of history and tried to become more strategic in his approach to Japan's international security policy. Although Abe's ideology was more consistently conservative than Koizumi's in terms of his view of Japan's history, he stopped making further controversial statements and decided not to visit the Yasukuni Shrine. As China regarded the history issue as the single most important and decisive issue in Sino-Japanese relations, Abe tried to strengthen Japan's position by making a concession on this issue. This approach worked. Abe was welcomed in Beijing in his first foreign visit in October 2006, and Chinese leaders were mostly silent on the history issue. Additionally, when Premier Wen Jiabao visited Japan in April 2007, he acknowledged that Japanese leaders had already made a number of apologies to the Chinese for the war and expressed appreciation for Japan's assistance to China's development.

Restoring normalcy in Tokyo's relations with Beijing, Abe and his advisors in the Ministry of Foreign Affairs (MOFA) found the theme of "universal values" to be a card that Japan could utilize in the diplomatic game. Abe, who possessed a more sober view of China and its rising military power than Koizumi, seems to have considered the theme of universal values useful as a means to soften the balance against China. Abe declared that his diplomacy was a "value-oriented" one and began to assert the importance of Japan strengthening ties with countries sharing the same universal values. He explicitly mentioned Australia and India as such countries in his first policy speech to the Diet. In late November 2006 Asō Tarō, Abe's foreign minister, introduced a new geographic concept to guide Japan's diplomacy: the "arc of freedom and prosperity"—the zone of countries on the rim of the Eurasian continent, from Northeast Asia, through Southeast Asia, to the Caucasus and Central and Eastern Europe. Asō emphasized the need for Japan to

support those countries on the "arc" that were trying to achieve freedom and prosperity.

In this context, TSD is a natural component of such value-oriented diplomacy. It is no accident that Abe and Howard agreed to issue the first Japan-Australia Joint Declaration on Security Cooperation in March 2007. Though the areas of cooperation were limited mostly to nontraditional security issues—as these were practically the only feasible areas Japan could pursue in the current legal framework, despite the recent normalization of Japan's security-related legislation—it was the highest moment in Japan-Australia defense cooperation in recent history.

Yet when Abe, partly at the suggestion of US vice president Dick Cheney, seriously started to consider the possibility of creating a quadrilateral initiative for security cooperation among the United States, Japan, Australia, India, and China reacted negatively. Abe believed the first and best way to strengthen ties to a country holding the same universal values was to extend the TSD to India. Relations between Tokyo and New Delhi had been abnormally weak and should thus be strengthened. Beijing, however, saw this approach as extending the ties of the Japan-US alliance to a country that had never been involved in the alliance. This quadrilateral initiative probably did not have a chance of success in any case because India did not wish to be entangled in a potentially anti-Chinese coalition.

Abe's international policy was more strategic than Koizumi's. Improving Japan's weak hand (i.e., by downplaying or making concessions on the history issue), Abe tried to utilize what he considered the strong cards that Japan held (i.e., shared universal values). His strategy seems to have worked to some extent. China was irritated by Abe's value-oriented diplomacy but had not shown any desire to downgrade its relations with Japan again. At the same time, how much Abe and Asō could follow through in their value-oriented diplomacy was not clear. India, Australia, and the United States sought to distance themselves a bit from Japan on the quadrilateral initiative out of fear of a possible negative reaction from China. Given domestic instability in Japan, it was not clear whether Abe could make a substantive international move such as sending troops for his value-oriented diplomacy; actual Japanese action might not live up to Abe's rhetoric. In any case, Abe did not have a chance to validate his strategy. In July 2007 he resigned as prime minister to take responsibility for his party's disastrous defeat in the upper house election.

Fukuda's Quiet Diplomacy

Fukuda Yasuo, who succeeded Abe in September 2007, held a less ideological and more cautious worldview than Abe. Though sharing with Koizumi and Abe the conviction of the fundamental importance of the alliance with the United States, Fukuda also believed in the intrinsic importance of Japan's relations with its neighboring countries, especially China. He emphasized the importance of creating "synergy" between relations with the United States and relations with other Asian countries. At the same time, Fukuda mentioned neither Australia nor India in his first Diet speech and rarely mentioned universal values. Fukuda's foreign minister, Komura Masahiko, ordered MOFA officials to remove mention of the arc of freedom and prosperity from the MOFA website. Fukuda refrained from any action that might have appeared as an attempt to isolate or encircle China.

If Abe had pursued an approach of soft-balancing against China, Fukuda's approach was more inclusive; in a speech to clarify his vision of Japan's Asia policy, he mentioned the necessity to regard the Pacific Ocean as an "inland sea" for the twenty-first century, just as the Mediterranean was depicted by Fernand Braudel as an inland sea in the sixteenth century. Fukuda's view of the players in this inland sea is very inclusive:

> If we take the Pacific Ocean for an inland sea, then whose "inland sea" is this, exactly? Clearly, it is an inland sea for Japan and the countries of ASEAN, yet also one for North and South America and for Russia if the development of its Far East region progresses. It is most certainly an inland sea for China and the nations of Indochina as well as Australia, and New Zealand, and in my view this sea also continues beyond India to connect to the nations of the Middle East.

The inclusive approach, when translated into actual policy—toward China, for instance—would appear to mean a kind of quiet diplomacy. When it was revealed that some frozen dumplings (*gyoza*) exported from China to Japan were contaminated with a poisonous pesticide, the Fukuda government—despite the uproar raised in the Japanese media—refrained from vocal accusations. Likewise, when many Western leaders, including President Nicolas Sarkozy of France, openly criticized China for its repression of the Tibetan riots, Fukuda said that it was not useful to make open accusations but rather that it was more productive to provide China with friendly advice to explore dialogue with the Dalai Lama.

Whether Fukuda's inclusive approach and quiet diplomacy were effective remains to be seen. With respect to Sino-Japanese relations, however, this approach achieved some positive results—the most significant of which was the Sino-Japanese agreement on the joint development of gas fields in the East China Sea. Despite involving questions of sovereignty, the issue was solved in a mutually agreeable manner in early July 2008. Fukuda seems to have applied this same inclusive approach to negotiations with North Korea on the abduction issue. Although North Korea finally agreed to renew investigations into the abduction of Japanese citizens, how satisfactory these investigations will prove remains uncertain.

Obviously, Fukuda's strategic approach is not a panacea for all diplomatic and strategic issues. It is, however, for now at least consistent with the new government of Australia and the current modus operandi of the Bush administration's Asia policy. The third TSD, held in Kyoto in early July 2008, indicated that all three partners use this mechanism mostly for cooperation in the humanitarian and nontraditional security areas. Depending on the results of the US presidential election, Japan's approach may need to be adjusted. Additionally, to the extent that the new US administration's Asia policy will be a function of Chinese behavior, China's foreign policy posture after the Olympics will also make a difference.

Further Normalization?

Despite successes on the diplomatic front, Fukuda Yasuo was not able to sustain his power domestically. He also made an abrupt declaration to resign as prime minister just one year after Abe's sudden resignation. In a hastily prepared presidential election, the LDP elected Asō Tarō to succeed Fukuda as its president. The lower house of the Diet, which was still under the control of the LDP and Kōmeitō, then selected Asō as succeeding prime minister. Originally, it was expected that Asō would dissolve the Diet immediately to hold a general election. Yet because of the financial crisis that shook the world in the autumn, Asō decided to ask the Diet to deliberate economic policy. On the foreign policy front, Asō seems to have continued the approach he took when he was foreign minister under Abe, but because of the overwhelming necessity of dealing with the financial crisis, he was slow to present his foreign and security policy agenda. Asō seems more interested than Fukuda in upgrading Japan's security relationship with Australia and India. The TSD thus may be given further impetus under the Asō administration.

A general election will be held by September 2009, when the term of the lower house expires. Asō may or may not serve as prime minister after the election. The Democratic Party of Japan (DPJ) may have a chance to obtain power. Depending on which party controls the government, Japan's foreign policy in general and its approach to the TSD in particular may change. Nonetheless, the basics of Japan's security policy, including the alliance with the United States, will not be questioned no matter who wins the election. The DPJ, the main opposition party to the LDP, also believes in the importance of the Japan-US alliance. The moderate application of such a "minilateral" mechanism as the TSD is expected to continue. The critical variables in Japan's international and security policy may include: (1) whether further normalization of the legal framework for this policy continues, (2) whether or not the Japanese government increases the power of the prime minister to formulate and implement international and security policy in a more integrated fashion, (3) whether China continues to adopt a moderate foreign and international policy, and (4) what kind of approach the new US administration takes toward international security in the Asia-Pacific. As these variables change, the scope and modes of operation of the TSD may vary.

Originally published by the National Bureau of Asian Research in a special report of *Assessing the Trilateral Strategic Dialogue*, no. 16 (2008).

Notes

1. Although what happened behind the scenes in China in the spring of 2005 has not been made clear, it seems impossible to have such large displays of violence in of all places Shanghai and Beijing without significant support in some quarters of Chinese power circles.

Bibliography

Fukuda Yasuo. "When the Pacific Ocean Becomes an 'Inland Sea': Five Pledges to a Future Asia that 'Acts Together'." Speech delivered at 14th International Conference on the Future of Asia, Tokyo, 22 May 2008. http://www.kantei.go.jp/foreign/hukudaspeech/2008/05/22speech_e.html.

Japan Ministry of Defense. "Joint Statement U.S.-Japan Security Consultative Committee." 19 February 2005. https://www.mofa.go.jp/region/n-america/us/security/scc/joint0502.html.

Ministry of Foreign Affairs of Japan. "U.S.-Japan Alliance: Transformation and Realignment for the Future." 29 October 2005. https://www.mofa.go.jp/region/n-america/us/security/scc/doc0510.html.

Tanaka Akihiko. "The Yasukuni Issue and Japan's International Relations." In *East Asia's Haunted Present*, edited by Hasegawa Tsuyoshi and Tōgō Kazuhiko, 119–141. Westport: Praeger Security International, 2008.

Japan-US Ties Crucial for East Asia

Shiraishi Takashi

ABSTRACT The Democratic Party of Japan (DPJ)-led government created uncertainties about the future of Japan-US alliance with Prime Minister Hatoyama Yukio's statements such as the creation of equilateral triangular relationship among Japan, the United States, and China. This essay points out the tension between the US-led regional security structure and the evolving trade and investment relations and underlines the importance of managing the tension.

Since the Democratic Party of Japan (DPJ) came to power with Hatoyama Yukio as prime minister, its foreign policy—above all its positions on the Japan-US alliance and East Asian community building—has come in for a spate of criticism at home and abroad.

Critics argue that it is contradictory to call for the building of an East Asian community while pledging to maintain the Japan-US alliance as the cornerstone of Japan's foreign policy. Some of them even wonder whether the new government's call for a "close and equal" alliance with the United States is but a Japanese version of the "equal partnership" with the United States that Roh Moon-hyun, the former South Korean president, had sought, with South Korea as a "balancer" between the United States-Japan and China-Russia relationships. And yet some others ask whether the Japanese government should prioritize the Japan-US alliance over East Asian community-building, or vice versa.

Such criticisms are wide of the mark. Neither the DPJ's manifesto nor the agreement the DPJ concluded with two other parties to form the coalition government calls for a strategic change in Japan's foreign policy such as reviewing the Japan-US alliance and forming a Japan-China axis. In fact, it is obvious from the party platform and the coalition agreement that the new government fully intends to keep its "mutually beneficial strategic relationship"—which is just another name for "friendship and cooperation"—with China while maintaining the Japan-US alliance.

Hatoyama stated, in his meeting with US president Barack Obama, that the Japan-US alliance is the basis of Japan's foreign policy on which Japan should strengthen its relationship of mutual trust with Asian countries and promote regional cooperation. In the trilateral meeting with leaders of China and South Korea in early October, Hatoyama once again stressed the importance of the Japan-US relationship while pursuing his Asia policy.

Why has Hatoyama come under such criticism then? To put it bluntly, it is because of the poverty of language. When we talk about international politics, we tend to treat countries as individuals, saying, for instance, "The United States thinks . . ." "China will react . . ." and "Japan should map out . . ." This language is anchored in the realist thinking of international politics in which achieving a "balance of power" in an anarchical world is a paramount concern that shapes the behavior of states. When this language is used, Japan's move to come closer to China automatically signifies a recalibration of its relationship with the United States. A typical example of this type of realist language is the call for an "equilateral" relationship among Japan, China, and the United States.

But relying solely on this realist language is not sufficient to capture the reality in East Asia and map out Japan's foreign policy. Let us take a look at the security and economic systems in East Asia. The regional security system is built on a "hub and spokes" system in which the United States has concluded bilateral security treaties and base agreements with Japan, South Korea, the Philippines, and other countries. This security system has remained basically unchanged in East Asia since the mid-1970s.

By contrast, the regional economic system in East Asia has changed significantly since the Cold War years. After World War II, the regional economy of "Free Asia" took the form of a triangular trade system among Japan, the United States, and Southeast Asia, along with South Korea and Taiwan.

This system underwent significant changes for two reasons. First, in the wake of the Plaza Accord of 1985, regional economic development driven by Japan's and other East Asian countries' enormous foreign direct investments has promoted de facto economic integration as Japanese and other East Asian multinational firms established their business operations across borders and expanded and deepened their regional transnational business networks.

This de facto economic integration has created "East Asia" as we know it today; that is, the region stretching from Japan and South Korea to the coastal areas of China, Taiwan, and Hong Kong to Southeast Asia. Second, during the same period, China (and then Vietnam) was integrated into the East Asian regional economy while successfully transforming its economic system from a socialist to a socialist market economy led by the Communist Party state.

Structural Tension

These developments have resulted in structural tensions between the US-centered hub-and-spokes security system and an East Asian economic system in which the United States is no longer the driving force. China and Vietnam are now part of the regional economic system and deeply involved in institution building with the Association of Southeast Asian Nations as the hub. But these socialist market economy states are not part of the US-led hub-and-spokes regional security system of East Asia. The resulting tension between the two systems will not vanish any time soon. In fact, the tension may increase as China's presence is felt in East Asian political and economic relations. The challenge for Japan, then, is how to manage this tension to ensure Japan's security and prosperity while promoting East Asian stability and economic growth.

Two things are crucial. First, all East Asian countries have formulated their security policies with the Japan-US alliance as a given. If the future of the Japan-US alliance were to come under question, security in East Asia would become unstable. In the worst-case scenario, the United States would withdraw its military forces to the Guam-Hawaii line and shift its strategy from the current forward defense to an offshore balancing act. Japan would then be forced to allocate far greater resources for its defense than it does now. If Japan chooses to strengthen its defense capabilities, China will likely would further accelerate its military growth, with South Korea and Vietnam following suit.

When East Asian countries have no choice but to prioritize defense expenditures over economic growth, the common political will to build an East Asian community will be lost. Keeping the current system in place heightens the predictability that security will be maintained. The government should bear this in mind as it decides on the kind of assistance it will extend to Afghanistan and Pakistan in their nation-building efforts and on the issues of cooperation with Washington on its military realignment plan and relocation of the US Marine Corps Air Station Futenma in Okinawa Prefecture.

Second, it is also important to promote regional cooperation and economic partnership in the name of East Asian community building. Most of the governments in East Asia have staked their legitimacy on the politics of productivity, in which achieving a national consensus on economic growth, job creation, poverty reduction, and higher standards of living is seen as the primary purpose of politics. Regional economic development is also crucial to Japan's growth strategy. Promoting economic partnership and increasing economic interdependence in the name of East Asian community building are the way to go.

What matters is not the form the proposed East Asian community might eventually take but the process of promoting regional economic interdependence. To do this, it is important to establish common norms and rules in such fields as currency and finance, investment, and trade, and professional qualifications to facilitate flows of people, goods, money, and information in the region. When all parties concerned are involved in creating common rules, each of them will find it difficult to infringe on those rules, even when it is convenient to do so. As East Asia's economic interdependence deepens, China and all other countries in the region will naturally have greater stakes in ensuring regional stability and prosperity. What should not be done? The answer is: Do not try to create a "closed" regional bloc of "Asia for Asians"—this concept is no longer tenable in the world we live in.

The Japan-US alliance is the basis for maintaining stability in East Asia. But for Japan's and other East Asian countries' economic growth (and the increasing importance China has in the regional economy), it is also important to create common norms and rules and promote regional economic interdependence. This can be pursued in the name of building an East Asian community. To keep the regional economic system open to the rest of the world, it is worth concluding a Japan-US free trade agreement as a harbinger of a collective APEC FTA for all the member economies of the Asia-Pacific Economic Cooperation forum. These are initiatives that Japan and the United States can take when they serve as chairs of the APEC talks in 2010 and 2011, respectively.

East Asia is now the world's growth center. For this reason, both the stability and the economic growth of the region are critical not only for Japan and other East Asian countries but also for the rest of the world. To understand the regional order in East Asia and map out Japan's foreign policy, we need both the realist language of the balance of power and the liberalist language of rule-making and interdependence.

Originally published by The Yomiuri Shimbun in *THE DAILY YOMIURI* "INSIGHTS into the WORLD" (1 November 2009).

II-(9) Twentieth-Century Japanese Diplomacy

Nakanishi Hiroshi

ABSTRACT Japanese diplomacy in the twentieth century can be roughly divided into five stages, each with its own distinctive characteristics: (i) emergence as a colonial power (1900–18), (ii) the fall of the empire (1918–45), (iii) rebirth as a nation state (1945–69), (iv) the economic power years (1969–91), and (v) post–Cold War foreign policy (1991–2000). At each stage, Japan has been somewhat successful in adapting to and meeting the goals posed by the international environment. On the other hand, Japan has typically been less successful in setting its own goals independently in accordance with the changes in the international situation and in considering how its own-setting goals would affect the international environment.

It is fair to say that Japan in the twentieth century, looked at objectively, followed a dynamic trajectory of a kind that has rarely been seen in world history. After being incorporated into the modern international system in the second half of the nineteenth century, Japan implemented a series of political, military, economic, and social reforms and became one of the few countries in the non-Western world to maintain its independence. In the early years of the twentieth century, Japan ranked as the only non-Western state to successfully implement an imperial policy and achieve a position of strength alongside the world powers. Following these early achievements, however, the country failed to respond to the changing international environment. Disarray in the country's domestic politics contributed to an unstoppable expansionist policy that led the country into a reckless war, as a result of which Japan not only lost all of its colonies but also suffered from catastrophic war damage and occupation and, for a time, even lost its sovereignty.

In the second half of the twentieth century, Japan swapped swords for spades. Through economy recovery and development, it worked to recover its lost international position. This policy was hugely successful in the postwar international environment, and by the 1970s, Japan had regained its position as one of the world's leading countries. It went on from there to achieve a position as an economic powerhouse second only to the United States and became one of the major poles within the Western alliance, alongside the United States and Europe. At the same, however, there were increasing signs of turmoil and disarray in domestic politics. The country's foreign policy, too, showed an increasingly conservative and diffident attitude that was content to concentrate on economic matters. In the years that followed, Japanese diplomacy struggled to escape from this essentially passive stance. These negative aspects of Japan's foreign policy became particularly clear at the end of the Cold War and the Gulf War. The final decade of the twentieth century was a decade of regret over lost opportunities.

Of course, it would be impossible to discuss in detail the turbulent history of Japanese diplomacy in the twentieth century in the limited space available to me here. At the risk of oversimplification, what I want to do is to look back at broad developments in Japanese foreign policy by dividing the twentieth century into five periods. I will then conclude with a summary of some tendencies that can be observed over the century as a whole.

1. Emergence as a Power: 1900–18

The early years of the twentieth century marked the high tide of an international order based on the imperialist system developed in Europe. In this period, the major powers competed to acquire colonies, and those peoples and societies in the non-Western world that refused to follow the path of modernization (or tried unsuccessfully to modernize) were reduced to the position of colonies or dependencies. During this period, Japan secured for itself a position as an imperial country alongside the Western powers.

The beginning of Japan's colonial expansion came with the Boxer Rebellion in Qing China and the dispatch of international troops in 1900 in response. The eight major powers with interests in East Asia cooperated to send a joint force to protect their diplomatic representatives and denizens. Japan provided an important part of the military force, contributing over 20,000 troops. This episode was symbolic of Japan's later international position. In terms of its diplomatic strategy, Japan was careful to appear noncommittal about dispatching troops so as not to arouse the suspicions of the other powers about its own interests in China, and it only sent troops when asked to do so by the other powers. Also, these troops behaved in a prudent manner, maintaining discipline and order and thus boosting international trust in Japan. Militarily, this incident was significant in demonstrating that Japan could outperform the other powers in terms of its ability to mobilize a sizable modern military force at short notice within Northeast Asia. These factors combined to qualify Japan as one of the world powers. Having met the requirements to be recognized as one of the "civilized nations" of Europe and America, Japan confirmed its position as a major nation alongside the Western powers, with superior military strength in East Asia.

Japan confirmed and strengthened this position through several diplomatic achievements. The system of extraterritoriality imposed on Japan by Western powers in the mid-nineteenth century had been scrapped in 1899, and Japan also regained tariff autonomy with the signing of the Anglo-Japanese Treaty of Commerce and Navigation in 1911, thus establishing itself as a totally sovereign state under international law. After entering an alliance with Great Britain in 1902, Japan was victorious in its war with Russia in 1904–05 and became the dominant power in East Asia. Following this, Japan renewed its alliance with Great Britain and signed a commercial agreement with France. Having improved its relations with Russia and reached an understanding with the United States, Japan incorporated the Korean Peninsula and acquired interests in Manchuria. By the 1910s, Japan had become a colonial empire.

Japan thus became a major power through its diplomatic and military successes. This happened at a dramatic speed. One negative aspect of this rapid ascent was that Japan had only a short window of time in which to decide how to deal with the fruits of these successes. This new challenge was in some senses more difficult than those it had already faced; achieving success and maintaining the results of that success in an appropriate manner required quite different policies.

This problem gradually became apparent in several ways. First, there was the question of the roles to be assigned to military power. After the Russo-Japanese War, Japan no longer faced any urgent military threats in Northeast Asia. Considering Japan's weak economic base at the time, it would not have been out of the question for Japan to have sought to reduce its military spending at this point. However, the period was one of a dramatic arms buildup around the world, symbolized by the arrival of the Dreadnought-class battleship in 1906. It was felt essential to keep up with these developments, and many people argued that Japan needed to increase its military strength in order to ensure stability within its newly expanded area of control. Another factor was that the lead-up to the Russo-Japanese War had increased the political prestige of the military. The military now became an unignorable political force as politics in Japan gradually became more democratic.

These factors pushed the country onto a path of military expansion. By all rights, the next question should have been to ask what strategic aims Japan wished to achieve through its new military might, and the leaders also recognized this question. The Imperial Defense Plan, formulated for the first time only in 1907, summarized the views of Japan's leaders at the time. The plan called for an offensive position: "In East Asia at least, it is essential to maintain the ability to take the offensive against any country that might try to invade our interests" (Takeharu 1973, 3). Behind this offensive stance, however, it was difficult to discern any clear objectives. Unless limits were set, it was possible to legitimize almost indefinite military expansion. Now that Japan no longer faced any immediate military threat, it had to address a more difficult problem, that of defining new strategic aims and deciding a level of military strength commensurate with those aims.

To some extent, the same thing happened on the diplomatic front. Once it achieved its aim of achieving independence as one of the world powers, Japanese diplomacy started to become too assertive. The best example of this was Japanese diplomacy during World War I, in particular the famous "Twenty-One Demands" issued to China in 1915. The Great War in Europe meant that the other powers were unable to divert forces to Asia. Japan entered the hostilities through its alliance with Great Britain, attacking German possessions in the Asia-Pacific and using the opportunity, and the excuse of the conflict, to expand its own interests. The turmoil in China following the Xinhai Revolution provided an ideal opportunity to force the government to swallow Japan's tough demands and allowed Japan to expand its interests in China. During the war, Japan reached agreements with Great Britain, France, and Czarist Russia on its right to control Shandong and the German-controlled Pacific Islands. It also decided that it had received approval for this from the United States through the Ishii-Lansing Agreement, though some ambiguity remained in this respect. Japan also built a cooperative relationship with the Peking government through the Nishihara loans and other measures, and for a while it appeared that its diplomatic policy of seizing World War I and the chaos in China as golden opportunities had succeeded. However, this position was rash and imprudent. The diplomatic policy that took advantage of the weakness of the Western powers and China led to increasing international suspicion and dislike of Japan and had serious costs in terms of Japan's diplomatic reputation.

This lack of diplomatic prudence was partly the result of rising rifts within Japan. It was increasingly felt that taking a powerful stance internationally was essential to maintaining order among quarreling factions at home. It seems likely, for example, that in issuing the Twenty-One Demands, Japan's Foreign Minister Katō Takaaki was trying to diplomatically make China agree to a demand that would satisfy the military, ensuring that the Ministry of Foreign Affairs would maintain its lead over the military with regard to Japan's interests in China. In fact, by this period Japan's colonial interests were already becoming a major cause of political turbulence. The colonies were the fruits of the success of Japan's imperialist policy, but they gave rise to problems that the Meiji constitutional system was ill-equipped to resolve. This had the effect of pitching the entire political system into disarray. Manchuria in particular became an almost insoluble problem. The primary reason for this is that Japan's leaders failed to provide a conclusive answer to an essential question: Were the country's interests in Manchuria limited to the South Manchuria Railway and areas adjacent to it or did they represent a foothold for future territorial control? There was also a lack of clarity about how the interests should be ruled: Should Japan prioritize its relations with China and acknowledge the leadership of the Foreign Ministry as diplomatic interests run in accordance with treaties, or should it prioritize military significance and place its interests under military control? This ambiguity over Manchuria was already surfacing by the time of the Conference to Discuss the Manchuria Issue in 1906, which brought civilian and military leaders together the year after the Russo-Japanese War. At this stage, the disagreement was limited to the level of debate, but it eventually grew to become a chronic disease that ravaged the entire political body of Japan as a colonial empire.

There is no question that Japan was responsible for several of the important reasons it was able to become a colonial empire so rapidly. Its success in establishing the systems necessary to a modern state and its acquisition of the power that made diplomatic and military successes possible were crucial parts of its rise, but there were also objective factors in the international situation that helped to make Japan's expansion possible. Geography was one key factor: Japan was, unlike other powers, the only major power located in East Asia. In the early years of the twentieth century, the focus of international politics began to shift away from imperial expansion to competitive rivalry among the European powers, while much of the non-Western world, including the Korean Peninsula and China, was in a state of chaos in terms of their internal politics. Instead of coolly analyzing these factors that had helped it achieve such a rapid ascent, however, and debating seriously how to deal with the changes brought by its rise, Japan instead became drunk on success.

2. The Fall of the Empire: 1918–45

Until 1918, Japan seemed to have used World War I to its advantage, achieving impressive results in terms of maintaining and expanding its colonial interests. As we have seen, however, Japan's actions in these years substantially increased international mistrust. In addition, several major changes both at home and abroad further increased the pressure on Japan's diplomacy in the years following 1918.

Internationally, the closing stages of the war brought fundamental challenges to the international order by colonial/imperial rule. The first of these was the rise of liberal universalism, as typified by the Fourteen Points speech of US president Woodrow Wilson in 1918. The Wilsonian position was not only supported by the colossal national might of the United States but was also linked to growing liberal forces and mass movements in various countries. These became powerful influences that leaders could not afford to ignore. The second challenge was socialism. In 1917, the Bolsheviks successfully took power following the Russian Revolution. Their criticism of imperialist foreign policy and advocacy of socialism linked these social movements together with international politics. The third challenge was nationalism. Aided partly by the good will and

support shown to nationalism by Wilson and the Soviet regime, nationalist movements gradually came to challenge colonial governments around the world. East Asia was no exception, as evidenced by two major uprisings in short succession in 1919: the 1 March movement on the Korean Peninsula and the 4 May movement in China.

Alongside these challenges to the existing international order, there were also major challenges within Japan itself, as social and economic factors became increasingly politicized. The Meiji political system was essentially dominated by a privileged elite but, during the first decade of the twentieth century, social movements became prominent. The Japanese economy boomed during the war, but the rice riots of 1918 soon revealed how flimsy were the foundations on which this growth had been built. Although the country had successfully modernized militarily, it was still underdeveloped economically. Socially, too, the process of modernization was far from complete. The problem of poverty became a social issue, with reportage such as Kawakami Hajime's essay "Binbō monogatari" (Tale of Poverty). It was in this context that the influence of American liberalism and Soviet socialism were felt. By the end of the war, the domestic situation in Japan was in turmoil, with many people clamoring for reform.

The influence of these various domestic and international factors on Japanese diplomacy was complex. On the one hand, domestic liberalist movements overlapped with Wilsonian internationalism. This can be seen, for example, in the arguments put forward by people like Yoshino Sakuzō.[1] This approach could be said to have provided the foundations for Shidehara diplomacy, which set the tone of Japanese foreign policy in the 1920s.[2] On the other hand, liberalism had tendencies that produced, and justified, social and economic inequalities both at home and abroad, giving rise to a view that prioritized the attainment of radical socialism rather than political liberalism. Some supporters of this view oriented themselves to socialism and became leftwing, while others became staunch statists. The famous essay "Reject the Anglo-American-Centered Peace," authored at the end of the war by Konoe Fumimaro, who was to become prime minister several times during the 1930s, reflects this radical evolution. Thus, there was opposition not only between conservative groups and progressives but also between supporters of incremental and radical reforms. These were tied up in complex ways with political power groups among the military, political parties, and bureaucracy as Japanese political history moved forward through the 1910s and 1920s into the prewar period.

These changes to political and social conditions within Japan and internationally posed huge challenges for Japanese diplomacy, but they only came to the surface later. For a time after the end of World War I, Japanese diplomacy achieved positive results. At the Paris Peace Conference in 1919, Japan was one of the major powers and continued to be one of the "big five" major powers at the League of Nations. At the Paris Peace Conference, Japan was able to overcome Chinese protests and achieve its aims with regard to its biggest concern: its claims to Shandong and the handling of the South Sea Islands in the Pacific. Following the treaty agreements made at the Washington Naval Conference, although the Anglo-Japanese Alliance was lost, it became possible to stabilize regional order in the Asia-Pacific and achieve a certain reduction in military spending. Japan's relationship with the Soviet Union, which had been poor since Japan's decision to send troops to Siberia, also stabilized after the signing of the Convention Embodying Basic Rules of the Relationship between Japan and the USSR in 1925. In the same year, a tariff convention was held in Peking between the major powers and China to implement the Washington Treaties. These developments helped to stabilize Japan's foreign relations. Militarily, the Imperial Defense Plan, revised in 1923, defined the United States, the Soviet Union, and China (in that order) as hypothetical enemies. In fact, though, the possibility of war seemed low and Japan felt increasingly secure, as can be seen from the fact that the military offered military spending proposals based on the assumption of fighting a short decisive war.

Nevertheless, the movement toward a fundamental shift in the global order that had been in evidence since the late stages of the war became increasingly difficult to ignore and brought increasing pressure on Japanese diplomacy. In China, the KMT nationalist government led by Chiang Kai-shek that was based in Canton made skillful use of the Chinese people's aspirations for nationalism and social reform and looked poised to unite the whole Chinese territory under its unified control in the second half of the 1920s. This required fundamental changes to the Washington System, which aimed to balance China's demands against the competing interests of the various powers in China. At almost the same time, the foreign policy of the United States, which had been introspective since the vote against joining the League of Nations, started to show signs of becoming more engaged again. For example, the Paris Peace Pact signed in 1928 was the result of a US-French initiative. Even if there were doubts about the effectiveness of the agreement, it demonstrated American readiness to engage with the global community again and make a major commitment. At the same time, it also showed that American foreign policy would not be oriented toward traditional power politics but would aim for radical change in the world order. Another factor was the Soviet Union. Although it had stabilized its diplomatic relations with all the major powers except the United States by the middle of the 1920s, the Soviet Union still used Comintern to control Communist movements around the world since the second half of the 1920s, exacerbating political instability in many countries. The pressure in this respect was especially intense in Japan, which was struggling with the lingering effects of the World War I bubble and the devastation caused by the Great Kanto Earthquake, on top of the tensions caused by social and economic modernization.

The various difficulties affecting Japanese diplomacy came to a head in the context of the country's interests in China, which were concentrated in Manchuria. The Washington System was gradually losing legitimacy and, with Japan now in difficulties, the lingering problem of Manchuria's ambiguous status became acute. By the 1920s, the view that Manchuria was more or less the only possible route to Japanese economic development was already widespread among the Japanese elite. A cabinet decision under Hara

Takashi on 13 May 1921 was typical: "It is hardly necessary to reiterate at this stage that Manchuria and Mongolia are intimately tied to our national defense and to the economic survival of our people. Accordingly, focusing on these two priorities and positioning our power in Manchuria and Mongolia are the essential fundamentals of our policy." Even if we accept the two goals of national defense and economic development, however, the actual policy to be followed will differ greatly depending on which of the two is made the number-one priority. However, Japan was not able to form a consistent strategy that would prioritize either national defense or the economy in Manchuria. In addition, because the Kwantung Army stationed in Manchuria performed an important political function, it became a hotbed for the politicization of the military. Japan's diplomatic, military, and economic development objectives became entangled. The involvement of Chinese warlords and other local powers further increased the chaos that marred Japan's management of its interests in Manchuria.

The system's rifts caused by the Manchurian problem eventually came to dominate the whole of Japanese politics. Following political disagreements, and with the military now involved as well as the political parties, the bureaucracy, and the Privy Council, Japanese politics became dysfunctional. The most frightening manifestation of this was the legitimization of the spirit of *gekokujō* (the spirit of the "lower overthrowing the upper") in the military, which eventually led to assassinations, coups d'état, and conspiracies in China, which allowed the military to manipulate domestic politics. Starting with the assassination of warlord Zhang Zuolin in 1927, the actions of a certain section of the military came to exert control over the government's foreign policy, as shown by the Manchurian Incident. In response, several attempts were made to unify the policymaking apparatus during the 1930s. These attempts only involved compromises by the major political players, though, and the lack of strong political leadership meant that only nominal changes were made. On the diplomatic front, Japan was pressed to respond to constantly evolving conditions, making do with compromises at home and continuing expansion overseas.

Of course, we should understand the difficult international environment in which Japanese diplomacy was placed. The international order in the interwar years was plagued with contradictions, with an international order based on the colonial empires continuing to exist alongside advocacy of universal values opposed to colonialism. This contradiction forced a particularly difficult choice on a country like Japan, which was relatively weak as a colonial empire and something of an unconventional presence in the international order. Japan was too weak to cast aside the interests it had already gained from its empire and practice universal values instead, but neither could it simply cling to its colonies and ride out the difficult situation.

With Japan lacking sufficient strength both militarily and economically, probably the only path forward would have been to make use of its voice within the international community to speak up about the contradictions in the global order. In fact, some appeals of this kind were made through international organizations such as the Institute of Pacific Relations. Still, Japan's ability to make its diplomatic voice heard was limited, partly for cultural reasons, and it struggled to express its difficulties in universal terms before the international community. It is possible to see the Greater East Asia diplomacy (to use Hatano Sumio's term) that was adopted after Japan had entered into the Pacific War—and the tide of the war had already started to turn for the worse—as an attempt to express Japan's position within the context of universal principles, but these efforts were too little too late.

The diplomatic and military complacency and systemic dysfunctionality that accompanied Japan's imperial expansion, which had been inherently present even in the period of Japan's first bloom as a colonial empire in the years leading up to World War I, were amplified in the interwar years by changes in the international environment and a series of domestic crises. Like a driverless steam train, Japan resorted to military means without any clear objectives and left diplomacy to cobble together plausible rationalizations for its military actions. Expansion without any strategy led to a destructive war, and Japan's colonial empire was dismantled and taken apart.

3. Rebirth as a Nation State: 1945–69

In World War II, Japan eventually ended up in a state of war with nearly all the world's major powers. The country suffered widespread strategic bombing and the dropping of two atomic bombs before it finally surrendered and lost all of its colonies. This was nothing less than a massive failure of the country's foreign policy and political leadership. However, as is almost always the case, this massive destruction also gave rise to a new hope for rebirth. By expanding geographically, Japan had brought chaos into its domestic politics and increased the number of its enemies. For Japan, the colonies were perceived like a nonperforming loan. Seen from the perspective of world history, the colonial period was coming to an end in any case, and in the long term, being forced to abandon its colonies after its defeat in 1945 was not a complete negative for Japan.

Several factors helped to give Japan an opportunity for rebirth. First, having passed through the tribulations of war, the people formed a kind of solidarity spirit among themselves. One of the reasons for the affection that most Japanese showed for the emperor immediately after the war was the image many people had of him as a savior who had rescued the people from the colonial imperial regime that had corrupted the Meiji constitutional system; second was the presence of the occupation forces, which possessed enormous authority to build new systems to harness this solidarity and convert it into energy for social and economic modernization. The occupying forces did not exercise power directly but were a presence that maintained a strict social order. Under this control, labor reforms and land reforms, which would have caused political chaos in prewar Japan, were pushed through in a short period of time. Japan was thus able to implement major systemic reforms peacefully and without causing major damage to national solidarity.

The international environment was also favorable to Japan. Unlike the closed prewar colonial imperial system, the America-centered Bretton Woods system was an open system in which Japan, too, would eventually be allowed to participate. Also, with East-West tensions gradually increasing, the victory of the Communists in China (which the US had initially hoped to make the pillar of order in postwar Asia) also increased the international importance of Japan in Asia. The need to station US troops permanently in the southern part of the Korean Peninsula following the Korean War further increased Japan's strategic importance and strengthened Japan's national security. This division of East Asia saved Japan from involvement in political chaos on the Korean Peninsula, in China, or in Southeast Asia, where the upheaval of decolonization was still ongoing, and freed it from the need to worry about political policy choices.

When we consider these factors, the choices taken by Yoshida Shigeru for peace and independence—that is to say, peace agreements with the Western powers, cooperation with the United States based on the Security Treaty, and a priority on economic recovery—may seem obvious. Nevertheless, Japan was fortunate to have Yoshida as its leader at that time. He was one of the few Anglo-American-oriented Japanese diplomats with experience serving in the colonial empire, as he had been consul general in Mukden. This experience gave him vital insights into governing as a statesman and allowed him to acquire a sense for the mechanics of diplomatic power. When he decided to delegate Japan's external national security to the United States, it was based on a careful analysis of the situation in which Japan was placed. Also, he had a different view on China than the US government at the time and tried to find a way toward closer rapprochement. Yoshida's affection for Anglo-American liberalism and his dislike of state intervention in the economy made him a good fit with the Bretton Woods system. More than anything, his decisiveness increased the trust placed in him by the people.

Of course, reforms under the foreign occupying forces resulted in all kinds of contradictions, which gradually came into conflict with peace after independence. The prime example is the Constitution. However, the content of these policies, including Article 9, was probably not far removed from the will of the various factions in the country at the time. The problem was that the enactment of the Constitution—the supreme act of political authority—was taken during a time of occupation, precisely when Japan was in a state in which neither authority nor politics really existed at all. This separated the Constitution from reality and overlooked the political bases for managing the Constitution by interpreting it to suit the changing times and to make amendments and changes. For example, although the new Constitution was based on a parliamentary cabinet system of government, many of the norms of the Diet continued unchanged from before the war, and the government was still weak. These defects were concealed under the occupation by the authority of the occupying forces, but once the occupation came to an end, they came to the surface in the form of Yoshida's rapid loss of political leadership.

This systemic crisis was only resolved after widespread protests over the Security Treaty in 1960. In this sense, the various results of 1960—the confirmation of the revised Japan-US Security Treaty, the resignation of Kishi Nobusuke, and the arrival in office of Ikeda Hayato, with his policy focused on economic development to double people's incomes—were final confirmations by the Japanese of postwar systems already in place. It is fair to say that the basic trajectory of postwar Japanese foreign policy, sometimes known as the Yoshida Doctrine, was laid down around this period. It was in this period that Japan decided to follow a policy of separating the defense of Japan from the wider regional security of the Far East. The former was treated as an issue of individual self-defense by legitimizing the Self-Defense Forces, while the latter was made a matter for collective self-defense, in which Japan would essentially remain uninvolved. It was also during this period that the choice was made to follow a policy that would avoid political disagreements, unify the people through economic growth, and strengthen Japan's standing in international politics—what might be called economic diplomacy in the broad sense.

This choice proved a great success. By the end of the 1960s, Japan boasted the second largest

Western GNP, behind only the United States. Its politics had also stabilized, as can be seen from the two terms (four years) Ikeda served as prime minister and the four terms (eight years) of Satō Eisaku. However, the Japanese were not aiming for economic growth alone. Economic growth was also a means for achieving another, higher objective in international politics. This was the revival of Japan's international prestige, which had reached rock bottom at the end of the war. Indeed, the Japanese showed an almost unusual eagerness to join international bodies. Apparently thirsting for a position as an advanced nation, Japan gradually acquired these memberships, sometimes at the cost of protecting its own domestic industry. Also, through its economic cooperation, which had started in the form of reparations, Japan developed positive relationships with the newly independent countries of Asia and slowly succeeded in achieving rehabilitation into the international community in Asia as well. The last of these objectives was the return of Okinawa. When Satō achieved the return of the administrative rights of Okinawa to Japanese sovereignty with President Nixon in 1969, the major aims that Japan had set after the war had been achieved. Like victory in the Russo-Japanese War in 1905, this was a time of triumph for postwar Japan and, at the same time, a new point of departure.

4. The Economic Power Years: 1969–91

Japan's rapid economic growth naturally attracted international attention. Numerous commentaries were written on Japan's economic "miracle," and many people who were not Japan specialists became interested in the country. One of these, Zbigniew Brezezinski, called Japan a "fragile blossom" in his study of the country and its systems. Brezezinski believed that the international and domestic conditions that made Japan's economic growth possible were changing and argued that there was a risk that these changes could have a negative impact on Japan.

These changes were first manifested in an expectation that Japan would adopt a more proactive position in its foreign policy. It could be said that this hope was already evident at the summit meeting between Satō and Nixon that decided the return of Okinawa to Japanese sovereignty. The so-called "Korea Clause" and "Taiwan Clause" included in the joint communiqué can be understood as expressing an expectation that Japan would play a bigger role in regional security. Also, it is almost certain that the two leaders discussed measures to deal with exports of Japanese textile goods to the United States. These two were both certainly difficult problems. Considering Japan's history as a colonial empire, it was understandable that it chose to be careful on the issues of Korea and Taiwan, at least in this period. The textile issue also had some negative aspects involving the president's political considerations. Nonetheless, for Japan, occupying a position of international significance meant it would need to come up with answers to these kinds of difficult questions. In the end, nothing concrete was ever achieved in relation to the Korea or Taiwan clauses, partly because of subsequent changes in the regional situation after the US-China entente, while an agreement was finally reached on the textiles issue after some complications. Already in this period the patterns of Japanese foreign policy were on display—adopting a passive stance on military and security issues and only taking steps to diffuse trade frictions, with a fine diplomatic line for bringing domestic opinions together using the excuse of outside pressure.

Part of the reason for this strong tendency to bring domestic opinions together using the excuse of outside pressure was the weak structure of political leadership. Rapid economic growth had weakened opposition parties that espoused socialism and anti-liberalism. The diminished ideological conflicts had also made the ruling party less attractive and damaged its ability to lead. In fact, after Tanaka Kakuei took office in 1972, the only person to stay in office as prime minister longer than two years was Nakasone Yasuhiro. Under the circumstances, it was difficult to implement an ambitious foreign policy, and there was an increasing tendency to try to maintain the status quo with as few concessions as possible.

Of course, Japan did act with greater energy in some areas. On currency, for example, Japan started to act as one of the world's leading countries from an early stage, and when the first

summit of leading industrialized nations was held in 1975, Japan's prime minister, Miki Takeo, took part, showing that Japan had now become one of the three major poles, coordinating the West's economic policy alongside the United States and Europe. Additionally, starting from the second half of the 1970s, Japan rapidly increased the amount of its overseas official aid assistance, which also helped to circulate its current account surplus. Part of this was used for "strategic assistance" that considered the security concerns and interests of the West. Also, growing attention was given to cultural exchanges—with the Japan Foundation, for example, founded in 1972.

One area to which Japanese diplomacy gave particular importance and in which it achieved a certain degree of success was the nurturing of international relations within the Asia-Pacific region. Already starting in the second half of the 1960s, terms like "Asia-Pacific" and "transpacific" came to be used in diplomatic circles but, with the Vietnam War and the Chinese Cultural Revolution still underway, there was little real development of any kind of international relations within the Asia-Pacific. In the second half of the 1970s, efforts such as the declaration of the Fukuda Doctrine by Prime Minister Fukuda Takeo and the concept of transpacific cooperation articulated by Prime Minister Ōhira Masayoshi, though they failed to attract much international attention at the time, with the benefit of hindsight, deserve to be recognized as the first to propose the basic foundations of the multilateral cooperation in the Asia-Pacific region today.

Taken in summary, Japanese diplomacy in this period was economic-centered diplomacy and can be said to have had certain characteristics that resembled the policy of the United States in the 1920s, sometimes called "dollar diplomacy" or "involvement without commitment." The results of this policy deserve to be given some credit, but we should probably be cautious about praising them excessively. The activities of Japanese diplomacy were totally dependent on the fact that the fundamental structure of international politics was ordered by the political, military, economic, and social relationship of opposition defined by the Cold War. This can be seen from the fact that Nakasone never received more international attention than when he spoke of the "solidarity" of the West at the Williamsburg Summit in 1983. It was within this order that Japan was able to concentrate on economic growth and use the proceeds of this growth to carry out economic diplomacy. Japan's diplomacy fundamentally matched the character of the world order at that time. Though it may have contributed to strengthening this world order in some aspects, it was never a diplomacy that would change the world order in any way. As an illustration of this, consider the fact that it was not possible to reestablish diplomatic relations with China until there was a change in the Sino-American relationship, notwithstanding the considerable economic ties between Japan and China that had already been built up before then. It is a fact that Japan's relations with China and South Korea were maintained on a relatively positive level, thanks to the yen loans to China started under the Ōhira cabinet and the economic cooperation with South Korea realized by Prime Minister Nakasone, but it would be hard to say that these were founded on any kind of spiritual reconciliation with Japan.

In Japan, the dominant rhetoric about national strength emerged, based on a distorted nationalism that combined pride in having become an economic superpower while being a small country in political and military terms. This was expressed in the opinion that it was because Japan had concentrated on pacifism and economic growth without spending on its military that it had been able to become an economic superpower, and the United States and the Soviet Union were doomed to decline and bankruptcy due to their huge military spending. This view became particularly pronounced in the 1980s, when there was even talk of Japan replacing the United States as a global superpower hegemon.

Seen from today's perspective, it is clear that the 1980s were a period in which globalization had started to promote change in global politics. The reforms carried out by Margaret Thatcher, Ronald Reagan, and others tried to reform stagnant political and economic systems, less by gradual transformations than by something closer to revolution. One side effect of this was prolonged turmoil and economic sluggishness. Still, these reforms gradually started to produce results, and by the end of the 1980s, even the Soviet Union and Eastern Europe had been absorbed into the wave of globalization and were on the path to decommunization. A certain amount of privatization also took place in Japan during this period under the Nakasone government, but this was less a response to the huge revolution brought about by globalization and more focused on international policy coordination and easy economic stimulus policies. These resulted in a bubble economy, and insensitive and excessive spending increased wariness of Japan and led to Japan revisionism.

The Persian Gulf crisis and the Gulf War that followed served to bring home to Japan the fact that the fundamental structure of global politics had changed with the end of the Cold War, and this made Japan aware of the limitations of the economic-centered diplomacy it had followed until then. Despite its provision of huge amounts of funding and some modest manpower contributions after the war was over, Japan was an almost invisible presence during the Gulf War.[3] As fundamental aspects of the global order were being questioned, Japan was made to realize that making peace through money and discussions alone was impossible. How it absorbed the lessons of this bitter experience would be the point of departure for Japanese diplomacy in the post–Cold War era from the 1990s on.

5. Post–Cold War Foreign Policy: 1991–2000

It is still too early to fully evaluate Japanese diplomacy from the 1990s on. However, we can perhaps point to several characteristics.

First, there was a new readiness to criticize previous Japanese diplomacy as "checkbook diplomacy" and "one-country pacifism" and to start gradually widening the parameters of engagement from purely economic matters to political and military questions. This began with the dispatch of the Self-Defense Forces (SDF) to join the United Nations Peacekeeping Mission Activities in Cambodia (United Nations Transitional Authority in Cambodia; UNTAC). The successful conclusion of this mission led to more systematic involvement of Japan's SDF in UN peacekeeping missions. Japan also began to express its ambitions to be admitted as a permanent member of the UN Security Council and started to request support for this move from countries around the world. In addition, it also redefined the terms of the Japan-US Security Treaty and reached an agreement on new defense cooperation guidelines with the United States. It also increased its involvement in regional security. In parallel with this, Japan stopped its aid to China in protest of China's nuclear weapons tests and postponed its funding for the Korean Peninsula Energy Development Organization (KEDO) in protest of missile tests carried out by the Democratic People's Republic of Korea (North Korea), demonstrating a readiness to use its economic power more politically.

The second point is Japan started to give greater importance to international relations within the Asia-Pacific region. Until this point, dialogue in the Asia-Pacific had concentrated on the economy alone, but Japan began to show signs of a willingness to broaden dialogue to include political aspects as well, as seen for example with the launch of the Asia-Pacific Economic Cooperation (APEC) in 1993 and the ASEAN Regional Forum (ARF) with the countries of Southeast Asia in 1994. There was an increasing tendency to strengthen regional relationships on a global level, and it is possible to see Japan's efforts in this direction as part of wider global trends. Yet it also meant the beginning of various multilateral relationships the likes of which had not previously existed in the Asia Pacific region. In particular, this new multilateralism aimed at bringing China onto the international stage and drawing it into greater involvement in regional affairs.

During the first half of the 1990s it was ASEAN and the developed countries on both sides of the Pacific who held the initiative in regional relations within the Asia-Pacific, but in recent years international relations in Northeast Asia have increasingly been the focus. Peaceful transitions of power in Taiwan, North Korea's increasingly engaged attitude toward the outside world, and Russia's move toward active diplomacy vis-à-vis

East Asia are examples of rapid developments in this part of the world in recent years. As an area that involves some of the world's major powers—Japan, the United States, China, and Russia—the Korean Peninsula has traditionally been a focus of international political attention. The shape that international relations in this region take will be important for international relations through out the Asia-Pacific region.

The third aspect we can note is the increasing importance of the need to respond to information technology and the globalization it brings in its wake in politics and diplomacy around the world. Globalization worked to the advantage of the West in bringing change to the balance of power and bringing the Cold War to an end, but it has become clear that this does not mean global markets are free of problems. Short-term movements of huge amounts of capital can cause considerable problems for small and medium-sized countries and, since this capital is often moved for speculative reasons, it often inhibits rather than encourages fair market mechanisms. The Asian currency crisis demonstrated the dangers of these negative aspects of globalization.

Globalization does not simply affect relationships among countries; it also has the potential to affect society at large. It will therefore be necessary to respond to this change on a number of different levels. We need to consider some level of international supervision and regulation to govern the liquidity and speculative movement of capital. Japan has argued this at the G7 Summit. Mechanisms to balance speculation and stabilize markets are also necessary, and some measures to this end are being taken, including the liquidity swap arrangement among ASEAN plus Japan, the United States, and China. There is a need for a society-wide response to the information gap created by globalization and the growing inequality that comes with it, ideally involving cooperation between NGOs and governments. NGOs in Japan are still weak in general, though they are gradually becoming stronger.

Japan has thus made responses to the post–Cold War world in a number of areas. However, the country still seems to be lacking in two important areas that are vital for maintaining a global position as the post–Cold War world order is constructed. The first is a lack of a worldview or philosophy regarding the situation now underway in which globalization is bringing about fusion and frictions between the world's diverse value systems. Around the time of World War II, Japan did make some efforts to articulate a worldview and philosophy but lacked the knowledge and ability to transform this into effective policy. However, today's Japan, although it does possess a certain amount of power, seems to me to lack the kind of profound philosophy that might enable it to pursue a vision of its worldview. There is a risk that this deficiency may make Japan's diplomacy a mere accumulation of tactics bereft of any unifying strategy. It will certainly not help to make Japan's presence felt in other countries.

Second is the problem of an adequate foundation for diplomacy within domestic politics. For diplomacy to carry weight in a mutually interdependent world, it is vital that the statements made by those in charge of implementing policy are supported within their own country and can realistically be put into practice. In modern diplomacy, almost everything depends on reciprocity, by which you accept a certain burden and expect the other party to shoulder its share of the burden in turn. In this situation, taking the initiative and shouldering one's own burden is an important diplomatic resource with regard to other countries. In Japan's case, the country has for some time actively taken up its burden in terms of contributing international funding, and this has not been entirely without significance. Still, this burden is not a question of funding alone. Other more politically challenging aspects, such as system reform and manpower contributions, can sometimes be more important. The only way to strengthen these aspects is for the government to have a consistent diplomatic strategy and to appeal to its people to shoulder their share of the burden. The 1990s were a decade of considerable confusion for Japan in terms of its domestic politics. Whether Japanese domestic politics will be able to reestablish itself on a stable foundation will hold the key to the success or failure of Japanese diplomacy in the early years of the twenty-first century.

Conclusion

In this paper I have provided a short review of the course followed by Japanese diplomacy in the twentieth century. In closing, I would like to make a few observations regarding Japanese diplomacy in this century.

In terms of diplomatic techniques and the pursuit of specific objectives, one can consider that Japanese diplomacy has in general achieved positive results. If we understand diplomacy to be the process by which a country develops cooperative relationships with other countries and decreases the number of its enemies, it is probably fair to say that Japanese diplomacy has achieved a degree of success.

Of course, part of the reason for this success has been the diligence of the people responsible for carrying out the nation's diplomacy. At the same time, though, we should not overlook another factor, namely, that when the international order has been stable and Japan has had a clear sense of direction and strategy, its people have pulled together, and the strength of the nation has been enhanced. It was not so much that Japan aimed specifically to become a military power during the Meiji era or an economic powerhouse during the postwar period of rapid economic growth. Rather, the country aimed to achieve its independence and status within the international community, and the Japanese people rallied around and concentrated their efforts to those ends.

However, it cannot be said that Japanese diplomacy has always been astute about how best to use the gains of its diplomacy and the efforts of its people. Successfully increasing its international influence required it to learn to exert diplomatic efforts across a more diverse range of areas and to put in place the decision-making systems vital for the major changes necessary to this end. Yet there was often insufficient understanding of the importance of these conditions, and Japan's structures tended to postpone these difficult changes. After achieving military and economic strength, both times Japan became too reliant on the strengths it had achieved and failed to pay sufficient attention to the negative aspects of this one-dimensional concentration on a single aspect of national strength. It also tended to underestimate the new problems brought by success and the need to learn how to manage the fruits of its success, and it only started to pay attention to these aspects once the situation had deteriorated quite seriously.

It is also true that Japan's success became a factor that changed the international order within which Japan existed and from which it derived its interests. From a long term perspective, the fact that Japan rose to become the only non-Western colonial empire destabilized the colonial empire system. Likewise, Japan's rapid rise to prosperity in the postwar period was one of the factors that produced change in the international economic order. In the twentieth century, Japan was in the ironic position of being forced to adapt to international factors that were changing because of its own success.

At times of dramatic change in international conditions, what is most important for a country like Japan is, first, a worldview that enables it to speak in universal terms and, second, a strong foundation in domestic politics that will allow it to implement a consistent diplomacy in a period of revolutionary change. These are both essential prerequisites for producing a long term foreign policy strategy, and Japan lacked both during the interwar period. As a result, its foreign policy became dominated by an internally focused expansionism that prioritized the logic of Japanese internal politics. Japan ended up with a passive diplomacy that was always playing catchup with situations after they had already arisen. Of course, history does not repeat itself exactly, but to some extent, Japan today resembles Japan of the interwar period. In this sense, the path that Japanese diplomacy followed over the course of the twentieth century has a number of important lessons to teach us today.

Originally published by the Japan Institute of International Affairs in the Resource Library, History (2017).

Notes

1. Yoshino Sakuzō (1878–1933): Political science professor at Tokyo Imperial University who became famous for advocating *Minpon-shugi*, a form of democracy with an imperial constitutional system, during World War I.

2. Shidehara diplomacy is named after Shidehara

Kijūrō (1872–1951). Shidehara originally joined the Ministry of Foreign Affairs in 1896. After occupying the highest positions of the ministry, such as the vice-minister, ambassador to the US, and the plenipotentiary to the Washington Conference in 1921–22, he served as the minister of foreign affairs repeatedly in the 1920s, pursuing cooperation with the US and UK.

3. E.g., the advertisement titled "Thanks America and the Global Family of Nations," *Washington Post*, March 11, 1991.

Bibliography

Ikei Masaru. *Santei Nihon gaikōshi gaisetsu* [A Summary of the History of Japanese Diplomacy, 3rd ed.]. Tokyo: Keio University Press, 1992.

Inoki Masamichi. *Hyōden Yoshida Shigeru* [Yoshida Shigeru: A Critical Biography]. 4 vols. Chikuma Shobō, 1995.

Iokibe Makoto, ed. *The Diplomatic History of Postwar Japan*. London: Routledge, 2010.

Irie Akira. *Nihon no gaikō: Meiji Ishin kara gendai made* [Japanese Diplomacy: From the Meiji Restoration to the Present]. Tokyo: Chūōkōron-Shinsha, 1966.

———. *Shin Nihon no gaikō: Chikyūka jidai no Nihon no sentaku* [New Japanese Diplomacy: Japan's Options in an Age of Globization]. Tokyo: Chūōkōron-Shinsha, 1991.

Kitaoka Shinichi. *Sengo Nihon gaikō ronshū: Kōwa ronsō kara Wangan sensō made* [Articles on Postwar Japanese Diplomacy: From Peace Treaty Controversy to the Gulf War]. Tokyo: Chūōkōron-Shinsha, 1995.

Kōsaka Masataka. *Kōsaka Masataka gaikō hyōronshū: Nihon no shinro to rekishi no kyōkun* [Collected Essays on Diplomacy by Kōsaka Masataka: Japan's Future Course and Lessons from History]. Tokyo: Chūōkōron-Shinsha, 1996.

Ministry of Foreign Affairs Centenary History Editorial Committee, ed. *Gaimushō no hyakunen* [100 Years of the Ministry of Foreign Affairs]. 2 vols. Tokyo: Hara Shobō, 1969.

Shimanuki Takeharu. "Nichi-Ro sensō igo ni okeru kokubō hōshin, shoyō heiryoku, yōhei kōryō no hensen, jō" [The Development of the Imperial National Defense Policy, the Estimate of Requisite Armament and the Outline of Strategy since the Russo-Japanese War], Article 1 of *Nippon teikoku no kokubō hōshin* [The Defense Policies of Imperial Japan] (1907). In *Gunji Shigaku* [The Journal of Military History] 8, no. 4 (March 1973).

Tobe Ryōichi. *Gyakusetsu no guntai* [The Paradox of the Military]. Tokyo: Chūōkōron-Shinsha, 1998.

Part III

China Rising

A Look Back on the Work of the Japan-China Joint History Research Committee

Kitaoka Shinichi

ABSTRACT When Japan was working to promote United Nations Security Council reform in 2005, China criticized Japan harshly for—so China said—failing to face up to its own history. Thinking this Chinese criticism was badly overblown, Japan responded by calling for the establishment of a committee of experts to examine the historical issues in question and to determine what exactly had happened. This then led to the establishment of the Japan-China Joint History Research Committee in December 2006. This committee toiled for three years before issuing its report in December 2009. Its work is summarized here by the Japanese co-chair.

Writing Parallel Histories

The author would first like to identify the genesis of this joint Japanese-Chinese historical research. The problems between Japan and China concerning history intensified between March and May 2005, when China objected vehemently to Japan's bid to reform the United Nations Security Council. The pretext for the protests that was cited at the time was that "Japan has not reflected on history." In April 2005, at the height of the protests, Japanese Minister of Foreign Affairs Machimura Nobutaka visited China and proposed that, if this were the case, the two nations should conduct joint historical research; however, the Chinese refused.

Subsequently, various behind-the-scenes moves led to an agreement at the October 2006 summit talks between Prime Minister Abe Shinzō and President Hu Jintao to commence joint Japanese-Chinese historical research. The details were then ironed out in November talks between China's Minister of Foreign Affairs Li Zhaoxing and Japan's Minister of Foreign Affairs Asō Tarō, and the first plenary session was held that December in Beijing.

The chief characteristic of this round of joint historical research is that it encompassed all the history between Japan and China—from ancient times to the present. Until this, the only history between the two nations that had been addressed was the history involving the wars between them. This meant, however, that there was a striking lack of balance. Undeniably, past wars have represented a significant dimension of Japan-China relations; however, in the modern era alone there have been several periods during which the two nations have not been at war and have cooperated with one another. Thus, any attempt to embrace the entire history of the Japan-China relationship represents important progress by its very nature.

Ten people from each country were then chosen for the committee. While there were five Japanese historians for the "ancient, medieval, and early modern" eras and five for the "modern and contemporary" eras, China allotted six of its representatives to the modern and contemporary eras. Moreover, since even the four committee members China allocated to the ancient, medieval, and early modern eras were actually historians who specialized in modern history, there were in reality no Chinese committee members who specialized in the eras prior to the modern and contemporary ones. This was rather unnatural and also served to show the high level of Chinese interest in the modern and contemporary eras.

The second plenary session was held in Tokyo in March 2007. The purpose of this key meeting was to determine how to proceed with the joint research. As the report's table of contents reveals, the decision was made to proceed by dividing the history of the ancient, medieval, and early modern eras by topic rather than by historical period. As is evident from the Japanese committee members' papers that are contained in the report, the Japanese research standard was higher.

Meanwhile, it was decided to subdivide the modern and contemporary eras by period. These eras were broadly divided into the period from the opening up of China and Japan to the eve of the Manchurian Incident, the period from the Manchurian Incident through the Second Sino-Japanese War to the Japanese surrender, and the postwar period. Each of these periods was further subdivided into three chapters. For example, the first period was divided into the time from the opening up of China and Japan until the eve of the First Sino-Japanese War, the time from the First Sino-Japanese War until the Chinese Revolution, and the time from World War I until the eve of the Manchurian Incident. Accordingly, nine chapters were devoted to the modern and contemporary eras alone.

For each chapter, the Chinese committee members would write one paper of approximately 25 A4-size pages, and the Japanese committee members would do the same. Points of mutual interest were established so that the two texts would not end up at cross-purposes. For example, around a dozen points of mutual interest were established for the time surrounding the Manchurian Incident, such as the September 18 Incident, Japan's withdrawal from the League of Nations, and the founding of the state of Manchukuo. Afterwards, the two sides would engage in discussion and—as far as possible—attempt to see each other's point of view. Despite this, however, a number of differences might remain, and these would be included as comments or in the form of a summary of the discussion. Thus, it was agreed that each chapter would consist of three elements: two papers and a set of comments.

It was also agreed that, for each chapter, the committee would investigate the general trends of the corresponding period (or the themes, in the case of eras prior to the modern and contemporary ones) and not simply delve into the various problems that characterized them. The purpose of this was to produce a general history of foreign relations between Japan and China.

Many newspapers described this structure by reporting that the views of both sides were written down side by side; however, this made it sound as if the two sides could not agree. However, it was known from the outset that agreement would be impossible. The objective was to first come to the same table (no simple matter in itself), with a view toward agreement and reconciliation in the ultra-long term. Parallel histories are a positive means to that end.

Our objectives were to use this technique to demonstrate that the disparities between Japan's and China's interpretation of history were not as polarized as was reported in the media (which has a tendency to report extreme statements in any event) and, in particular, to be able to demonstrate to the Chinese people that it is possible to hold points of view other than the official Chinese line.

In light of the above explanation, it can probably be understood that assessments such as "there are points of contention and the gap between the two sides' interpretations is not closing" and "the views of both sides were written down side by side" are stereotypes and miss the point. A handful of academics debating for a mere two or three years are never going to reach a shared perception of the two countries' histories. There remain huge differences between Japan and China. However, it is doubtful that there is any point in reporting only these differences. Simply writing these differing interpretations down represents important progress in itself, and the author would like to emphasize at the outset that—irrespective of the differences that remain between the two nations—the two sides were able to affirm to each other that they are capable, to a certain extent, of sharing perceptions.

Also, given that the joint research should emphasize the overall picture, reporting that focuses on individual events, such as the Nanjing

Massacre (Incident), misses the point. [The author's thinking on the Nanjing Massacre (Incident) will be described later; however, it was originally set out in a paper of approximately 25 pages.] This overall picture needs to include an overview of the four-year period from the outbreak of the Second Sino-Japanese War to the attack on Pearl Harbor. Since the committee was writing these types of papers and basing its discussions on them, it was impossible to engage in a lengthy debate devoted solely to the Nanjing Massacre (Incident).

When it comes to history, it is important to maintain a sense of proportion. Reducing the Second Sino-Japanese War to the Nanjing Massacre (Incident) does not seem like an appropriate method of covering it.

Repeated Close Consultations

In practice, writing the papers following the conclusion of the second plenary session in March 2007 took considerable time. Subsequent meetings were held (starting close to the end of 2007) to discuss these papers as they were completed; including subcommittee meetings for the modern and contemporary eras group led by the author, meetings were held in November 2007 (subcommittee meeting, Fukuoka), January 2008 (plenary session, Beijing), March 2008 (subcommittee meeting, Kagoshima), and May 2008 (subcommittee meeting, Jinan in Shandong Province). Hence, meetings were essentially held at two-month intervals. Over the course of these repeated discussions the specific content the two sides could essentially agree on and that which they could not agree on emerged; the comments were then drafted afterwards. Comments for a single paper stretched to two or three pages (around 10% of the length of the paper). The comments from both the Japanese and Chinese committee members would thus total around five or six pages.

In May 2008 President Hu Jintao visited Japan, and the importance of joint historical research was affirmed in the talks he held with Prime Minister Fukuda Yasuo. Here, too, the discussion between the two parties is understood to have been of a relatively amicable and academic nature. At this juncture, the Japanese committee members were intending to publish the results of their research in July or August 2008.

Japan-China Joint History Research Committee—Summary of Meetings

17 April 2005
Minister of Foreign Affairs Machimura Nobutaka visits China in response to anti-Japanese demonstrations and proposes that Japan and China conduct joint historical research.

8 October 2006
Prime Minister Abe Shinzō visits China. At summit talks with President Hu Jintao, an agreement is reached to commence joint Japanese-Chinese historical research.

16 November 2006
Talks are held in Hanoi between Foreign Ministers Asō Tarō and Li Zhaoxing. An agreement is reached on an implementation framework for joint historical research.

26–27 December 2006
First plenary session is held in Beijing.

19–20 March 2007
Second plenary session is held in Tokyo.

24–25 November 2007
First research symposium for the modern and contemporary eras subcommittee is held in Fukuoka.

5–6 January 2008
Third plenary session is held in Beijing.

14–16 March 2008
Second research symposium for the modern and contemporary eras subcommittee is held in Kagoshima.

20–23 March 2008
Research symposium for the ancient, medieval, and early modern eras subcommittee is held in Fukuoka and Tsushima.

5–6 May 2008
Research symposia for the ancient, medieval, and early modern eras subcommittee and the

modern and contemporary eras subcommittee are held in Jinan in Shandong Province.

7 May 2008

President Hu Jintao visits Japan. At summit talks with Prime Minister Fukuda Yasuo, there is agreement to continue joint research in the future.

24 December 2009

Fourth and final plenary session is held in Tokyo. This completes the current phase of joint historical research. There is agreement on the method of publication of research results and some results are published. (Papers are to be published in the original Japanese or Chinese in January 2010 and then in translation a few months later.)

31 January 2010

Papers in the original Japanese or Chinese (that comprise the report) are published by the committee members from the respective countries.

A Sudden Change of Attitude by the Chinese

However, after this, the situation took a turn for the worse. At the start of July 2008, the Chinese responded half-heartedly regarding the staging of the next plenary session, and the author traveled to Beijing in early August.

There, the author met with a few Chinese leaders who said they wished the comments section of each chapter remain unpublished. It is of course the comments that throw the differences between the Japanese and Chinese committee members into sharp relief. They asserted that "Academics can understand that there are differences between them, but the general public cannot understand this properly and we anticipate a negative reaction. We wish to avoid giving prominence to the differences."

One purpose of joint research is for both sides to candidly clarify the differences between their respective views. Accordingly, the Chinese proposal was most unfortunate; however, rejecting it would probably have meant the report could not be published. This would have meant that it would have been impossible to relay the results of the joint research back to the general public and the intelligentsia of each country. In any case, reading the text of the papers would reveal the differences. With this in mind, the author acceded to the Chinese proposition.

However, after a coffee break, the Chinese came out and said they did not wish to publish any of the papers either. They stated that they wished to halt publication of all 14 papers on the ancient, medieval, and early modern eras, and all 18 papers on the modern and contemporary eras. They wished instead to publish a few pages summarizing the findings of the joint research and to defer publication of the papers until the second period of joint research.

We rejected this absurd request, canceled the dinner scheduled for that evening, and returned to our hotel. The next day produced more of the same. We requested the Chinese specify which paragraphs or sentences or words of which papers they were concerned about publishing, and why, and brought the meeting to a close.

We never received any subsequent clarification from the Chinese. Although there was repeated haggling and, at times, intense discussion over this point, no conclusion was ever reached. Over the course of approximately one year, as many as four top-level meetings involving a few select committee members were held. Around the summer of 2009, the Chinese came out and stated that they were prepared to accede to the publication of all the papers except the six papers that comprised the last three chapters of the volume on the modern and contemporary period, which dealt with the postwar period.

In the wake of this, top-level talks were held in Tokyo on 25 August 2009. With one year having already been wasted, we accepted the Chinese proposal in the belief that further delay had to be avoided, and it was agreed that the final plenary session would commence on 4 September 2009. Accordingly, it was agreed that a summary of the joint research—consisting of a few pages—would be published, and a report, including all the papers except for those on the postwar period of the modern era, would then be issued within one month.

On 1 September, however, word came from the Chinese that they were canceling the plenary session. Some on the Japanese side responded by asserting that since both sides had agreed to this meeting, it could not be postponed without Japanese agreement, and they would stage the meeting anyway. If the Chinese arbitrarily chose not to attend, so be it. Although the author shared their anger, he judged that to do so would put too much pressure on the Chinese committee members and would have highly disadvantageous consequences. He thus agreed to the postponement—albeit with extreme reluctance.

On this occasion in fact, the leader of the Chinese committee members did apparently go to the Ministry of Foreign Affairs and endeavor to arrange for the meeting to go ahead. Battling external pressure, the Chinese committee members also wanted the joint research to proceed. In fact, at our meetings the author increasingly heard from them that they did wish to publish our research results, but they were under strong pressure from various quarters.

It was not made clear why the meeting was canceled. One possible reason was that, with the October anniversary of the founding of the People's Republic approaching, the Chinese government wished to avoid internal unrest at all costs. Alternatively, there has also been conjecture that China was anticipating that Japan's perceptions of history might change to become closer to the Chinese view in the aftermath of the landslide victory by the Democratic Party of Japan. Hard as it is to imagine in a free country, the fact of the matter is that the answer is not known.

The 24 December Tug-of-War

We on the Japanese side of the committee subsequently continued to try persuade the Chinese side to resume the meetings quickly. As a result, we obtained their agreement that the final meeting would be staged during 2009, and it was thus agreed that a preparatory meeting would be held on 15 December and the final plenary session would commence on 24 December. Since there would not be time to fully complete the detailed report by 24 December, it was decided that it would be published within a month of the final

meeting (that is, just before the end of January 2010). However, this would not include the six papers comprising chapter three. It was also agreed that the following four documents would be published at the plenary session: (i) a simple one-page description of the development of the joint research to date; (ii) a foreword to the entire report, written jointly by the author and Bu Ping, the Chinese chair of the committee and head of the Institute of Modern History at the Chinese Academy of Social Sciences; (iii) an introduction to the section on the ancient, medieval, and early modern eras by Yamauchi Masayuki, professor at the University of Tokyo, and Jiang Lifeng, head of the Institute of Japanese Studies at the Chinese Academy of Social Sciences; and (iv) an introduction to the section on the modern and contemporary eras by the author and Bu Ping. With the final meeting in sight, the meeting on 15 December ended well.

However, on the evening of 22 December, the Chinese telephoned to say they wanted these four papers to be published in Japanese only. It seemed that they were extremely wary of these papers being read by Chinese people. This seemed like a pointless exercise to us, as the four documents were short and could be translated swiftly; however, we acquiesced. Having awaited our response, the Chinese flew to Japan early on the morning of 23 December.

After arriving in Japan, Bu Ping, the chair of the Chinese committee, telephoned the author that day to say he would like to discuss the following day's plenary session. Hence, that evening the author paid Bu Ping a visit at the hotel where he was staying. Bu Ping said he wished to publish only the first of the four documents (the one that described the development of the joint research) at the following day's plenary session, and not the remaining three. Although the author rejected this completely ridiculous suggestion, Bu Ping insisted repeatedly and would not allow the author to leave. After a rather heated exchange, the author left the hotel.

The following morning, the author received a further telephone call from Bu Ping. He wished to discuss the matter again, and so we met at the University of Tokyo. He reiterated his request from the previous evening. Naturally, the author refused. Bu Ping had been in frequent contact with China by telephone—presumably with the Ministry of Foreign Affairs.

Finally, the Chinese wished to delete part of one of the four documents (the introduction to the volume on the modern era)—the part that summarized the agreements and discrepancies between the Japanese and Chinese views of the modern era. It seemed that they did not wish these to be made clear.

After concluding the meeting at the University of Tokyo by telling Bu Ping the Japanese would give their reply at the final meeting, the author conferred with the other Japanese committee members. The decision was that they would acquiesce to the Chinese request. Since the agreements and discrepancies between the two sides' views would be apparent when the two versions of the reports were published, there was no major disadvantage in conceding this point, and so the Japanese compromised in the belief that this was preferable to Chinese nonattendance. As a result, the final meeting was held that same evening and concluded without incident.

After the plenary session, the four documents were submitted to Minister of Foreign Affairs Okada Katsuya, and a press conference was staged, at which Bu Ping responded to a question on the Nanjing Massacre (Incident) by stating that "The Nanking/Nanjing Tribunal established a figure of 200,000 victims of the massacre, and the Tokyo Trials established a figure of 300,000. These figures must be respected." The author immediately objected to this, saying that, firstly, it is our job as historians to carefully scrutinize such figures, and secondly, this had not been discussed at any plenary session or subcommittee meeting. By way of retraction, Bu Ping replied that "No, this is my own personal view." In other words, although he was seizing every possible opportunity to push the official Chinese line, he was inadvertently admitting that the Nanjing Massacre (Incident) had not been the subject of in-depth discussions in the course of the joint research. Subsequently, as the reader may know, the papers written by both the Japanese and Chinese committee members (with the exception

of the papers on the postwar period) were published in the form of a report on 31 January.

Looking back over the events to date, we have been made painfully aware of how difficult it is to conduct discussions with a country like China, which does not have adequate freedom of speech. However, it is probably Bu Ping and the rest of the Chinese committee members who have felt this most acutely. Under pressure from various quarters, they expended great effort and worked extremely hard on the joint research.

The Clear Reality of Japanese Aggression

Finally, the author would like to address a number of criticisms that came from the Japanese media and other quarters after the publication of the report.

First, the acknowledgment that Japan waged a war of aggression against China has attracted heavy criticism. The author simply cannot accept this criticism, as it seems clear that, in reality, Japan was the aggressor. Quite apart from the results of the joint research, the author has held this view for a long time (for example, see *From Party Politics to Militarism in Japan, 1924–1941*, Lynne Rienner Publishers, 2021). Nor is the author alone in this view. There seem to be virtually no Japanese historians who believe Japan was not the aggressor against China.

There are some people who maintain that since the definition of aggression has only been established relatively recently (prior to which the boundaries of what constituted aggression were not clear), Japan's conduct at that time cannot be termed "aggression." However, the reason why it took so long to come up with a definition for "aggression" was that there is a fine line between "aggression" and "nonaggression," and it took time to decide where the boundary actually lies. Japan's actions in the wake of the Manchurian Incident did not fall into any such gray zone, and by any definition, they constituted a clear case of aggression. Whatever the legal arguments, to historians this was clearly aggression.

In addition, there have recently been some people who have said the assassination of Zhang Zuolin was a conspiracy by the Comintern and the Manchurian Incident was not aggression.

As far as the assassination of Zhang Zuolin is concerned, this is total misinformation. As far as the Manchurian Incident is concerned, there are some who say the Chinese infringed upon the legal interests of Japan. In terms of balance, however, it is impossible to justify the huge scale of the actions taken by Japan—occupation of territory three and a half times the size of Japan—on the strength of Chinese treaty violations.

It is also necessary to take a precise look at the assertion that Japan had interests in Manchuria for many years. The only Japanese interests that were widely and indisputably acknowledged internationally consisted of a relatively limited area surrounding the South Manchuria Railway. The basis for Japanese claims to any territory outside of this area was rather vague. Even more pertinent, Japan never claimed to have any rights or interests in Northern Manchuria, which it took possession of on the strength of the Manchurian Incident. As a teacher of history, the author finds it lamentable that there are people who fail to comprehend these basic realities and maintain the Manchurian Incident was not an act of aggression.

The Nanjing Massacre (Incident)

With regard to Nanjing, the acknowledgment that the Japanese army engaged in a massacre has been criticized as outrageous. As mentioned earlier, there was no specific time allocated for discussion of Nanjing in the course of the joint research. As is clear from the report, the Japanese committee members simply introduced the fact that there are different casualty figures in Japan.

However, it is impossible to accept the view that no massacre took place. There are virtually no Japanese researchers in modern history who fail to acknowledge that a considerable number of illegal killings and acts of violence took place in Nanjing. It was even regarded as a scandal by some in Japan before the war. Although the Chinese Nationalist Party (Kuomintang/Guomindang) certainly used Nanjing for propaganda, this did not cause people to discount the idea that a massacre had taken place.

In fact, the records of many units describe the "disposal" of prisoners of war. Much—if not all—of this "disposal" was carried out in the form of human executions. Given that there is an obligation under international law to treat prisoners of war humanely, they should never ever be killed for minor insubordination. It is also an absurd leap of logic to say that it was acceptable to kill soldiers in plainclothes because they took off their uniforms and slipped off into the general population instead of surrendering in uniform, as they normally were supposed to do.

In every country in the world, the most patriotic organizations are groups of former servicemen, such as veterans' associations. The Kaikōsha, an association of former Japanese army officers, falls into this category. However, despite intense criticism from the members of the association, after its investigation of Nanjing, the Kaikōsha acknowledged that a massacre had taken place (see *Nankinsenshi* [The History of the Battle of Nanking]). It is this intellectual courage to face up to such unpleasant facts that should be a source of pride for Japan, and it would be shameful not to acknowledge the misconduct of the past.

In addition, we pointed out in our report that although Japan bears the lion's share of responsibility for the Nanjing Massacre (Incident), there were also problems with the way the Chinese handled the situation. Chiang Kai-shek (Jiang Jieshi) decided to defend Nanjing with the knowledge that he was almost certain to lose, and he escaped from the city before the battle. Tang Shengzhi, the general who was in charge of the defense of Nanjing, also escaped just before the battle. Normally a unit would surrender when it became clear it could not win. This would probably have led to a death sentence for the commanders in a court martial, but it would have saved the lives of the ordinary soldiers. The report stipulates that the failure of the Chinese commanders to follow this combat protocol, and their irresponsible behavior in escaping, was a major contributing factor to the massacre. Unlike the last three chapters of volume two, the Chinese committee members did not reject this one.

Although in overall terms the Chinese committee members did not appear very flexible in their attitudes, on this issue there seemed to be signs of change. This softening in the Chinese stance was also alluded to in an article in the *Sankei Shimbun* newspaper on 1 February 2010 by Professor Hata Ikuhiko—as might be expected from a historian regarded as a leading authority on historical research on the Shōwa era.

What Were the Problems with the Post-war Section?

The Japanese and Chinese committee members agreed not to publish the postwar section. This was agreed to reluctantly; however, as it was part of an overall agreement, it is impossible to go into detail here. The story broke in the morning edition of the *Mainichi Shimbun* on 10 February in a report that was extremely regrettable in terms of its likely damaging effect on the relationship of mutual confidence between Japan and China. Moreover, the report was inaccurate because the draft featured was not the draft that ultimately caused the breakdown in the agreement but a comparatively early draft. This was bad for the experts, who were asked to comment on the wrong draft.

One of the main points of contention in the postwar section was the Tokyo International Military Tribunals. Our contention was that there were considerable problems with the Tokyo Tribunals; they were seriously flawed in terms of procedure. At the same time, Rikkyo University Professor Awaya Kentarō's comment that "the Tokyo Tribunal has been virtually repudiated" does not represent legitimate criticism. The author cannot go into detail since the papers have not been published, but it was not due to any of the Japanese committee members claiming the Tokyo Tribunal was invalid or meaningless. However, there are problems regarding the legitimacy of the Tokyo Tribunal, and these are not simply procedural problems involving ex post facto law. For example, when crimes against humanity and peace are considered, who should be held accountable for the Great Tokyo Air Raids and the atomic bombing of Hiroshima and Nagasaki? In addition, it was improper for the Soviet Union, which invaded Japan in violation of the nonaggression pact between the two nations, to supply one of the judges for the tribunals. These points

would have been unacceptable to the Chinese, who hold an unequivocally favorable view of the Tokyo Tribunals.

The newspapers also actively discussed the 1989 Tiananmen Square incident; however, the coverage did not reflect reality. The committee did not discuss the Tiananmen Square incident in the course of the joint research. Instead, the discussion focused on why Japan-China relations had taken a downturn, as exemplified by the anti-Japanese demonstrations of 2005, after the comparatively favorable relationship that the two nations had enjoyed in the period following the emperor's 1992 visit to China.

China's "patriotic education" system must be cited as a reason for this. The Chinese committee members asserted that there is no specific anti-Japanese intention behind this. Whatever their intention might have been, however, our belief is that it does in effect serve as anti-Japanese education. However, there are still people in China, both within the government and without, who are involved in patriotic education, and it was probably difficult for the Chinese committee members to discuss this issue.

Finally, the Japanese committee members clearly described the differences between Japan and Germany in terms of history education and historical perception, which were supposed to be topics in the third chapter of section three. Although Germany has sincerely apologized for the crimes committed by the Nazis, it has not clearly taken overall responsibility for the war. Hence, the Japanese committee members take the view that it is unacceptable to assert unconditionally that Japan has not acknowledged responsibility or has not apologized as unequivocally as Germany. The Chinese committee members could not comprehend this point and made no effort to.

Essentially, these were the disputed points in the postwar section. Since any further elaboration would violate the agreement between the two sides, the author will refrain from discussing the matter any further.

First-Stage Report of the Japan-China Joint History Research Committee

A Dispassionate Assessment of the Successes and Challenges

Japan and China are not alone in that their mass media are quick to closely cover extreme debate, while commonsense views that find broad agreement do not make for good newspaper copy. Although many in China believe Japan does not acknowledge its responsibility for the war, the reality is different, as the majority of Japanese do in fact acknowledge the nation's responsibility. The way in which this acknowledgment is expressed, however, differs in many respects from how the Chinese Communist Party would interpret such acknowledgment. It is the attempt to compare the interpretations to see where and how they differ, the attempt to establish where they can be reconciled and where they cannot, and the clarification of these aspects that constitute the fruits of this round of joint historical research.

Naturally, on certain points, it is no wonder China misunderstands Japan. When the report was published, the only views reported were that Japan was not the aggressor in the war and there was no massacre at Nanjing. In the end, there will be a few people saying things like "Japan was not the aggressor, so it must be a splendid country." The author believes that Japan has been an aggressor in the past, but it is a wonderful country. There are many countries around the world that acknowledge their past responsibilities and are doing fine (or are doing fine precisely because they acknowledge their past responsibilities). Japan must think more seriously about the way it conducts research into, and teaches, modern Japanese history in order to ensure that such fallacies hold no sway.

It is often said that Asia is slow to reach historical reconciliation in comparison with Europe. However, even the relationship between France and Germany required enormous time and effort before it was able to attain its present state, and problems remain even now. A few years ago there was an uproar when Günter Grass admitted to having formerly been involved with the Nazis. There has also been little headway in research on Nazi collaborators in the French Vichy government. Reconciliation between Germany and Poland did not start in earnest until Poland joined the ranks of free nations. In Europe, too, then, the road to reconciliation has seen many twists and turns.

In Latin America, the Spaniards annihilated the Inca in the sixteenth century. In addition to the Inca, there have been many peoples and cultures around the world that have been obliterated or debilitated by Europeans without being able to voice any protest. Most of the large-scale conflicts around the world today are taking place in regions where the residual effects of colonial rule still remain. Sudan, the Democratic Republic of Congo, and Afghanistan all fall into this category.

By contrast, the situation in Asia is currently peaceful, with China, the Republic of Korea, and Taiwan all boasting spectacular growth. Japan bears great responsibility for the war and still retains significant scars; however, Japan's overall progress since the war is in no way inferior to that of Europe. As we appreciate this progress, we should continue to engage in joint research.

Kitaoka, Shinichi. "A Look Back on the Work of the Japan-China Joint History Research Committee." *Asia-Pacific Review* 17:1 (2010), 6–20. © Nakasone Peace Institute reprinted by permission of Taylor & Francis Ltd, https://www.tandfonline.com on behalf of Nakasone Peace Institute.

This essay is based on one published in Japanese in the April 2010 issue of *Gaikō Forum*.

III-(2) Pendulum Swings Back to Asia-Pacific from East Asia

Shiraishi Takashi

ABSTRACT The ASEAN Summit held in Hanoi in 2010 decided to invite the United States and Russia to the East Asia Summit to be held in 2011. It was largely in response to China's aggressive attempts to establish effective control over the South China Sea which China claims as its own. The essay argues it is the question of what risk ASEAN states face to hedge that is decisive in the shift in the regional framework for cooperation.

The year 2010 will be remembered as a significant turning point in the history of regional cooperation in East Asia and the Asia-Pacific. In 1989, the Asia-Pacific Economic Cooperation (APEC) forum was inaugurated, heralding the beginning of regional cooperation. Eight years later, in the wake of the Asian economic crisis, the Association of Southeast Asian Nations (ASEAN) as well as Japan, China, and South Korea launched the ASEAN+3 Summit, marking the ascendancy of East Asia over the Asia-Pacific region as the framework for regional cooperation. However, the pendulum swung back in 2010, with the emergence of multilateral cooperation encompassing the Asia-Pacific region as a whole.

Why did the pendulum swing back?

One reason is that China has acted unilaterally in pressing territorial claims to islands in the East China and South China Seas. Japan encountered this in September when a Chinese fishing boat rammed Japan Coast Guard patrol vessels off the Senkaku Islands in Okinawa Prefecture. Beijing's activities in the South China Sea were taken up at a meeting of the ASEAN Regional Forum (ARF), of which China is a member, in Hanoi last July.

China's enactment of the Law on the Territorial Sea and the Contiguous Zone in 1992 triggered territorial disputes in the South China Sea between ASEAN members and Beijing. On the strength of this law, China regards various islands in the South China Sea as its territory. It also has territorial disputes with Vietnam, Brunei, Malaysia, and the Philippines over various islands in the region. In response, ASEAN adopted the Declaration on the South China Sea in 1992, emphasizing "the necessity to resolve all sovereignty and jurisdictional issues by peaceful means, without resort to force" and calling for the establishment of "a code of international conduct" over the disputed waters. But in 1995, China, advocating the bilateral approach in settling the disputes, occupied Mischief Reef, which is claimed by the Philippines.

In 2000, China modified its policy toward ASEAN. As a result, China and ASEAN in 2002 concluded the Framework Agreement on Comprehensive Economic Cooperation and the Joint Declaration on Cooperation in the Field of Nontraditional Security Issues and signed the Declaration on the Conduct of Parties in the South China Sea. In 2003, China subscribed to the Treaty of Amity and Cooperation in Southeast Asia—ASEAN's signature pact of association.

However, the 2002 declaration on the conduct

of parties is not legally binding and China has refused to accede to any binding code with ASEAN in this respect. Since 2007, tensions have heightened between China and the ASEAN countries, especially Vietnam, over the South China Sea. For instance, Chinese fishery patrol ships seized one Vietnamese fishing boat after another in waters around the Paracel Islands, which are claimed by Vietnam but effectively controlled by China. In waters around Indonesia's Natuna Islands, a showdown occurred between an Indonesian patrol vessel trying to seize Chinese boats engaged in illegal fishing operations and an armed Chinese vessel protecting them. During the ARF conference in July, ASEAN insisted that a joint statement contain a clause calling for the parties to formulate a binding code of conduct in the South China Sea. However, China has stuck to its policy of dealing with territorial disputes through bilateral talks.

In the hope of defusing friction, ASEAN has turned to major countries not involved in the disputes, seeking their engagement in South China Sea affairs. This was one of the reasons ASEAN took the initiative during the fifth East Asia Summit in Hanoi in October to bring Russia and the United States into the EAS this year. Before that initiative, the EAS brought together ASEAN+6 (i.e., Australia, China, India, Japan, New Zealand, and South Korea).

Active US Reengagement

The other reason for the swing back from East Asia to cooperation with the Asia-Pacific region is that Washington has become more actively reengaged in East Asia. In a speech in Tokyo in November 2009, President Barack Obama confirmed his country's continuing engagement as a Pacific nation with East Asia. At the ARF conference in July, Secretary of State Hillary Clinton said: "The United States, like every nation, has a national interest in freedom of navigation, open access to Asia's maritime commons. The United States supports a collaborative diplomatic process by all claimants for resolving the various territorial disputes without coercion. We oppose the use or threat of force by any claimant." Furthermore, Washington dispatched a US aircraft carrier to the South China Sea off Da Nang, Vietnam, when the Chinese sent warships to disputed waters and staged massive naval exercises in a show of force.

Beijing, of course, reacted angrily to Washington's deployment of the carrier. Nonetheless, Clinton, speaking just ahead of the start of Chinese president Hu Jintao's state visit to the United States, made it clear that "there is no such thing as a G2," ruling out the possibility of Washington and Beijing forming a Group of Two to lead the world. Instead, she reaffirmed Washington's policy of improving its links with its allies and partners by saying, "America has renewed and strengthened our bonds with our allies—Japan, South Korea, Thailand, Australia, and the Philippines . . ."

Indeed, the United States has deepened its engagement in East Asia. I can cite a number of recent examples: the complete resumption of military exchanges with Indonesia, the launch of Vietnam-US defense policy dialogues at the deputy ministerial level, the second US-ASEAN Leaders Meeting, and the US agreement to provide India with missile-related and civilian nuclear technology.

The deepening of the US commitment to the Asia-Pacific region also is evident in the field of trade. The proposed Trans-Pacific Partnership (TPP) free trade framework originally surfaced in 2006 as a four-nation economic partnership agreement involving Brunei, Chile, New Zealand, and Singapore. The United States, Australia, and Peru expressed their willingness to participate in the new regional trade architecture, embarking on negotiations in 2010 to subscribe to the TTP pact. As a process to form a new Asia-Pacific free trade zone on an APEC scale, the TPP initiative may become as important as, or even more important than, the ASEAN+3 framework advocated by China and the ASEAN+6 backed by Japan.

With this major turning point in the history of regional cooperation, it seems collaborative efforts are now shifting back to Asia-Pacific from East Asia. When Asia plunged into the 1997–98 economic crisis, many Asian countries pursued East Asia-centric regional cooperation by keeping the United States at arm's length as they were wary of Washington's intervention. Now, however, China's unilateral actions have made the region more worried, making it essential to realize Asia-Pacific regional cooperation with the participation of the United States.

What do these developments mean for Japan? Japan is actively involved in the pendulum swinging back to the Asia-Pacific region. Prime Minister Kan Naoto's foreign policy speech on 20 January lends credence to this. He reaffirmed "the Japan-US alliance as the cornerstone of Japanese foreign policy," while adding, "At the same time, there are areas in China's strengthening of its national defense in which transparency is somewhat lacking, and we are concerned by its increasingly ambitious maritime activities."

Kan went on to say, "I intend to determine around June of this year whether or not Japan will participate in negotiations aimed at joining the [TPP] agreement." Throughout the speech, Kan did not refer to his predecessor Hatoyama Yukio's East Asian Community initiative at all.

The swing of the regional cooperation pendulum back to the Asia-Pacific, however, is not meant to contain China. As China is deeply integrated into the world economy, containment is no longer viable. But China should not try to coerce other countries to follow its rules no matter how powerful it becomes. To ensure robust regional cooperation, countries in the region must join hands to encourage China as a responsible nation to help maintain order and further develop East Asia. Such an approach will undoubtedly help strengthen the position of mainland Chinese policymakers who attach importance to international cooperation.

Originally published by The Yomiuri Shimbun in *THE DAILY YOMIURI* "INSIGHTS into the WORLD" (7 February 2011).

III-(3) The Three Principles on Arms Exports

Shiraishi Takashi

ABSTRACT The Japanese government decided to revise its policy on weapons exports and introduced the new "Three Principles on Transfer of Defense Equipment and Technology." This essay argues that the most important question that needs to be addressed is how to maintain the technological and industrial base for Japanese defense in a time of declining budgets and in view of expanding inter-operativity between Japan's self-defense forces and the US military.

At a meeting of Japan's National Security Council on 11 March 2014, the government approved the draft outline of a new set of rules to replace the existing Three Principles on Arms Exports. Dubbed "Three Principles on Transfer of Defense Equipment and Technology," the new restraints would: (1) ban transfers (exports) of defense-related equipment that would clearly impede the maintenance of international peace and security, (2) implement careful screening and restrict the transfers that are approved, and (3) allow transfers only where there is assurance of appropriate controls to prevent the equipment from being used for unintended purposes or transferred to third countries. If the new principles are officially adopted by a cabinet decision in April, it will become possible to transfer defense-related equipment to foreign governments and international institutions like the United Nations, provided that doing so will "contribute to peace and be helpful for the active promotion of international cooperation" and "be helpful for Japan's national security." This will represent a substantial relaxation of the existing Three Principles, which have effectively banned almost all arms exports.[1]

After the draft was adopted by the NSC, the government submitted it to the Liberal Democratic Party (LDP) and New Kōmeitō, the two parties of the ruling coalition. At a meeting of an LDP-Kōmeitō project team on national security, the government officially presented an operational framework for the new rules: the NSC will determine whether or not to allow exports of weapons or related technologies in important cases and will publish its decisions; with regard to other cases, the government will compile and publish an annual report on export numbers and destinations. In addition, as an example of the sorts of exports that would be allowed, the government cited exports of equipment for rescue, transport, warning and surveillance, and minesweeping to countries with which Japan has a cooperative relationship in the national security field. The government indirectly indicated its intention to allow exports to coastal countries along Japan's sea lines of communication, but apparently in deference to the Kōmeitō, which has been wary about relaxing the existing rules, it refrained from explicit mention of these sea lines. The two parties gave their overall approval to the proposed revision.

It is apparent that great attention is being paid to the question of how to delimit and place restraints on exports of defense equipment. This is fine if it will help people both in Japan and elsewhere to understand the objectives of the new set of principles. But looking at the stories on this topic in the press, I cannot but wonder how well people understand the basic issue of why it is necessary at this point to replace the existing Three Principles on Arms Exports with a new framework.

Maintaining the Industrial Base of Japan's Defense Power

The move to revise the Three Principles actually started a couple of years ago, when the Democratic Party of Japan was in power. In December 2011, the administration of Prime Minister Noda Yoshihiko decided to allow participation in international joint development and the production of defense equipment like fighter jets and to permit the transfer of defense equipment for peace-building activities (such as UN peacekeeping operations) and for humanitarian purposes as exceptions to the general ban on arms exports.[2] The Abe administration's move to replace the old Three Principles with a new set is a continuation of the revision process that began under Noda. Why was this process seen to be necessary?

One of the foundations for defense power is industrial power. In many countries state-owned enterprises handle defense-related production, but Japan depends entirely on the private sector for this purpose. The value of the defense industry's output (including the development, manufacture, and maintenance of defense-related equipment, along with logistical support and assistance with repairs) for the Ministry of Defense comes to less than ¥2 trillion a year, a mere 0.8% of Japan's total industrial production. The scale of the industry is determined by the size of the ministry's annual budget for procurement and maintenance of defense equipment. Given the critical state of public finances, these appropriations cannot be increased substantially. But as equipment becomes more sophisticated, unit costs rise; this results in smaller numbers of items being ordered, which in turn hurts the profitability of the defense industry. Over the medium to long term, private-sector companies are likely to find it increasingly

difficult to sustain their defense-related research and production operations.

If it is not going to be possible to keep up the entire foundation of defense production and of related technologies within Japan, what should be done to deal with the situation? Something like the following set of policies is probably the only practical option: (1) identify the core areas of defense production and technology that should be kept within Japan and concentrate on maintaining and developing them so as to sustain the country's defense power steadily over the medium to long term; (2) strengthen cooperation with the United States and its allies and participate in joint technological development and production activities for next-generation defense equipment so as to help expand the market for parts makers and strengthen the business base of defense-industry companies, aiming to maintain, develop, and enhance Japan's defense-related production and technological foundations. This was the thinking behind the move to reconsider the old Three Principles and formulate a new set of rules to replace them.

National Security and Scientific Innovation

Though not directly related to the new set of principles on defense equipment transfers, I would like to note that the Fourth Science and Technology Basic Plan adopted by a cabinet decision in August 2011 also refers to the nurturing of the industrial base for defense power, citing "strengthening national security and key technology" as a priority for research and development, to be pursued by having the government itself take a long-range view, building up results by promoting R&D on an ongoing, broad, and long-term basis.[3]

Here is a quote from the relevant section of the basic plan:

The government will promote R&D into technologies for ocean exploration and development aiming to develop and secure useful natural resources, technologies for space transportation and satellite development and utilization that help to ensure national security, public safety, etc., including information collection, technologies for new energies with the aim of securing independent energy sources . . . high-performance computing technology of the world's top level, technologies for geospatial information, and technologies concerning active and dependable information security.

These technologies are critically important both for the private sector and for national security purposes, but neither private-sector companies nor universities can be expected to develop them. Ever since the start of the current Abe administration, the government has been placing great emphasis on policies to promote scientific and technological innovation as part of its drive to revitalize the Japanese economy and boost the competitive strength of Japanese industry. This is fine. At the same time, however, we should note the need for a government commitment to investment on a major scale over the long term and on an ongoing basis in developing core technologies, such as technologies for high-efficiency aircraft engines, unmanned underwater research vehicles, development and production of oceanic energy and mineral resources, observation satellites, and radioactive waste processing (volume reduction, hazard level reduction).

Originally published by Nippon Communications Foundation online at *Nippon.com* (2014).

Notes

1. (Ed.) "The Three Principles on Arms Exports" were created by Prime Minister Satō Eisaku in 1967. Pressured by opposition insistence on the spirit of the pacifist Constitution in the House of Representatives Audit Committee, Satō crafted the Three Principles to ban the export of arms to (1) Communist bloc countries, (2) countries subject to arms export embargoes under United Nations Security Council resolutions, and (3) countries involved or likely to be involved in international conflicts. In 1976, Prime Minister Miki Takeo submitted a so-called Unified View of the Government to the House of Representatives Budget Committee. This confirmed the pledge "not to permit the export of arms to the countries or regions restricted in the Three Principles and 'to refrain from arms export to other areas not included in the Three Principles in conformity with the spirit of the Japanese Constitution and the Foreign Exchange and Foreign Trade Act.' The Three Principles thus became an official arms export ban" (excerpted from Murayama 2012).

2. See Murayama, op. cit. and Shiraishi 2012 for related information.

Bibliography

Council for Science and Technology Policy. "Japan's Science and Technology Basic Policy Report." 24 December 2010. https://www8.cao.go.jp/cstp/english/basic/4th-BasicPolicy.pdf.

Murayama Yūzō. "A Review of the Three Principles on Arms Exports." *Nippon.com*, 9 February 2012. https://www.nippon.com/en/currents/d00016/.

Shiraishi Takashi. "Revision of the Three Principles on Arms Exports, Assistance for Myanmar." *Nippon.com*, 14 May 2012. https://www.nippon.com/en/column/f00008/.

III-(4) Japan Should Partner with Indo-Pacific Region

Tanaka Akihiko

ABSTRACT The mid-twenty-first century international framework may well be characterizable as the Indo-Pacific Age. Ensuring the Indo-Pacific region's peace and prosperity is thus crucial to Japan's long-term national interest. While private-sector initiative and innovation are key here, Japan needs an international strategy that centers on revitalizing summit diplomacy and other foreign policy activities, creates economic partnerships conducive to trade and investment liberalization, and enhances its official development assistance (ODA). Looking specifically at ODA, it is of the utmost importance that ODA be promoted to foster development, to underwrite human security, and to contribute to peace-building.

Prime Minister Abe Shinzō recently held a series of meetings with India's new prime minister, Narendra Modi, during the latter's visit to Japan. Over the weekend, Abe was on a three-day tour of Bangladesh and Sri Lanka. These events can be described as part of his globe-trotting diplomacy, which took him to Africa in January and five Latin American countries in late July, among other destinations. Media often interpret his style of diplomacy as a response to China's growing influence in various parts of the world.

However, those who peddle such an interpretation ignore long-term and strategic implications in favor of short-term and tactical maneuvers. For Japan, attaching importance to its relationships with South Asia, Africa, and Latin America is derived from its long-term national interests that reflect a game-changing direction in the world system in the mid-twenty-first century. This has little to do with the short-term situation in Japan-China relations.

Indo-Pacific Growth Hub

What will the world system be like in the coming decades of the twenty-first century? One of its major features will be the economic rise of the coastal areas of the Indian Ocean; with the continuing economic dynamism of the Pacific Ocean's coastal areas, the world will have ushered in what could be dubbed the Indo-Pacific age.

Looking back, Western Europe and North America were the world economy's key players from the nineteenth century to the third quarter of the twentieth century, a period that is called the Atlantic age. The last quarter of the twentieth century saw the rise of Pacific Rim economies, a development that led to the Pacific age or Asia-Pacific age. As we are 14 years into the twenty-first century, countries bordering on the Indian Ocean are joining their Pacific Rim peers as they expand economically.

Look at the International Monetary Fund's World Economic Outlook database or similar global economic data provided by other institutions and you will notice the location of countries with economies projected to grow by an annual average rate of 5% or more over the next several years. The growth regions are East Asia, comprising China and Southeast Asian countries, South Asia, including India and its neighbors, eastern and southern Africa, and the Pacific side of Latin America. Indeed, many developing countries Abe has traveled to are located in this Indo-Pacific region.

Over the past 20 years or so, the world's airport rankings in terms of international passenger traffic have undergone a drastic change. In 2000, only three airports relatively close to countries bordering the Indian Ocean—Hong Kong, Bangkok, and Singapore—were ranked in the top 30. However, in the January–April 2014 rankings, Dubai airport in the United Arab Emirates, which joined the club in 2007 for the first time, was ranked third. In addition to Hong Kong, Bangkok, and Singapore, the latest top 30 list also included Jakarta and Kuala Lumpur, both of which are in close proximity to the Indian Ocean.

If Japan is to prosper continuously, it should enhance its linkage with countries in these dynamic emerging regions and secure extensive business relations with them. The business sector of Japan is obviously aware of the importance of this necessity. That is why Abe has been accompanied by top executives of leading Japanese companies on his overseas tours, such as his visits to Africa and Latin America, as well as this weekend's tour of South Asia.

In other words, Japan should help ensure prosperity and peace in the Indo-Pacific region, as the region's high potential for further growth can help safeguard its long-term national interests.

The key to the realization of this major goal lies in the Japanese private sector's vitality and innovation. Without them, it will be impossible for Japan to stay competitive in the world's growth regions. On top of such private-sector efforts, the government should put in place a three-way global strategy.

First, the Japanese government should bolster its diplomatic activities, including the prime minister's "summit diplomacy." In the six-year period from 2006, when Koizumi Junichirō's administration ended, the country had six prime ministers, each of whom lasted about a year. During this period, very few Japanese leaders visited developing countries, especially those in the Indo-Pacific region. As a result, Japan's presence in this region of great importance inevitably waned. At that time, Japan was seen as having effectively "abandoned the game" from the beginning.

Globe-trotting Abe has dramatically changed Japan's diplomacy. When he visited the United States in February 2013, he declared in a speech that "Japan is back." In fact, thanks to his diplomatic efforts, Japan "has come back" to other parts of the world, too.

The second part of Japan's international strategy is to formulate frameworks for multilateral economic partnerships to facilitate the liberalization of trade and investment. For this, Japan should contribute to the establishment of a "high-quality" mechanism for trade liberalization under the proposed Trans-Pacific Partnership (TPP) free trade pact. A TPP breakthrough of this kind should be used as leverage to realize the geographical expansion for economic partnerships through related frameworks, such as the proposed Regional Comprehensive Economic Partnership involving East Asian countries, including China, India, and Japan.

ODA as a Peace-Building Instrument

The third part of the international strategy is to make better use of official development assistance (ODA), which often is referred to as the "best instrument" for Japan's diplomatic endeavors. How then should ODA be utilized to generate the best possible results in the Indo-Pacific age? I think we have three viable approaches.

The first is using ODA to ensure economic growth. In the Indo-Pacific region, Japan should assist those countries reaching middle-income status to move toward high-income or developed status. For example, Japan should extend cooperation in the fields of science and technology, high-level human resources development, and structural reforms to help middle-income countries avoid the so-called middle-income trap, a situation where they attain a certain income level but are stuck there.

Moreover, Japan should expedite cooperation in broader, region-wide infrastructure development by including low-income countries. To do so, it should present visions for infrastructure improvement covering a greater region, ranging from Southeast Asia to South Asia to Africa, while incorporating development projects tailored to individual countries.

The second ODA-related approach in the

Indo-Pacific age is to use ODA to enhance "human security." Economic growth is the best way to reduce poverty, yet growth without a human security framework could only widen the social divide, keep society vulnerable to disasters, and make the hardships of the disadvantaged even worse.

The Indo-Pacific age is just starting. Therefore, Japan needs to cooperate with developing countries in the Indo-Pacific region, particularly to help them, for example, strengthen disaster prevention and improve sanitation and hygiene practices so that every citizen, including women and the physically handicapped, will be able to live less precarious lives.

The third ODA approach is to use assistance for peace-building purposes as well. Earlier, I touched on the rise of the Indo-Pacific region as one of the attributes of the world system today. I cannot help discussing the destabilization of international politics and the lingering existence of areas prone to conflict as another factor in the current world system.

The world remains perturbed by the Ukraine conflict; civil wars in Syria, Iraq, and Libya; post-civil war turmoil and instability in Afghanistan, Somalia, South Sudan, and Mali; the fragile internal systems that have caused unabated disturbances in the Central African Republic and the Democratic Republic of the Congo; and the failure on the part of West African countries to quickly contain the Ebola outbreak.

Look at these highly volatile areas and the Indo-Pacific region on a map and you will find many countries in the former group that are either located in or close to the northern edge of the Indo-Pacific region. Should turmoil or instability in those volatile areas spread to the Indo-Pacific region, it would inevitably cast a shadow over the future of the region. Any threat of spreading turmoil to the Indo-Pacific region should be prevented, and efforts must be made to reduce troubled areas.

Military options could be needed to keep the Indo-Pacific region from being embroiled by conflict and turmoil. However, ODA as a non-military solution can play an extremely important role in this regard. Japan should help troubled areas through ODA. This is Japan's responsibility for the human community, but it also serves its own national interest of ensuring the safety of a region of great importance to Japan.

Originally published by The Yomiuri Shimbun in *The Japan News* "INSIGHTS into the WORLD" (9 September 2014).

A "Proactive Contribution to Peace" and the Right of Collective Self-Defense

III-(5)

The Development of Security Policy in the Abe Administration

Kitaoka Shinichi

ABSTRACT The Abe administration scored an impressive number of successes in the national security policy area, including creating the National Security Secretariat and formulating the National Security Strategy in 2013 and reimagining the principles governing the export of defense hardware (basically relaxing the three principles forbidding weaponry exports and expanding the allowable categories) in 2014. While this earned him the "hawk" label from critics, there were also many people who hoped these reforms would have a major policy impact. In reality, however, there were only modest easings of the unnatural constraints on Japanese national security policy and there is still much more that needs to be done.

The second cabinet headed by Abe Shinzō took office on 26 December 2012. Between then and the summer of 2014, there were many important developments in the area of security policy.

First, on 4 December 2013, the National Security Council (NSC) was established. The NSC's membership consists of four cabinet-level officials: the prime minister, the chief cabinet secretary, the foreign minister, and the defense minister. The National Security Secretariat, an administrative office that supports the NSC, was established on 7 January 2014, with former vice-minister for foreign affairs Yachi Shōtarō as its secretary-general. Thus, the NSC was established as an organ spanning government departments and shouldering the responsibility for an integrated foreign and security policy under the guidance of the prime minister.

In a similar vein, the Act on the Protection of Specially Designated Secrets was promulgated nine days after the establishment of the NSC, on 13 December. (The law was passed on 6 December. The floor vote in the House of Councillors, according to the *Yomiuri Shimbun* newspaper, was 130 ayes to 82 nays.) Information leaks are common in Japan, and they have acted as barriers to effective security policy, particularly when Japan has cooperated with other countries; the new law introduced harsher punishments for leaking secrets relating to security and is intended to safeguard such information.

On 17 December, the government, via the NSC and the cabinet, decided on a National Security Strategy to serve as a document guiding Japan's security and defense policies. This was the first document of its kind in post–World War II Japan—and nearly without precedent even prior to the war. The National Security Strategy presented a "proactive contribution to peace" and international cooperation as its central concepts.

The same day, the government reviewed its guidelines for the defense of Japan with the resulting document titled "National Defense Program Guidelines for FY2014 and Beyond." The National Defense Program Guidelines were first established in 1976 and were subsequently revised in 1995, 2004, and 2010, thus making this the fifth iteration. The central concept of the 2014 guidelines is "dynamic joint defense force."

On 1 April 2014, a new policy concerning the export of defense equipment—The Three Principles on Transfer of Defense Equipment and Technology—was established. For the past 40 years, Japan had virtually banned the export of arms, but this was changed with the new policy.

Next, on 15 May 2014, the Advisory Panel on Reconstruction of the Legal Basis for Security[1] submitted its report, which proposed a new constitutional interpretation permitting the partial exercise of the right of collective self-defense—a right whose invocation previous interpretations of the law deemed impossible. The report also noted defects in the current legal frameworks for individual self-defense and collective security and suggested remedies for these problems.

The government proceeded to debate the panel's suggestions, deciding on 1 July to set a new policy[2] for the system underpinning Japan's security, including partial exercise of the right of collective self-defense.

Based on this new policy, the government is attempting to revise the Japan-US defense guidelines; it also plans to move forward with legislation implementing the new policy in 2015.

Within the context of Japanese politics, all these changes were hard-fought, to the extent that, at the time, it was an open question whether even one of them could be achieved during a single cabinet's tenure. That the government succeeded in all of them is a tremendous accomplishment. What do these changes constitute, specifically? What made the overturning of the prevailing policies possible? How will the new policies affect Japan's future? These are the three questions that this essay will consider.

To state the conclusion up front: these policies, even if fully implemented, will contribute to global peace and security; far from leading Japan down a path of militarism. The problem is that such a shift in policy has, until now, been impossible. Thus, as this essay explains, the shift in security policy under the Abe administration, the peculiar nature of the security policy that has long prevailed in postwar Japan, will be revealed in stark contrast to what is now proposed.

The Act on the Protection of Specially Designated Secrets

Of these policy shifts, it was the Act on the Protection of Specially Designated Secrets that first became actual law. The Liberal Democratic Party (LDP) submitted the bill to the Diet on 25 October 2013, after first obtaining the agreement of its junior coalition partner, New Kōmeitō. While the bill was under deliberation, an amendment resulting from discussions between the Japan Restoration Party (JRP) and Your Party was passed, and these two parties came to support the bill (though the JRP eventually abstained on procedural grounds). The Democratic Party of Japan (DPJ) submitted a competing bill and opposed the government bill. Three other opposition parties, the Social Democratic Party (SDP), the People's Life Party, and the Japan Communist Party (JCP), also opposed the bill, but on 6 December, it passed with a comfortable majority and was promulgated on 13 December 2013.

Public opposition to the bill was strong—so much so that, after it became law, the approval rating for Abe's cabinet dropped by about 10 points. (According to a poll conducted by Jiji Press from 6 to 9 December, the approval rating was down 9.5 points from the previous month, to 47.1%. This was the first time since Prime Minister Abe's return to power that the government approval rating dipped below 50%, and the government disapproval rating also rose past 30% for the first time. However, it was the media that spurred public opposition to the law. As shown above, only three extremely minor opposition parties were completely against it, with two larger opposition parties supporting the bill and the leading opposition party—the DPJ—opposing the bill but not in its entirety. Indeed, this law had been debated for some time; under DPJ-led governments, expert panels were established and the issue was discussed. Having taken the reins of power, the DPJ had begun to feel a sense of responsibility about security.

The National Security Council

The next development to be discussed here, the National Security Council, has overcome the infamous tendency of Japanese governance to have individual departments that are internally strictly hierarchical but that externally conflict rather than coordinate with one another. The NSC is an organ intended to promote flexible and unified foreign and security policy. The view that such an organ is necessary has existed for some time.

However, it was not until the first Abe administration that actual work on the issue began. In December 2006, the Council on the Strengthening of the Functions of the Prime Minister's Office Regarding National Security[3] was created, with Abe as the council's president. Following discussions within the council, a bill was submitted to the legislature in April 2007. However, the subsequent instability of the political landscape resulted in the bill not becoming law.

The succeeding Fukuda Yasuo administration issued an official cabinet decision not to continue Abe's policy of designing a new security apparatus, on the grounds that the existing Security Council was functioning sufficiently well. The Security Council of the day was generally recognized as a mere rubber stamp for the reports and proposals of the administrative office in charge of it, and thus the decision by Fukuda's government was widely criticized.

Rather than post-Abe cabinets headed by the LDP, it was instead the DPJ-led administrations that came to power in 2009 that responded favorably to proposals for overhauling Japan's management of security-related issues. When, at the end of 2010, the National Defense Program Guidelines were being debated, the DPJ agreed that a National Security Council was necessary. On 30 November 2010, the DPJ released a document with the title "The Basic Stance of the Democratic Party of Japan." The sixth item in this text stated: "The DPJ will go forward with organizing intelligence capabilities and a crisis management system that are uniquely Japanese to serve as the bases for political judgment."

The 2010 National Defense Program Guidelines called for "strengthen[ing] [Japan's] information security system that extends across ministries and agencies so as to facilitate information sharing among them" and stated that "in the event of various contingencies, the Cabinet, led by the Prime Minister, will make rapid and appropriate decisions." The document also established that "after examining the current organization, functions, and structure of the Cabinet related to security issues, including the Security Council, the Government will establish a body in the Prime Minister's Office which will be responsible for national security policy coordination among relevant ministers and for providing advice to the Prime Minister."

As the culmination of these events leading up to the establishment of the NSC, in November 2013, the second Abe administration submitted a bill to the legislature. The bill passed with the support of not only the LDP's coalition partner, New Kōmeitō, but with also that of the DPJ, the JRP, Your Party, and others. (A total of 231 votes were cast on the floor of the House of Councillors on 27 November with a result of 213 ayes and 18 nays.)

However, some negativity toward the bill coming from among the ranks of the civil service could not be ignored. For instance, some criticized the bill on the grounds that the hierarchical and partitioned nature of the Japanese government was so entrenched that the creation of an NSC would not eliminate it. To be sure, this administrative tendency would not vanish overnight. That said, unified governance would become vastly simpler if, for example, the defense and foreign ministries came together at the section chief level to share information and policies, rather than each ministry first building consensus internally and only then meeting and reconciling their respective positions.

Another criticism was that Japan's intelligence-gathering capabilities were lacking, so the establishment of an NSC would be pointless. Japan's intelligence-gathering apparatus is indeed deficient. But it will be bolstered if the NSC is established as a consumer of intelligence that, so to speak, places orders with that apparatus for the intelligence Japan requires, providing the demand that should create its own supply. The notion that the NSC was pointless because decent intelligence-gathering organs did not exist was patently reactionary.

Yet another view was that there would be no one suitable to assume the role of secretary-general of the NSC. However, with the NSC now in existence, former foreign affairs vice-minister Yachi—a man with the full confidence of the prime minister—is performing this function admirably.

Simply put, those criticisms were nothing but

expressions of a cynicism that stems from a mentality inherent in the bureaucracy, which clings to precedent and wants to maintain its own authority. If the NSC were to come into being, then the bureaucracy would be forced to relinquish some of its power. At the time, many civil servants were negatively disposed toward this prospect. Such passive resistance to change, which is inherent in the bureaucracy, cannot be broken without political will. The general consensus is now that, because Abe and his cabinet used their political will to act decisively, the NSC is functioning comparatively well.

The National Security Strategy and an Active Contribution to Peace

The Council on Security and Defense Capabilities (Security and Defense Council, not to be confused with the NSC) was formed as a panel with the purpose of formulating a National Security Strategy. (The decision to create the council was made on 10 September 2013, and the body first met two days later.) The author of the present essay served as the council's chair. The rest of its membership consisted of three other scholars; a former vice-minister of defense; a former chief of staff, Joint Staff Office of the JSDF; a former ambassador to the United Kingdom; and a special advisor to the cabinet (former vice-minister for foreign affairs Yachi).

The council had two duties: to draw up the National Security Strategy and to draft the National Defense Program Guidelines. The National Security Strategy is a document that sets the course for Japan's security policy and diplomacy—something that did not previously exist. Before World War II, there were security-related documents such as the Imperial Defense Policy (adopted in 1907, 1918, 1923, and 1936), but all of these were essentially just the respective positions of the Imperial Army and the Imperial Navy, written independently and displayed side by side and thus did not present a unified vision. The army considered the Soviet Union to be the hypothetical enemy in its scenarios, with the navy instead imagining war with the United States. Japan did not possess sufficient might to resist either of these enemies, and yet its official defense

policies envisioned scenarios in which Japan fought both. It is thus clear that these were not documents with any true efficacy.

In terms of documents dealing with both diplomacy and defense, there was, among others, the 1936 Fundamentals of National Policy (*Kokusaku no kijun*), but this, too, did nothing more than compile the respective positions of the Foreign Ministry, the army, the navy, and various other organs.

Postwar, there was a "Basic Policy for National Defense" issued in 1957, which described, inter alia, cooperation with the United Nations, a gradual increase in defensive power commensurate with Japan's strength as a nation, the gentle encouragement of patriotism, and the Japan-US alliance as a bedrock. To that extent, this policy was a decent start. But it was a brief document of only around 10 lines, and it no longer plays any meaningful role in Japanese policy.

To remedy this situation, the Security and Defense Council, which drew up the current National Security Strategy, introduced within that document the concept of "a proactive contribution to peace" (literally, "active pacifism" in Japanese). This phrase may sound unusual, but it did express one thing clearly: A passive form of pacifism would not do. Passive pacifism—a passive contribution to peace—is, simply put, the notion that disarmament is the road to peace. It is the idea that the fewer arms in existence, the better and safer the world would be, and it is the ideal of Article 9, Paragraph 2 of the Japanese Constitution. However, a balance of power is necessary for peace in the real world; the idea that disarmament is the road to peace is, as a rule, a delusion.

The second thing that the phrase implies is that, for there to be peace, countries must not withdraw into themselves but should instead take active steps. Since the postwar years of the 1950s, Japan has made strides in offering ODA support and contributing to the stability and development of the East Asian region. Development occurred because of stability, leading to the emergence of middle classes and, eventually, democratization. Furthermore, since 1992, Japan has participated in peacekeeping operations (PKO), thus contributing to global stability. From the latter half of the 1990s onward, Japan has advocated the concept of "human security" at the UN and other venues, contributed funding for human security, and appealed that the security of the masses of the world's poorest countries is the foundation for security in the world as a whole.

It is as an extension of these actions that Japan has named the idea of further contributions to global stability "a proactive contribution to peace." Moreover, the new phrase accords with the preamble to the Japanese Constitution, which proposes that Japan should not be indifferent to the international society.

However, the idea that Japan should actively contribute to peace in some respects recalls the concept of "peace enforcement" espoused by former UN secretary-general Boutros Boutros-Ghali. It might also be misinterpreted as the idea that Japan will engage in the creation of peace all by itself. Therefore, it has stressed that Japan will act in concert with the rest of international society and referred to the idea in English as "a more proactive contribution to peace."

One aspect of the Security and Defense Council that deserves note is the style of the debates within it. Typically, in Japan the prime minister or another minister of state will commission an advisory committee, which will submit a report that will then be cherry-picked—policy thus being decided through the political process.

In this particular council, however, the procedure went differently. Panels of experts discussed issues two or three times, but, in this case, the opinions expressed in those meetings were then taken up for debate in joint meetings between the experts and five cabinet ministers, namely the prime minister, deputy prime minister, chief speaker of the cabinet, foreign minister, and defense minister. Next, there was another round of two or three expert panel meetings, followed by another joint meeting with cabinet members. Finally, the cabinet made its decision. As a result, there was no such document as "The Report of the Expert Panel."

The prototype for this sort of council can in fact be found in the era of DPJ-led governments. When the National Defense Program Guidelines

were revised at the end of 2010, a meeting was held among four ministerial-level officials (the ministers for foreign affairs, defense, and finance, as well as the chief cabinet secretary). One scholar (the author)[4] also participated, so the conclusions concerning how to revise the guidelines were drawn from several de facto "4+1" meetings. Thus, these meetings benefited from some apolitical wisdom; the politicians and the experts joined forces to make a decision. The LDP has continued the DPJ's stance of gathering wisdom from those other than politicians and civil servants.

The National Defense Program Guidelines and Dynamic Joint Defense Force

The National Defense Program Guidelines were then revised based on the discussions that had occurred in the Security and Defense Council. Such revisions often happen when there has been a shift in the international situation. The guidelines were first established in 1976 and—after a considerable interval—revised in 1995, 2004, and 2010.

It is because the international situation has changed and Japan's roles on the world stage have shifted considerably that new guidelines have been decided relatively frequently since 1995. All decisions to review the guidelines have been grounded on previously established expert panels.

In 1995, the fundamental question was whether the Japan-US alliance was still necessary after the end of the Cold War. Prime Minister Hosokawa established an expert panel in February 1994 (its chair was Higuchi Hirotarō), and the panel submitted its findings to Hosokawa's successor's successor, Prime Minister Murayama in August of the same year. In the intervening period between the establishment of the panel and the publication of its findings, there were increasing suspicions that North Korea had been developing nuclear weapons since late 1993. Because of this and other reasons, it was a foregone conclusion that the panel's recommendation would be that the Japan-US alliance was still necessary after the end of the Cold War. The 1995 guidelines (officially headed "The National Defense Program Guidelines for FY1996 and Beyond") were adopted at the end of the year. The Hashimoto administration's redefinition of the Japan-US alliance, among other things, happened with these guidelines in effect.

In 2004, the fundamental question was what form Japanese defense should take during an era in which 9/11-style attacks were feared. The idea that Japan, too, should play a role in dealing with terrorism, based on the October 2001 Anti-Terrorism Special Measures Law and other policies, was included in the 2004 guidelines ("The National Defense Program Guidelines for FY2005 and Beyond"). Meanwhile, the 2010 guidelines ("The National Defense Program Guidelines for FY2011 and Beyond") were predicated on Chinese expansionism.[5]

It has already been described how scholars were unofficially involved in the drafting of the 2010 guidelines because of the criticism that previous guidelines had ultimately been drafted at the discretion of civil servants from the Ministry of Defense who allegedly did not adequately incorporate the findings of the expert panel reports.

The area to the southwest of Japan was the focus of the 2010 guidelines. The plan was to shift from the previous concept of a "basic defense capability" or "basic defense force" that was meant to counter incursions by the Soviet Union to something more focused on Japan's southwest. To do so, it was necessary to cut Ground Self-Defense Force (JGSDF) personnel and to divert the cost savings to the Maritime and Air Self-Defense Forces (JMSDF and JASDF, respectively), as well as to redeploy the Self-Defense Forces (JSDF) overall, concentrating personnel in the southwestern area of Japan. However, the JGSDF was strongly opposed to the cuts, so the eventual personnel reduction was only 1,000 troops. There was also strong opposition to the JSDF deployment shifts. To counter this opposition, the concept of "dynamic defense" was adopted mainly to accelerate troop movements to the southwest.

The 2013 guidelines were unchanged in their focus on the southwest. The new guidelines planned for some upgrades to JMSDF and JASDF equipment. However, the LDP was opposed to basing its policy on ideas the DPJ had conceived,

so it explained these plans using its own notion of a "dynamic joint defense force." This was, however, progress in the sense that the idea of a more integrated structure was included.

However, the LDP has strong ties with the JGSDF—traditionally the JSDF's core force—and, as a result, the JGSDF also received an increase of 5,000 troops.

There were various debates at the time, with some arguing that Japan should abandon the concept of a defense-only posture, or that—rather than responding to North Korean missile threats with missile defense systems alone—Japan should possess offensive or counteroffensive capabilities. However, debate on these questions was shelved.

That is why the 2013 guidelines attempt to respond to threats from China and others but largely maintain the status quo. As will be seen from the history of the Advisory Panel on Reconstruction of the Legal Basis for Security presented in the next section, the National Defense Program Guidelines themselves were previously regarded as mere pieces of paper, and only their appendices—that is, the lists of the arms with which Japan should equip itself—were considered of any consequence. However, it will be shown that this is not now the case, and the understanding of international affairs described in the guidelines, among other things, is also important.

The Principles Concerning Defense Equipment Exports

On 1 April 2014, the Three Principles on the Transfer of Defense Equipment and Technology were established, thus revising previously strict regulations on exports and setting a course toward allowing overseas trade to contribute to peace.

The former Three Principles on Arms Exports were first mentioned in a reply by Prime Minister Satō Eisaku in an April 1967 meeting of the House of Representatives Auditing Committee. Satō stated that Japan would not export arms to Communist countries, those under UN sanctions, those that were parties to international disputes, or those likely to become such parties. However, in February 1976, Prime Minister Miki Takeo gave a reply in the House of Representatives Budget Committee stating that Japan would additionally "refrain" from exporting arms to regions other than those mentioned previously by Satō. Thus, in the repetition of government replies to questions in the Diet, somehow the Three Principles had transformed into a de facto statement that Japan would have no arms exports whatsoever. Subsequently, in January 1983, the Nakasone administration's chief cabinet secretary, Gotōda Masaharu, stated in a speech that the provision of military technology to the US, Japan's ally, would be treated as an exception, and in November of that year, Japan and the US exchanged a bilateral document concerning the provision of arms to the US. Other arms exports, however, were even more severely restricted, becoming virtually forbidden.

This led to some absurd practices. For instance, when the JSDF were dispatched on PKO missions, their troops would, of course, be carrying weapons overseas. Every single time this happened, the chief cabinet secretary would have to release a statement to the effect that doing so did not violate the Three Principles on Arms Exports.

The recent revision of the Three Principles, like other recent changes in Japanese defense policy, was debated from the era of DPJ-led administrations onward. There were two reasons for the change.

First, the development of modern weapons is extremely expensive, and thus it is frequently conducted in international joint-development projects. If Japan were to participate in such projects, it would then be engaging in the export and import of weapons or weapons technologies. Thus, the first reason the principles were changed is that it was unavoidable due to the considerable cost of weapons.

The second reason is related to Japan's goal of a proactive contribution to peace. The following scenario is at least conceivable: A certain country is subject to a threat from another country and requires arms for defensive purposes. Japan is able to supply such arms at a reasonable price, so offering them would be more conducive to peace than not offering them.

Underpinned by this type of thinking, the word "arms" was replaced with the term "defense equipment." This made it possible to provide defensive equipment—with limitations on transfers to countries other than the US and only after assessment of the country and the situation. Even if this new export regime were to develop further, Japan would still remain the country with the most limits on arms exports of all the major world powers.

The Advisory Panel on Reconstruction of the Legal Basis for Security Submits Its Report

The Advisory Panel on Reconstruction of the Legal Basis for Security (the Panel) was established in April 2007 by the first Abe administration. (Its chairman was former vice-minister for foreign affairs and later ambassador to the US Yanai Shunji.) As Prime Minister Abe had resigned before the Panel could complete it, the report was submitted to Prime Minister Fukuda Yasuo in 2008. Prime Minister Fukuda put the report on the back burner, and his administration did not consider its findings.

Having returned to power in 2012, Abe reestablished the Panel in February of the following year. The membership of the body in 2013 was nearly identical to its membership in 2007–08. However, the Panel's president, Yanai, was abroad—after having become president of the International Tribunal for the Law of the Sea—so it continued its discussions while the present essay's author acted as chair. Finally, on 15 May 2014, the new report was ready for submission.

The goal of the Panel was to consider whether there are any flaws in the current legal system for security, and, if there are, to suggest how these should be corrected. The Panel did not discuss only matters related to the right of collective self-defense. It also touched on defects in the law concerning the exercise of the right of individual self-defense, something already considered to be constitutionally permitted. It is simply that, in a variety of areas, the Cabinet Legislation Bureau's (CLB) interpretation that the right of collective self-defense cannot be exercised has frequently acted as an impediment to establishing an effective legal system for security. Because of this, the Panel ended up devoting considerable space to the topic of collective self-defense. Discussed below are these issues as they relate to, in order, the right of individual self-defense, the right of collective self-defense, and collective security.

1. Concerning the right of individual self-defense, there are issues that exist in the so-called gray zone. For instance, the prime minister is permitted to order defense mobilization in the event that Japan has suffered an armed attack, but this refers to cases in which an organized, planned encroachment by a foreign country has occurred. Nowadays, there are often times when it is impossible to tell whether an incursion counts as that sort of clear invasion. So-called low-intensity conflicts are much more likely to happen. But the Self-Defense Forces Act does not stipulate anything regarding the right of self-defense in such cases. The Panel has recommended that this state of affairs be resolved by all means necessary.

2. Concerning the exercise of the right of collective self-defense, the Panel's report advocates that constitutional provisions be reconsidered as follows: Article 9, Paragraph 2 of the Japanese Constitution bans the maintenance of "land, sea and air forces, as well as other war potential." When the Constitution was written in 1946, this was interpreted to mean that Japan could possess no armed forces whatsoever. However, in 1954, another interpretation was proposed: Because it is an inherent right of sovereign states to possess the minimum level of armed forces they require, there was no such sweeping ban. This interpretation was accepted as valid in the Supreme Court's 1959 decision in the Sunagawa case. However, in October 1972, the government interpretation became that "the minimum level required" referred specifically to the right of individual self-defense— that is, the right to repel an attack on one's own country— and that, therefore, if another closely related country were to be attacked, the right to exercise force to remove the threat would not be included in the "minimum level."

The Panel believes that there are substantial problems with this interpretation. With the exception of the military superpowers, the majority of countries in the world are incapable of defending themselves with only their own

strength—that is, with only the right of individual self-defense. These countries thus cooperate with other states with which they are in close relationships to maintain security. Consequently, Article 51 of the UN Charter permits all states to exercise the rights of both individual and collective self-defense. In the case of Japan, it may have indeed been possible to protect the nation while exercising only the right of individual self-defense during a time when the position of the US was overwhelming. However, this has now become difficult. The 1972 interpretation is unacceptable both in theory and in practice. To begin with, "the minimum level required" changes, depending on developments in military technology and international affairs, making it impossible to draw a hard and fast line in legislation. This fact forms the core of the Panel's recommendations. Doubts have been raised about amending the interpretation of the Constitution in the way the Panel recommends, but, compared to the change that happened in 1954, the shift would be small, so the Panel considers that there would be no real problem in doing so.

Based on this, the Panel recommended that, if a country in a close relationship with Japan suffers an armed attack and that country requests Japan's cooperation, and if leaving the situation as it stands would likely have a significant effect on Japan's security, then the prime minister— after deliberations with the NSC—should be able to make a determination of necessity and proportionality in a comprehensive manner and gain the consent of the Diet—either before or after the fact—and exercise the right of collective self-defense. In such cases, the Panel recommended that Japan gain the consent of countries en route to the conflict area if Japan's forces should pass through their territories.

There are numerous concrete examples of circumstances that would be covered by this, including (a) if US vessels were attacked outside Japanese territory but close to Japan, and (b) if sea lanes were closed off, such as with mines. But further discussion of these shall be omitted here.

3. Concerning collective security and peacekeeping operations (PKOs), the Panel has advocated the following. Article 9, Paragraph 1 of

the Japanese Constitution stipulates that Japan will not use, or threaten to use, armed force as a means of settling international disputes. However, the phrase "international disputes" referred to here comes from the Kellogg-Briand Pact (1928) and the UN Charter (1945)—which were the sources of the language in the provision—and should be interpreted as international disputes in which Japan is one of the directly involved parties. Consequently, there is no constitutional restriction on participation in collective security or PKOs. In terms of PKOs in particular, a problem would arise only with regard to the use of weapons, and it is extremely unlikely there would be any exercise of national sovereignty or large-scale force in such cases. Until now, Japan has not permitted itself to use weapons to defend other countries' forces or civilians or to eliminate interference with JSDF operations; the Panel advocates that this be changed to the UN standard.

Based on concepts such as those described above, the Panel's report calls for revising the Self-Defense Forces Act, the PKO Act, and the Act on Measures to Ensure the Peace and Security of Japan in Perilous Situations in Areas Surrounding Japan, as well as for taking further legislative steps as necessary. These bills would be submitted by the cabinet (though in theory they could also be submitted as private member bills), and they would conflict with the current constitutional interpretation of the CLB. Therefore, it would be necessary first to make some adjustments to constitutional interpretations within the cabinet, as the Abe administration would go on to do.

In any case, if the cabinet or an individual Diet member were to submit a bill, if the Diet were to debate it, and if it were to become law, then it would be part of the democratic process to submit any concerns about the law to the judiciary's discretion. There are some in the opposition in the Diet who argue that the interpretation of the Constitution should not be changed via the cabinet, but they are off the mark. The criticism that the change is sudden is also entirely beside the point and inaccurate: There have been discussions since 2007, and the Panel released its first report in 2008, which already included the gist of what is contained in the 2014 report.

A Cabinet Decision Relating to the Legal System for Security

On 15 May 2014, the day the Panel submitted its report, Prime Minister Abe held a press conference. He stated that he supported the part of the report that recommended permitting the exercise of the right of collective self-defense, he agreed with several of the Panel's assessments that there were defects in the legal system relating to the right of individual self-defense, and he intended to implement the recommended policies via a cabinet decision. Compared to the report itself, Abe's statements were much more tepid; he devoted little attention to collective security and PKOs.

This was in deference to New Kōmeitō, which is extremely cautious when it comes to security. However, New Kōmeitō is not negatively disposed toward PKOs in absolutely all cases. Thus, discussion of PKOs was subsequently reinvigorated, albeit with conditions, through discussions between the LDP and New Kōmeitō, such as those in which the latter agreed to permit so-called *kaketsuke-keigo* (defined as coming to the aid of PKO troops from other countries and civilians under fire).

The focus of the discussions between the two ruling parties was whether to permit the exercise of the right of collective self-defense. Traditionally, New Kōmeitō's position was that cooperation with the US military in Japan's environs, among other things, could probably be dealt with merely as extensions of the right of individual self-defense. As the Panel's report made clear, the expansion of the right of individual self-defense is far more dangerous than exercising collective self-defense and should thus not be permitted. In response to LDP arguments to this effect, New Kōmeitō eventually settled on a stance of partial approval of collective self-defense.

As a result of this change in New Kōmeitō's stance, the cabinet issued a decision concerning the future of the legal system for security on 1 July. This decision permitted—with limitations—the exercise of the right of collective self-defense in circumstances that pose an existential threat to Japan, in responses to incursions that fall short of armed attacks, in *kaketsuke-keigo* during PKOs, and in other possible actions.

The *Yomiuri Shimbun* newspaper and the *Sankei Shimbun* newspaper supported these developments, as did the *Nihon Keizai Shimbun* newspaper, more or less. Other newspapers, however, including the *Asahi*, *Mainichi*, and *Tokyo*, were strongly opposed. Public opinion was strongly against the changes; the government approval rating dropped somewhere between 5 points and 10 points. (According to a poll that Jiji Press conducted from 11 to 14 July, the government's approval rating was down 6.4 points from the previous month, to 44.6%, the lowest ever during Abe's second tenure as prime minister.)

Looking at each of the non-LDP Japanese political parties, members of the ruling coalition partner New Kōmeitō were generally in favor of the changes in security policy, as were those of the conservative opposition parties the Party for Future Generations (which consists of members who broke away from the JRP), Your Party, and the JRP. Members of the Unity Party (which broke away from Your Party) were somewhat critical. The DPJ was also negative toward the changes overall, although there is a faction within it that supports them, and it has yet to work out a clear position. The opposition microparties—the People's Life Party, the SDP, and the JCP—were all opposed. In other words, the composition of support and opposition to the cabinet decision resembled that concerning the Act on the Protection of Specially Designated Secrets; the two cases also similar in that the media and public opinion were more negative than the stances of the various political parties.

Conclusion

As mentioned above, the Act on the Protection of Specially Designated Secrets is, compared to legislation in other major countries, perfectly typical—if not down-right tepid. It is also clear that the NSC, the National Security Strategy, the National Defense Program Guidelines, the principles concerning defense equipment exports, the Advisory Panel on Reconstruction of the Legal Basis for Security's report, and the recent cabinet decision concerning security are all, relative to what exists in other major countries, more pacifist.

Of the major world powers, no government

other than those of China and the two Koreas, criticizes Japan's policies. The countries of Southeast Asia and others subject to Chinese pressure in particular are supportive of Japan. Even China's own response has not been quite so hard-line. There have been no bilateral top-level summits between Japan and China for some time. Though this atypical state of affairs has continued, what China wants is for Japan to recognize the Senkaku Islands as a territorial issue and for the prime minister to promise not to visit the Yasukuni Shrine. In other words, China's demands are unconnected to security. Even in South Korea, there are loud voices calling for a resolution of historical issues, and yet the country itself has not objected to Japan's security policy outright.

Upon reflection, this is only natural; all countries engage in the same behaviors, so there is no reason to criticize Japan for exhibiting them.

Therefore, the strongest opposition to Japan's security policy comes from Japan's own public opinion and the media. The passive pacifism of Article 9, Paragraph 2 of the Japanese Constitution has become stubbornly fixed in the minds of the Japanese people. Some in the media, too, complacently toe the same line. There has been no change since—during a time when US power was absolute—the media faced off against the government with concerns that Japan could be drawn into US wars. It is quite interesting indeed that the same media that report on tensions in the South China Sea, practically daily, are so skeptical of any suggestion by Prime Minister Abe that Japan's security environment has worsened.

The media also criticize the liberal faction of the LDP as impotent, and they similarly criticize the opposition parties as powerless. However, LDP liberals have merely chosen not to turn a blind eye to China's rise and its aggressive policies. The DPJ, for its part, has experienced holding the reins of power, so it is no longer capable of saying things that are quite so irresponsible. It once again seems that it is the politicians who are facing reality.

There are not quite so many new things that Japan is now able to do as the result of the series of policies described in this essay, as one would understand from the way the media describe them. However, it is still profoundly meaningful that Japan is questioning the ideas about the Japanese Constitution that are at the root of Japan's merely passive contribution to peace, which has persisted until today, as well as meaningful that the country is now moving toward putting the document to use in a way that conforms with reality. In other words, one giant leap—from an idealistic sense of safety conferred by worship of the Constitution to a realistic system for true security—is what could give the recent policy changes real significance. On that note, it appears safe to say that great changes are indeed in the process of being achieved.

Kitaoka, Shinichi. "A 'Proactive Contribution to Peace' and the Right of Collective Self-Defense: The Development of Security Policy in the Abe Administration." *Asia-Pacific Review* 21:2 (2014), 1–18. © Nakasone Peace Institute reprinted by permission of Taylor & Francis Ltd, https://www.tandfonline.com on behalf of Nakasone Peace Institute.

Notes

1. The Advisory Panel on Reconstruction of the Legal Basis for Security consisted of 14 experts: Iwama Yōko, professor, National Graduate Institute for Policy Studies; Okazaki Hisahiko, director, Okazaki Institute; Kasai Noriyuki, chairman emeritus, Central Japan Railway Company; Kitaoka Shinichi, president, International University of Japan, and professor, National Graduate Institute for Policy Studies; Sakamoto Kazuya, professor, Graduate School of Law and Politics, Osaka University; Sase Masamori, professor emeritus, National Defense Academy; Satō Ken, president, Institute for International Policy Studies (former vice-minister of defense); Tanaka Akihiko, president, Japan International Cooperation Agency; Nakanishi Hiroshi, professor, Graduate School of Law, Faculty of Law, Kyoto University; Nishi Osamu, professor emeritus, Komazawa University; Nishimoto Tetsuya, chairman, Self-Defense Force Veterans Association (former Self-Defense Forces Joint Staff Council chairman); Hosoya Yūichi, professor, Keio University; Murase Shinya, professor emeritus, Sophia University; Yanai Shunji, president, International Tribunal for the Law of the Sea (former vice-minister of foreign affairs).

2. "Cabinet Decision on the Development of Seamless Security."

3. The Council on the Strengthening of the Functions of the Prime Minister's Office Regarding National Security: 14 members, including Prime Minister Abe:

Council president

Abe Shinzō	Prime Minister
Aihara Hironori	Chairman of the Board, Transcutaneous Technologies, Inc.
Ishihara Nobuo	President, Research Institute for Local Government
Okazaki Hisahiko	Director, Okazaki Institute
Ogawa Kazuhisa	Military Analyst
Kitaoka Shinichi	Professor, University of Tokyo
Koike Yuriko	Special Advisor to the Prime Minister (for national security affairs) (Acting chair of the council)
Sassa Atsuyuki	Former Director General, Cabinet Security Affairs Office
Satō Ken	President, Institute for International Policy Studies
Shiokawa Masajūrō	Former Chief Cabinet Secretary
Shiozaki Yasuhisa	Chief Cabinet Secretary
Massaki Hajime	Special Advisor, Nippon Life Insurance Company
Morimoto Satoshi	Chairman, Institute of World Studies, Takushoku University
Yanai Shunji	Judge, International Tribunal for the Law of the Sea

Source: The Prime Minister's Office

4. A team of several young scholars was organized under the author's direction and held symposia with civil servants from the foreign, defense, and finance ministries. The 4+1 meetings were held to discuss the research conducted in the symposia, as was a session of the Security Council. As the final step of the process, the cabinet officially accepted the findings of these meetings.

5. In 2009, the Asō administration established an expert panel with the aim of revising the guidelines at the end of the year, and the panel submitted its report. However, the general election in September resulted in a DPJ victory, so a new expert panel was established, and it formed the basis for the new guidelines that were eventually formulated. The conclusions in the report of the 2009 expert panel did, however, resemble those of the 2010 panel.

Bibliography

Cabinet Secretariat. "Kuni no sonritsu o mattou shi, kokumin o mamoru tame no kireme no nai anzen hosho hosei no seibi ni tsuite" [Cabinet Decision on Development of Seamless Security Legislation to Ensure Japan's Survival and Protect Its People]. http://www.cas.go.jp/jp/gaiyou/jimu/pdf/anpo-hosei.pdf.

Prime Minister's Office, The. "Anzen hoshō to bōeiryoku ni kansuru kondankai no kaisai ni tsuite" [Regarding the Council on Security and Defense Capabilities]. http://kantei.go.jp/jp/singi/anzen_bouei/pdf/konkyo.pdf.

———. "Press Conference by Prime Minister Abe." 15 May 2014. https://japan.kantei.go.jp/96_abe/statement/201405/0515kaiken.html.

Reorienting Japan? Security Transformation under the Second Abe Cabinet

Nakanishi Hiroshi

ABSTRACT This paper reviews the Japanese foreign policy under the second Abe administration from the mid-term perspective of early 2015. Though the national security legislation has yet to be enacted, it seems Abe has accomplished much in a relatively short time, such as (i) establishment of the Japanese National Security Council, (ii) formulation of the National Security Strategy, (iii) revision of the National Defense Program Guidelines, and (iv) Cabinet approval of a new interpretation of the Constitution's Article 9. This paper discusses how these achievements were consistent with the tendency to de-emphasize Japan's involvement in issues on the Asian continent and to instead be more involved in that broad region from Southeast Asia to the Indian Ocean.

In this essay, I provide an overview of the major security and defense changes achieved by the second Abe Shinzō cabinet and analyze why Abe was reasonably successful. Based on an analysis of the major Japanese strategic guidelines, the new National Security Council (NSC), and legal arguments on interpretations of the Constitution, I argue that Abe's security and defense reforms are not unique to his ideology or political stance but follow the general trend Japan has pursued in the last two decades. What is unique about Abe is his drive and political tact to ram through these reforms. These reforms are also suited to shifting Japan's geopolitical focus away from the Asian continent and toward the Eurasian littoral and maritime areas, where Japan sees more economic and political opportunities without the historical controversies it faces in East Asia.

When Abe Shinzō returned as prime minister in December 2012, foreign and security policy was not the thing that most concerned the Japanese people. After the severe economic recession that followed the Lehman Brothers shock, the 11 March earthquake in eastern Japan, and the revolving door phenomenon of six prime ministers since 2006, the Japanese people voted for the comeback of the Liberal Democratic Party (LDP)

cabinet, hoping for the recovery of stability and confidence. After the short-lived and generally disappointing mismanagement of the Democratic Party of Japan (DPJ) government, the LDP was viewed as a return to stability and economic recovery. Abe's own comeback did not augur well initially, as people remembered his abrupt resignation in September 2006 when he first served as prime minister and his well-known enthusiasm for dealing with foreign and national security policy rather than domestic economic management.

Now, after more than two years as prime minister, Abe has maintained a relatively high popular approval rating and has succeeded in stemming the initial skepticism. No doubt, the so-called Abenomics has been the key policy that has allowed Abe to rule in general comfort. But he has already achieved several important security and defense reforms, overriding domestic political debate.

In this essay, I provide a brief overview of the major security and defense changes the second Abe cabinet has implemented and analyze why Abe was reasonably successful despite domestic criticism. I argue that Abe's security and defense reforms are not unique to his ideology or political stance but follow the general trend Japan has pursued in the last two decades. What is most unique about Abe is his drive and political tact to ram through these reforms. At the same time, Abe's conservative ideology on history and education has gathered criticism and wariness from both within and without, leading Japan's geopolitical focus away from the Asian continent and toward the southwest maritime areas. There, Japan sees a more economic frontier and political associability with much less historical controversy.

As a result, Abe's "proactive contribution to peace" policies do not mean simply moving away from the postwar Yoshida Doctrine of not resorting to force beyond Japan's borders. Combined with an overall foreign policy reformulation, Abe's security and defense policies both reflect and initiate a long-term foreign policy change that goes beyond the traditional East/West dichotomy or simplistic postwar orthodoxy/revisionism.

Security and Defense Reforms under the Abe Cabinet

In fewer than 30 months since returning to power, Prime Minister Abe has undertaken more security and defense reforms than any previous prime minister. The Abe cabinet has changed the doctrinal, institutional, and legal frameworks of Japanese security and defense policy. Whether one likes or dislikes these changes— according to recent polls, 51% of the Japanese public remain wary of the collective defense legislation, against 31% supporting it—the Abe cabinet unquestionably has been quite efficient in bringing these changes about (*Nikkei Asian Review* 2015).

But extraordinary efficiency does not mean the changes made are truly novel or pathbreaking. Indeed, despite the rhetoric of the administration, the changes made are more the result of the debate and incremental policy changes that took place in the last two decades. The reforms under the Abe cabinet, at least so far, are more of the climax than the start of the security reforms.

The security and defense reforms under the current Abe cabinet can be summarized in four categories: (1) doctrinal changes published in the key strategic documents, such as the National Security Strategy (NSS 2013) and National Defense Program Guidelines (NDPG 2013); (2) institutional changes by establishing the NSC; (3) legal changes—revising previous interpretations of the Constitution and other legislative and regulatory codes; and (4) operational changes in formulating new Japan-US defense guidelines.

Doctrinal Changes

Just after returning to power, Abe's cabinet expressed its willingness to revise the NDPG issued by the previous DPJ government in 2010. Following a decision by the newly established NSC, the cabinet, on 17 December 2013, approved the NSS and NDPG documents and the new Medium-Term Defense Program (MTDP 2013), the last of which directs defense procurement plans for the next five years.

Before this, the successive NDPGs operated as the only basic strategic document for Japanese security and defense policy. The new NSS enlarges the "strategic" part of its predecessor, while the 2013 NDPG revises the "defense policy" part of the same document.

The key phrase of the NSS, the basic formulation of the security doctrine of the Abe cabinet in general, is *sekkyokuteki heiwashugi* (proactive contribution to peace). According to the NSS (2013), surrounded by an increasingly severe security environment and confronted by complex and grave national security challenges, it has become indispensable for Japan to make more proactive efforts in line with the principle of international cooperation. Japan cannot secure its own peace and security by itself, and the international community expects Japan to play a more proactive role for peace and stability in the world, in a way commensurate with its national capabilities.

The reference to an "increasingly severe security environment" is meant, the NSS states, to highlight global issues: changes in the global balance of power, proliferation of weapons of mass destruction, international terrorism, risks to global commons, human security challenges, and economic risks. It also refers to Asia-Pacific regional issues, specifically North Korea's military buildup and China's rise.

The NSS assessment generally reflects the Japanese people's current mindset. An opinion poll conducted by the Cabinet Office shows that the Japanese people have become more interested in the Self-Defense Forces (SDFs) and defense affairs in the last two decades. Those who are interested increased from 56.8% in 1994 to 71.5% in 2015, and those who are not interested declined from 40.8% in 1994 to 28.2%. The chief reason given by those who are interested has also shifted, from "disaster relief operations and other matters closely connected to people's lives" (36.3% in 1997) to "problems relating to Japanese peace and independence" (46.1%).

According to the same poll, the top five major concerns of the public are: China's military modernization and maritime activities (60.5%); the situation on the Korean Peninsula (52.7%); activities of international terrorist organizations (42.6%); the military posture of US forces in areas surrounding Japan (36.7%); and relations between the United States and China (32%). In addition, an interesting change has occurred in the leading agenda, from the Korean Peninsula (the top concern in 2012 at 64.9%) to Chinese military modernization (second in 2012 at 46%). The survey conforms with other polls in Japan, suggesting that the NSS follows the general trend of public feelings about the deterioration of Japan's security environment, particularly on matters relating to peace and independence and China's rise and its maritime activities, rather than solely reflecting the Abe cabinet's perceptions.

In order to cope with these changes in the security environment, the NSS proposes to: (1) strengthen and expand Japan's own capabilities and roles; (2) strengthen the Japan-US alliance; (3) strengthen diplomacy and security cooperation with Japan's partners for peace and stability in the international community; and (4) proactively contribute to international efforts for peace and stability.

The 2013 NDPG provides more details. It introduces the concept of "Dynamic Joint Defense Force," replacing the "Dynamic Defense Force" concept proposed in 2010 under the DPJ government. But as the name shows, the two concepts are roughly the same. According to the National Institute for Defense Studies report, the "2013 NDPG can be viewed as a continuation" of the 2010 NDPG and the longer trend of Japanese defense transformations in the post–Cold War era (National Institute for Defense Studies 2014, 56–59). The clear change, the report judges, is that the 2013 NDPG reverses the declining trend of the defense budget for the first time in 10 years.

Therefore, the difference between the 2013 NDPG and its recent predecessors is more of quantity rather than quality. The document emphasizes increased jointness among the air, land, and maritime forces; prioritization of air and maritime superiority; and strengthening of deterrent capability in gray-zone situations. The gray-zone situations refer to "confrontations over territory, sovereignty and economic interests that do not escalate into wars." A typical case of a gray-zone situation is the low-level intrusion by Chinese vessels into the Senkaku/Diaoyu Islands maritime areas, which intensified drastically after the Japanese government announced the transfer of ownership of some of the Senkaku Islands to governmental hands in 2012. The 2013 NDPG announces that Japan intends to "clearly express its resolve not to tolerate the change of status quo by force."

The defense procurement plan shows clear emphasis on maritime and air capabilities. Diesel-propelled Sōryū-class submarines are to increase from 16 to 22 units, two Izumo-class helicopter destroyers are already in production, and the number of Aegis destroyers equipped with SM-3 missile systems is to increase from four to six. In addition to the F-35 combat aircraft the DPJ government decided to procure, the Abe cabinet will establish an amphibious unit and purchase 17 V-22 Osprey aircraft. The government has also begun to build a radar station on Yonaguni Island, 100 kilometers east of Taiwan and around 150 kilometers from the Senkaku Islands (Sakaki 2015). But because of well-known fiscal constraints, the government needs to streamline less prioritized sectors. For example, the number of tanks and artillery pieces will be cut to 300 each from the current 700 and 600, respectively (Yoshihara 2014).

Institutional Change: The Japanese Version of the NSC

Less than a month before the NSS and NDPG

were approved, the Abe cabinet legislated to establish the Japanese version of the NSC. This was another long-term project. The first Abe cabinet was enthusiastic about establishing this organization, but political confusion and Abe's resignation ended the effort. Nonetheless, later prime ministers continued to pursue prime minister-centered foreign policy planning and decision-making organization (Sunohara 2014).

When Abe returned to power, he quickly restarted the effort to establish the NSC. In late 2013, the NSC was formally established, followed by the creation of the National Security Secretariat. To head it, Abe nominated Yachi Shōtarō, the former vice-minister in the Foreign Ministry during the Koizumi Junichirō and first Abe cabinet periods, from 2005 to 2008. The intended roles of the NSC are stronger policy integration to cope with security environment change, higher priority on crisis management, strengthening the capability of the prime minister's office, and international synchronization at the institutional level (Research Institute on Peace and Security 2014).

The first three roles overlap. In the post–Cold War era, security issues have become quite diverse compared with the Cold War period, where the avoidance of East-West military conflict was the highest priority. In order to cope with the various types of risks and emergencies, interagency flexibility and integration under the top leadership have become indispensable.

The Japanese NSC actually combines three types of minister-level conferences. The first is the 9-minister conference, which has been around since the 1950s to secure civilian control over the SDFs. The four-minister conference is the core of the new NSC; it consists of the prime minister, the ministers of foreign affairs and defense, and the chief cabinet secretary. The conference decides the basic strategic policy, such as the NSS, and discusses important matters relating to diplomacy and security. The third type is the emergency situation conference, whose members are flexibly designated by the prime minister along with the cabinet secretary. Upon invitation by the prime minister, top uniformed staff such as the chairman of the joint staff can participate and make comments in any of the conferences (Research Institute on Peace and Security 2014).

The National Security Secretariat is authorized to have wide-ranging authority to coordinate the cabinet secretariat. At the time of its creation in January 2014, the secretariat had 67 staff drawn mainly from the ministries of foreign affairs and defense and six units (general coordination, policy units one to three with geographical specialization, strategic planning, and intelligence). One of the secretariat's roles is to handle secret intelligence, including intelligence shared with the United States and other friendly powers. Yachi, as head of the secretariat, is the official designee to meet with his US or other counterpart. The Abe cabinet created the Act on the Protection of Specially Designated Secrets in order to increase intelligence sharing, but the act created greater havoc among the public than the creation of the NSC.

Legal Changes Surrounding the Constitution and Other Regulations

Legal Politics on Article 9

Interpretation of Article 9 of the Japanese Constitution has been one of the most contentious political issues in postwar Japan. After the Cold War, many people called for changing the article or its interpretation so that Japanese defense forces could play more roles abroad. But such views were still in the minority in public opinion.

Ever since his first cabinet, Abe Shinzō has been intent on tackling this politically divisive issue. He has been quite explicit in declaring that revising the Constitution is his ultimate objective; but his initial objective is to revise the interpretation of the Constitution so that Japan can exercise the right of collective self-defense, an interpretation that postwar leaders have so far rejected. In his first cabinet, Abe commissioned experts to review the legal basis for a constitutional reinterpretation. The group's report was finalized after Abe resigned, and it was shelved by later prime ministers; but Abe reassembled the expert group in the second cabinet. The group issued a new report in May 2014. On 1 July, the Abe cabinet approved the Cabinet Decision on Development of Seamless Security Legislation to Ensure Japan's Survival and Protect Its People (Nakauchi 2014).

Detailed legal debate aside (which is almost unintelligible beyond Japanese linguistic phraseology), the crux of the matter is political consensus on the legal allowance for the exercise of force. Postwar Japanese security and defense policy was based on the consensus that Japan will not resort to force except for its own self-defense. This was the politico-legal basis of the so-called Yoshida Doctrine. At the same time, it needs to be noted that revising this self-restraint has been a long-running issue in Japan. Yoshida Shigeru, the prime minister in the early postwar period, wanted to change the interpretation (Choong 2015).

After the end of the Cold War, Japan decided to send the SDF on UN peacekeeping operations or on disaster relief missions. Tokyo also dispatched noncombat units to post-conflict Iraq and on anti-piracy operations along the Somalia coast. However, Japan kept to the principle of not using force beyond its own defense, partly because of the wariness of the public and partly because of opposition within the government to changing the interpretation of the Constitution.

The May report of the commission proposed that the exercise of collective self-defense and participation in UN collective security activities are both permissible under the current Constitution. The July cabinet decision, by contrast, allowed only partial exercise of the right of collective self-defense and limited use of arms and logistical support in international peace activities. The decision thus denied full-fledged participation in collective-security measures involving the use of force. Why Abe did not follow the report completely is unclear. It may have been a result of compromise with the governmental legal staff or the Kōmeitō Party, the LDP's coalition partner. Another possible reason is that Abe, who prefers to revise the Constitution, wanted to keep some room for further revision (Sakaki 2015).

Whatever the reason, the cabinet decided that the exercise of self-defense is permissible "not only when an armed attack against Japan occurs" but also "when an armed attack against a foreign country that is in a close relationship with Japan occurs and as a result threatens Japan's survival and poses a clear danger to fundamentally overturn people's right to life, liberty and pursuit of happiness." In other words, the attack on a foreign country needs to be a clear danger to the survival of the Japanese people for Japan to exercise force.

On paper, therefore, Abe's policy is not as clear a break from the past interpretation as political circles and the media, both for and against the revision, make it appear. Rather, the policy is a result of the long-term debate within the Japanese foreign policy community and academia on adjusting the legal basis on security for the post–Cold War era. Nonetheless, the new policy is a milestone in Japanese security and defense history, since it implies that Japan will exceed the strict limitation of its use of force beyond territorial self-defense.

Arms Exports

Just before the July cabinet decision, the government made another significant revision on foreign defense equipment and technology. Since the late 1960s Japan had imposed strict limitations on arms exports with the exception of technological cooperation with the United States. But in view of the changing nature of arms production and the desire to enhance security cooperation with allied and friendly powers, the defense industry sector had long called for relaxing the near-prohibition on arms exports. Indeed, in December 2011, under the DPJ government, the previous arms export restriction was virtually abolished by the cabinet secretary.

The Abe cabinet further formalized this revision in April 2014 by adopting "Three Principles on the Transfer of Defense Equipment and Technology." According to the new principles, the transfer of defense equipment and technology to other countries is prohibited when: (1) the transfer violates obligations under treaties and other international agreements that Japan has concluded, (2) the transfer violates obligations under United Nations Security Council resolutions; or (3) the defense equipment and technology is destined for a country party to a conflict (a country against which the UN Security Council is taking measures to maintain or restore international peace and security in the event of an armed attack) (Sakaki 2015).

Practically speaking, this policy change has opened the way to promote security and defense cooperation not only with the United States but also with other friendly powers such as the United Kingdom, France, Australia, India, and the 10 member countries of the Association of Southeast Asian Nations (ASEAN) (Japan Ministry of Defense 2014).

The July cabinet decision requires changes to be incorporated into Japanese domestic law. As of April 2015, the LDP-Kōmeitō discussion on the possible legislation is ongoing. Media reports indicate that the laws governing armed attack, the surrounding situation (i.e., conflict in areas near Japan), and international peace cooperation are being revised and a new law to support foreign militaries will be enacted (*Asahi Shimbun* 2015).

Alliance Coordination

Seeking a Strong US Security Commitment

The Abe cabinet has put strong emphasis on deepening the Japan-US alliance. Indeed, just after Abe returned to power, he desired to visit the United States first, but the US government responded that it was not ready so soon after the reelection of President Barack Obama. There is no doubt that Abe's "proactive contribution to peace" is in response to the request of US Japan-handlers, as the first Armitage-Nye report originally recommended (Armitage et al. 2000). In October 2013, at the Security Consultative Committee (2+2) under the second Abe cabinet, the United States generally endorsed the actions taken by Japan on security and defense affairs (US Department of State 2013).

Strengthening the Japan-US bilateral alliance becomes even more important for the United States as it starts the so-called pivot or rebalance to the Asia-Pacific. Responding to the rise of China, particularly regarding maritime activities in the East and South China Sea areas, the United States finds it necessary to clarify its commitment to maintaining the status quo and rejecting changes in it by force. When Obama made his first visit as president to Japan in April 2014, he declared that the Senkaku Islands are subject to

Article 5 of the Security Treaty, which states that the two countries will act against an attack on "territories under the administration of Japan" (Singh 2014).

After the 2+2 meeting, the crux of the security and defense reforms of the alliance under the Abe cabinet has boiled down to the revision of the Guidelines for Japan-US Defense Cooperation. The guideline has been regarded as the key document directing the basic operational cooperation between the defense forces of the two countries. The initial agreement in 1978 mainly applied to the defense of Japan. The revised version in 1997 applied cooperative defense to "surrounding situations," particularly Japanese logistical support to future US operations on the Korean Peninsula. The second revision was initially expected to be completed by the end of 2014, but because of the necessity of Japanese legislation after the revision of constitutional interpretation, the deadline was shifted to sometime in 2015.

New Guidelines and the China Factor

What most interests Japan is ascertaining the US commitment to the defense of Japan, including the gray-zone cases involving the offshore islands. For the United States, the expectation is increased Japanese support of US military activities at both the regional and global levels. In October 2014, the two governments issued the "Interim Report on the Revision of the Guidelines for Japan-U.S. Defense Cooperation" (US Department of Defense 2014). The report declares that the two governments share: recognition of the importance of seamless and effective whole-government alliance coordination; measures to prevent the deterioration of Japan's security; enhanced bilateral cooperation to generate a more peaceful and stable international security environment; cooperation in space and cyberspace in an alliance context; and mutual support in a timely and effective manner. In addition, the report mentions enhancing their bilateral planning mechanism, which suggests the establishment of a new military-to-military planning body.

Cooperation to strengthen the bilateral alliance does not mean that the security interests of the two countries are completely identical, particularly on China. For Japan, the rise of China has vital importance both politically and militarily. Politically, the competition for Asian leadership in the context of a power transition in Asia has the broadest implications for Japan's influence, not only in the Asia-Pacific but also globally. Militarily, the modernization of China, particularly in disputed maritime areas, means that Japan is increasingly dependent on Chinese maritime control if the US maritime presence recedes. Thus, keeping the US commitment in the region is of vital importance for Japan.

For the United States, the peace and stability of the Asia-Pacific has strategic importance. Japan is the linchpin of its security commitment in the region, but the US has long desired that China become a strong partner within US global leadership. Therefore, the United States consistently pursues an "engagement and hedging" policy toward China and does not want Japan to provoke China for fear of precipitating a dangerous confrontation. That concern is why Washington expressed "disappointment" when Abe visited the Yasukuni Shrine in December 2013 and showed some displeasure about his "historical revisionism." It has become customary, particularly among Western observers, to depict Abe as having two faces, one being the pragmatic realist and the other being the conservative ideologue (Rozman 2015). According to this picture, the realist Abe seeks to strengthen Japan's status and presence in the world and is willing to commit Japan to universal and sometimes progressive values, such as the promotion of women's status. However, the ideologue Abe pursues a conservative agenda by emphasizing the virtues of traditional Japan, including idealizing prewar Japan and denying war guilt.

No doubt Abe's stance has some contradictions, such as his strong attachment to the US-Japan alliance and his denunciation of the postwar Constitution. Both these themes are part of Japan's "postwar regime." This sort of contradiction and ambiguity, along with Abe's conservative ideology, has made him a polarizing figure domestically and a difficult leader to deal with abroad, including in relations with the United States.

However, Abe maintains high popularity domestically despite his specific agenda on national security and even though Abenomics does not get high public approval. And internationally, despite skepticism about his conservative revisionism, he has generally made headway toward improving relations.

The explanation for this Abe paradox seems to lie in the condition that what Abe pursues in his second cabinet, intentionally or less intentionally, follows the spirit of the age, reflecting the grand-scale transformation besetting the world. Geopolitically, the retreat of Russia as an imperialistic power in Asia is the consequence of the Soviet collapse in East Asia. This has changed the basic framework within which Japanese foreign policy has operated since the nineteenth century. In order to cope with the Russian advance, Japan made large commitments to the Asian continent, both on the Korean Peninsula and in China, which later resulted in atrocious warfare. As South Korea modernizes and China rises, Japan no longer considers a continental commitment to be vital to its own security, particularly so long as the United States remains committed to the defense of both Japan and South Korea.

When it comes to Japanese security interests on the Korean Peninsula, over the last two decades Japan has reaffirmed that it does not have an inherently strategic stake there. True, Japan is very concerned about North Korean nuclear and missile development, but the most effective way to cope with this threat is to enhance the US commitment to the Korean Peninsula rather than deeply involve Japan. The prospective update of the US-Japan guideline will broaden the 1997 guideline, which was mostly dedicated to the Korean situation, but in reality the new guideline suggests the lowering of the Korean Peninsula's priority in the Japanese security agenda.

This lower priority is partly the consequence of the historical issues between Japan and South Korea, but the change is more deep-seated and realistic. First, the relative decline of Japan and South Korea as trading partners has made the relationship more one between economic competitors. Second, the geopolitical status of Japan and South Korea has structurally diverged. For

Japan, the maritime rivalry due to the rising naval and maritime power of China gets top strategic importance because Japan is surrounded by sea and dependent on sea routes. For South Korea, deterring the North Korean threat and preparing for future unification make harmonious management with both the United States and China vital. Therefore, Japan is likely to be involved in the peace and security of the Korean Peninsula within the Japan-Korea-US trilateral framework and in various regional groups, but the United States and China come first in strategic importance.

Japan's security and economic interests are increasingly connected with the southwestern world—"China plus one." China is the number-one trading partner for Japan, but Japanese business is seeking alternatives to China in Southeast Asia, India, the Middle East, and Africa, where future economic growth is expected. In security affairs, Japan's traditional strength in peace-building activities and humanitarian relief efforts can be important resources for its global diplomacy. These activities also buttress the United States by supplanting the receding US presence and indirectly securing the US commitment in the Asia-Pacific, including Japan.

Ideologically, too, Japan has reason to strengthen its ties with southern Eurasia and Africa. Historical memory in these regions concerning Japan is very different from the Asia-Pacific. Generally, the Japan of the past is seen as another imperial power along with the Western colonial powers. Japan is guilty of imperial expansion and war, but the West shares the guilt. This was the stance Indian judge Radhabinod Pal took at the time of the Tokyo War Crimes Tribunal (Tokyo Saiban Kenkyūkai 1984).

Pal's judgment has received somewhat skewed treatment by Japanese conservatives, who have tried to make it seem that he was declaring Japan innocent of war crimes. Actually, he took the stance that Japan cannot be judged guilty because the Tokyo War Crimes Tribunal was organized by the victorious powers, who were also imperialists. Of course, Pal's stance is debatable, but politically it is convenient to argue that Japan was just one of the guilty parties. Given Japan's heightened nationalistic rivalry with South Korea

and China, finding agreement on history with Asian countries southwest of Japan is much easier and more strategically important than resolving the orthodoxy-versus-revisionism dichotomy currently prevalent in the Asia-Pacific.

Nakanishi, Hiroshi. "Reorienting Japan? Security Transformation under the Second Abe Cabinet." *Asian Perspective* 39:3 (2015), 405–421. © Institute for Far Eastern Studies, Kyungnam University. Reprinted with permission of Johns Hopkins University Press.

Bibliography

Armitage, Richard L. et al. "The United States and Japan: Advancing toward a Mature Partnership." INSS Special Report. Washington, DC: Institute for National Strategic Studies, National Defense University, October 2000. http://purl.access.gpo. gov/GPO/LPS22906.

Asahi Shimbun, The. "Anpo hōsei jikō kyōgi ga ketchaku" [Security Legislation, LDP-Kōmeitō Consultation is Finalized]. 22 April 2015.

Cabinet Public Relations Office. "Jieitai, bōeimondai ni kansuru yoron chōsa"[Summary of the Public Opinion Poll on the Self-Defense Forces and Defense Affairs]. 2015. http://survey.gov-online. go.jp/h26/h26-bouei/gairyaku.pdf.

Choong, William. "Defense and Japan's Constitutional Change." *Survival* 57, no. 2 (March 2015): 173–192.

Japan Ministry of Defense. "Bōei sōbi, gijutsu iten ni kakaru shokadai ni kanrusu kentō kai" [On the Status and Task of Defense Equipment and Technology Transfer]. PPT slide, 18 December 2014. https://warp.da.ndl.go.jp/info:ndljp/ pid/11591426/www.mod.go.jp/j/approach/ agenda/meeting/materials/sobi-gijutsuiten/giji/ pdf/01.pdf.

Nakauchi Yasuo. "Shūdanteki jieiken no kōshi yōnin to anzenhoshō hōsei seibi no kihon hōshin: Kakugi kettei o uketeno kokkai ronsen no gaiyō" [Admission of Exercise of Collective Defense Right and Basic Direction of Security Legislation: Summary of Diet Debate after the Cabinet Decision]. *Rippō to Chōsa*, no. 356 (2014): 23–40.

National Institute for Defense Studies (NIDS). "Japan: New Development of National Security Policy." *East Asian Strategic Review* (2014): 37–72. http:// www.nids.mod.go.jp/english/publication/east-asian/pdf/2014/east-asian_e2014_01.pdf.

National Security Council and the Cabinet. "Medium-Term Defense Program (FY2014–FY2018)." 17 December 2013. https://warp.da.ndl.go.jp/ info:ndljp/pid/11591426/www.mod.go.jp/j/ approach/agenda/guideline/2014/pdf/Defense_ Program.pdf.

———. "National Defense Program Guidelines for FY 2014 and Beyond (Summary)." 17 December 2013. www.cas.go.jp/jp/siryou/131217anzenhoshou/ndpg-e.pdf.

———. "National Security Strategy (English translation)." 17 December 2013. https://www.cas.go.jp/jp/siryou/131217anzenhoshou/nss-e.pdf.

Nikkei Asian Review. "Less Than a Third of Japanese Support Defense Policy Change." 23 March 2015. https://asia.nikkei.com/Japan-Update/Less-than-a-third-of-Japanese-support-defense-policy-change.

Research Institute on Peace and Security. *Saiki suru Nihon kinchō takamaru Higashi, Minami Shinakai: Nenpō Ajia no anzenhoshō (2014–2015)* [Recovering Japan, Rising Tensions in the East and South China Seas: Annual Report on Asian Security 2014–2015]. Tokyo: Asagumo Shuppansha, 2014.

Rozman, Gilbert. "Realism vs. Revisionism in Abe's Foreign Policy in 2014." *The Asan Forum*, 5 February 2015. www.theasanforum.org/realism-vs-revisionism-in-abes-foreign-policy-in-2014.

Sakaki, Alexandra. "Japan's Security Policy: A Shift in Direction under Abe?" SWP Research Paper, *Stifung Wissenschaft und Politik* (2015). https://www.swp-berlin.org/fileadmin/contents/products/research_papers/2015_RP02_skk.pdf.

Singh, Bhubhindar. "Obama, the Senkaku/Diaoyu Islands, and the US-Japan Security Treaty." *Pacific Forum CSIS*, 7 May 2014. https://csis-website-prod.s3.amazonaws.com/s3fs-public/legacy_files/files/publication/Pac1436A.pdf.

Sunohara Tsuyoshi. *Nihonban NSC towa nanika* [What Is the Japanese NSC?]. Tokyo: Shinchōsha, 2014.

Tōkyō Saiban Kenkyūkai. *Kyōdō kenkyū Paru hanketsusho* [Joint Study on the Judgments of Radhabinod Pal]. 2 vols. Tokyo: Kōdansha, 1984.

US Department of Defense. "The Interim Report on the Revision of the Guidelines for U.S.-Japan Defense Cooperation." 2014. https://dod.defense.gov/Portals/1/Documents/pubs/20141003_INTERIM_REPORT.pdf.

US Department of State. "Joint Statement of the Security Consultative Committee: Toward a More Robust Alliance and Greater Shared Responsibilities." 2013. https://archive.defense.gov/pubs/U.S.-Japan-Joint-Statement-of-the-Security-Consultative-Committee.pdf.

Yoshihara Toshi. "Japanese Hard Power: Rising to the Challenge." *American Enterprise Institute*, 25 August 2014. https://www.aei.org/research-products/report/japanese-hard-power-rising-to-the-challenge/.

III-(7) Japan Seventy Years after World War II
From a Challenger to a Supporter of the International Order

Kitaoka Shinichi

ABSTRACT Prime Minister Abe having been subjected to an unceasing torrent of criticism as a right-wing historical revisionist, the statement that he issued in 2015 on the 70th anniversary of the war's end was closely scrutinized and compared with the statement Prime Minister Murayama had issued in 1995. The Abe Statement clearly recognized that Japan had engaged in aggression, was frankly contrite over this, and pledged that Japan, having earlier challenged the international order, was fully committed to upholding the postwar international order. It was a powerful statement laying to rest much of the criticism of both Japan as a nation and Abe personally over how historical events are perceived and presented.

The Advisory Panel on the History of the 20th Century and on Japan's Role and the World Order in the 21st Century (the "21st Century Advisory Panel") released its report. The "Abe Statement"—presumably drafted with reference to this report—was issued on 14 August 2015. I served as acting chair of the advisory panel on behalf of its chairman, Nishimuro Taizō, and was involved in compiling the panel's report.

At the start, there were questions as to whether it was necessary to make a statement marking the 70th anniversary of the end of World War II and whether a new statement should be issued every 10 years. However, given that expectations—or concerns—have been on the increase, it seemed appropriate for Prime Minister Abe to present Japan's official stance directly. Thus, the advisory panel was established to provide historical analysis for reference when presenting the Abe administration's position.

The name of the advisory panel indicated the directions it would take: First, it describes Japan and the broader world together, and, second, it not only considers the wartime era but also places this period within a larger historical context.

Initially, media interest focused exclusively on the question of whether the four key words,

namely "aggression," "colonial rule," "remorse," and "apology," would appear in the prime minister's statement. These are certainly important words, each of which has its own meaning and origins, but it would be absurd to judge the statement solely on whether or not they were included. In the extreme, does it mean that as long as these words were included, it did not matter what other content the statement contained? Further, I think it is natural that a statement marking 70 years since the war and one marking 50 years would differ in some aspects. To demand exactly the same content in both is to face history disingenuously.

The Issue of "Aggression"

That being the case, how Japan recognizes the past is a crucial issue. I believe the key to this issue is the concept of "aggression." I received a great deal of criticism after saying at a symposium in March that "of course what Japan committed was aggression. I want the prime minister to say that we committed aggression." I was aware that the prime minister had said, "I have never said that we did not commit aggression." However, I wanted him to take one step further when I said, "I want him to say that Japan committed aggression." I did not necessarily mean that he should write down the exact word in his statement, and I believe that a term other than "aggression" would be equally appropriate.

Listening to the reaction to my statement, I was struck by the considerable number of people who opposed the use of the word "aggression." It would appear that, once again, the matter requires a thorough explanation.

First, some people say that, because the term "aggression" is undefined, it cannot be said that Japan committed aggression. This is utterly incorrect. The word "aggression" has a dictionary definition. Picking up the nearest dictionary, one finds it defined as the act of entering another country on the offensive and plundering land or property or as the act of using force to control another country's sovereignty. The definitions of "aggression" used in political science, history, and international politics are all similar. In none of these areas has the term ever been a controversial concept.

If one maintains that one cannot say Japan committed aggression on the grounds that it is not a strictly defined concept, then that would mean there is no such thing as aggression, and thus, Hitler and Stalin never conducted aggression either. It would also mean that the Soviet Union's incursions into Manchukuo and the Chishima (Kuril) Islands could not be called aggression.

If one requires strict definitions, then, for instance, one can no longer use the word "peace." One could not even use the phrase "a proactive contribution to peace." Nothing could be so foolish.

However, in the field of international law, the definition of aggression is somewhat vague. There is a UN General Assembly resolution that relates to the definition of aggression, so the term is tentatively defined. However, there is a rather broad gray area, and it can sometimes be difficult to judge whether something is an aggression. For example, the question of whether Israel's offensives against Hezbollah in Lebanon constitute aggression or self-defense against terrorism does not permit a simple answer one way or the other.

Regardless of what criteria one uses, however, it is clear that Japan, prior to World War

II, committed aggression. One instance is the Manchurian Incident. It is certainly true that the fact that Japan possessed treaty-backed special rights and interests in southern Manchuria and the eastern part of Inner Mongolia has been frequently ignored and that these interests were even encroached upon. However, as a result of the Manchurian Incident, Japan occupied a region three and a half times the size of the Japanese mainland and established Manchukuo. This state included northern Manchuria, where Japan had not previously possessed any special rights or interests. This cannot in any way be explained as self-defense. An act of self-defense requires proportionality; anything beyond what is proportional becomes an aggression.

Concerning treaties that Japan had concluded at the time: the Covenant of the League of Nations (1919) imposed on its parties the obligation not to resort to war. The Nine-Power Treaty (1922) called for respecting the independence and integrity of China. Furthermore, the Kellogg-Briand Pact (1928) repudiated war as a means of resolving international disputes. Japan's behavior during the Manchurian Incident contravened all these agreements, and its policymakers knew that it would be difficult to explain their actions. That is why the Kwantung Army made it appear as though Chinese nationals had bombed the South Manchuria Railway. It is also the reason that Japan presented itself, not as annexing Manchuria but, instead, as guaranteeing the independence of Manchukuo as if it was based on the voluntary will of its residents.

It should be noted that, in the Manchurian Incident, Japan did not declare war, and so, from an international law perspective, it was not a war. Japan did not declare any wars between the Second Sino-Japanese War (then known in Japan as the "China Incident") and Pearl Harbor. This was because, due to the US Neutrality Acts, a declaration of war would have made it difficult to import supplies from the US. However, both the Manchurian Incident and—obviously—the Second Sino-Japanese War were indeed de facto wars. The reason that, following World War II, the United Nations Charter and the Japanese Constitution banned not "war" but the "exercise of armed force" was to not allow such pretexts as: "It is an incident, not a war."

In his essay "Nation, Class and War," written in November 1931, Yoshino Sakuzō criticized the Kwantung Army, stating that, even if the Manchurian Incident had started as an act of self-defense, the scope of the army's actions had already far exceeded that of self defense, and given that events had progressed so far, they could be termed nothing but aggression. Yoshino noted that, at the time, the military had maintained not so much that it was engaging in self-defense but was instead acting out of necessity to ensure Japan's survival. To this, Yoshino rejoined by asking whether it was permissible to take another country's land just because it was deemed necessary. As children were we not given moral education that one should not drink from another's well? These were truly brave things to say at that time.

Some people who say that Japan did not commit aggression give other reasons to support their argument. For instance, some maintain that saying something that implies Japan did something bad means that one cannot be proud of Japan. This is a curious view. Is there any major country that has not waged an aggression at some time in its past? Regardless of whether or not Japan has ever committed aggression against another country, it is still a remarkable nation. There may be some countries where people rewrite their history because they love their homelands, but Japan ought not to be one of them.

There are also some people who say that because Japan fought with all its might against Russia over Manchuria, the territory belonged to Japan. To be sure, had Japan not fought the Russo-Japanese War, perhaps Manchuria would have ended up belonging to Russia. However, that does not imply Manchuria therefore rightfully belonged to Japan. Near the end of the shogunate, there was an incident in which a Russian corvette (the *Posadnik*) suddenly arrived at the island of Tsushima. The ship remained there illegally, and its crew engaged in various illicit behaviors. Japan then gained British assistance in driving the ship away. If one subscribed to the logic outlined at the start of this paragraph, then it would mean that Great Britain thus gained an interest over Tsushima.

Some people attempt to ignore the importance of the Manchurian Incident on the grounds that there was little criticism of the event at the time. The criticism from the great powers was, in fact, so weak as to be scarcely in the same category as that to which they leveled against Japan following the Shanghai Incident, which occurred the following year, in January 1932.

It is not, however, tenable to argue that, therefore, the Manchurian Incident was not an aggression. The strength of the international community's condemnation following an act is not necessarily proportional to the degree of its illegality. When the actor is strong, criticism is tepid. If a country's position is weak, or if it has weak ties to a given region, its disapproval of an aggressor's actions will be restrained. Many countries were yet to recover from the Great Depression, and, furthermore, Manchuria was a faraway place. By contrast, Shanghai seemed nearby to the great powers.

Some people also say it was not just Japan that challenged the international order. Italy intruded into Ethiopia. Germany forced incorporation of Austria in the Austrian Annexation, annexed part of what was then Czechoslovakia, and invaded Poland. The Soviet Union annexed the Baltic states and invaded Finland. However, the first of this series of aggressions was the Manchurian Incident. These aggressions all succeeded in the short term, and so each followed from the previous one. The Manchurian Incident thus struck a greater blow to the international relations of the day than some people in Japan realize.

Some people argue that, if Japan recognizes this as aggression, it will have to apologize once more, suffering a disadvantage. This, too, is mistaken. That Japan committed aggression against other countries was long ago decided at the Tokyo War Crimes Tribunal. The Tokyo Tribunal had numerous procedural problems, and they cannot be said to have been legally proper trials. However, they were unavoidable if Japan was to be welcomed back into the international community. Consequently, Japan promised at the San Francisco Peace Conference that it would not challenge the decisions of the Tokyo Tribunal.

Following the conference, Japan lost territory

and paid compensation, or the other party waived its right to compensation, or Japan provided economic assistance that was, in a sense, reparations. The other parties accepted these outcomes, and thus all matters were settled. No further apologies are required.

Japan's prime minister represents its people today. The vast majority of the Japanese alive today were born after World War II. Surely, many people would be reluctant to apologize further for events that happened even before the war. In an opinion poll conducted in the US, a combined total of 61% of respondents thought Japan had either apologized enough or did not need to apologize. Even what China is seeking is not an apology but for Japan to face up to its history. There are only two groups that are calling for more apologies: South Korea and some of Japan's media.

On the other hand, despite having recognized the fact up to this point, if Japan were to reverse course and cease to recognize that it committed aggression against other countries, then that would be a major problem. Some people have said that if Japan recognizes it has waged aggression, it would be as if it were providing aid and comfort to the enemy. To the contrary, the fact is, were Japan to say it has not committed aggression against other countries, it would find itself treated as an enemy, not only by the countries with which it had previously waged war but by practically the whole world. After all, the majority of countries have faced aggression in the past.

Historical recognition must begin with facing the reality of aggression head on and clearly admitting to it.

Colonial Rule

Another one of the terms at issue is "colonial rule." At the start of the twentieth century, colonial rule blanketed the globe. It was Japan's victory in the Russo-Japanese War that applied the brakes to colonialism. The war resulted in the shattering of the myth of the unbeatable white man, and there was a rise in independence movements in numerous colonies around the world. Many leaders of nations that achieved independence from colonialism after World War II had

heard of Japan's victory in the Russo-Japanese War as children and were thus galvanized.

However, at that time, Japan never stood on the side of the colonized. It was fully engaged in standing as an equal among the great powers. The second Anglo-Japanese Alliance, concluded in the final stages of the Russo-Japanese War, called for respect of British rule over India, and the Franco-Japanese agreement of 1907 similarly called for respect of French rule over Indochina; both agreements called on the European party to respect Japan's interests in Korea and Manchuria. Japan cooperated with British and French colonial rule to help dispose of the massive foreign debts it incurred as a result of the Russo-Japanese War. Also with the United States, a secret agreement was signed between Prime Minister Katsura Tarō and William H. Taft (Secretary of War, Civil Governor of the Philippines) in July 1905 in which Japan expressed it had no ambition toward the Philippines and the US recognized Japan's leading position in Korea. Field marshal in the Imperial Japanese Army and former prime minister Yamagata Aritomo argued that Japan's victory represented a win by an Asian nation, which had learned Western technology well, over a Western nation that had not done so itself. However, he stated this by no means demonstrated that Asia was superior to the West, and Japan should absolutely refrain from doing anything that might incite notions of racial animus between the West and Asia.

The next wave of independence from colonialism came with the end of World War I. The great powers had needed the cooperation of their colonies in order to wage total war. This accelerated movements toward independence. One of the Fourteen Points for Peace that President Wilson proposed during the final stages of the war called for the self-determination of peoples. This was originally a principle that applied to peoples within Europe, but it had effects on other regions as well, sparking the March First Movement in Korea and the May Fourth Movement in China in 1919.

There were even movements in response to the principle of self-determination in Japan. Following the annexation of Korea, Governors-General

Terauchi Masatake and Hasegawa Yoshimichi instituted a regime that had direct control over the people by military police. Following World War I, this regime was abolished, and those qualified to be governor-general of Korea expanded from only active-duty army generals so that even a civilian could be appointed. It also became possible for the governor-general of Taiwan to be a civilian official. Admiral Saitō Makoto, a naval reservist, was named governor-general of Korea, and a civilian, former communications minister Den Kenjirō, was appointed governor-general of Taiwan. At the farewell party on the occasion of Saitō's appointment to his post in Korea, Saionji Kinmochi, a genro (extra-constitutional elder statesman), requested that His Excellency conduct a civilized government.

Among the intelligentsia, there were even some, such as Ishibashi Tanzan, who advocated independence from colonialism. Realist politicians, such as Hara Takashi, also showed signs that their thinking was beginning to move toward autonomy.

However, in the 1930s, when the Second Sino-Japanese War intensified, Japan's colonial rule became harsher. The year 1940 saw the institution of the *sōshi-kaimei* policy (requiring Koreans under Japanese rule to take surnames and "encouraging" them to adopt Japanese names). Mobilization of Korean laborers began around 1939.

Even in Taiwan—which was thought to be less turbulent—the Wushe Incident occurred in 1930, resulting in more than 1,000 deaths. The extent of the rebellion was such that the Japanese military deployed cannons to suppress it. It is said that the cause of the incident was discriminatory attitudes toward the Gaoshan tribes.

Colonial rule is not pleasant for those who are ruled. During the US occupation of Japan, there was considerable opposition from those occupied. Many nations' peoples have effectively said that they would choose an impoverished independence over an affluent colonialism. The same could be said of Japan.

Compared to rule by Great Britain, Spain, Portugal, Belgium, and the other colonial great powers, it could be argued that Japan's colonial

rule was much preferable. However, that does not mean one could say it was good or right.

An accurate evaluation is also needed of the influence of the Pacific War on Asia. Some people considered the war to be for the liberation of Asia, and there were people who fought under that understanding. For instance, after Japan's defeat, some of its soldiers fought the Netherlands on behalf of the Indonesians.

However, of the various decisions made in the lead-up to the war in the Pacific, none were made with Asian liberation as the principal goal. The majority of decisions were aimed at the self-preservation and self-defense of Japan—that is, Japanese interests. Ironically, though, the result of these decisions was the opposite of self-preservation and self-defense.

It was because of oil that Japan did not grant independence to Indonesia—which then was most ready for it. Japan desired direct rule. Because the German-collaborationist Vichy government that controlled French-ruled Indochina was on the Axis side, Japan could not make Indochina independent. What Japan could have made independent were British territories in Burma and Malaya and the US-ruled Philippines.

The reason Japan concluded an equal treaty with the Wang Jingwei–led Reorganized National Government of the Republic of China and held the Greater East Asia Conference was that the war situation had become severe, and thus Japan required the cooperation of the areas it occupied.

Nevertheless, it is a fact that Japan's actions shattered British, US, and Dutch rule, therefore advancing independence. Great Britain, France, and the Netherlands intended to reinstitute their colonial rule after World War II. France fighting the Vietnam War is well known. The Netherlands started a war to regain its colonies, ultimately not recognizing their independence until 1949. Although Japan did not pay particular attention to the Netherlands one way or the other, it was on Indonesia's side, and in a 1960 border-issue conflict between Indonesia and the Netherlands, when the Netherlands requested the use of Haneda Airport as a temporary port of call for dispatching marines, Japan refused.

In *The Issue of War*, historian Christopher

Thome argued that the greatest consequence of the war was independence from colonialism in the Asia-Pacific region, and perhaps this is an appropriate evaluation.

How, then, should one think about responsibility for the aggression and colonial rule described above?

As already noted, the vast majority of Japanese people currently living were born after the war. They should not bear any direct responsibility. There is no need for the prime minister to formally apologize to other countries. This is because Japan has already apologized on numerous occasions, and other countries have accepted those apologies. However, as a separate matter, this reasoning should not go so far as to exclude the possibility of apologizing to individuals who were actually victimized, including comfort women and POWs.

Remorse and reflection are perhaps more important than apologies. Japan should reflect again on having committed tremendous mistakes and ensure that this reflection is communicated to the countries against which those mistakes were perpetrated.

To ensure that this reflection proves fruitful, above all, Japan must not forget its history of past aggression and must keep that history in its collective memory.

Public understanding of modern history is disappointingly shallow—and not just among young people. I am ashamed of this as a researcher of history. Therefore, I would like to energize historical research and create courses on modern history that go beyond the limits of mere "Japanese history" or "world history" and that, instead, cover the findings of specialists in areas such as political science, international politics, and geography. I would like to make these courses required subjects.

When it comes to history, joint research is also crucial. I have participated in Japanese-South Korean and Japanese-Chinese joint research. Although I am well aware of the difficulty of such endeavors, if one takes the time to deliberate the issues, then a certain degree of dialogue is possible, even with a totalitarian China or a fiercely nationalistic South Korea. It is not necessary to

force everyone's historical understandings to match. However, if we debate issues based on historical sources, then extremely exaggerated views should eventually be weeded out.

It would still be difficult to have identical understandings of history. Nevertheless, it is important to know what others believe. I think that, if possible, it would be beneficial to create booklets—not textbooks but supplementary readers—that print side by side what Japan and South Korea each think of the March First Movement, for instance, so as to enable each to understand the other's standpoint.

If possible, it would be preferable to have the participation of researchers from other countries. So far, China, in particular, has tended to try to limit the scope of dialogues to bilateral issues. However, one cannot, for instance, discuss postwar Japan-China relations without touching upon the Korean War, and it is utterly impossible to discuss postwar international relations in East Asia on a bilateral basis alone.

Next, it is important to never again start such a war. However, it is almost inconceivable that Japan would ever be the side that starts a conflict. Japan current prosperity is premised on the existence of a liberal and stable world order. Surely no one in Japan believes that prosperity should be attempted through expansionism by force.

A more realistic question to ponder is what Japan can do to prevent conflict around the world. I would now like to list a few answers to that question.

Japan's Role in the Twenty-First Century

First, there is UN reform. The Security Council, which is the main player in conflict prevention and resolution, is starting to become paralyzed. There are two types of reforms to the Security Council: expanding its membership and amending the way it deliberates (such as by putting limitations on veto power). I would like for both reforms to take place and for Japan to contribute from a permanent or semipermanent position.

Second, in consideration of the fact that poverty can be the root of conflict, Japan should contribute to economic development worldwide. It would be desirable to increase considerably the amount Japan spends on ODA. Japan should, based on the ideal of human security, provide active assistance for those in absolute poverty.

Third, Japan should support democratization around the globe. Dictatorships are hotbeds for conflicts, and Japan should strictly monitor the suppression of freedom of speech in particular. Had restraints on speech not been tightened in Japan during the middle of the Second Sino-Japanese War, it is possible that criticism of the war might have grown stronger.

Fourth, Japan should resolve conflicts through laws, not force. Because of this, Japan should not remain a spectator to conflicts around the world but should, instead, actively speak out about them. A Japan that violated the Nine-Power Treaty and the Kellogg-Briand Pact and destroyed the world order should especially commit to this point.

Fifth, Japan should intensify its cooperative efforts, including PKOs. Japan currently has too many constraints on its participation in PKOs; it must remove these constraints and contribute more actively.

Sixth, the hindrance of the development of global trade in the 1930s became a major reason why Japan went down the wrong path. Thus, Japan should always participate in trade liberalization.

Seventh, regional instability can cause conflicts. There is also a danger that vulnerabilities could lead to attacks. It is thus necessary to remove any vulnerabilities by enhancing Japan-US security cooperation. Japan-US security cooperation is also an international public good, so Japan should focus on making sure this strengthened cooperation contributes to the stability of East Asia.

These are all well-known issues. However, if one considers why Japan undertook expansionism in the 1930s, one should understand why these issues must be dealt with. In other words, these ways in which Japan should play a more active role are grounded in reflection over the errors that Japan made before World War II. Japan at that time became a challenger to the international order, and it destroyed that order. Since the end of the war Japan has developed into a beneficiary of the international order. Now it is Japan's turn to become a country that supports that order. Reflecting on past misdeeds and determining one's future are thus one and the same effort.

Kitaoka, Shinichi. "Japan Seventy Years after World War II: From a Challenger to a Supporter of the International Order." *Asia-Pacific Review* 22:2 (2015), 3–13. © Nakasone Peace Institute reprinted by permission of Taylor & Francis Ltd, https://www.tandfonline.com on behalf of Nakasone Peace Institute.

This essay is based on an essay published in Japanese in the September 2015 issue of *Chūō Kōron* by Chūōkōron-Shinsha.

III-(8) Sustainable Development Goals and Japan's Official Development Assistance Policy

Human Security, National Interest, and a More Proactive Contribution to Peace

Kitaoka Shinichi

ABSTRACT Japan's official development assistance policy was revised in 2015 to explicitly include consideration of Japan's national interest. That said, this is not a narrowly defined "national interest" but should be understood as national interest in the broadest sense—focusing on the maintenance of the international order providing for free trade, the peaceful settlement of disputes, and more. The Sustainable Development Goals adopted by the United Nations in September 2015 are broadly compatible with Japan's national interest, this paper argues, and Japan should actively engage with this SDG effort.

Introduction: Adoption of SDGs

With the spread of terrorism, interminable conflicts, increased number of refugees, and heightened nationalism, today, a somber mood is often cast over our lives.

On the other hand, there has been an increased move toward international cooperation. "The 2030 Agenda for Sustainable Development" was adopted at the UN Summit in September 2015. This is a grand-scale project in which global scale development issues requiring the collaboration of the international community between 2016 and 2030 were compiled as SDGs. The SDGs consist of 17 goals and 169 targets. As the content is too broad to describe here, let me focus solely on the 17 goals:

1. No poverty
2. Zero hunger
3. Good health and well-being
4. Quality education
5. Gender equality
6. Clean water and sanitation
7. Affordable and clean energy
8. Decent work and economic growth
9. Industry, innovation, infrastructure
10. Reduced inequalities
11. Sustainable cities and communities
12. Responsible consumption, production
13. Climate action
14. Life below water
15. Life on land
16. Peace, justice, and strong institutions
17. Partnerships for the goals

Shortly after the adoption of the SDGs by the UN, the 21st Session of the Conference of the Parties (COP21) to the United Nations Framework Convention on Climate Change was held in Paris from November to December of the same year, and the Paris Agreement that holds all countries accountable was signed. This is another extremely significant agreement. The issue of climate change is also indicated in goal 13: "climate action." In other words, the Paris Agreement can be considered a partial actualization of the SDGs. Both the SDGs and the Paris Agreement may make 2015 remembered in the future as the year when an important step toward international collaboration was taken.

From MDGs to SDGs

The SDGs succeed the Millenium Development Goals (MDGs) adopted in 2000. The MDGs aimed to halve worldwide poverty by 2015, and eight goals (eradicate extreme poverty and hunger; achieve universal primary education; promote gender equality and empower women; reduce child mortality; improve maternal health; combat HIV/AIDS, malaria, and other diseases; ensure environmental sustainability; and global partnership for development) and 21 targets were established. Although they look more modest than the SDGs, in the beginning quite a few people had a cynical view of such voluminous and ambitious targets. However, it would be safe to say that substantial progress has been made; the population living in extreme poverty has been reduced to one-third and infant and maternal mortality has been nearly halved in the past 15 years.

Having said this, there remain many unsolved issues. First, in some regions, such as sub-Saharan Africa, there are still some unachieved MDGs, such as maternal and child health and access to safe sanitary facilities. Further, the world's population in extreme poverty was reduced due largely to development in China and India. Second, internal disparities between regions, between males and females, races, and persons with disabilities have actually expanded even in countries that have shown numerical improvements as a whole. And third, important issues, such as climate change and natural disasters, that had not been anticipated earlier have come to the surface. Therefore, the SDGs were developed as goals geared not only toward developing countries but also toward advanced nations by succeeding the MDGs and introducing a new agenda.

Human Security and the SDGs

The SDGs have quite a lot in common with Human Security, which Japan has been promoting for many years. It was in the latter part of the 1990s that Japan incorporated this concept into its foreign policies, and in 1999 it donated the "Trust Fund for Human Security" to the UN.

Despite such efforts, however, Japan had difficulty gaining understanding from the international community. One of the reasons was that the concept was confused with Responsibility to Protect (R2P). The idea underlying R2P is that, basically, a country must bear responsibility for

the safety of its people, but if the government is unwilling or unable to do so, the international community has the responsibility to protect those people. The UN is run by states and sets out the principle of noninterference in a state's internal affairs. Therefore, intervention beyond national boundaries was not justified up to that time. Developing countries were seriously concerned that approving this concept of R2P would mean acceptance of intervention from the developed nations.

The same applies to human security in terms of cross-border obligation. Human security holds that all human beings have the right to live their lives with dignity, and the international community has a duty to support this. R2P and Human Security have some features in common. However, R2P carried a connotation of forced intervention, while Human Security put more emphasis on low-key support.

The then closely watched Darfur issue in Sudan was an important test for R2P. The Sudanese government was suspected of neglecting, tacitly approving of, or being a party to the attack by Muslims/nomads on indigenous farmers as part of the clan-based rivalry in the Darfur region of western Sudan. Backed by international opinion, the UN Security Council decided to send PKOs in April 2005 to contain the opposition of the Sudanese government and its supporter, China. This was an example of R2P.

In September of the same year, a UN reform document was adopted at the 60th Anniversary UN General Assembly, when R2P and Human Security were introduced as important concepts that should be studied separately. Human Security was accepted, for the first time, in the UN official document as a concept distinct from R2P, although full understanding of it was yet to be obtained.

Subsequently, the progress in R2P became stagnant. Various conflicts occurred as part of the Arab Spring that erupted in 2011, and military intervention was undertaken against the uprising in Libya in 2011. From the international community's perspective, however, it was the extremely objectionable Muslim extremists affiliated with Al-Qaeda who confronted the dangerous and irresponsible government in the chaotic circumstances of Syria, and the scheme devised by the international community to intervene in the Syrian government has run up against major difficulties. In 2013, President Barack Obama delivered a stark warning to the Assad regime in Syria over its possible use of chemical weapons by using the ultimatum of a "red line." However, even after running into a situation indicating that chemical weapons were actually used, the international community was unable to resort to military intervention. Subsequently, the "Islamic State" was created by an anti-government force in Syria, and the international community ran into the fundamental major obstacle of how and for what purpose an intervention should be conducted. In the end, R2P turned out to be inapplicable in a situation like Syria.

On the other hand, Human Security was steadily accepted. At the UN, the General Assembly Resolution in September 2012 created a shared understanding about "Human Security" among the member countries. Human Security is defined as "the right of people to live in freedom and dignity, free from poverty and despair."

In Japan, Human Security was introduced into the Official Development Assistance (ODA) Charter in 2003 as a fundamental perspective. It remained the core concept of the Development Cooperation Charter that was revised last year.

Although the phrase "Human Security" is not found in the SDGs, "people-centered" is mentioned. In addition, "no one will be left behind," the principle also valued by Human Security, is clearly specified. The SDGs attach importance to the efforts to improve the safety net and reinforce ability (empowerment) so that the people who escaped from poverty will not be drawn back to where they were before due to disaster, unemployment, accident, and so on. This idea is also close to that of Human Security.

The Development Cooperation Charter (2015) and Human Security

Let me now describe how the Development Cooperation Charter developed in February 2015.

Human Security is explicitly stated as the basic concept of the Development Cooperation Charter. On the other hand, the phrase "Proactive Contributor to Peace" and explicit use of "national interest" have gathered attention.

The words "national interest" can be interpreted as follows in the current global context; that is, national interest boils down to the safety, freedom, and prosperity of the Japanese people. Furthermore, it means preserving the good traditions of Japan (though what is meant by "good traditions" leaves room for further discussion) and for the country to be respected by the international community.

In this sense, it is different from the nineteenth-century interpretation of national interest. Japan has neither vast territories nor abundant resources, nor does it have hundreds of millions of people. In other words, as Japan does not have strategic depth and alternatives, it must coexist with the international community or the above-mentioned basic national interest requirements will not be satisfied. Japan should support the peace and stability of the international community, and the world needs to be a place in which free trade is ensured and international disputes are solved in a peaceful manner. To this end, Japan needs to make a certain level of contributions. It goes without saying that Japan is unable to make contributions to such an extent that may threaten the safety, freedom, and prosperity of Japan. However, a self-centered policy that is solely focused on the pursuit of the country's own interests goes against the national interest of Japan.

From this viewpoint, Prime Minister Abe's cabinet developed the National Security Strategy (NSS) at the Council on Security and Defense Capabilities in 2013 and announced a "Proactive Contribution to Peace" policy.[1]

Although this "Proactive Contribution to Peace" policy drew criticism that it could partly increase Japan's international military role, that notion is completely mistaken. It is true that strengthening the role of the Self-Defense Forces is absolutely necessary as part of the "Proactive Contribution to Peace" policy. The enhancement was actually enabled by the security-related laws enacted in 2015, and its legal foundation was discussed by the Council on the Reconstruction of the Legal Foundation of Security.

The increase in the role of the Self-Defense Forces is primarily geared toward cooperation with the US forces in the areas surrounding Japan. It is absolutely necessary that the relationship with US forces be strengthened in the face of the exponential military buildup of China and North Korea. The lack of a strong relationship would be detrimental to all nations that are threatened by an expansive China. This is why the passage of the security-related laws in 2015 was welcomed not only by the US and Australia but also by ASEAN nations.

Secondly, the strengthening of the Self-Defense Forces has brought its PKO and other international roles a little closer to international standards. The Self-Defense Forces engaged in PKOs were traditionally placed in an extraordinary position in which they were not allowed to come to the aid of other countries' forces under attack, but they may receive support from them. Bringing this situation slightly closer to international standards is one of the essential features of the security-related laws. Although details are yet to be completed, it is safe to say that the activities of the Self-Defense Forces will be extremely limited under the new Rules of Engagement.

In light of the above, the Self-Defense Forces are indispensable in promoting the "Proactive Contribution to Peace" policy. However, their involvement is only a very small part of it. The leading promoter of the "Proactive Contribution to Peace" policy is the ODA, which is based on the core concept of Human Security. As outlined above, the "Proactive Contribution to Peace" policy, Japan's national interest, and Human Security are interrelated.

Contribution in the Health Sector

Japan has a long tradition of international cooperation, and its policies often reflect its own history. One area in which Japan has traditionally contributed is health. Since the premodern age, Japan has put a great deal of effort into medicine and health. During the Edo period (1603–1868), the widely shared ethic that "medicine is a benevolent art" recognized the humanitarian nature of medicine and suggested that all people should have access to medical care.

In and after the Meiji era (1868–1912), Japan investigated the old customs and practices throughout the nation and started to accept modern medicine. It has also learned from the social policy mapped out by Otto von Bismarck in response to negative effects of industrialization.[2] Although sufficient results were not necessarily obtained due to the inadequate economic power of Japan at that time and the path to war, the introduction of the universal healthcare system in 1961 after the war was a remarkable accomplishment.[3]

The mother and child health handbook was a significant achievement in the health sector. It is a simple system in that important data concerning the birth and growth of a child is recorded from the time a woman becomes pregnant. However, the degree of the contribution it has made to the health of the people is immense. In many Western countries, churches had control over the birth of children, and the role of the government in reproductive health was limited. As outlined above, the unique history of Japan's health care system, its tradition, and the government's intervention enabled the development of the mother and child health handbook.

This mother and child health handbook has become the key element in Japan's international cooperation in the health sector. The system of the mother and child health handbook has been implemented by various countries, including Thailand, Indonesia, and Kenya.

Going back to the overall issue of health, the most important effort is prevention. Prevention is more affordable and effective than treatment. Some basic practices for prevention are to wash hands, gargle, get proper nutrition, and have moderate exercise. While the mother and child health handbook provided basic education for mothers, these preventive practices were taught in schools in Japan. This example reflects how two seemingly unrelated sectors, health and education, are actually linked and influence one another.

In short, Japan's initiatives in the far-reaching and complex SDGs in the health and education sectors are considered to be one of the most effective cross-sectoral approaches and can lay the foundation for the achievement of other SDG targets. In this respect as well, Japan is also positioned to lead the international community in the initiatives aimed at achieving SDGs by leveraging the concept of Human Security.

Significance of Partnership

However, we should not be fully satisfied with what we have undertaken so far. For instance, there is the issue of partnership. While Human Security and MDGs also emphasize partnership, the SDGs highlight more clearly the significance of diverse forms of partnership, not only between governments, international organizations, and supporting institutions but also between business enterprises, NGOs/NPOs, universities and research institutions, local governments, and so on.

Conventional methodologies are considered insufficient to address SDG agenda items, such as the reduction of greenhouse gas emissions, development of vaccines for infectious diseases, ensuring food supply, and water purification, so the role of science and technology innovation are underscored. Of particular note are the sophisticated technologies owned by companies. In other words, tremendous business opportunities exist in the SDGs. It is believed that there is a strong possibility that companies' core technologies can contribute to solving problems. Good examples include the practical realization of a "waterless toilet" promoted by LIXIL, a Japanese company specializing in the housing and building industry, in Kenya and the introduction of contactless IC card technology (FeliCa), developed by Sony, in urban public transportation systems. The FeliCa system was also introduced by a state-owned bus company in Bangladesh through the cooperation of the Japan International Cooperation Agency (JICA).

It will even be possible for venture companies and small- and medium-sized companies with limited manpower and economic clout to contribute to achieving a sustainable society by leveraging their innovative technologies.

Domestic Efforts also Contribute to SDGs

Expectations for Japanese companies are not exclusive to their businesses overseas. The SDGs are universal goals that all countries, including advanced nations, are engaged in achieving. Therefore, the perspective that domestic efforts can also contribute to the achievement of the goals of other countries is also necessary. Here again, companies can function as "nodes" in their efforts for achieving the SDGs in partnership with consumers, investors, employees, affiliated companies, and so on.

The issue of food waste that surfaced as a problem in Japan is included as a target under SDG 12: "responsible consumption, production." In addition to this, "control of chemical substances and disposal, reduction in emissions," "reduction in wastes," and "sustainable lifestyle" are also included in the targets.

Furthermore, many of the initiatives launched in Japan, such as activities of elementary/junior high/high schools and local governments, regional development activities led by residents, environmental conservation activities, consumer movements, and so on are also tied to the global issues. The SDGs are closely related to our daily lives; each one of us is required to position the SDGs as our own goals and do whatever we can.

The Agenda of International Cooperation

According to the estimate by the UN Conference on Trade and Development (UNCTAD), the annual investment required to achieve the SDGs is US$3.9 trillion, of which only 1.4 trillion can be mobilized by developing countries through their own efforts. In contrast, the ODA from developed countries totals only US$137.2 billion (2014). Innovative ingenuity is required more than ever in order to use the limited resources effectively.

The Copenhagen Consensus Center, a think tank based in Denmark, published the results of their analysis on the cost-effectiveness of each of the SDG targets last year. The list of the targets proven to have the highest cost-effectiveness, thus calling for concentrated ODA investment, was narrowed down to 19 items, which include many of the unachieved MDGs. The think tank suggests that efforts should be first focused on unsolved issues under the MDGs, such as health and education in the low-income African nations. Priority would also be given to the eradication of violence against women, the promotion of female education, and the attainment of gender equality. These are the areas Japan has always emphasized in Human Security. As for gender equality, although much needs to be improved in Japan, support for female education is an area in which Japan has a long tradition, and it has been a focus of effort.

This year, the G7 Ise-Shima Summit is scheduled for May, and the Sixth Tokyo International Conference on African Development (TICAD VI) will be held in August. The agenda the Japanese government has been advocating, such as "universal health coverage," "a society where women can shine," "high-quality infrastructure partnership," and "African development," are considered higher-priority issues, for which Japan will be able to contribute greatly, achieving the SDGs through the strategic investment of ODA.

In the 1990s, Japan was the world's biggest ODA donor. However, the ODA budget continued to decrease in the past 16 years to half of its peak. Japan now ranks fourth globally in terms of aggregate spending and 18th in Gross National Income (GNI) and thus remains at a low level compared with other Development Assistance Committee (DAC) member nations. However, the government's draft budget for this fiscal year has shown a small increase. Japan should play a leading role in the SDGs to achieve results and once again become the world's foremost, world-proud donor nation by further increasing ODA. By doing so, Japan will be able to "occupy an honored place in an international society," as stated in the preamble to the Constitution of Japan.

Notes

1. Having presided at this council, the author is in no small part committed to both the National Security Strategy (NSS) and the "Proactive Contribution to Peace" policy. Although the ultimate author of this document and concept is Prime Minister Abe Shinzō himself, the author is positioned, so to speak, as a coauthor. This note was added for the purpose of maintaining fairness in discussion.

2. An icon in this connection would be Gotō Shinpei (1857–1929). Gotō learned Western medicine as a doctor, joined the Home Ministry's medical bureau to contribute more widely to people's health, and studied Bismarck's social policy in Germany as a policy to address social health. Gotō, who later rendered distinguished service in the colonial administration in Taiwan and Manchuria, attached much value on hygiene from the beginning; he set up a hospital and achieved great results of eradicating opium in Taiwan (Kitaoka 1988).

3. However, this does not mean that the introduction of the universal healthcare system had no harmful effect. For instance, it has been pointed out that medical development has stagnated compared with the US, where a fierce competition principle prevails; and the too successful system has imposed a heavy financial burden on the government. However, these are the results of a successful universal healthcare system, and the system itself should not be blamed for such an outcome. If there had been any adverse effect of the system, it is that the countermeasures were not sufficient. It would be irrelevant to call the universal healthcare system a failure.

Bibliography

Kitaoka Shinichi. *Gotō Shinpei: Gaikō to vijon* [A Biography of Gotō Shinpei: Diplomacy and Vision]. Tokyo: Chūōkōron-Shinsha, 1988. Published in English as *Gotō Shinpei, Statesman of Vision: Research, Public Health, and Development* (Tokyo: Japan Publishing Industry Foundation for Culture, 2021).

From the "1972 System" to "Strategic Mutual Benefits":
Japan's Foreign Policy toward China

Kokubun Ryosei

ABSTRACT For the first two decades following the normalization of diplomatic relations in 1972, Sino-Japanese relations developed on a foundation of bilateral friendship. Japan actively supported China's economic modernization and worked to facilitate China's integration within the international community. Since then, however, relations have deteriorated due to divergent understandings of historical events, differences related to Taiwan's status, and other points of disagreement. Seeking to reverse this worrisome trend, the two countries moved in 2006 not to revert to the neighborly friendly relations of old but to structure a forward-looking strategic mutually beneficial relationship. This was, however, derailed by the dispute over the Senkaku Islands and the bilateral relationship again turned chilly. While the United States is an important external factor in Sino-Japanese relations, it is increasingly clear that the two countries' domestic situations are more important.

During the 20-plus years since the end of the Cold War, the Japan-China relationship seems to have entered a long, dark tunnel that obscures the future. As is well-known, the two sides at times seem to be in competition over how low each can take its view of the other. As Figure 1 (p. 212) shows, over 70% of Japanese indicate, on a long-term basis, that they do not feel any affinity for China, and there are few signs of improvement in this trend. The major influence behind this deterioration is bilateral political problems. For instance, they would include: the crisis in the Taiwan Strait around the mid-1990s and the redefinition of the Japan-US security relationship; a renewed sense of history since President Jiang Zemin's visit to Japan in 1998 and early in the twenty-first century; the Japanese prime minister's visit to Yasukuni Shrine to pay respects to the war dead commemorated there; the attempts by North Koreans fleeing their country to take shelter in the Japanese consulate in Shenyang; China's opposition to Japan's membership in the UN Security Council; gas field development by China in the East China Sea; food poisoning caused by frozen dumplings from China; two Japanese patrol boats' collision with a Chinese trawler off the Senkaku Islands; a landing

conducted in the Senkakus by Hong Kong activists; and the Japanese government's purchase of the Senkakus.

Such incidents have been widely reported by the mass media, amplifying their effect in each country and contributing to a mutual decline in image. Since the 1990s, with the arrival of the IT revolution, individuals have come to vent their feelings toward these numerous developments across the Internet, producing a snowball effect. The concept of a mutually beneficial relationship based on common strategic interests was introduced in 2006 to stop this vicious cycle, but as one generation of politicians has been replaced over time by the next, the political network has been weakened and the new arrangement has had little or no effect on blocking further deterioration.

The overall Japan-China relationship, however, has shown a very different picture, corresponding to the broadening and deepening in interdependence in the bilateral economic relationship. Since the end of the Cold War, the Japan-China economic relationship, swept along by waves of globalization, has taken on a new and different appearance. As shown in Figure 2 (p. 213), despite growing opinions around the world about the potential threat from China,

Japanese investment in China began to pick up toward the middle of the 1990s, and while there was a gradual decline thereafter, investment once again began to expand rapidly with the start of the twenty-first century, undeterred by the worsening of bilateral relations over the Yasukuni visit. Despite the establishment of a mutually beneficial relationship based on common strategic interests in 2008, the results of that new setup faltered somewhat, but rapid growth began again even after the serious bilateral problems in the Senkakus. We can reasonably observe that such political problems do not seem to be useful variables in explaining the course of Japanese investment in China.

The investment in China by Japanese enterprises can be easily explained if looked at in terms of economic rationality. During the first half of the 1990s, China called itself a socialist market economy, substantially taking steps toward becoming a market economy. As a result, companies from around the world started to enter China. The Asian currency crisis, which occurred during the second half of that decade, also came as a heavy blow to Japan, which had been on the economic upturn, and investment in China fell. In 2001 China joined the World Trade Organization (WTO), which brought a shift toward China by foreign companies, and Japanese enterprises followed suit. The sharp slowdown in the US economy in the wake of the subprime mortgage crisis and the Lehman Brothers bankruptcy there around 2007 and 2008, and the accompanying European economic crisis, resulted in international investment in China going from growth to just marking time. Japanese companies' investments in China briefly declined during this period, but given the abnormal strength of the Japanese yen, a steady stream of companies, manufacturers mainly but others as well, found themselves with little course but to increase investment in China. There were, however, a good number of companies who sensed that Chinese investments would prove unstable in the future, so that investment in ASEAN also grew rapidly.

As a rule, when economic interdependence grows, it also becomes easier for frictions to appear, but it is believed that such frictions are

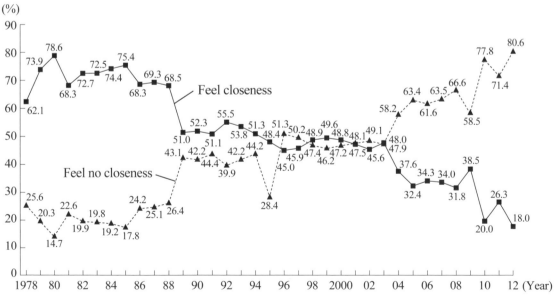

Figure 1. Feelings of closeness toward China

Source: Cabinet Office, "Gaikō ni kansuru yoron chōsa" [Survey on Public Opinion toward Diplomacy], October 2012

also steadily absorbed by mutual dependence. In Japan-China relations, however, the friction is increasing with no sign of abating. At one point the saying *sei rei kei netsu* was popular in Japan to describe Japan-China relations—"cold political relations but hot economic relations." The "20 lost years" and more have passed since the collapse of Japan's bubble economy, and with the 30th year quickly approaching, this is by no means favorable. Japan-China relations have worsened, and when anti-Japan demonstrations break out in the streets of China, it is Japanese-capital enterprises that are threatened and damaged. The source of Japan's strength lies in its economic power, and if exercise of that economic strength is blocked by the two sides' political relationship, Japan's economic recovery is also blocked.

Looking back, we can see that a variety of frictions had already appeared in the Japan-China relationship during the 1970s and 1980s. Examples would include the Japan-China air transport agreement, the bilateral Peace and Friendship Treaty, the Senkaku Islands, plant cancelations, problems with school textbooks, the question of official visits to the Yasukuni Shrine, trade frictions, the Kōkaryō Dormitory court ruling, the Tiananmen Square incident, and so on and so on. Despite such frictions, these problems inflicted no major damage on the bilateral relationship, as they were either resolved or reduced to minimal proportions or simply set aside. And that was even before the relationship of economic interdependence had taken on substantial form. This process of having political and economic relations develop interconnectedly actually contributed to the stable development of the bilateral relations. So, what happened after the Cold War to lead to the breakdown of this relatively smooth development in the relationship? In this essay, I will attempt an explanation through reference to Japan's diplomacy toward China. I would of course need to include reference to China's policies toward Japan to reach any comprehensive conclusions, but I will reserve that subject for another examination.

If we look back at the development of Japan's diplomacy toward China following World War

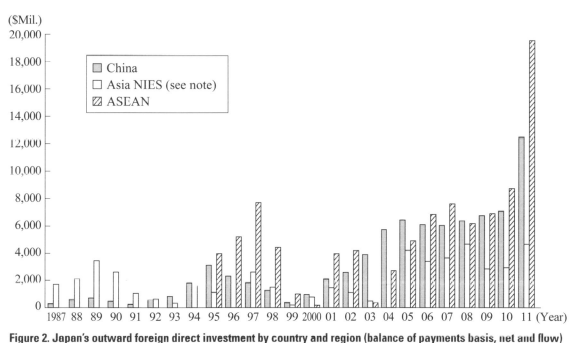

Figure 2. Japan's outward foreign direct investment by country and region (balance of payments basis, net and flow)

Note: Asia NIES data is for South Korea, Taiwan, Hong Kong, Singapore; Singapore excluded after 1995. Prepared from materials on JETRO's main site (20 December 2012).

II, we can see a number of periods based on what standards are taken for judgment, but it would seem effective to use the following three periods. Just by coincidence, each of these periods covers about 20 years. First would be 1952 to 1972. During this period, Japan restored diplomatic relations with the Republic of China on Taiwan (which we will just refer to as Taiwan) and had no diplomatic relations with the People's Republic of China on the mainland (hereafter China). Relations with China were limited to the private sector and consisted primarily of economic interchanges. The second period would be 1972 to 1992, during which time Japan normalized and expanded its relations with China, including both a treaty of peace and friendship as well as a number of working agreements. At the same time, however, historical problems and new developments, such as the Tiananmen Square incident, caused frictions. In 1992, China set itself on the road to economic growth via a socialist market economy and the Japanese emperor visited China, two factors representing a kind of turning point in Japan's diplomacy toward China. From 1992 to the present would represent the third period. In 1993, the Liberal Democratic Party (LDP) lost its singlehanded grasp on the government for the first time since 1955, and since then, Japanese governance has undergone a variety of changes and lost a great deal of stability. As the world has undergone ever greater globalization following the end of the Cold War, China has experienced very rapid economic growth and has expanded its national capabilities, making itself a presence to be reckoned with on the international scene; in contrast, Japan continues to find itself unable to completely recover from the bursting of the economic bubble. During this period, the Japan-China relationship has been beset by frictions, and despite the establishment of a mutually beneficial relationship based on common strategic interests as a new framework for Japan-China relations in 2006, the relationship today remains in the dark regarding its future path.

The focus of this article will be on the third period, the post–Cold War period. A full appreciation of Japan's diplomacy toward China, however, requires an understanding of its historical background. In particular, without an understanding of the true nature of the relationship established through normalization of ties in 1972 and of the international and domestic aspects of that relationship—the "1972 system"—it would be impossible to pursue the nature and problems of the relationship today. A number of considerations of the 1972 system have been conducted (Kokubun 2001), and in general, while Japanese scholars appreciate the historical significance of the 1972 system, they have strongly tended to point to its limitations since the 1990s, in particular since the end of the Cold War, Chinese scholars tend to stress the universal significance of the 1972 system (Mori 2006). Here, consideration will first be given to the normalization of relations during the second period so as to shed light on the 1972 system and the various preconditions it supported (regarding the first period, refer to the article by Inoue Masaya) (Inoue 2013).

1. Normalization of Relations and the "1972 System": 1972–92

Setting up the "1972 System"

On 29 September 1972, Prime Minister Tanaka Kakuei and Premier Zhou Enlai issued a joint Japan-China communiqué and normalized diplomatic relations between the two countries. Regarding the Taiwan issue, the communiqué took the position that Japan was "normalizing" rather than "realizing" its relations with the People's Republic of China, since Japan had already "restored relations" with the Republic of China in 1952. In addition, Japan recognized the government of the People's Republic of China as the sole legal government of China and attested that it fully understood and respected its stand that Taiwan was an inalienable part of the territory of the People's Republic of China. At the press conference following the release of the joint communiqué, Foreign Minister Ōhira declared a break in relations with Taiwan, stating that the peace treaty between Japan and the Republic of China had lost its rationale for continuing and had been brought to an end (Kazankai 2008, materials 7). In addition, before Prime Minister Tanaka's visit to China, Shiina Etsusaburō, one of the leading members of the LDP's pro-Taiwan group, had been dispatched to Taiwan in an act of "farewell diplomacy" that laid the groundwork for continuing private-sector exchanges after the breaking of diplomatic relations.

Regarding historical problems, the joint communiqué noted that "the Japanese side is keenly conscious of the responsibility for the serious damage that Japan caused in the past to the Chinese people through war, and deeply reproaches itself," in regard to which China declared that "in the interest of the friendship between the Chinese and the Japanese peoples, it renounces its demand for war reparation from Japan" (Kazankai 2008, materials 6). The fact that the communiqué renounced the "demand for reparations" rather than "the right to demand reparations" was due to Japanese insistence that, since the Republic of China had already renounced the right to demand reparations, the People's Republic no longer had such a right.

Regarding the developments during this period, Hattori Ryūji describes the political leadership of Tanaka Kakuei, the political negotiating abilities of Ōhira Masayoshi, and the support which they received from Ministry of Foreign Affairs personnel such as Treaties Bureau Director Takashima Masuo, China Division Director Hashimoto Hiroshi, and Treaties Division Director Kuriyama Takakazu (Hattori 2011). Inoue Masaya argues that, in the course of such negotiations, while the two sides achieved "agreement" on historical factors and Taiwan, or in a more ambiguous sense on some issues including the Senkakus, what they achieved was actually agreement to disagree (Inoue 2010). It is related that during the talks, Tanaka asked Zhou, "What do you think about the Senkakus?" Zhou is said to have replied, "I don't want to talk about that now. It's not good for us to talk about that now" (Ishii et al. 2003). Some have insisted that there was a tacit understanding that there was a problem involving the Senkakus, but the Japanese government holds that the problem has not been formally recognized.

Whatever the case, the Japan-China 1972 system that was set up at this time took, from Japan's viewpoint, a perception of history and Taiwan as its two fundamental principles and was based on:

first, the changes that had come to pass in the international environment forming an encircling net around the Soviets as the United States and China came ever closer as a result of the electrifying policies followed by the Nixon administration since 1971; second, the domestic Japanese sense that an increasingly important China should be welcomed into the international community; and third, Japanese domestic political agreement to that goal. As is frequently pointed out, an important role was played by highly individual politicians such as Tanaka Kakuei, Ōhira Masayoshi, and Takeiri Yoshikatsu, but the most important actor in the normalization of diplomatic relations was public opinion during that era, as it was broadly aroused throughout society by politicians, bureaucrats, business leaders, academics, and the mass media. That normalization of relations permitted an opening of channels between the governments of the two countries, so that Japan's foreign policies toward China thereafter were to be led mainly by the Ministry of Foreign Affairs.

China's Path to Modernization and Japan's Diplomacy

Following the normalization of diplomatic relations between Japan and China, Prime Minister Tanaka turned his attention to improving relations with the Soviet Union, but in 1974 Tanaka's own financial affairs came into question, and those problems triggered his retirement. In December 1974 the Miki Takeo cabinet was formed. During that period a number of government-to-government agreements had been reached primarily through bilateral diplomatic channels on fishing and air transport, and since the adoption of the civil air agreement sparked much disagreement about aircraft from Taiwan landing in Japan, it was finally decided that China would use Narita International Airport and Taiwan would use Haneda.

This series of governmental agreements was followed by the start of negotiations for a Japan-China treaty of peace and friendship, but the Lockheed scandal set Japanese politics on its heels, resulting in the July 1976 arrest of former prime minister Tanaka. In December of that year,

Fukuda Takeo replaced Prime Minister Miki, and China faced the last stages of the Great Cultural Revolution with the deaths of Zhou Enlai and Mao Zedong and the arrest of the Gang of Four, among other occurrences. These situations delayed negotiations on a peace treaty, and the main points of contention were over reference to "anti-hegemony." The Chinese side argued that including an "anti-hegemony" clause was appropriate since it appeared in the joint communiqué, while the Japanese side insisted that such language could not be included so long as it might be interpreted as aimed at the Soviet Union. The treaty negotiations were delayed, but when Deng Xiaoping came to power, the pace picked up greatly; in August 1978, Foreign Minister Sonoda Sunao visited China on order of Prime Minister Fukuda, and the treaty was concluded. In the end an "anti-hegemony" clause was included after it was agreed that Article 4 of the treaty would carry a third-party clause (i.e., language specifying that this treaty was not directed at any third-party nation) (Tanaka 1991).

At this stage in the Japan-China relationship, it was relatively simple on the Japanese side for relations to be guided by politics given the LDP's hold on the government and the political balance among the various factions. This was true on the Chinese side as well. Although the government faced a period of confusion as the Great Cultural Revolution ran its course, its policy toward Japan was consistently driven by political leadership under both Zhou Enlai and Deng Xiaoping. In April 1978, a large number of Chinese trawlers intruded the waters of the Senkaku Islands, but Deng immediately withdrew the vessels and indicated the intention to put the problem on the back burner for the next generation to deal with. It is theorized that the invasion of the Japanese territorial waters was actually the work of remnants of the Cultural Revolution supporters, but this is still unclear.

Subsequently, the Japan-China relationship entered its honeymoon period. Economics in particular began to pick up. This was largely the influence of the bilateral Long Term Trade Agreement concluded in February 1978. This agreement seemed to be a typical north-south arrangement, where China would export raw materials such as petroleum while Japan provided advanced science and technology, but it provided a step toward greater economic cooperation with China by Japanese financial circles. Because of China's long years of political contention, its economy was not highly built up, and perhaps it was impatience with the economic development that spurred the Hua Guofeng government to adopt a highly ambitious 10-year plan for economic development that called for constructing a momentous 110 categories of projects, with Japan-China trade at their core. Deng Xiaoping, who visited Japan, saw the reality of modernization there and took Japan as China's model for development. The Baoshan iron and steel plant (nicknamed the Baogang plant) built outside Shanghai with the full cooperation of Nippon Steel was viewed as a symbol of Japanese and Chinese friendship.

Such ambitious plans, however, were frustrated by China's shortage of foreign exchange and problems increasing oil production. Hua Guofeng faltered amidst the struggle for political power and was made to bear the burden of blame for those problems. Domestically, the rapid transition to construction for the purpose of modernization made the shortage in financial resources suddenly very evident, and it became unavoidable for China to adopt economic adjustment policies in spring 1979. Early in 1981, China began to cancel a variety of projects contracted with Japanese and West German companies among others. Pessimistic attitudes toward the Chinese market began to surface in Japan, and surprised by this reaction, Deng Xiaoping approved a full return to projects based on loans denominated in Japanese yen.

Turning to Official Development Assistance (ODA) provided to China, in December 1978 Prime Minister Fukuda resigned and was followed in office by Ōhira Masayoshi, who had worked in tandem with Tanaka on diplomacy with China, and under Ōhira's direction, more substantive attention was paid to ODA. This resulted in the first yen-denominated ODA loan for China, a five-year loan announced during Ōhira's visit to China in December 1979 amounting to ¥330.9 billion. Japanese ODA for China is frequently pictured as a means of atonement for China's dropping demands for reparations, but nothing can be found in any official government documents to back up such a claim. The rationale presented in official statements by Ōhira and others was that, by providing support for the Chinese modernization policies so recently instituted, Japan was keeping China from retreating to a period like that of the Cultural Revolution (Suh 2004; Xu 2011), This came shortly before the United States established diplomatic relations with China, meaning that Japan was a step ahead of the United States in diplomacy with China, and given the rapid pace of Japanese economic growth at that time, there were worries on the part of the United States and other countries that Japan might monopolize economic relations with China. For this reason, Japan in particular took such US and European anxieties into account when providing China with ODA and stressed that the aid was "untied," with no strings attached.

The Heyday of Japan-China Relations

Looking back, we can see that the 1980s was the heyday of the Japan-China relationship. During that decade, Japan was recording the world's greatest economic growth, as typified by Ezra Vogel's bestseller *Japan as Number One*, and some even ventured to call the twenty-first century Japan's century. Although factional strife had become the norm in domestic politics, the LDP had a stable hold on government. Prime Minister Ōhira's sudden death brought Suzuki Zenkō to office, followed by the long-term administration of Nakasone Yasuhiro, which, starting in November 1982 and lasting until November 1987, represented the most stable direction for the LDP under a single-party head. At the end of the Nakasone government, Takeshita Noboru took office in November 1987, and Unō Sōsuke became prime minister for a mere two months in June 1989, but he stepped down in the wake of a personal scandal and the losses suffered by the LDP in the House of Councillors elections, thus bringing in the cabinet of Kaifu Toshiki. During this period, Japan's trade with China consisted largely of importing petroleum and other primary products and exporting iron and steel, machinery, electronic goods, and the like, and all this trade grew rapidly during those years. Investment in China increased as well in keeping with the opening-up policies. During the Nakasone years, contracts were signed in 1984 alone for secondary yen-denominated loans amounting to ¥840 billion over six years. The Plaza Accord reached in 1985 gave greater momentum to a strong yen and weak dollar, and Japanese enterprises were left with little choice but to relocate abroad. The yen loans to China thus stood as a sort of Japanese national guarantee for such Japanese enterprises' moving to China.

Under Deng Xiaoping, China had just taken its first steps toward economic "reform and opening up" to the outside world and was vitalizing its economy via many twists and turns as it adopted a market economy even as it maintained a socialist system.

To move these efforts forward, China promoted a policy of opening itself to the outside world. Hu Yaobang played a central role in these efforts, having been named Chinese Communist Party general secretary at the 12th CCP National Party Congress in September 1982. Over the strong objections of party conservatives, Hu actively pursued economic reform and opening. Further, the two national leaders, Nakasone and Hu Yaobang, used the ties of personal trust they had established to agree to set up the Japan-China Friendship Committee for the 21st Century and promote bilateral youth exchanges, among other activities, to consolidate the friendly relations between their two countries. Hu was removed from office in January 1987 on claims that he had been overly tolerant toward student demands for democratization, but he was followed by reformer Zhao Ziyang, so this change had relatively little influence on the Japan-China relationship. Later, students took the death of Hu Yaobang as an opportunity to increase their demands for democracy, and the Tiananmen incident of June 1989 threw China into international isolation. During this same period, the waves of democratization in other regions brought the Cold War to an end and moved the Soviet Union toward dissolution in 1991.

"History" and "Taiwan" Raise Their Heads Again

It is undeniable that Japan-China relations experienced occasional problems during the 1980s. The first would involve school textbooks. In June 1982, during the Suzuki administration, a disagreement arose between Japan and China over descriptions in senior high school history textbooks, but the problem was finally resolved by releasing remarks by Chief Cabinet Secretary Miayzawa Kiichi that thereafter Japan would pay more attention to the position of its neighbors. A similar textbook problem appeared in 1986 during Nakasone's term, and 1985 saw contention between Japan and China over the first official visit to Yasukuni Shrine by a sitting prime minister. Prime Minister Nakasone did not conduct an official visit the following year, 1986, and the problem died away. Nakasone noted that the reason for not visiting was that such visits had presented a dilemma by opening General Secretary Hu, whom Nakasone viewed as a strong partner, to attack from Chinese conservatives (Hattori 2012).

Another major point of contention arising during the 1980s was the question of who owned the Kōkaryō Dormitory in Kyoto where Chinese students lived. Since 1952, this dormitory was owned by the Republic of China (ROC), but since the students living there included a group supporting the mainland, in 1967 the ROC government brought suit to have those students evicted from the dormitory. In 1972 Japan switched diplomatic recognition from the ROC to the People's Republic of China, and the courts in Kyoto denied Taiwan's claim in 1977. In 1982, however, the Osaka High Court responded to an ROC appeal and ordered that the denied claim be returned to the Kyoto courts. In February 1986 the court in Kyoto repeated its earlier decision and denied the claim, but in February 1987 the higher court in Osaka handed down a decision that Taiwan owned the dormitory. China vigorously criticized that decision, but the Japanese government did not respond, insisting on the principle of the separation of powers among the three branches of government (Kojima 2012).

During the Nakasone years, 1984–85 saw considerable shaking in the political world. That shaking represented ruptures in the LDP Tanaka faction, which had played the key role in Japanese policy toward China. In 1984, Nakasone named Kanemaru Shin, who had been the "captain of the guard" in the Tanaka faction, as the LDP's chief cabinet secretary; a step that surprised Tanaka Kakuei. When Kanemaru set up an organization called the Sōseikai in 1985, aimed at establishing Takeshita Noboru as Kanemaru's successor within the Tanaka faction, Tanaka got so angry that he suffered a stroke. In July 1987 the group was renamed the Keiseikai. This newborn group became the Takeshita faction, and Takeshita took office as prime minister in November. Later, large-scale bribery detected within the bureaucracy developed into the Recruit Scandal and also led to the scandal involving illegal political contributions by the Tokyo Sagawa Kyūbin trucking company. This marked the start of a breakup within the Takeshita faction and a rearrangement in political circles, with the result that the LDP's policies toward China lost coordination.

Contention in the Japan-China relationship during the 1980s centered on two major points, history and Taiwan, which supported the 1972 system. Such contention notwithstanding, the LDP's monopolistic control over Japanese politics provided a steady pipeline of communication to Deng Xiaoping, Hu Yaobang, and others in China's leadership, which drove the enthusiasm in Japanese financial circles toward the Chinese market and, at the same time, provided substance to the Japan-US-China relationship, which sought to form a net aimed at the Soviets. During this stage, ODA served as a symbol of friendship between Japan and China, with new assistance frequently announced during Japanese leaders' visits to China. Japan's public position was that it would be in Japan's interest and benefit the world as a whole for China, still a developing country, to be modernized and drawn into the international system; very likely this was the private opinion of many as well. This situation showed its effectiveness most clearly during the Tiananmen Square incident of 1989.

Tiananmen, a Southern Inspection Tour, and an Imperial Visit

A student movement demanding democracy for

China seized the opportunity offered by the death of Hu Yaobang on 15 April 1989. Due partly to what was essentially support by Secretary-General Zhao Ziyang, the participants in the movement rapidly increased to a million by mid-May. On 20 May, however, Deng Xiaoping and the other top leaders placed Beijing under martial law and on 4 June, in the so-called Tiananmen incident, used force to clear Tiananmen Square of the students who had massed there, resulting in clashes between the martial law troops and the students and other citizens there. During that period the democracy movement was making headway in Eastern Europe, and in the Soviet Union as well. Gorbachev was pushing rapidly ahead with the perestroika reform policy, making China's reaction to a similar phenomenon just the opposite. As a result, China became isolated internationally.

The United States and many other Western countries were severely critical of China. Japan was no exception. It announced it would freeze plans for providing ODA. Compared to other countries, however, Japan's reaction was rather mild. This was because Japan as a whole and the Foreign Ministry in particular took a broadly consistent stand against isolating China from the international community. It was partly due to geographical proximity but more a product of the pragmatic realization that Japan would not be able to change the emerging power that was China solely through its own efforts, and inclusion of China in the international community could solve China's systematic problems, including human rights. At the Summit of the Arch held in July 1989, while the other Western nations gave priority to human rights from their various domestic perspectives, Japan stressed hopes for support for China's reform and opening and the need to avoid putting China in isolation, with the result that such matters were included in the meeting's final declaration. Japan played the same role at the Houston Summit the following year, and in November 1990, Japan decided to remove the freeze on tertiary yen loans.

Perhaps due to some extent to such approaches from the outside, China launched itself on a path decided by Deng Xiaoping for audacious reform and opening up. Those policies were pronounced by Deng during his "southern inspection tour" in 1992 and in later declarations on a socialist market economy. This represents the moment when China determined to strengthen its foundation for such development, making the decision to participate actively in the market economy, which constituted the international system, based on the lesson drawn from the Soviet Union's collapse. This became the greatest inducement for investment from around the world and ushered in an age of annual growth rates over 10%. In April General Secretary Jiang Zemin visited Japan, where he met with the emperor and gave Prime Minister Miyazawa a formal invitation for the emperor to visit China.

The long-hoped-for imperial visit to China materialized in October 1992. In advance of the visit, some strong opposing views were expressed in Japan that the visit would be used for political purposes, but it came off problem-free. It is said that Deng Xiaoping had promised Japan that the emperor's visit would be a success. When speaking at the welcoming banquet, the emperor spoke of the historical friendship between Japan and China and of some personal thoughts on the matter, later noting that "in the long history of relationships between our two countries, there was an unfortunate period in which my country inflicted great suffering on the people of China. About this I feel deep sadness" (Kazankai 2008, materials 156). To the Japanese side at least, that moment represented the closing of a curtain on the two countries' postwar relations.

During this period, China sought to cleanse itself of the aftereffects of the Tiananmen incident and show a readiness to take active part in the international community, but at the same time, as shown in the process of drawing up the Law on the Territorial Sea and the Contiguous Zone (the "Territorial Sea Law") in February 1992, China began to work to strengthen its maritime interests and increase its naval capabilities. The Territorial Sea Law naturally defined the Spratly (Nansha) and Paracel (Xisha) islands as Chinese territory but also did the same for the Senkaku Islands, which belong to Japan. During this period, Japan faced such distractions as the bursting of the economic bubble and political disruptions, so the territorial issue was not made into a major problem.

2. Post–Cold War Diplomacy with China: 1992 to the Present

The Bursting of the Bubble and Redrawn Political Lines

During the latter half of the 1980s, in particular after the Plaza Accord, Japan found itself in a roiling bubble economy of rising asset prices centering on real estate. This situation did not last long, however; with 1989–92 as a peak, the sharp tightening of credit brought plummeting stock prices, and after the 1991–92 period, there was no way to put the brakes on the precipitous decline in land prices and the sudden increase in bad debts. Despite such developments, an overly optimistic outlook meant that government policy was slow to address these issues, setting off the move toward recession. All of Japan's financial institutions found themselves faced with failures and reorganizations into the second half of the 1990s. Japan went from a golden age in the 1980s into its 20 lost years. Following Deng's "southern inspection tour" of 1992, however, China suddenly found a foothold for a market economy and went all-out to launch itself on the path to growth.

The economic impasse in Japan caused political divisions. The Tokyo Sagawa Kyūbin political contributions scandal came to light in 1992 during the Miyazawa administration, shaking up Japanese political circles. The scandal began with the discovery of ¥500 million in under-the-table political contributions to Kanemaru Shin, but that was just the tip of the iceberg. It triggered Kanemaru's unwilling resignation from the Diet, and in the struggle over who would then head the Keiseikai group, which served as the Takeshita faction, Ozawa Ichirō and Kajiyama Seiroku found themselves in contention. Takeshita proposed Obuchi Keizō for the position, supported by Kajiyama, and as a result, in December 1992, Ozawa joined with Hata Tsutomu, Watanabe Kōzō, and others in forming Reform Forum 21. This development split the Takeshita faction, the biggest faction in the LDP. The opposition parties launched a no-confidence motion against the Miyazawa cabinet in June 1993, which passed with support from Ozawa and Hata, and Miyazawa dissolved the Diet's House of Representatives.

Amidst all this, Takemura Masayoshi and others left the LDP and formed the Shintō Sakigake (New Party Sakigake, also called the New Harbinger Party). Triggered by this, Ozawa and others also left the LDP to set up the Shinseitō (Japan Renewal Party). In general elections the following July, great gains were recorded by the Shinseito and the Shintō Sakigake as well as the Nihon Shintō (Japan New Party), which had been formed in 1992 centering on Hosokawa Morihiro, and in August 1993 these three parties put together a coalition government with Hosokawa as prime minister. This brought a close to the LDP's 55 years single-handedly heading the government. Contention later grew between Chief Cabinet Secretary Takemura and Ozawa over the national welfare tax, and this confusion was compounded when Prime Minister Hosokawa suddenly resigned in April 1994. Hata then became prime minister, but when the LDP introduced a motion of no confidence in his cabinet, the cabinet resigned en masse in June, less than two months after taking office. In the subsequent election to name a new leader, the LDP threw its votes to Murayama Tomiichi, chairman of the Socialist Party, resulting in a defeat for the Shinshintō (New Frontier Party), which had been set up by Ozawa as a coalition of opposition parties. (The party dissolved in December 1997.) The Shintō Sakigake joined up as well, allowing the formation of a three-party (LDP-Socialist-Sakigake) coalition and giving birth to the Murayama Tomiichi administration, headed by a socialist.

We can see that policies designed to handle the situation since the bubble burst have been delayed by the political confusion. At the same time, foreign policy could not be decided by political leadership, so there was no choice but to rely on the Foreign Ministry for diplomacy. In the past, policy toward China had been guided by the Tanaka faction of the LDP, the party's largest faction. The chaos within the Keiseikai, however, and the resultant structural weakening of the

LDP took away a strong foundation for China policy. Nakasone had already lost an important channel of communication when Hu Yaobang left the scene. The exposure of scandals such as that involving Recruit in 1988 and Tokyo Sagawa Kyūbin in 1992 brought rigid enforcement of the laws already in place in relation to political contributions, making people again clearly aware of such regulations, and Japan thereafter moved toward requiring political groups to reveal their assets and forbidding companies from making political contributions. The cleansing of politics moved forward and also worked toward removing that predisposition toward coziness between bureaucrats and companies, which served as a step toward splitting politics from economy in Japan's foreign relations. Beset by the post-bubble economy and the recession caused by the high yen, Japanese enterprises did relocate abroad, but this was not the result of any strategies tying the economy to politics.

New Guidelines and the Taiwan Strait Crises

The Hosokawa cabinet took a clear stand regarding the history issue. In his 1993 general policy speech, Hosokawa called the Sino-Japanese War an invasion and offered an apology. China welcomed these statements, but during the Hata administration, which took over after Hosokawa's resignation, Justice Minister Nagano Shigeto called the Nanjing Massacre a "fabrication" and was forced to resign for the characterization. This and other occurrences rocked the Japan-China relationship. In 1995, the 50th anniversary of the end of the war, Prime Minister Murayama of the Socialist Party sought a Diet resolution renouncing war, but the proposition made little headway and turned into a discussion which touched on history issues (Yakushiji, ed., 2012). This was preserved as Murayama's statement "On the Occasion of the 50th Anniversary of the War's End." Here, Murayama said, "During a certain period in the not too distant past, Japan, following a mistaken national policy, advanced along the road to war, only to ensnare the Japanese people in a fateful crisis, and, through its colonial rule and aggression, caused tremendous damage and suffering to the people of many countries,

particularly to those of Asian nations. In the hope that no such mistake be made in the future, I regard, in a spirit of humility, these irrefutable facts of history, and express here once again my feelings of deep remorse and state my heartfelt apology. Allow me also to express my feelings of profound mourning for all victims, both at home and abroad, of that history." (Kazankai 2008, materials 158).

Earlier, the Murayama cabinet had to face the problem of Chinese nuclear testing. In June and October 1994, China conducted two underground nuclear tests, testing again in May and August of the following year. These tests took place somewhat hurriedly, as if China wanted to get them out of the way before it signed the Comprehensive Test Ban Treaty. China's hardline position generated strong opposition in Japan, bringing much criticism of a fourth round of yen-based loans to China.

During 1993–94, suspicions that North Korea was developing nuclear weapons made Japan starkly aware of the need to restructure its post–Cold War security arrangements, bringing Japan and the United States to make a joint reaffirmation of their security commitment. This reaffirmation took place during the Hashimoto Ryūtarō administration, which replaced Prime Minister Murayama's government after Murayama's resignation in January 1996. During Hashimoto's discussions with President Clinton in April, the two leaders agreed on the need to elevate the Guidelines for Japan-US Defense Cooperation, which had been agreed upon in 1978 for use in a Japanese emergency; the goal of the revised guidelines would be to appropriately define the forms US-Japan cooperation could take during other emergencies in the area surrounding Japan. It was also about this same time that conditional agreement was reached on the relocation of facilities from the Futenma airfield in Okinawa.

In September 1997, the new Guidelines for Japan US Defense Cooperation were released after approval from the two governments, and the Diet was presented with drafts for revising the laws needed to put the new guidelines into practice, including the *Shūhen Jitai-hō*, known in English as the Law Concerning Measures to Ensure the Peace and Security of Japan in Situations in the Area Surrounding Japan, and the revised Self-Defense Forces Act. The *Shūhen Jitai-hō* was particularly important and generated considerable discussion of the sections defining "situations in the area surrounding Japan." The government did not view this as a geographical concept but rather focused on the nature of the situations concerned. Much was made in the media of speculation that the rather ambiguous wording employed in such sections was related to the Taiwan problem. North Korea was clearly a problem for Japan, but Taiwan was a much more nuanced matter. In addition, the democratization in Taiwan was making progress during this same period under President Lee Teng-hui, and Taiwan's first popular presidential election had taken place in March 1996. As a threat to Taiwan during these developments, China had conducted military exercises in 1995 and 1996 just before the presidential election, including missile tests.

China reacted strongly to the movement toward a set of new US-Japan guidelines, seeing them as policies for the joint defense of Taiwan. After the Taiwan Strait crisis, China was perhaps wary of setting off discussion not only in Japan but internationally as well about a "threat from China," and it went on the offense diplomatically to deal with a post–Cold War world where the United States alone was predominant. China was able to bring about the 1997 visit to the United States by President Jinag Zemin and President Clinton's visit to China in 1998, building up a "strategic partnership." Since Clinton's visit to China covered almost 10 days but did not include even a short stop in Japan, an old American ally, the visit resulted in discussion of whether it was a form of "Japan passing."

Jiang Zemin visited Japan in November 1998. The Japanese prime minister position at that time had switched from Hashimoto to Obuchi Keizō, and the Jiang visit proved quite displeasing to the Japanese (Kokubun 2000). This was because Jiang took every opportunity, including a banquet at the Imperial Palace, to criticize Japan's past militarism and otherwise unnecessarily raise questions concerning Japan's history. In China, the level of trust in socialism and the Communist

Party had fallen after its adoption of a socialist market economy; beginning around 1994, Jiang had raised calls for patriotic education, also using the 50th anniversary of the end of the war in 1995 to stress the importance of the anti-Japanese war that testified to the legitimacy of the Communist Party's authority in China. Japan considered that, after the emperor's visit to China and Prime Minister Murayama's statement on the occasion of the 50th anniversary of the war's end, history issues had more or less been put to rest, but to the contrary, on the Chinese side history issues seemed to remain in the leadership's thoughts and grow to new dimensions.

On 2 April 2000, Prime Minister Obuchi collapsed partway into his term of office and died on 14 May. Obuchi had been aware of the trends toward globalism and regionalism since the end of the Cold War, and even as regionalism was picking up momentum in Europe and North America, Obuchi was also sensitive to the trend toward regionalism in Asia. It was Obuchi who had promoted a framework consisting of ASEAN and the Japan-China-Korea triad. The personal relations that grew up between Obuchi and President Kim Dae-jung of South Korea played an important role during the Obuchi administration, and summit conferences among Japan, China, and South Korea became regular events. It was also Obuchi who decided to hold summit conferences in Kyushu and Okinawa.

The Koizumi Administration Period

When Obuchi fell ill, he was replaced as prime minister by Mori Yoshirō, but given his various slips of the tongue and inappropriate statements, Mori resigned in April 2001 after about a year in office. After Mori's resignation, Koizumi Junichirō entered the election for the head of the LDP, in what was actually a head-to-head battle with Hashimoto; Koizumi won and became prime minister. Koizumi had belonged to the old Fukuda faction and understood quite well the difficulties of a small, weak grouping, and so he sought to dissolve the party's factional politics with calls to "break up the LDP," putting pressure in particular on the Keiseikai. In the election he gained the support of the Japan War-Bereaved

Families Association, and at that time, he promised he would officially visit Yasukuni Shrine on 15 August, the anniversary of Japan's surrender (The Yomiuri Shimbun Political News Department 2006).

Perhaps to avoid creating a commotion, or perhaps to try to lessen sharp criticism from China and South Korea even a little, Koizumi made his visit to Yasukuni early on 13 August. China of course criticized the visit. But then, less than two short months later in October, Koizumi made a day trip to Beijing and visited the Anti-Japanese War Memorial Hall at the Marco Polo Bridge (Lugouqiao). There, he expressed his heartfelt apology and regrets to all the people of China who became victims in Japan's invasion (Kazankai 2008, materials 217). Koizumi had clearly been entertaining plans for a visit to Yasukuni, and it is likely that people in the foreign affairs community in each country, acting in advance of the visit, planned an early call on China as a form of damage control. In short, at this level the situation was open to management by the Foreign Ministry personnel in the two capitals. In the same month of October, Koizumi visited Shanghai to participate in an unofficial APEC summit meeting, and while there he met with Jiang Zemin. Further, on 12 April 2002, Koizumi was invited to attend the Boao Forum for Asia, a gathering seeking status as a Chinese Davos. Even though it was not to be a meeting at the national leader level, Koizumi decided to attend.

Very shortly after he returned home, however, on 21 April 2002, Koizumi unexpectedly visited Yasukuni. Koizumi had intended his attendance at the Boao Forum and other similar gestures to demonstrate in advance to the Chinese the attention he was paying to their country, but China seemed to view the Yasukuni visit as a betrayal. The foreign ministries in the two countries could do little about this event since they had no advance notice. It was this second visit to Yasukuni, even more than the first, which turned Yasukuni into a real point of contention (The Yomiuri Shimbun Political News Department 2006; Kokubun 2010). Prime Minister Koizumi conducted further visits to Yasukuni Shrine on 14 January 2003, 1 January 2004, 17 October 2005,

and, shortly before his resignation, on 15 August 2006.

Domestically, viewpoints were divided regarding the appropriateness of such visits to Yasukuni Shrine, and during the five years from 2001 to 2006, Japanese society seemed to have nothing else to occupy its attention other than Yasukuni. Globalization of the international economy moved on apace, and countries around Asia came more and more to the fore, with China in particular starting to emerge during this stage both politically and economically. Koizumi's diplomacy with the United States was delivering great results, but his diplomacy with other Asian countries was merely marking time. Domestically, however, Koizumi was extremely popular, and in the September 2005 general elections, called the "Koizumi Theater" by some, the LDP made the most of the single-seat constituency system and the attention to the privatization of the postal service to bring home a major victory.

During March and April of 2005, the question of the reform of the UN Security Council, in particular the expansion of the number of permanent members of the council, sparked large anti-Japan demonstrations around China every weekend, and the police, anxious to keep the demonstrators from having cause for major violence, stood by and allowed the demonstrations. During this period, summit-level talks were being held during regularly scheduled international meetings and similar events, but they had no success in improving relations. The Japan-China relationship was thus at an impasse, and in the United States, the Bush administration, especially after the 9/11 attacks in 2001, was greatly concerned about a possible worsening of Japan-China relations and began to hope for some stabilization.

Economic relations, however, fared just the opposite of political relations, and Japan rapidly leaned more and more toward China. One major reason for this trend was China joining the WTO in December 2001. Japan played an important role in China's membership. This was in keeping with Japan's policy of encouraging China's internationalization by inviting its active participation in the international community. As Figure 2 indicates, despite the Yasukuni problem and being virtually unaffected by it, Japanese investment in China grew rapidly beginning in 2001. This was Japanese companies' way of responding to how China's membership in the WTO had influenced other countries to increase the pace of their entry into the Chinese market, and it also was a reflection of the problems caused for Japanese companies by the strong yen. This separation of political and economic affairs was indeed an example of the saying *sei rei kei netsu*—"cold political relations but hot economic relations."

During the Koizumi administration, the problem of resource development in the East China Sea became a steadily more intense element in the Japan-China relationship. Following the establishment of the Territorial Sea Law in 1992, China began to greatly step up its oceanographic surveys so as to expand its maritime interests. A system was set up in February 2001 for advance notice of plans to conduct oceanographic survey activities, but soon after taking shape, the system began to shift toward empty formality. In 2003 China began to develop natural gas fields near the mid-point between Japan and China in the East China Sea, and while Japan rigorously objected, it could do nothing to stop these activities. In addition, China continued to modernize its military and conduct its own foreign aid, raising growing doubts and criticisms in Japan over ODA for China. Prime Minister Koizumi announced in 2004 that China had "graduated" from receiving yen-based loans, and the two countries' governments later agreed that the loans would aim for completion by the 2008 Olympic Games in Beijing. It was at this point that the two countries' relations ceased to be a north-south relationship.

Reviving Summit-Level Interchange and a Strategic Mutually Beneficial Relationship

Koizumi resigned in September 2006, and the search for his successor narrowed down to his chief cabinet secretary, Abe Shinzō. Even before rising to prime minister, Abe had given the job of coordinating the Japan-China relationship to Vice-Minister for Foreign Affairs Yachi Shōtarō. Within the Foreign Ministry and elsewhere in the foreign policy community, considerable

criticism was directed at the "China School," the China hands with a background in China and the Chinese language, and Yachi tried to handle foreign policy toward China himself. At this time, an important role was played by the comprehensive foreign policy dialogue (a strategic dialogue) between Vice-Minister Yachi and Dai Bingguo, a vice-minister in the Ministry of Foreign Affairs who had direct access to Hu Jintao. These dialogues were held from time to time starting in May 2005, in anticipation of developments after Koizumi's departure. Against the background of such behind-the-scenes diplomacy, soon after Abe became prime minister on 26 September 2006, he paid visits to China and South Korea between 8 and 10 October. As a result, the visit to China by Abe served to improve the damaged bilateral relationship in a single stroke. During this "ice breaking" visit to China, the Japanese remained ambiguous about Yasukuni, not touching on whether a visit had or had not been paid to the shrine and not commenting on whether visits would or would not be made in the future. Needless to say, the decision was made on the Japanese side by Prime Minister Abe and on the Chinese side by President Hu Jintao, who was able to keep the hardliners at bay, but behind the scenes were the unobtrusive efforts by Yachi and Dai (Kokubun 2008).

The results of the visit were presented in a joint press statement. Here was the first appearance of a reference to a mutually beneficial relationship based on common strategic interests as a new stage in the Japan-China relationship. Such a relationship was somewhat different from the neighborly friendly relations between Japan and China, in other words the 1972 system, that had been pictured for the two countries since the normalization of relations. More than a bilateral approach with an emphasis on the past in the form of pledges to deal with the issues of history and Taiwan, the new approach turned toward the future as indicated by using the term "strategic." It expressed a more multilateral approach of dealing together with affairs in the region which further uses the expression "mutually beneficial" to symbolize that emphasis is being placed on real benefits for each side. Where problems of history were involved, the emphasis came to be placed on giving Japan rightful credit for its peacefulness and development since the war rather than on the prewar situation.

The next year, in April 2007, Premier Wen Jiabao visited Japan. Dubbed an "ice-melting" trip, this visit's highlight was an address to the Diet. In his speech, Premier Wen made minimal reference to history or Taiwan and lauded Japan's postwar peacefulness and development, also positively highlighting the fact that the Japanese government had repeatedly apologized for problems in history. This visit also gave more substance to the meaning of a strategic mutually beneficial relationship, with agreement reached on such areas as expanded exchanges between the leadership, high-ranking officials, youth, and other groups; promotion of a security dialogue and joint research into history; and greater interchange involving finance, agriculture, energy, environmental protection, intellectual property, and telecommunications.

In September of that year, Prime Minister Abe abruptly resigned for health reasons, and Fukuda Yasuo was installed after him. Fukuda had a well-developed pipeline of contacts with China and worked hard to strengthen that relationship. He paid a formal visit to China from 27–30 December and sought to speed up progress toward realizing that sort of strategic mutually beneficial relationship, focusing in particular on improving relations through cooperation on the environment and energy and through youth exchanges. On the East China Sea, it was announced that it could be made "a sea of peace, cooperation, and friendship." This visit, by the way, was christened Fukuda's "ringing in the spring" trip.

From 6 through 10 May 2008, President Hu Jintao made a state visit to Japan. This allowed completion of a cycle of visits by heads of state and was in turn christened Hu's "warm spring trip." Because Hu was a state visitor, he met with the emperor three times, a welcoming call on the emperor, a state banquet in the Imperial Palace, and a farewell meeting. The visit to Japan was marked by release of a Joint Statement between the Government of Japan and the Government of the People's Republic of China on Comprehensive

Promotion of a "Mutually Beneficial Relationship Based on Common Strategic Interests," which laid out in more detail some specific measures to further such a relationship. This arrangement would serve as a contribution to matters of bilateral importance, including: the promotion of mutual trust in political areas through exchanges of visits by the countries' leaders and a security dialogue; exchanges between the public media and youth as well as cultural exchanges; cooperation for the common good in energy and the environment, food safety, trade and investment, and East China Sea resources development; and concerns of global significance as well, including climate change, energy security, poverty, and infectious diseases.

Actually, during this visit Hu gave China's agreement to joint development with Japan on natural gas fields in the East China Sea near the halfway mark between the two countries, resources on which China was already at work. This was not announced at that time, however, due to strong Chinese domestic resistance, and it was only made public in June. The Great Sichuan Earthquake, 8.0 in magnitude, took place on 12 May, just two days after Hu Jintao's return to China. China permitted emergency assistance teams from a wide range of countries to enter China, but at Hu's personal direction, the team from Japan was the first admitted. Chinese media reported prominently on the Japanese emergency team's activities. This was one fruit of the strategic mutually beneficial relationship.

On a daily, working-level basis, however, the Japan-China relationship declined in ways seemingly unconnected to this sort of accommodation at the very top. One example was the food poisoning from frozen dumplings, which occurred in January 2008, where food products manufactured in China's Hebei Province contained the organic phosphorous insecticide methamidophos, which poisoned several families in Japan's Chiba and Hyōgo prefectures who had eaten these products. The incident provoked the temporary disappearance of all Chinese frozen foods from Japanese supermarkets. Another example involved the Olympic sacred flame relays through various countries leading up to the 2008 Beijing

Olympics; protest demonstrations were held internationally by Tibet independence movement groups, and protest demonstrations were also held in Japan, timed to the Hu visit. Both of these two examples led to a deterioration in China's image. In short, the strategic mutually beneficial relationship agreed upon at the governmental level did not contribute to an improvement in Japan's image of China.

Birth of a Democratic Party of Japan (DPJ) Administration and Chinese Trawler Collisions Near the Senkakus

The Olympics were held in Beijing in August 2008. This was an opportunity for China to enhance its national prestige, and it also outranked the United States in the number of gold medals captured. It was a moment when one could imagine that China's day had arrived at last. Very shortly thereafter, beginning on 15 September, the world economy suddenly went into a dive—the much-discussed "Lehman shock." China, acting like the big power it saw itself as, immediately declared that would lay out 4 trillion yuan (roughly ¥56 trillion or US$586 billion) to support the economy. China not only felt its international presence was growing stronger, it was trying to match its words and actions to the ever more obvious picture it presented of itself as an international power. In contrast, while Japan was attempting to recover from its recession, it once again fell into stagnation and was seeing a decline in its prestige. Then in 2010, Japan's GDP was surpassed by China's to fall to third internationally. It was said that in 2000 Japan's GDP had been four times that of China, and this happened in just about 10 years.

After Koizumi's resignation, Japan's LDP administrations changed at yearly intervals. From Abe the office went to Fukuda, then, in September 2008, falling support rates caused Fukuda to resign and Asō Tarō was installed as prime minister. The different factions all shared the common concept that foreign policy toward China should seek a strategic mutually beneficial relationship, so that goal stayed in focus despite the changes in leadership. Foreign policy in the Asō administration envisioned an "arc of freedom and prosperity" and tried to strengthen relations with India. This approach at one point caused China to worry that Japan was seeking to encircle it, but Asō was aware of the importance of attention to China, which he supplied by active visits there among other gestures. Prime Minister Asō, however, put off domestic general elections, and because of problems related to some unfortunate statements during this period, popular support for Asō plummeted.

General elections were at long last held on 30 August 2009, and Asō's LDP was far outpaced by the Democratic Party of Japan (DPJ). But rather than being a major victory for the DPJ, this was the result of the voters' sense of disappointment in the LDP, as reflected through the single-seat constituency system. Still, the DPJ government also had to face a variety of problems, such as intraparty discord and lack of experience and the disastrous results of the March 2011 Great East Japan Earthquake and the subsequent accident at the Fukushima Number 1 nuclear reactor, as well as the party's inability to provide stable government management as represented by the annual shift in prime minister from Hatoyama Yukio to Kan Naoto to Noda Yoshihiko. There was no change in a strategic mutually beneficial relationship as the premise of foreign policy toward China, but the Japan-China relationship still deteriorated greatly. And bilateral contention shifted from history and Taiwan to the Senkakus.

Hatoyama's DPJ administration, coming into power atop the great LDP failure, tried to thoroughly disavow the pattern and style of policy under the LDP. One example was the way in which it tried to limit involvement by bureaucrats, putting matters thoroughly under political leadership from the very start. Important government policy formation, including foreign relations, excluded bureaucrats, and regularly scheduled meetings involving deputy-level administrative vice-ministers were halted. Plans were scrapped for reducing the burden on Okinawa by relocating the Futenma airfield to Henoko, Nago City, replaced by calls for locating the facilities outside of Okinawa Prefecture. At the November summit talks with President Obama, Prime Minister Hatoyama asked Obama to "trust me" to find a solution by the following May, even though he had no particular course in mind.

In foreign relations, the DPJ government invoked a "spirit of fraternity" (*yuai*) and stressed the ties to China and South Korea, also urging an East Asian community. China and South Korea of course expressed their welcome for these ideas, but in combination with the Futenma problem, US lack of trust in Japan grew and the stability of the US-Japan alliance was questioned. DPJ policies, both domestic and international, seemed out of touch with reality, and as growing attention was directed to the party's own pronounced political fundraising problems, support for the Hatoyama administration fell sharply. On 2 June 2010, in a joint meeting of DPJ Diet members from both houses, Hatoyama announced his resignation as prime minister; on the 4th an in-party election for a new DPJ leader selected Kan Naoto, who was sworn in as prime minister on 8 June.

On 7 September, the Kan administration ran up against a major problem in relations with China. Chinese fishing vessels entered Japanese territorial waters off the Senkaku Islands and began operating illegally there. When Japan Coast Guard patrol boats warned them off, a Chinese trawler deliberately collided with the Japanese vessels. The Coast Guard arrested the captain of the trawler for interference in official duties, whereupon the Chinese government immediately demanded the release of all crewmembers. Under direction of Chief Cabinet Secretary Sengoku Yoshito, all the crewmembers except the captain were returned to China on the 13th and the trawler was also released. At first it was decided to keep the captain in custody for a longer period, but then, on the 25th, the Naha public prosecutor's office released the captain without indictment and returned him to Fujian Province. During this period China engaged in retribution, such as limiting Chinese tourism to Japan, restricting rare earth exports to Japan, and taking four personnel from the Fujita Corporation into custody. Protest demonstrations broke out in both countries during October, further complicating the relationship, but on 30 October, Prime Minister Kan and Premier Wen briefly held talks during the East Asian Summit conference in Hanoi, and Kan also met briefly with President Hu Jintao on 13 November during the Yokohama APEC conference, confirming that the two countries had returned to a strategic mutually beneficial relationship.

Setbacks for the DPJ, Revival for the LDP

On 11 March 2011, the Great East Japan Earthquake struck, and Japan was forced to respond to the consequences of the subsequent major tsunami and the accident at the Fukushima 1 Nuclear Power Plant. President Hu Jintao sent the emperor a telegram expressing China's sorrow and condolences, as did Premier Wen to Prime Minister Kan, and they also offered to send an international aid team. Premier Wen inspected the site of the destruction while in Japan for the May bilateral summit conference. Prime Minister Kan, who had been severely criticized for his response to the earthquake and the nuclear plant accident, announced his resignation on 26 August, and on the 29th, the DPJ leadership elections selected Noda Yoshihiko as its leader, giving birth to the Noda administration. Counting from Prime Minister Abe, Noda was the sixth prime minister in five years.

The Noda administration got off to a good start with China, visiting there in December and repeatedly holding summit talks while attending various international conferences. Eventually, however, Noda was beset by the situation in the Senkakus. In April 2012, while visiting Washington, DC, Tokyo Governor Ishihara Shintarō unexpectedly announced that the Tokyo Metropolitan Government planned to buy Uotsurishima, Kitakojima, and Minamikojima islands in the Senkakus. The Noda administration watched the situation and eventually, in July, decided in favor of having the country make those purchases. During this period, criticism by the Chinese Ministry of Foreign Affairs was relatively softer, perhaps thanks to the Foreign Ministry working-level talks that were held intermittently, but when activists from Hong Kong landed in the Senkakus on 15 August, China exploded with criticism on the Internet, and anti-Japanese demonstrations took place around China every weekend. When the Japanese government made the official purchase on 11 September, anti-Japanese demonstrations took place throughout the country every weekend during September. The demonstrations became violent, and some Japanese businesses and products were destroyed.

Prime Minister Noda also had a brief talk with President Hu Jintao on 9 September at the APEC Leaders' Meeting in Vladivostok. Tang Jiaxuan, a former state councilor, complained that it had been impolite to make the purchase immediately after the earlier talks, but it is said that the Japanese side's interpretation had been that China had already been informed of the plans for the purchase and had taken part in the talks right before the fact only to drive home its point.

The question is why the Chinese reaction, which at first had been relatively restrained, suddenly became so pronounced after the middle of August. The answer is closely tied to Chinese domestic politics. China had its 18th CCP National Party Congress in the fall of that year, and a fierce internal struggle for power was going on behind the scenes. It appears that Bo Xilai, party secretary at Chongqing, was thought likely to be promoted to standing member of the CCP Central Committee Politburo, but something major occurred in February 2012, which led to his downfall, and Hu Jintao was able to consolidate his own authority in the process. The list of seven Politburo standing members at this point is thought to have consisted almost completely of members with roots in the Communist Youth League, Hu's power base. Since Hu at the time had been engaged in developing a conciliatory approach to Japan, his advantaged position in CCP circles may have made him unwilling to put much emphasis on the Senkakus. During the first half of August, however, the annual party summer meeting was held in Beidaihe, where CCP personnel matters were given a final adjustment, including matters affecting elder statesmen. There, conservatives centering around Jiang Zemin and Zeng Qinghong were able to reclaim authority, and in a stroke, the list of names of the seven members of the Politburo Standing Committee changed to people close to the conservatives. It is thus very likely that this development largely undercut Hu Jintao's power base, and his conciliatory policies

toward Japan, such as joint development of East China Sea resources, came under criticism.

The Noda cabinet, while trying to deal with the confusion in the political situation, also had to respond to such great difficulties. The relations between Prime Minister Noda and the bureaucratic structure of the Foreign Ministry and other agencies did improve greatly, and the prime minister was able to keep his position and policies in focus. However, the Chinese gave up attempts to conduct talks with Prime Minister Noda and instead seemed to start looking to discussions with whatever new administration followed Noda after the general elections. Prime Minister Noda dissolved the House of Representatives on 16 November 2012, as promised, and general elections were held on 16 December. The result was disaster for the DPJ and a resounding victory for the LDP. An election for party president had already been held in the LDP, with Abe Shinzō winning over such candidates as Ishiba Shigeru, and the general election results meant that Abe was made prime minister on 26 December. The second Abe cabinet was formed in coalition with the Kōmeitō.

3. From the "1972 System" to a "Strategic Mutually Beneficial Relationship"

As touched on earlier, tracking the course taken by Japan's policies toward China reveals that while interdependence in economics and other areas has deepened, there has also been a negative correlation in that political friction has also grown. Economic interdependence does not provide support for a political relationship. Rather, friction between Japan and China grew along with progress toward interchange and globalization in the various areas of contact, beginning with economics. In short, that is because the relationship does not include any stabilizing mechanism that can prevent the various types of friction from arising as bilateral contacts grow, or at least to hold the friction to the smallest possible level. Looking back, we can see that, at least until the 1980s, such a function was being performed despite the fact that interdependence was not growing.

Why did that mechanism cease to work? It

is possible to find an answer to that question in terms of the limits to the 1972 system and the immaturity of the mutually beneficial relationship based on common strategic interests that was agreed upon to take over from the earlier system. As discussed earlier, the 1972 system, as seen from the Japanese viewpoint, consisted of two fundamental principles, the perceptions of history and Taiwan. It was premised upon changes in an international environment where the growing closeness of the United States and China was taking on the form of a net to encircle the Soviet Union, on Japan's domestic awareness that as China became more important it should be welcomed into the international community, as well as on agreement in Japan's domestic politics on that latter point.

Phases of History Issues and the Taiwan Problem

We can conclude that there has been no change in the basis for these two fundamental principles. Looking at the perceptions of history, Japan has not changed its basic position regarding the wars and aggressions of the past, and Murayama's statements on the 50th anniversary of the end of World War II still stand. To the Japanese, Murayama's public statements and the emperor's visit to China in 1992 marked an end to an era on the issue. To the Chinese, however, due to growing lack of trust in the Communist Party and other domestic circumstances, as well as the Taiwan problem, or even just because of an individual leader's personal preferences, the war against Japan again became a topic of attention. As a result, the Japanese side came to feel tired of patriotic campaigns by the Communist Party, which were expanded by using domestic sentiment or playing the Japan card.

This phenomenon came to a peak with the visits to Yasukuni Shrine right during the Koizumi years. Domestically, there are arguments in Japan on both sides of the question of the political leadership visiting the shrine, but there was a spreading aversion to how China was interfering with Japanese internal affairs. Right after Koizumi's retirement, the Abe government was born, and its ability to reach a kind of historical accommodation with Hu Jintao freed the bilateral relationship

from the spell cast on it in the past; this was because of the intention to sublimate a mutually beneficial relationship based on common strategic interests with an eye to the future and the overall situation. While resistance from the Jiang Zemin faction, which maintained a very unsparing attitude toward Japan, continued to be strong, Hu Jintao continued to try to avoid references to historical problems and adopted a magnanimous, conciliatory policy toward Japan, which focused on Japan's peacefulness and development since the war. There are a number of rationales offered for why Hu adopted this approach. For example, some say that Hu Jintao's attitude was related to how, as the person responsible for carrying out General Secretary Hu Yaobang's youth exchange during the mid-1980s, he made repeated trips to Japan. In that sense, an important topic for future attention will be just how Xi Jinping, the successor to Hu Jintao, will deal with history matters and promote the strategic mutually beneficial relationship.

Looking at the positioning of the Taiwan problem, as confirmed under the 1972 system, even today Japan continues to support the One China principle and has firmly maintained its stance of not supporting independence for Taiwan. There have, however, been some great changes in Taiwan between 1986 and the present. Taiwan, during the Chiang Kai-shek and Chiang Ching-kuo days, was under dictatorial rule of the Kuomintang, but from around 1986, toward the end of Chiang Ching-kuo's time in office, Taiwan suddenly entered a period of democratization, which took on more momentum with the start of the Lee Teng-hui era in 1988. As a result, the democratization of Taiwan—which actually was a "Taiwanization" of the ROC—developed rapidly, switching in 1996 to a democratic system where the president was chosen through popular elections. This development did not bring changes in the fundamental structure of relations between Japan and Taiwan, but in addressing the question of Taiwan, Japan has come to emphasize that the future of Taiwan should reflect the will of the people.

Lee Teng-hui spoke positively about the past when Taiwan was under Japan's control. Jiang

Zemin was incensed by this, categorizing it as Japanese aggression against China and as part of the historical problem. Later, during the Hu Jintao years, Taiwan played a much smaller role in the mutually beneficial relationship based on common strategic interests, due to progress made on concepts such as "maintaining the status quo" and "dialogue." We can now watch to see whether the Taiwan problem will be kept at this relatively low level under Xi Jinping. Or will Xi's administration, which has been emphasizing the unity and superiority of the Chinese people, once again raise the Taiwan problem as a priority theme?

Shifts in the International Environment

Japan's postwar diplomatic engagement with China started in a Cold War framework. The Yoshida government, which had just recently secured independence for Japan, could not turn its back on its ally, the United States, and it was against such a backdrop that Japan gave priority to its diplomatic relationship with the Republic of China on Taiwan. The fact that the normalization of relations in 1972 became possible was also a result of the US-China rapprochement. In other words, it was wholly natural under the Cold War structural setup that Japan should stay in step with the United States. This all means, in short, that the 1972 system was due to coordination among Japan and China and the United States and represents the design of a relationship to resist the Soviet Union.

In that sense, the end of the Cold War in 1989 held a more profound meaning when looked at in reference to international relations. The hypothetical enemy that was the Soviet Union evaporated, and Japan, China, and the United States lost the Soviet Union as a common target that the three had shared. With the coming of the 1990s, situations such as the Taiwan Strait crises and China's rapid economic growth raised the specter of a "Chinese threat," and in response, China became wary of the strengthening of the Japan-US alliance. This situation, in reality reflected the flux in the international environment that followed the Cold War. As the twenty-first century began, China displayed an even stronger orientation toward modernization of its economic power,

and its military might as well, a phenomenon which added momentum to the situation.

Against a background of the globalization of the economy since the start of the 1990s, with the exception of the Asian currencies crisis of 1997, there has been more and more of a leveling effect for Asia's economies as their growth rates increased, and in addition to China, South Korea and the ASEAN countries have rapidly increased their ability to make themselves heard. In addition, the growth of the Asian economy as a whole brought up a wide range of topics of common interest, including finance, the environment, energy, intellectual property, poverty, and contagious disease, and each country needed to find ways to deal actively with such concerns. This in turn created a background for Asia's rapidly growing interest in the premise of globalization in regionalism, including free trade agreements and comprehensive economic partnership agreements.

A strategic mutually beneficial relationship between Japan and China was proposed to reflect these Asian realities. In short, the existing Japan-China relationship had each partner focused squarely on the other partner, with little interest in looking at the bilateral relationship more broadly to include Asia or the world. When Japan and China gave some thought to correcting this situation by placing more emphasis on how they, as the two largest powers in the region, could jointly contribute to such common concerns of the region and the world, the result was a mutually beneficial relationship based on common strategic interests. Without a doubt, there were many topics of common regional concern, some of which had reached a stage calling for common action. Both Japan and China were able to recognize this. But it was not easy to shift from the inertia of bilateralism built up over the years, and there was still little concrete content to the strategic mutually beneficial relationship.

From North-South Relations to a Level Relationship

If we look at the political system in China around the time of the normalization of relations, we see that instead of being authoritarian, it was more of a sort of totalitarianism. Under the dictatorial rule of Mao Zedong, the Great Cultural Revolution devastated the country. It was, in the end, a war over authority. So how was it possible for relations with China to be normalized at this stage, followed by a sudden improvement in Japan's domestic image of China? That is hard for us to imagine looking at the situation today. But as already mentioned, that was the vox populi of the day; the trend of the times.

It was in December 1978 that China had the opportunity to shift course from the revolutionary road to the path toward modernization and move toward a policy of reform and opening up. That was the time of the 3rd Plenum of the 11th CCP Central Committee. Provision of yen-denominated ODA to China had begun, with the goal of bringing China, which had just barely started its efforts at modernization, into the international community. Around that time China had taken Japan as its model of development and at a stroke was moving forward, promoting trade and the import of technology. Under the long-term trade agreement concluded between Japan and China, Japan would provide China with science and technology while China would give Japan petroleum and other basic resources and materials—a typical north-south arrangement between an advanced country and a developing one. This phase of relations continued from the 1980s to the 1990s. During this period China continued to decrease its production of oil until, in 1993, it turned into a net importer of petroleum. It experienced rapid economic growth starting in 1992 with the shift to a market economy, which presented an opportunity for a flood of foreign capital seeking a cheap labor force in China. Such developments are not so different from such a pattern.

Doubts about ODA for China started to appear in Japan after Tiananmen Square, and while it froze the ODA at first, Japan did not want to isolate China and was quicker than other countries in restoring the aid. During the first half of the 1990s, while Japan suffered through the aftermath of its burst economic bubble, China celebrated its rapid economic growth. From around the middle of the 1990s, when China was conducting nuclear tests and sparking crisis in the Taiwan Strait, doubts began to appear

over whether China could indeed be counted as a developing country. Later, as China continued on its course of military modernization and it became apparent that China itself had begun to assist developing countries, criticism of the ODA for China rose to new levels. With the arrival of the twenty-first century, in the face of such occurrences as China's unannounced start of resource development in the East China Sea, Prime Minister Koizumi began to allude to China as having "graduated" from ODA. Later the two countries agreed to move toward ending ODA, with the Beijing Olympics of 2008 as a goal.

In 2010, China outstripped Japan in GDP, becoming second internationally. China was already devoting twice Japan's expenditures to national defense. China even now still considers itself a developing country, but the Chinese marketplace overflows with the world's biggest companies, and it is the world's largest holder of US national debt. It is increasing its presence on every economic stage around the world. In short, the relationship between Japan and China has shifted from a north-south relationship to a level one, and if China's momentum and its political influence are taken into account, one might wonder whether the positions have been reversed. This phenomenon means that the two countries are entering into a difficult phase, where realizing the "mutually beneficial" in their strategic mutually beneficial relationship presents a challenge.

Changes in Agreement on Policy (Political, Bureaucratic, Financial)

If we look at the policymaking process regarding Japan's diplomacy toward China, we can see that over the 40 years since normalization, there have been some major changes. Before normalization, Japan did not have relations with China, and accordingly, the role of the Foreign Ministry and other bureaucratic institutions and financial circles was relatively minor, with the top elite instead playing an overwhelmingly large role. The views of the elite toward China carried great weight. That is plain if we look at the periods identified with Yoshida, Kishi, Ikeda, Satō, and others. In the normalization process itself, parties, such as those led by politicians including Tanaka and Ōhira, bureaucratic institutions centering on the Foreign Ministry, and the members of financial circles who supported the Japanese economy as it grew, were able to participate broadly and pretty much at will. This trend continued at least until Nakasone's years in power. We could even say that during this period, political leadership, bureaucratic institutions, and Japan's economic growth represented a unified "trinity" of their own.

Following the 1990s, however, as the Cold War ended and the bubble economy collapsed, the political scene in Japan fell into confusion. Internal divisions in the LDP resulted in its fall from power in 1993. While the Hosokawa coalition government did take office, it proved unstable, which resulted in an LDP-Socialist Party coalition government. That coalition was dissolved, but the LDP was incapable of exercising a monopoly on forming a government. With Japan's entry into the twenty-first century, the Koizumi government did last for a long period, but it was followed by the reappearance of a situation where the administration changed annually.

Then, in 2009 a Democratic Party government was born, and the LDP was again removed from power. The prime minister, however, changed annually, from Hatoyama to Kan and then to Noda, and after that, the LDP bloomed again in December 2012 and the second Abe Shinzō administration was born. During this period there was a string of political scandals and examples of political corruption, which brought a tightening of the laws restricting political contributions to block the relationship between money and politics. In the relationship with China, the links between politics and the business community have been weakened, a separation of politics and economics has continued, and bureaucracies no longer shine as brightly as they once did. As the once powerful trinity has collapsed, attention is somehow still continuing to be paid to the so-called mutually beneficial relationship based on common strategic interests, but efforts to make these words into reality are lagging behind.

Conclusion

When we consider Japan's diplomacy toward China, we need to keep in mind three factors, Japan's domestic situation, the international environment, and the situation in China in terms of a feedback function. Here, we have conducted an analysis based on Japanese domestic circumstances and the international environment, excluding the situation in China. We have placed the focus on Japanese domestic circumstances. What is most important in foreign relations is having enough political stability to permit a cool analysis of the world and the situation in the other country along with one's own standpoint, then to formulate specific foreign policies based on both a grand vision and strategic considerations and carry that out. This is because foreign policy is an extension of domestic politics. It bears repeating that such fundamentals must not be forgotten.

Looking back, the international environment factor seems to have played a relatively small role in Japanese foreign policy toward China. Conditions in the world economy or China's economy were indeed major background factors influencing corporate activities within economic circles, but the US factor was overridingly influential on the political aspects of Japan's foreign policy toward China. That fact, of course, does not explain all that took place, but the fundamental structure of that foreign policy has not changed from the immediate postwar period to the present. In that sense, the Japan-China relationship in an international context essentially was Japan-US-China relations. The reason that the influence of the international environment was relatively small in the Japan-China relationship was that the weight of history was an ever-present underlying factor in the relationship, including with Taiwan. So long as the Chinese Communist Party in particular maintains its political control over China, prewar history, and particularly the CCP's role in the war against Japan, will preserve the legitimacy of its authority. China continues to insist that Japan is belittling its unfortunate history, and in Japan, distrust of China continues to grow as the Japanese wonder how long China intends to continue to pursue anti-Japanese education. That fact in particular explains why it is difficult to bring changes in the 1972 system and its emphasis on bilateralism.

The significance of a strategic mutually

beneficial relationship lies in how it includes the possibility of an escape from that sort of vicious cycle. It has become possible to give a formal name—"a mutually beneficial relationship based on common strategic interests"—to the framework to which Japan and China will gravitate in the end. What remains is the question of how to move forward, steadily creating something to fill in that framework. The essential elements for Japan and China will be a sense of reality and a broad perspective.

English version originally published by the Japan Institute of International Affairs in the Japan Digital Library, Japan and the World Series (2017).

This article was originally published in 2013 as "'1972 Shisutemu' kara 'senryakuteki gokei' e: Taichū gaikō," in *Nihon no gaikō dai 4 kan* [Japan's Diplomacy vol. 4], edited by Kokubun Ryosei (Tokyo: Iwanami Shoten), 111–42.

Bibliography

Hattori Ryūji. *Nitchū kokko seijōka: Tanaka Kakuei, Ōhira Masayoshi, kanryōtachi no chōsen* [Japan-China Diplomatic Normalization: The Challenge of Tanaka Kakuei, Ōhira Masayoshi, and the Bureaucrats]. Tokyo: Chūōkōron-Shinsha, 2011.

———. "Nakasone-Ko Yōhō kankei to rekishi mondai 1983 1986nen" [The Nakasone-Hu Yaobang Relationship and the History Problem 1983–1986]. In *Nitchū kankeishi, 1972–2012, I, seiji* [The History of Japan-China Relations, 1972–2012, I, Politics], edited by Takahara Akio and Hattori Ryūji. Tokyo: University of Tokyo Press, 2012.

Inoue Masaya. *Nitchū kokkō seijōka no seijishi* [Political History of Japan-China Diplomatic Normalization]. Nagoya: University of Nagoya Press, 2010.

———. "Nitchū kankei no keisei: Nikka heiwa jōyaku kara Nitchū heiwa yūkō jōyaku made" [Shaping the Japan-China Relationship: From the Treaty of Peace between Japan and the Republic of China to the Treaty of Peace and Friendship between Japan and the People's Republic of China]. In *Nihon no gaikō dainikan gaikōshi sengohen* [Japan's Foreign Diplomacy, Volume 2, History of Diplomacy, Postwar], edited by Hatano Sumio, 71–96. Tokyo: Iwanami Shoten, 2013.

Ishii Akira, Zhu Jianrong, Soeya Yoshihide, Lin Xiaoguang, eds. *Kiroku to kōshō: Nitchū kokkō seijōka, Nitchū heiwa yūkō jōyaku teiketsu kōshō* [Documentation and Investigation: Normalization of Japan-China Diplomatic Relations and Negotiations for Conclusion of the Treaty of Peace and Friendship between Japan and the People's Republic of China]. Tokyo: Iwanami Shoten, 2003.

Kazankai. *Nitchū kankei kihon shiryōshū: 1972–2008* [Basic Materials in the Japan-China Relationship: 1972–2008]. Tokyo: Kazankai, 2008.

Kazuko Kojima. "Kōkaryō mondai, 1987–88 nen" [The Kōkaryō Dormitory Problem: 1987–88]. In *Nitchū kankeishi, 1972–2012, I, seiji* [The History of Japan-China Relations, 1972–2012, I, Politics], edited by Takahara Akio and Hattori Ryūji. Tokyo: University of Tokyo Press, 2012.

Kokubun Ryosei. "Shiren no jidai no Nitchū kankei: Ko Takumin hōnichi kijitsu" [The Japan-China Relationship in a Time of Ordeal: Records of Jiang Zemin's Visit to Japan]. *Hōgaku kenkyū* [Journal of Law] 73, no. 1 (2000): 65–81.

———. "Reisen shuketsugo no Nitchū kankei: '72-nen taisei' no tenkan" [The Japan-China Relationship after the End of the Cold War: Transition of the '72 System']. *Kokusai Mondai* [International Affairs], no. 490 (2001): 42–56.

———. "Nitchū kankei to kokunai seiji no sōgo renkan: Kinnen no kankei kaizen o megutte" [The Relationship between Sino-Japanese Relations and Domestic Politics: Recent Efforts at Diplomatic Rapproachement]. *Hōgaku kenkyū* [Journal of Law] 81, no. 6 (2008): 1–21.

———. "The China-Japan Relationship, East Asian Community, and the Dynamics of Trilateral Relations." In *Getting the Triangle Straight: Managing China-Japan-US Relations*, edited by Wang Jisi, Gerald Curtis, and Kokubun Ryosei. Tokyo: Japan Center for International Exchange, 2010.

Mōri Kazuko. *Nitchū kankei: Sengo kara shinjidai e* [The Japan-China Relationship: From the Postwar Period to a New Era]. Tokyo: Iwanami Shoten, 2006.

Suh Seung-Won. *Nihon no keizai gaikō to Chūgoku* [Japan's Economic Diplomacy and China]. Tokyo: Keio University Press, 2004.

Takahara Akio, Hattori Ryūji, eds. *Nitchū kankeishi, 1972–2012, I, seiji* [The History of Japan-China Relations, 1972–2012, I, Politics]. Tokyo: University of Tokyo Press, 2012.

Tanaka Akihiko. *Nitchū kankei 1945–1990* [The Japan-China Relationship 1945–1990]. Tokyo: University of Tokyo Press, 1991.

Wang Jisi, Gerald Curtis, Kokubun Ryosei, eds. *Getting the Triangle Straight: Managing China-Japan-US Relations*. Tokyo: Japan Center for International Exchange, 2010.

Xu Xianfen. *Nihon no taichū ODA gaikō: Rieki, pawā, kachi no dainamizumu* [Japan's ODA Diplomacy toward China—The Dynamism of Interest, Power, and Values]. Tokyo: Keisō Shobō, 2011.

Yakushiji Katsuyuki, ed. *Murayama Tomiichi kaikoroku* [Murayama Tomiichi, a Memoir]. Tokyo: Iwanami Shoten, 2012.

Yomiuri Shimbun Political News Department, The. *Gaikō o kenka ni shita otoko: Koizumi gaikō 2,000 nichi no shinjitsu* [The Man Who Turned Diplomacy into a Quarrel: The Reality of 2,000 Days of Koizumi Diplomacy]. Tokyo: Shinchōsha, 2006.

III-(10) | What the "Indo-Pacific" Means for Japan

Shiraishi Takashi

ABSTRACT Prime Minister Abe Shinzō started to use the term "Indo-Pacific" to capture the regional arena whose security, stability, and prosperity is crucial for Japan. This essay notes that the United States put more emphasis on geopolitics, while the Japanese government underlines the importance of both geopolitics and regional economic cooperation.

In recent decades, Asia's regional framework has been shaped and reshaped according to the region's perceived underlying risks.

In the 1990s, when the Japanese economy outstripped the combined gross domestic product of all other countries in Asia, the "Asia-Pacific" emerged as a regional framework for East Asian countries and the United States, as well as for Mexico, Chile, and Peru. This was intended to prevent Asia from becoming Japan's backyard.

After East Asia suffered an economic crisis in 1997–98, "East Asia" emerged as a regional framework, with countries in the region viewing the United States as a risk. This development was a response to Washington's hard nosed, interventionist approach in pressuring Thailand, South Korea, and other crisis-stricken economies to comply with overly demanding structural reform policies.

Now, what about the "Indo-Pacific" concept? The Australian government adopted the "Indo Pacific" term in 2012 as a pivotal idea in its diplomacy. Prime Minister Abe Shinzō used the same term for the first time in August 2016 during the Sixth Tokyo International Conference on African Development (TICAD VI), held in Nairobi, when he unveiled a "Free and Open Indo-Pacific" strategy.

Abe said, in effect, that vital sea lanes in the Pacific and Indian Oceans connect Asia and Africa, and the world's stability and prosperity hinge on the dynamism that is brought forth through "the union of [the] two free and open oceans and two continents." He urged that the Pacific and Indian Oceans be turned "into peaceful seas" and "a place that values freedom, the rule of law and the market economy, free from force or coercion."

US president Donald Trump used the "Indo-Pacific" term for the first time in Da Nang, Vietnam, in November last year when he participated in the summit meetings of the Asia-Pacific Economic Cooperation (APEC) forum. He supported the vision of "a free and open Indo-Pacific—a place where sovereign and independent nations, with diverse cultures and many different dreams, can all prosper side by side, and thrive in freedom and in peace."

Why is the "Indo-Pacific" now the focus of attention as a regional framework? What is the risk that gives urgency to the "Indo-Pacific" vision?

Considering Asia's economic growth and Africa's growth potential, the vast region that stretches from the Pacific to the Indian Ocean has a good possibility of becoming the center of prosperity in the twenty-first-century world. However, China, under the leadership of President Xi Jinping, aims to become hegemonic in Asia through its military build-up and regional economic cooperation in the name of the "Belt and Road Initiative" (which still is called "One Belt One Road" in Chinese) that envisages the creation of a vast geo-economic zone. This is the risk against which the "Indo-Pacific" concept is meant to hedge.

Japan and US Differ

Nonetheless, Japan and the United States differ significantly in their approaches to the "Indo-Pacific" vision.

To realize a "free and open Indo-Pacific," Abe has called for improving infrastructure, promoting trade and investment, and fostering human resources development, while seeking to deepen the Japan-US alliance and strengthen security partnerships with Australia and India, among other countries. He thus attaches importance to the economic growth of the region while ensuring the regional power balance in response to China's military buildup. In this context, it is of great significance that Japan and 10 other countries signed a new Trans-Pacific Partnership, also known as TPP11, in March.

Trump, meanwhile, emphasizes negotiating bilateral free trade agreements (FTAs) instead of multilateral trade pacts like the TPP. In its "National Security Strategy (NSS)" issued in December last year, the Trump administration defined the "Indo-Pacific" as an arena for geopolitical competition between the United States and China.

In the Indo-Pacific region, the United States and China are in competition to shape the regional order in their own favor. As the US National Security Strategy puts it, "China is using economic inducements and penalties, influence operations, and implied military threats to persuade other states to heed its political and security agenda." Its "infrastructure investments and trade strategies reinforce its geopolitical aspirations. Its efforts to build and militarize outposts in the South China Sea endanger the free flow of trade, threaten the sovereignty of other nations, and undermine regional stability. China has mounted a rapid military modernization . . . Chinese dominance risks diminishing the sovereignty of many states in the Indo-Pacific." The report states that the United States will exercise leadership "in a collective response that upholds a regional order respectful of sovereignty and independence."

There exists a clear and important difference between Japan and the United States as to the "Indo-Pacific" regional vision.

Japan opposes China's moves to impose its political will on other countries in the region by force and coercion, while, nevertheless, cooperating with China wherever possible. This approach is based on Japan's principle of ensuring "freedom, the rule of law, and market economy."

The United States has been rebalancing its military assets toward Asia since the early 2010s. Responding to this pivot, Japan has deepened its alliance with the United States and strengthened strategic partnerships with Australia and India. As for the territorial disputes in the South China Sea, Japan opposes Beijing's claim over the entire South China Sea and activities to build and militarize artificial outposts there.

On the economic front, however, Japan has adopted a more accommodating approach, as in the case of China's Belt and Road Initiative. In June 2017, Abe offered a positive evaluation of the Chinese scheme for its "potential to link diverse areas," while demanding that the principles of transparency and fairness prevail in choosing and funding infrastructure projects and that recipient countries' fiscal soundness be maintained.

US-China Confrontation

On the other hand, the Trump administration is more inclined to adopt a confrontational stance on China. The NSS document labeled both China and Russia as "revisionist powers" challenging "American power, influence, and interests" and intent on "shap[ing] a world antithetical to U.S. values and interests." To be specific, the United States accused China of seeking to "displace the United States in the Indo-Pacific, expand the reaches of its state-driven economic model, and reorder the region in its favor."

On the economic front, the United States is now pursuing bilateral free trade agreements in its own favor by employing its overwhelming economic might. Washington now does not hesitate to resort to coercion as witnessed in recent FTA negotiations with South Korea. In other words, from the perspective of countries in the Indo-Pacific region, the United States under Trump seems to be behaving like the "revisionist power" it accuses China of being.

If this kind of situation continues to prevail, it will remain difficult to realize a "free and open Indo-Pacific." The "Indo-Pacific" unites an immense region, stretching from the western shores of the Americas to the eastern coast of Africa. The region has two main geographic spines—the east-west line running from Japan to India via the Philippines and Indonesia, and the north-south line stretching from Malaysia and Singapore to Australia. As such, the backing of these countries is crucial for the realization of a "free and open Indo-Pacific."

These countries want to ensure their sovereignty and security and improve their standard of living by achieving economic growth. The peace and stability of the region are supported by the US-led regional security system. Therefore, US efforts to reinforce the security system will be greatly appreciated.

But the "Indo-Pacific" strategy of the United States is overly preoccupied with Trump's "America First" trade policy.

What each country should now do is not to prioritize its own interests but to cooperate with one another to enable every country in the region to enjoy peace, stability, and prosperity. In this regard, Japan should take the initiative, together with Australia, India, and the Association of Southeast Asian Nations (ASEAN) member states, to promote and deepen such regional cooperation.

Originally published by The Yomiuri Shimbun in *The Japan News* "INSIGHTS into the WORLD" (8 May 2018).

III-(11) Changes to the International System Due to the Rise of China

From Trade Wars to a New Cold War

Tanaka Akihiko

ABSTRACT With the inauguration of the Trump administration, Sino-American relations stopped being just a trade war and developed into a new Cold War with systemic disputes including ideology as well as military and national security clashes. Concern over China has spread and is now pervasive throughout American society, and the United States has recognized it made a mistake in supporting China's development in the hope prosperity would be accompanied by internal liberalization. China is showing the developing countries that there can be a path to development that does not include adopting Western freedoms and democracy. This new Cold War between the US and China will persist so long as China maintains its current political structure. Accordingly, Japan is being called upon to state unequivocally that it is in the freedom-and-democracy camp and to respond to China in concert with the Euro-American states—even as it needs to create areas of peaceful coexistence with China to ensure the new Cold War not become a Hot War.

Four Characteristics of the Trump Administration Compared to the 1980s

Is this the beginning of a new Cold War? It has now become usual to characterize US-China relations using the term "trade war." But is the conflict affecting that relationship really limited to trade alone? During the 1980s and 1990s, the United States turned Japan's trade surplus with the United States into a problem, and trade friction between the two nations intensified. But can we really describe the ongoing US-China trade war as a contemporary version of Japan-US trade friction? Rather, if the current clash between the United States and China is not simply a trade war, and if we were to seek a similar phenomenon, could we not compare it to the Cold War between the Soviet Union and United States? In other words, should it not be considered the ongoing evolution of a systematic conflict that encompasses both ideology and military and security issues?

President Trump often makes statements to the effect that a balance of trade reflects a nation's loss or gain. In this respect, the current US-China trade war is similar in many ways to 1980s Japan-US trade friction.

The US trade deficit with the rest of the world during the 1990s was US$124.3 billion, while its deficit with Japan was US$44.5 billion, accounting for 36% of the whole (according to IMF, Direction of Trade data). Despite the fact that most economists said there was no point, from the perspective of economics, in making an issue of the trade deficit between the two countries, the majority of American politicians thought that Japan should reduce exports to the United States and increase imports. As a result, there was a series of voluntary export restraints on automobiles and other goods, as well as talks on opening Japan's market to goods such as oranges and beef. During the final stage of Japan-US trade friction, numerical targets were set for the import of US-made semiconductors. Then, in 1989 the Japan Structural Impediments Initiative took place: talks that treated the makeup of the Japanese market itself as an issue.

The United States' current trade deficit with China is also enormous. Looking at the 2017 figures, the United States had a US$797 billion trade deficit with the rest of the world, including a US$375.2 billion trade deficit with China that accounts for 47% of the whole (according to IMF, Direction of Trade data). The visit to China this May by a large group of US economic officials, and their demands to the Chinese side regarding various areas of the economy, is a scene that reminds us of past Japan-US trade friction.

Even from the limited perspective of trade negotiations, however, there are aspects to the current US-China trade war that were not seen in the Japan-US trade friction of the past.

Firstly, President Trump rarely refers to the multilateral trade system and has no hesitation in moving forward with bilateral trade negotiations. No previous US president has shown this lack of interest in the multilateral trade system.

Secondly, the Trump administration is pushing on with bilateral negotiations, not just on trade with China but with all the countries and regions with which the United States has a trade deficit, such as Canada, Mexico, South Korea, the EU, and Japan. What is more, every one of these countries has said that the United States is engaged in "unfair" behavior.

Thirdly, in the case of negotiations with each of these countries, the United States suddenly said it will impose tariffs but then forced the other side into talks. In the case of negotiations with China, too, the United States suddenly imposed approximately US$50 billion of tariffs on Chinese goods exported to the United States and said that, should China retaliate, it would impose a further approximately US$200 billion of tariffs on exported goods or, if necessary, put tariffs on all the Chinese goods exported to the United States. During the Japan-US trade friction, various points of agreement were reached before retaliatory tariffs were set.

And fourthly, the United States has demanded that China put in place regulations to protect intellectual property rights and securely implement them and stop demanding intellectual transfer accompany investment from overseas. Furthermore, the nature of its demands has greatly exceeded the scope of previous trade negotiations, including that China stop state support for what one might describe as China's industrial strategy: Made in China 2025. (According to reports, the United States has even demanded withdrawal of the plan itself.)

An Incoherent President Versus a Judicious Political System

When we look at the Trump administration's trade policies as a whole this way, there seems to be no clear establishment of priorities and, to put it negatively, the strategy appears incoherent. Probably, it is the personality of President Trump that has given rise to these characteristics, as well as the obscurity and uncertainty that distinguishes the running of his administration. It seems that President Trump is not unduly concerned about appearing incoherent. That is because it seems he believes the secret of successful "deal making" is not to allow the other party to understand his real intentions.

However, according to media reports since the start of the administration, the book recently published by Bob Woodward, and a newspaper column written by an anonymous writer claiming to be an administration official, it is a situation in which the making of decisions and implementing them is chaotic. The "adults" in the administration are using persuasion and sabotage to somehow avoid President Trump's impulsive and ill-thought out decisions and to ensure that decisions made by its government do not cause damage to the US national interest.

We really do not know the truth. But it is gradually becoming clear that there are considerable checks on President Trump's ability to decide policy. Since he is the president, he has considerable legislative authority. Yet, various political and administrative processes must be gone through for the personal statements of the president to be implemented as decisions made by the United States. The appointments made by the Trump administration to date have been exceptionally unusual, and the appointment of officials to many key departments still has not taken place. Furthermore, appointed officials continue to resign or leave their posts. Meanwhile, the view of the anonymous writer is that a "quiet resistance" is working to prevent the country from making mistakes. Of course, it is not impossible for President Trump to overcome this quiet resistance and see that his orders are implemented. But to date, policies that have not had the agreement of this quiet resistance have been sabotaged or, even when they have been imple-mented, it seems only to have been in a suitably watered-down form.

Moreover, the administration is not the only entity that can decide US policies. So far, in vari-ous ways the US judiciary has checked the imple-mentation of Trump administration policies. Also, Congress has a decisive role regarding US policy. Article I, Section 8, Clause 3 (Commerce with Foreign Nations) of the US Constitution gives authority for tariffs and trade negotiations to Congress. While it is possible for an adminis-tration to negotiate trade with various countries, ultimately it is Congress that has the final say. Accordingly, when an administration conducts trade negotiations it is under pressure to make sure the contents of those negotiations are within the limits of Congress's agreement.

President Trump probably dislikes constraints such as these. But that is exactly why the anti-Trump camp in the US consider him dangerous to the nation's freedom and democracy. If it were possible for Trump to act in a way that fundamen-tally defeated these constraints, he would com-pletely overturn the US constitutional system and destroy the nation's system of freedom and democ-racy. Should something like that happen, it would be a massive threat for all those living in systems of freedom and democracy around the world—a much greater disturbance than the rise of China.

While one cannot completely deny the possi-bility of freedom and democracy being destroyed in the United States, I do not think it will happen. So far, the Trump administration has not been able to overcome these constraints, and while an anti-democratic trend is not completely absent among hard-line supporters of President Trump, there is no particularly obvious anti-democratic movement. If, as anticipated, the Democrats gain a majority in Congress following the November midterm elections, these constraints will become even stronger. It will probably become hard for the administration to implement most of its con-troversial policies.

In other words, these are the safety valves that the founding fathers incorporated into the US Constitution at the end of the eighteenth century. The US Constitution was drafted by James Madison in accord with his assumption that "Enlightened statesmen will not always be at the helm." When an "enlightened statesman" is absent, preventing despotism due to the entire government becoming dysfunctional is a concept that lies right at the heart of the system of freedom and democracy and a function such as this may be operating right now.

China's Erosion of Intellectual Property Rights and High-Tech Industries

When it comes to trade policy, too, it is very unclear what would ultimately happen should such dysfunction occur. Practically speaking, no trade negotiations result in completely free trade or completely protective trade; and there are deals with different degrees of freedom or protec-tion for various goods and services.

Although the deal agreed at the end of August between the United States and Mexico was not desirable from the perspective of those who advocate for completely free trade, as a political settlement it was not improbable. The "quiet resistance" may have decided that if they com-promise this far, things will not be that bad.

In any case, since the long-term economic effects will not appear immediately, if President Trump wishes, he can say that it is a victory for the United States and end negotiations. I believe that ultimately there will be a similarly vague agreement when it comes to Canada, the EU, and Japan, too.

So, what about the trade war with China? Since the United States' trade deficit with China is far larger than with other countries, resolu-tion of the issue will not be easy. Furthermore, a decisive factor is that US demands of China are qualitatively different to trade issues with other countries. When the Trump administration said it would impose tariffs on steel and aluminum products from the EU and Japan "for security reasons," many commentators pointed out that it was strange to raise the issue of security regarding steel and aluminum products from ally nations. At the end of the day, should trade issues with ally nations not be about regulation issues such as jobs rather than security issues? It seems that the first and second distinct features of the Trump administration's trade policies mentioned above ultimately do not reflect the US national interest, while they push the whole of US society (including forces of resistance) toward a weakened state.

What is more, the United States is not currently just seeking action related to jobs through its demands on China. Even assuming that President Trump personally thinks job issues are the absolute priority, Chinese industrial development capacity in cutting edge fields is more important from the perspective of the overall US national interest.

This June, the White House issued a report titled: "How China's Economic Aggression Threatens the Technologies and Intellectual Property of the United States and the World." According to this report, China steals technology and intellectual property using both physical and cyber means, as well as forcing the transfer of technology by foreign-owned companies by various regulations and domestic measures. In addition, it is collecting information via the huge number of students and researchers based in research institutions in the United States and other nations. What is more, it is attempting to buy overseas companies with advanced technology through the use of foreign investment by state-owned companies. The report argues that through these activities China seeks to "Acquire key technologies and intellectual property from other countries, including the United States, and capture the emerging high-technology industries that will drive future economic growth and many advancements in the defense industry."

The US National Security Strategy, released at the end of 2017, expresses a similar view. It states that "China and Russia challenge American power, influence, and interests, attempting to erode American security and prosperity. They are determined to make economies less free and less fair, to grow their militaries, and to control information and data to repress their societies and expand their influence." It indicates the same perception as the White House report that "Every year, competitors such as China steal US intellectual property valued at hundreds of billions of dollars."

Also, it seems that these worries about China regarding security are not just evident in Trump administration documents but are shared by US society as a whole. This spring, a supply of US semiconductors to the Chinese communications equipment maker ZTE was halted due to the company's illegal exports to Iran and North Korea. It is rumored that, due to the stop in supply of US parts, ZTE was no longer able to manufacture its own products and went bankrupt. At that time, President Trump was aiming for a deal with North Korea and hinted that he might relax sanctions at the request of Xi Jinping. Concerning this, Congress and others were critical of the Trump administration.

The economist Paul Krugman was also critical, saying "[Trump is] a president using obviously fake national security arguments to hurt democratic allies, while ignoring very real national security concerns to help a hostile dictatorship." (*New York Times*, 28 May 2018.) Yet even Krugman, who has been repeatedly and fiercely critical of Trump, considers China a "hostile dictatorship" and clearly a "very real national security concern." At present, for the Democrats and their supporters, the technological challenge from China (i.e., the unfair means used), is becoming a shared threat to the whole of the United States.

The United States' current stance toward China has not arisen simply from the Trump administration, still less from President Trump's own temporary assumptions. (Lately, there has been an inclination in the United States to cooperate with the EU and Japan to create a WTO rule framework regarding the protection of intellectual property rights, technology transfer, and state support for industrial policy. In this, too, we can see the direction of overall US national interest.)

Changes to the Global System over the Last Twenty Years

Ultimately, this view of China in the United States has arisen and been formed due to changes in China itself over the last 20 years or more. When the Cold War ended, China's GDP (exchange rate adjusted) was around a quarter of Japan's, but by 2010 it had overtaken Japan's. Around 1990, China's official military spending, too, was far less than Japan's, but now it is more than three times as much. China has improved its naval and air capacity, and since the beginning of the 2010s, it has not hesitated to take a confrontational stance toward Japan in the East China Sea, while also moving forward with the establishment of advantageous "facts on the ground," such as the building of artificial islands in the South China Sea.

The United States has continued to reevaluate its understanding of China in the face of a nation that does not hesitate to wield power overseas. A typical example of this is the National Security Strategy mentioned above.

According to the strategy document: "For decades, U.S. policy was rooted in the belief that support for China's rise and for its integration into the postwar international order would liberalize China. Contrary to our hopes, China expanded its power at the expense of the sovereignty of others. China gathers and exploits data on an unrivaled scale and spreads features of its authoritarian system, including corruption and the use of surveillance." Moreover, Kurt M. Campbell and others have demonstrated a similar perception when implementing South Asia policy during Democrat administrations.

For some time, I have asserted that countries' behavior within the global system becomes generally easier to understand when they are categorized according to freedom of political system and level of living standards. Countries with high living standards and high levels of political freedom (the "free world") are accorded the "peace of democratic nations," and the free movement of people becomes possible based on economic interdependence. Meanwhile, I have posited the possibility of conflict among other countries (the "realist world" and the "fragile world") themselves or with the countries of the free world. Based on these ideas, I have made a graph that plots political freedom and living standards in nations of the world against two axes. I used indicators from Freedom House (an American NGO that monitors freedom and democracy) for the freedom axis and the United Nations Development Program human development indicator for the living standards axis.

Figure 1 (1995) on the next page shows both political freedom and living standards, with the size of the circle representing a nation's GDP. Countries that have high political freedom and high living standards are located at the graph's top right. The United States, Japan, and other countries are here. Looking at the overall distribution, the higher living standards are where the more political freedom exists, and we can also see a tendency for economies to be larger. In other words, just after the end of the Cold War in 1995 we could observe a trend in which democratization progresses as living standards rise (the so-called modernization theory). Just prior to this, the once authoritarian states of South Korea and Taiwan had achieved democratization as their economies grew; developments that served as evidence to back up this trend. Then, China was still poor and located at the bottom left of the graph. Post breakup of the Soviet Union, Russia was seeing democratization and had a relatively high degree of political freedom.

Figure 2, however, shows the distribution in 2015. We can see how India and Indonesia have moved toward the top right of the graph. At the same time, China did not see any increase in political freedom at all, yet living standards went up as the economy greatly increased in size. Russia, meanwhile, has seen a gradual decrease in political freedom as it moves toward the bottom right of the graph, but it has also recovered in terms of economic size. In other words, while in Figure 1 many countries tended to move toward the top right of the graph, in Figure 2 there is a striking move toward the bottom right as well as a shift toward the top right.

Just as these changes to the world system were gradually becoming apparent, General Secretary Xi Jinping made the following statement at the 19th National Congress of the Communist Party of China.

This is what socialism with Chinese characteristics entering a new era means . . . It means that the path, the theory, the system, and the culture of socialism with Chinese characteristics have kept developing, blazing a new trail for other developing countries to achieve modernization. It offers a new option for other

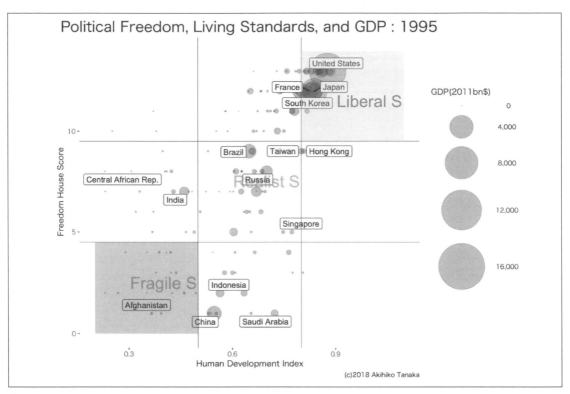

Figure 1. 1995

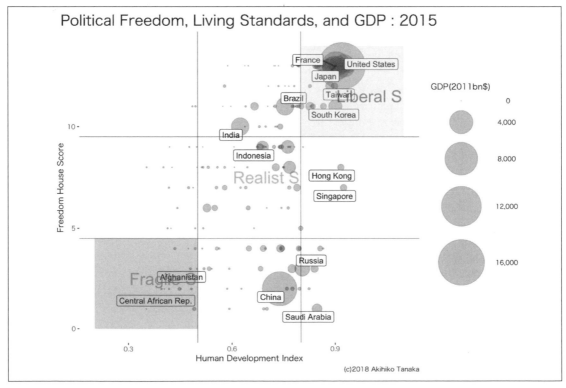

Figure 2. 2015

countries and nations who want to speed up their development while preserving their independence; and it offers Chinese wisdom and a Chinese approach to solving the problems facing mankind.

In short, China has demonstrated that there is a potential path toward the bottom right of the figure 2 graph; namely, a development model for developing countries. But are Xi Jinping and the leaders of the Chinese Communist Party really serious? Considering the Chinese Communist Party system of rule and the nature of its decision making, it is inconceivable that the language that appears in the general secretary's statement was included only at the whim of the leaders.

From a chronological perspective, the US National Security Strategy, announced exactly two months after this statement, acknowledged that the US policy to date (i.e., that supporting the Chinese economy would lead to liberalization in China) had been mistaken. If it is true that current US-China relations are really entering a new Cold War, Xi Jinping's statement may have been the declaration of the new Cold War's start.

The Start of a New Cold War and Japan's Position

Of course, it is possible that US-China relations will not face any particularly intense conflict, much less military confrontation. The US National Security Strategy also states that, while the United States is in competition with revisionist states such as China and Russia, this will not immediately lead to conflict or military confrontation. From approximately spring 2018, China has also worked extremely hard to moderate the tone of its external hard-line stance. On occasions, China has also made some fairly bold compromises in its trade war with the United States, so it may respond to the US issues of protecting intellectual property rights and technology transfer.

Yet, as long as the Chinese Communist Party tries to maintain its current political system, a new Cold War will continue under the surface. When the leaders of a country with as huge an economy and as influential as China offer a development model to replace liberal democracy, we

can only say that the world has entered a kind of ideological conflict. After the end of the Cold War, for a while challengers to liberal democracy in the form of political ideologies disappeared. In terms of its economic possibilities, Islamic fundamentalism did not really possess a development program that could go up against liberal democracy. But that is not the case for the development model proposed by China . . . because it has already shown results.

Yet, because China's domestic model is based on a hard-line authoritarian system that denies freedom to its people, and because of the huge size of China's economic system and military power, it can be a threat to liberal democratic nations in terms of both external security and internal politics. Should domestic forces that support Chinese-style ideology spring up, there is a danger that something like a "domestic cold war" might occur, as it has in the past.

If this new Cold War intensifies, it will not be possible for liberal democratic countries like Japan to see it as someone else's problem. Japan has no choice but to make its position clear. On the other hand, depending on shifts in China's stance going forward, this new Cold War may appear to have slipped under the surface. Nevertheless, the relationship with China is unlikely to continue as it has in the past. When it comes to security-related high-tech fields in particular, it will be necessary to take careful action to ensure that important technology is not transferred. Together with the United States and the countries of Europe, Japan needs to make the necessary demands of China in the areas of protecting intellectual property rights, the issue of technology transfer, and data management.

In any case, it is inconceivable that China would give up on its dream of further advancing its economy. The ZTE incident may have actually strengthened China's resolve to bring high technology within China. This new Cold War will continue both as a battle between ideological systems and as a contest over advanced industrial technology. As a key liberal democratic nation, Japan needs to ready itself to make sure it does not lose the contest over science and technology.

Nevertheless, even if the new Cold War is a

"cool" battle, we must prevent it from becoming a "hot" one. From the Japanese perspective, we need to strengthen the Japan-US alliance and maintain our deterrence capability, as well as create a space for peaceful coexistence with China. If we decide, as a basic principle, that the recently discussed cooperation between Japanese and Chinese companies in the Indo-Pacific will contribute to the development of emerging nations in that region, there is no reason for Japan to hesitate with our cooperation. Regarding projects in third countries, as long as irresponsible external loans are not made and sustainable development that considers the environment and human rights happens, this will not be seen by emerging nations as an exported Chinese model. Also, if such joint projects influence the actions of Chinese companies, it may contribute to a change in the Chinese model itself.

Even within China there are those raising the alarm regarding the "arrogant" external stance expressed last year in Xi Jinping's statement and who do not consider the strengthening of internal suppression a good thing. Although Japan cannot base its China policies and its security policies on the premise that China will move toward liberalization, we must not forget that there are people in China who seek liberalization. There is no need to think that the path to liberalization in China is completely barred.

Courtesy of Chūōkōron-Shinsha.

English version originally published by Japan Journal in *Discuss Japan: Japan Foreign Policy Forum*, no. 51 (2019).

Translated from "Chūgoku taitō de henyōsuru kokusai shisutemu: Bōeki sensō kara 'atarashii reisen' e" [Changes to the International System Due to the Rise of China: From Trade Wars to a New Cold War], in "Beichū gekitotsu to Nihon no kiki" [The US-China Clash and the Crisis for Japan], special feature, *Chūō Kōron* (November 2018): 26–37.

Bibliography

Hamilton, Alexander, James Madison, and John Jay. *The Federalist Papers*. New York: Bantam, 1982. Translated into Japanese as *Za Federarisuto* (Tokyo: Iwanami Shoten, 1999).

Krugman, Paul. "Trump's Manchurian Trade Policy." *New York Times*, 28 May 2018. https://www.nytimes.com/2018/05/28/opinion/trump-china-trade-policy.html.

The White House. "National Security Strategy of the United States of America." December 2017. https://trumpwhitehouse.archives.gov/wp-content/uploads/2017/12/NSS-Final-12-18-2017-0905.pdf.

White House Office of Trade and Manufacturing Policy. "How China's Economic Aggression Threatens the Technologies and Intellectual Property of the United States and the World." June 2018. https://trumpwhitehouse.archives.gov/wp-content/uploads/2018/06/FINAL-China-Technology-Report-6.18.18-PDF.pdf.

III-(12) The Western Nations Must Increase the Appeal of Liberal Democracy

Nakanishi Hiroshi

ABSTRACT The greatest challenge the West faces today is that posed by China's rise. Since Xi Jinping's inauguration as president, the Chinese government has steadfastly maintained its control of the economy and society, promoted science and technology, and created what has come to be known as digital dictatorship. It is strikingly at odds with the Western ideal of liberalism, which embodies the separation of state and market and of economic policy and national security. It is important Japan and the rest of the free world be fully cognizant of Chinese realities, but it is also important not to wantonly impose freedom and democracy on other countries and important to lead a world to the spirit of freedom and tolerance which allows cultural diversity.

As the speech made by US vice president Mike Pence on 4 October 2018 makes clear, the issues at the center of the confrontation between the US and China extend far beyond trade and technology. As China moves toward achieving the dominant position in key technological areas, including 5G (the goal of Huawei) and AI, for the US, China is becoming not merely an economic and technological competitor but also a threat at the level of national security.

On the other hand, for China's current regime, information technology is not merely an issue of external competitiveness but is also enormously significant as a means of domestic governance. Since the Song dynasty, the Chinese political system has been an imperial one in which authority is concentrated in the hands of the emperor, and it has stabilized the country by this means. Under its policy of reform and openness, China's Communist Party under Deng Xiaoping and later leaders legitimized its control based on the precondition of economic development, but the Xi Jinping administration appears to be returning to the traditional system of imperial despotism as the growth rate declines. While claiming to maintain the safety of the Chinese people by applying the latest information management technologies,

the Xi administration appears to also be using it to realize a system of internal control exceeding even that of the former imperial system. If we take this to be the case, we can see that it will be extremely difficult for China to relax its control of information technology.

Expressed differently, at the root of the confrontation between the US and China is a competition between two systems—the Western system of liberal democracy and China's 1,000-year-old system of imperial despotism—being conducted using twenty-first century technology. Given that China is confident in its technological power, there is every possibility that the confrontation between the two nations could last a long time.

Chinese-style technological despotism is attractive to the leaders of authoritarian regimes, and these nations are prone to embrace the influence of China. Looking back, the hasty imposition of liberal democratic systems on developing nations and formerly Communist nations in the post–Cold War period by the Western advanced nations (including Japan) was imprudent, and the rising skepticism and disillusionment with liberal democracy in those Western nations themselves in the wake of the global financial crisis is adding to the appeal of Chinese-style governance.

It is necessary for the Western nations to counter the increasing appeal of authoritarianism in China's domestic system and the entrenchment of China's influence internationally, and to apply pressure for the acceptance of Western values. But rather than insisting on imposing a formal system of liberal democracy on the rest of the world, the West should demonstrate the attractiveness of its system by making it a priority to embed a spirit of freedom and tolerance in other societies based on a recognition of the existence of diverse cultures and taking the initiative in addressing the issues and problems caused by the development of information technology.

English version originally published by the Nippon Institute for Research Advancement in *My Vision* 41 (2019).

This is a translation of a paper originally published in Japanese, for which NIRA bears full responsibility. Translated by Michael Faul. © 2019 Nippon Institute for Research Advancement.

Turbulence in the Postwar Order and Issues in Japanese Diplomacy

Nakanishi Hiroshi

ABSTRACT The post–World War II international order is in danger of unraveling in the latter half of the 2010s. This international order was founded upon the "politics of productivity," the United Nations as a universal institution led by the great powers, the multilateral free trade regime, and the progressivism of industrial civilization. This order was sorely tested in the 1970s, but the United States and other Western powers overcame the challenges by promoting globalization. Today, we face serious challenges caused by further globalization, such as the "risk society," the rise of non-Western states, and the deterioration of political leadership in democratic countries.

Few would deny that a sense of insecurity is growing across the world today. Of course, this is a question of perception, and one might also say that compared with the terror of nuclear war between the US and USSR during the Cold War era, there are presently no huge threats, and the modern world has escaped from the danger of major disaster.

However, the fact that there is no clear object of fear is itself amplifying the present sense of uncertainty. At the time this is being written (late November 2017), the world is facing multiple unpredictable political risks, including tensions regarding North Korea's nuclear missile program, developments in Saudi Arabia in the Middle East, and the outlook for the Angela Merkel administration in Germany. On the other hand, the global economy is favorable and stock markets continue to post record highs. Does this mean that the world's investors anticipate that the impact of such political risks will be limited and that this has resulted in such a situation? Or should it be interpreted as an indication that investors are closing their eyes to political risks and concentrating on financial speculation alone? The source of the anxiety today is that our fundamental conceptual framework for understanding

and interpreting the current situation is being shaken. To quote the famous words of US president Franklin Roosevelt's inaugural address, "The only thing we have to fear is fear itself." Nevertheless, this undefined fear is what makes us most afraid.

One might say that at the root of such global conditions lies the upheaval in the postwar order, which has been the basis of the peace and prosperity that the world has enjoyed for more than 70 years. We have a tendency to focus on particular individuals and phenomena, such as the withdrawal of the United Kingdom from the European Union (EU), the election of President Trump, and the North Korean nuclear missile tests. However, distinctive individuals and events are the signs—in other words, the superstructure—of changes that are both structural and long-term. In this paper, I present an overview of the trajectory of changes in the postwar order and touch on issues in Japanese diplomacy.

1. History of the Postwar Order

The framework of the present international order was formed during and just after World War II. At its core are universal international institutions such as the United Nations and the Bretton

Woods institutions. Following two world wars which caused tens of millions of casualties during the first half of the twentieth century, as well as the horrors of the development and use of nuclear weapons toward the end of World War II in a project that gathered the best of modern science, humanity has spent more than 70 years without experiencing large-scale war.

From a long-term perspective, one might conclude that the continued peace brought about by the postwar international order was actually founded on the long-term and large-scale destruction and violence experienced prior to that time. Then why did such destruction and violence occur? One interpretation is that the changes sparked by the Industrial Revolution, which developed full-scale in nineteenth-century Europe, burst apart the nineteenth-century order and these horrors occurred in the process of seeking a new equilibrium.

Formation of the Postwar Order

From the nineteenth century forward, the Industrial Revolution promoted industrialization throughout the world. Industrialization brought multiple huge changes to human society. These changes may be summarized as (1) a dramatic increase in production capacity, (2) an expansion of the state's administrative ability to control society, (3) a rapid increase in the population, and (4) the diffusion of power from Europe to the rest of the world.

From the end of the nineteenth century through the beginning of the twentieth century, these changes created nations with robust state bureaucratic systems, including large-scale military forces, in the advanced nations where industrialization had progressed, and they also rapidly deepened cross-border exchange. Meanwhile, the empires of the Qing dynasty, Spain, Ottoman Turkey, British India, and Russia, which had ruled over most of the non-European world up until that time, could not bear military rivalry with and economic penetration by the advanced nations that had industrialized, and they gradually weakened.

Such changes led to wars such as the First Sino-Japanese War, the Spanish-American War, and the Boer Wars, as well as such revolutions and anti-government movements as the First Russian Revolution, the Young Turk Revolution, the Xinhai Revolution, and self-government by the Indian National Congress. In World War I, a terrorist incident in the Balkans at the border of the weakened Austro-Hungarian and Ottoman empires triggered war among European industrialized countries and eventually spread into a global war in which Japan and the US also participated. The Russian, Austro-Hungarian, German, and Ottoman empires were brought to collapse one after another.

After World War I, efforts were made to restore the international order with the formation of the League of Nations and the reconstructed gold standard, but with the beginning of the Great Depression (1929), the capitalist economies led by the US and UK were at the brink of failure. The USSR and fascist nations adopted planned economies or controlled economies, and the acceptance of market intervention by the state rose in the free market countries as well. In the course of political and economic crises, the advanced nations proceeded along the path to becoming administrative states with large-scale bureaucratic organs responsible for wide-ranging functions, such as national security and social security, and with the tax collection systems to support them.

World War II provided another opportunity, especially for the US and Great Britain, to shape a new international order. As presented in the Atlantic Charter, which was issued in August 1941, that international order was fundamentally one pursuing liberal ideals. Having said that, national power was also emphasized to facilitate the achievement of those liberal ideals and to uphold them. The solid foundations of the postwar international order were established by combining liberal ideals with practical elements of power.

Specifically, the postwar order had four main pillars. The first was the realization of the "politics of productivity" (Charles Maier), which enabled both industrialization and stable popular government. The second was the founding of a universalistic United Nations with mechanisms for the great powers to maintain the international order. The third was the multilateral free trading system, which mostly promotes trade in industrial products. And the fourth was a progressivism that affirms industrial civilization, along with a share of anti-war sentiment transcending region and systems based on the tens of millions of victims of the two world wars.

These four pillars underwent revisions as the Cold War began and the advanced industrialized world was split into the two camps of East and West shortly after the end of World War II. The security order was mainly maintained by mutual restraint between the two camps, rather than by collaboration among the great powers, and the free trade system was shared exclusively among Western industrialized nations as a hegemonic framework for which the US carried the burden. Regardless, throughout the early 1970s, these four pillars continued functioning to a substantial extent as the basic framework of the international order.

Japan, which was defeated in World War II, also walked the path to reconstruction within this postwar order. Japan lost its regional hegemony in Asia and its military, but the Western open economic system resolved the lack of resources and markets that had troubled prewar Japan as a newly industrializing country. Japan was able to advance rapid industrialization under this system. With the "politics of productivity" as the foundation, Japan was also able to construct the stable political framework known as the "1955 System."

On the other hand, Japanese foreign policy was facing two issues up until the early 1970s. The first concerned Japan's security policy. Under the Constitution of Japan enacted just after the war, the security of Japan, as a former enemy nation, was prescribed assuming it was under the control of the United Nations. In the subsequent transition to the Cold War regime, however, Japan accepted US forces as an ally, concluded the Japan-US Security Treaty, and began rearmament within certain limits without revising its Constitution. This tension did not generate any specific problems as long as the mutual deterrence structure between East and West avoided actual wars among the industrial powers, but

a fundamental vagueness remained in Japan's national security structure.

The second issue was that the postwar Asian region became the focus not only of the Cold War regime but also of decolonialization, which was another global-scale transformation. While Japan positioned itself as "a member of Asia," interaction between the Cold War and post-decolonization politics prevented Japan from establishing formal relations with divided China and Korea, with which it had deep ties as former war theaters and colonies. As a result, the emphasis in Japan's foreign policy was placed overwhelmingly on its relations with the US, Europe, and their former colonies.

Changes in the Postwar Order

The postwar order reached a turning point in the 1970s. While the industrialized nations were suffering from skyrocketing resource prices, reduced economic growth rates, high inflation, and rising unemployment, the East-West framework of the Cold War could no longer grasp the whole of international politics, including changes such as an intensification of the North-South divide and shifting relations among the US, China, and the USSR.

The basis of these changes was the undercurrent that subsequently came to be called globalization, that is, technological advances made it possible for various actors in society to greatly amplify their capabilities, and the quality and quantity of transnational activities rapidly expanded. Such phenomena had begun gradually progressing from the 1960s. Advances in transportation and telecommunications technologies enabled the new wave of movement of people, goods, and money, eluding the net of government regulations. New communication networks and technological developments also awakened hitherto embedded senses of identity based on ethnicity and religion. One might say that the strengthened domestic solidarity and increased cross-border interdependence that had progressed and centered on the state from the nineteenth century through the first half of the twentieth century emerged at this time with a focus on social actors.

Yet, in the 1970s, the Cold War framework

was still steadfast, and the Western capitalist nations were able to maintain solidarity. The Western countries stepped up their vigilance over the advance of the USSR and other Communist countries, such as Cuba, as developing nations and collaborated to strengthen defense capabilities and maintain free trade to avert protectionism and division into bloc economies.

Then from the 1980s, new political coalitions that would lead the West were formed in the US and UK. In contrast to the Liberal and Labour Party forces that had led politics since the end of the war, political conservatism and market-oriented liberalism fused into new political alliances that attacked large government, labor unions, and other vested interests. US president Ronald Reagan and British prime minister Margaret Thatcher brought together conservative political alliances while also establishing market-oriented economic policies.

In this way, the postwar order was maintained, overcoming the crisis of the 1970s. Nevertheless, the postwar Cold War framework was weakened. The mutual deterrence between East and West through nuclear weapons morphed into competition in high-tech weapons, and the confrontation between capitalism and socialism, which shared industrial civilization, turned into a moral battle of good against evil and between democracy and despotism. The deregulation line led by the US and the UK transformed into a globalization policy of removing all economic barriers to free trade that centered on the manufacturing industry, and as the relocation of manufacturing overseas advanced, the stable middle class and organized interest groups, such as industrial societies or trade unions, gradually broke down, and the trend whereby public relations and image strategies determine election results intensified. Manufacturing firms relocated to developing countries, which had started moving away from their former closed development policies and had begun adopting market economy policies, and rapid industrialization was achieved in the East Asian countries in particular.

Mikhail Gorbachev, who became the secretary-general of the Communist Party of the Soviet Union in 1985, eased the USSR's tense foreign relations and worked toward the revitalization of its domestic society. He achieved some measure of success at the former but failed at the latter, which ultimately brought about the separation of Eastern Europe from the Communist Bloc, as well as the eventual dissolution of the USSR and its withdrawal from Communism. In foreign relations, his "new thinking" diplomacy eased East-West tensions and was well received, but the domestic revolution became frustrated and this approach ultimately allowed Eastern Europe to abandon Communism, leading to an attempted coup d'état by Communist Party members and the collapse of the USSR. In a nutshell, those efforts ultimately failed.

As the Cold War was coming to an end, when Saddam Hussein of Iraq attempted to annex Kuwait by force, miscalculating the US reaction, the US and USSR collaborated to confront this by restoring the pre-Cold War UN collective security mechanism, and the multilateral forces dispatched based on a UN Security Council resolution won an overwhelming victory with the full use of US high-tech weaponry. The images of the war broadcast live across the globe gave the impression that the liberal international order originally conceived in the aftermath of World War II had been realized through US initiative. While happenstance, it was also symbolic that it was President George H.W. Bush, the last president to have fought in World War II, who proclaimed "a new world order."

During this period, Japanese diplomacy followed a path of growth and setbacks. From the 1960s through the 1970s, Japan had overcome its prior restraints for the time being and constructed a foreign policy framework as the second largest economy in the free world. First, this was a comprehensive security policy whereby, while keeping self-defense capabilities within a limited range, economic influence was used as a means for a diplomatic security policy for the purposes of international cooperation and development assistance, instead of linking economic power to building up military capabilities overseas. Second, it succeeded in setting Japan's relations with Asian countries, including China and South Korea, with economic relations as the foundation, and promoted Asia-Pacific regionalism by combining free trade among advanced nations around the Pacific Rim with development assistance to Asian countries. These became systematic during the Ōhira Masayoshi administration in the late 1970s, which called for Pan-Pacific regional cooperation and established the Pacific Economic Cooperation Caucus (PECC) in 1980. Based on this foundation, in the 1980s the Nakasone Yasuhiro administration worked to solidify Japan's ties with the West, reinforce the Japan-US security alliance, and improve relations with China and South Korea under the slogan of Japan as an "international state."

However, the direction of such successes changed in the late 1980s when the Japanese economy became bloated from an economic bubble and Japan became viewed as an outlier, mercantilist power by other Western countries. Moreover, in the Persian Gulf crisis and the Gulf War, Japan presented no clear policy on the potential use of force and, in the end, could only share the burden with a financial contribution of US$13 billion. Coming on top of the collapse of the bubble economy, this experience made Japan feel a deep sense of frustration and begin seeking reforms to catch up with the new post–Cold War world order.

2. The Dissolving Postwar Order

However, expectations of the new world order rapidly fell by the wayside. Looking back today, one cannot help but see the Western world's euphoria and pride, as well as its failures. This period gave rise to two theses: Francis Fukuyama's 1989 "The End of History?" and Samuel Huntington's "The Clash of Civilizations?"[1] Reading these again today, while they naturally have some defects because of the limitations of the times, one notes how the world, and the Western world in particular, failed to take the warnings voiced by these two authors seriously. While stressing the victory of liberal ideology, Fukuyama points out that contemporary liberalism is limited because of its inability to give people aspirations that transcend utilitarianism and everydayness. Meanwhile, Huntington argues that while for the time being Western civilization should work at reinforcing

its own influence versus non-Western civilization, especially Confucian and Islamic civilization, over the long term it is necessary to anticipate the emergence of non-Western civilization, transcend cultural differences, and reach a deep understanding. Despite the debates sparked by both of these essays, the West did not earnestly respond to such reservations or warnings. The conditions today nearly 30 years after the fall of the Berlin Wall, in which walls that separate people are being built in all parts of the world, including cyberspace, must be seen as the consequences of the complacency of the advocates of liberalism. More specifically, three factors overlapped to gradually hollow out the postwar order from the inside, just as termites destroy buildings by consuming their pillars.

Emergence of a Risk Society

What manifested in the 1990s following the conclusion of the Cold War was the risk society[2] that accompanies globalization. While globalization greatly expanded the scope of activity of social actors, by removing various boundaries and linking them as a network, it also caused new risks, which had been buried during the Cold War era, to emerge.

The rapid advance of identity politics was one of the sources of these risks. Through examinations of historical relics and records, the information technologies that enabled globalization also made it possible for the masses to gain awareness of memories that had been forgotten in the past. In contrast to the post–Cold War liberal worldview, which tended to deny a communitarian sense of belonging to certain groups, groups that rallied for particular ethnicities and religious interpretations provided identity awareness and gained a strong ability to mobilize.

What is more, with the progress in globalization, which made it possible for people, money, goods, and information to move across national boundaries, society approached a complex system (chaos) of multilayered spider web like networks linking various and diverse factors. In complex systems, local phenomena gain the potential to exert large-scale changes and influences going beyond the range that can be controlled by technological causal inference (the butterfly effect).

Such conditions were demonstrated time and again, as typified by the financial crises of Black Monday (1987), the East Asian financial crisis (1997), and the Lehman crisis (2008). What is more, the power of entities that devoted themselves to destroying the existing order at the local level gained force relative to that of systems managers responsible for overall stability, such as the major powers. Small-scale challenges and disruptions of order by terrorists and rogue states came to cause risks for overall systems.[3]

In that sense, the 11 September 2001 terrorist attacks in the US were an epoch-making event. A terrorist group using just the low-level technology of hijacking airplanes struck a blow in the heart of the US, which apparently took pride in being invincible. The psychological impact of these attacks was far greater than the physical damage.

Following the 9/11 attacks, the administration of President George W. Bush placed the "war on terror" at the center of US foreign policy and not only invaded Afghanistan, which had become a base for Al-Qaeda, and toppled the Taliban regime but also designated Iraq, Iran, and North Korea as the "axis of evil'" and went to war to overthrow the government of Saddam Hussein in Iraq. The Tony Blair administration in the UK mediated in assembling cooperation from the international community for the "war on terror" and ultimately exercised force together with the US.

Overturning the Hussein administration was easily achieved given the US military capabilities. However, the failure to make any preparations for government after the collapse of that administration reflected the simple optimism of liberal democracy as the historical winner, and the US and UK, who took the initiative in the war, paid a high price for their excessively optimistic outlook. The confusion of the postwar governance pulled down the international prestige of the US and UK, and insufficient attention was given to the development of nuclear weapons in Iran and North Korea.

Because the burden of the "war on terror" turned out to be much heavier than initially anticipated, the Bush administration then had to give particular attention to upholding domestic economic conditions. Because a real estate bubble

had been tolerated and those loans were turned into financial products when the real estate bubble collapsed, that spread into a general financial crisis. The emergence of the Lehman crisis in September 2008 reconfirmed the fragility inherent in globalization.

The Rise of the Rest

The "rise of the rest"[4] progressed in parallel with the prolongation of the war on terror and concerns about a global depression, starting in the US, caused by the collapse of Lehman Brothers. A 2003 report by the largest US securities company Goldman Sachs used the term "BRICs" to refer to Brazil, Russia, India, and China and hinted at the potential for these countries to surpass the industrialized nations in the future global economy, drawing a great deal of attention.[5] These four countries, plus South Africa, subsequently came to be called the BRICS, and various other terms were proposed to refer to the BRICS together with other emerging nations.

At that point in time, the West mostly viewed the emergence of the newly industrializing economies not as a challenge to the international order but rather as a demonstration that the cooperative framework would be maintained because these countries also benefited from the open order created by the West.[6] To be certain, up until the 2008 Lehman shock, the basic policy in these countries as well was to pursue economic growth within the international order led by the industrialized nations. For example, in the case of China, the Hu Jintao administration, which came to power in 2002, initially called for the "peaceful rise" of China and emphasized the stance that the emergence of the Chinese economy was not a threat to the existing order but was rather in line with that framework.

Just after the 2008 Lehman crisis, there were growing calls for the industrialized nations and the newly industrializing economies to reinforce the international cooperation framework with new foundations. The strengthening of the G20 is a representative example. The G20 Summit, first held at the invitation of the US in November 2008, was made into a regular event. After the crisis settled down somewhat, however, cracks emerged between the advanced nations and the emerging economies, and the stagnation of the G20 became conspicuous. The background to this included a sense among the emerging economies that Western leadership was in decline as they gained confidence in their own economic power, along with an emphasis on strengthening authoritarian systems to avert domestic social discontent over growing economic disparities and to control freedom of speech. Consequently, albeit only partially, the newly industrializing countries began to make clear their critical stance toward the existing order led by the West.

The trends in China and Russia were particularly important. The Beijing Olympics was held just before the Lehman crisis, and in China at this time there were growing calls among the leadership to switch from the line of "keeping a low profile and biding time" to a policy of actively "striving for achievement," and a struggle for power emerged in relation to Xi Jinping's succession to power. Once Xi took power in 2012, China turned increasingly proactive in its foreign policy. Under the banner of "the great revival of the Chinese nation," while strengthening its voice within the existing international economic order through such initiatives as including the renminbi as one of the currencies that comprise the International Monetary Fund (IMF) Special Drawing Rights (SDR), China launched its "great maritime power" and "Belt and Road" initiatives, established the Asian Infrastructure Investment Bank, and otherwise began building up a framework to compete with the existing framework led by the West. Meanwhile, domestically, the Chinese government tightened its stance on controlling the spread of outside influences and stepped up its control over free speech, which had been tolerated to some extent under the reform and opening-up policy.

The glorification of nationalism and regression of freedom have also proceeded in Russia under Vladimir Putin, who has suppressed the opposition, placed the media under control, and grasped the foundations of power of the *siloviki* (persons related to the security or military services) and of energy and other industrial conglomerates. Furthermore, the Putin administration has strong suspicions regarding Western penetration of Russia and nearby regions and has taken stances opposing the West in its territorial dispute with Georgia (2008) and in the Russian military intervention in Ukraine and annexation of Crimea (2014).

However, the newly emerging economies are not strongly united: India was absent from the 2017 Belt and Road Forum for International Cooperation, and there is some overlap between the Belt and Road Initiative and the Eurasian Union advocated by President Putin. At least for the time being, the effect of the rise of the newly emerging economies will likely be limited to eroding and weakening the postwar order, and the construction of an opposing order will not be straightforwardly pursued.

Decline in the Political Leadership of the Democratic System

While the newly emerging economies began to distance themselves from the postwar order led by the West, domestic politics were destabilized in Western nations, especially in the US and UK, which had served as the core leaders of the postwar order, and their international leadership declined. This trend, which had been noted just after the end of the Cold War,[7] rapidly accelerated after the Lehman crisis. While the recurrence of a global depression has been averted since the Lehman crisis by nontraditional financial policies and a large-scale expansion in fiscal spending, the fracturing of society has deepened over that time, and the political support for anti-globalism can no longer be ignored. While the anti-globalism movement does not have a systematic worldview, it does embody the sense of the downfall of the middle class, which enjoyed prosperity during the period when the postwar order was fixed, and this movement has also become mixed with a backlash against the elite who pushed globalization forward, animosity toward immigrants, ethnic and religious chauvinism, and fear of terrorism. Although the majority of people do not actively support anti-globalism, its influence in democratic politics is rising due to its ability to mobilize politically since the use of social networking services (SNS) and other new communications means outside the mass media have become widely available.

In 2016, such political changes brought about major shifts in the foreign policies of the US and UK, which had been in charge of the postwar order. Barack Obama, who became the first Black president of the US in 2009, declared that the US is not the world's policeman and pursued diplomacy without relying on military power and with an emphasis on multilateral cooperation. While Obama's idealistic vision calling for a "world without nuclear weapons" had the power to appeal to public opinion, he failed to completely bridge the gap with China and Russia, which stepped up their challenges against the West and were becoming increasingly authoritarian, and while he did achieve the withdrawal of US combat units from Iraq, that invited the rise of the Islamic State (IS). Nonmilitary responses to the mountain of problems, including the governance of Afghanistan, the North Korean nuclear missile development, and the Iraqi nuclear development, had its limits and conversely led to a decline in international prestige and the intensification of domestic opposition. In the 2016 US presidential election, Hillary Clinton, who inherited the Obama line, lost to Donald Trump, who called for an America-first policy, which implied destroying the postwar international order based on American liberal leadership. In the United Kingdom as well, Prime Minister Tony Blair, who had a middle-of-the-road line, resigned amid criticism regarding the Iraq War. The Labour Party lost its cohesiveness, and after the brief Gordon Brown administration, the government switched to the Conservative Party and David Cameron. However, in order to achieve unity within his own party, Cameron rather capriciously proposed a national referendum on the United Kingdom leaving the EU. To the shock of the British and the world, the "leave" vote narrowly outnumbered the "remain" vote in the referendum of June 2016.

The Brexit referendum under the Cameron administration and the selection of the real estate agent Donald Trump as the Republican Party candidate and then as president revealed cracks in the alliance between neoliberalism and conservative patriotism that had been central to US and British politics since the 1980s. Neoliberalism and conservative patriotism had been united under the great causes of criticizing the administrative state and confronting Communism, but after the end of the Cold War, internal tensions intensified due to a sense of the downfall of the conservative middle class and debates regarding war leadership. As a result of this split among the conservatives, Prime Minister Cameron was forced into holding the Brexit referendum, while in the US, the split within the Republican Party enabled the selection of Trump as the Republican candidate. Of course, turmoil in domestic politics is not limited to the US and UK: the emergence of anti-EU factions and separatist movements can be seen in other European countries as well.

It should be possible to argue from a logical and utilitarian viewpoint against President Trump's assertions that the present international order places excessive burdens on the US, allows free-riding by other countries, and harms US interests. Nevertheless, it is undeniable that the US and UK, and the US in particular, have borne an asymmetrical burden (admittedly with certain privileges) in the postwar international order, and a utilitarian counterargument based on profit-and-loss arithmetic will not resonate with the feelings of those who seek more than utilitarian value. In addition to the emergence of a risk society and the rise of newly emerging economies, the postwar order is now being challenged from inside the states that have served as its main axis. This is the greatest trial the postwar order has ever faced.

Conclusion

In this paper, I have reviewed the developments in the postwar order from its formation up until the present time. Although the postwar order has provided peace and stability for more than 70 years, its shaking is gradually growing stronger. The postwar order is a system that was conceived at the peak of industrial civilization, and there is no question but that it has become a presence that no longer matches the age of postindustrialization. The issue is whether the transition to a new order will take place peacefully and gradually or if we shift to a new order by passing through devastating shocks, including war. Of course, the former is clearly desirable, but we cannot overlook the reality that this path is gradually narrowing.

Japan, which has received great benefits from the postwar order, has a particularly great interest in a peaceful transition. Even though Japan lacks the power to determine the fate of the international order by itself, its decisions may have a large influence on important aspects of it.

In that regard, what will be most important is the ability to make strategic judgments that determine the allocation of limited resources. The environment Japan finds itself in includes potential conflict areas, such as North Korea and the Taiwan Strait, and is a region where US, Chinese, and Russian influences intersect and where it is becoming increasingly difficult to project the future overall. Consequently, Japan's efforts to reinforce its security system should be prioritized to enhance Japan's own safety and also as a means of diplomatic influence. Yet, considering the present level of the technologies, there are clearly limits to Japan's own resources that can be devoted to defense, and Japan should allocate substantial resources to its diplomatic capabilities and information collection and analysis capabilities. In particular, in this age of fake news and conspiracy theories, accurate information analysis capabilities may determine the fate of nations.

Also, geopolitically, the Indo-Pacific region may gain importance as a region where US and Chinese interests compete, and Japan may also need to build up its own network of influence in this region as well. That may require a dramatic expansion of people-to-people exchanges, including the acceptance of immigrants from this region.

From a longer-term perspective, as the world transitions to an information civilization, the decision on whether the unit that comprises a stable order will be the nation-state or some other form is important. The modern nation-state framework is presently the most rational and universal political order. Nevertheless, it is also certain that the modern nation-state system, which is premised on the demarcation of strict national boundaries and ethnic integration, cannot be applied to a substantial part of the world. In the international order that will be formed now, a choice will have to be made on whether to greatly reform the nature of the twentieth-century nation-state or to find new principles of order that differ from the sovereign state, or to adopt some mixture of both. Even if the territory of Japan, which is surrounded by the sea, remains unchanged, the type of principles of order to be adopted will have decisive importance on Japan's living environment.

Devising and implementing long-term strategies is an area where Japan has not been strong. But if we do not deal with this issue amid the intensifying upheaval of the postwar order, the danger that Japan's peace and prosperity may be lost will only grow stronger.

English version originally published by the Japan Institute of International Affairs in *Japan Review* 2, no. 4 (2019).

This essay was originally published in *Kokusai Mondai* [International Affairs], no. 668 (Jan–Feb. 2018). NB: Parts of the original essay include revisions to "Yūkai suru sengo chitsujo no raireki to kadai" [History and Issues of the Dissolving Postwar Order], *Journal of the Research Bureau* (Secretariat of the House of Representatives), no. 14 (Dec. 2017): 1–8.

Notes

1. Fukuyama 1989; Huntington 1993. Both papers were subsequently published as books: Fukuyama 1992 (Jp. same year); Huntington 1996 (Jp. 1998).

2. This term is based on the concept suggested in Beck 1986 (Jp. 1998).

3. Early works that attempted to apply the concept of chaos to international politics include Nagai and Tsuchiyama, eds. 1993 and Jervis 1997. Nassim Nicholas Taleb's work stressed the concept once again just before the Lehman crisis, Taleb 2007 (Jp. 2009).

4. Zakaria 2008.

5. Wilson and Purushothaman 2003

6. As a representative advocate, see Ikenberry 2006 (Jp. 2012).

7. A political analyst who proposed the "southern strategy" to the Republican Party in the past drew a picture of the political deterioration of Anglo-Saxon society. See Phillips 1994 (Jp. 1995).

Bibliography

Beck, Ulrich. *The Risk Society: Towards a New Modernity*. London: Sage, 1992. Translated by Azuma Ren and Itō Midori as *Kiken shakai: Atarashii kindai e no michi* (Tokyo: Hosei University Press, 1998). Originally published in German in 1986.

Fukuyama, Francis. *The End of History and the Last Man*. New York: The Free Press, 1992. Translated by Watanabe Shōichi as *Rekishi no owari jō: Rekishi no "shūten" ni tatsu saigo no ningen* (Tokyo: Mikasa Shobō, 1992).

———. "The End of History?" *The National Interest* 16 (Summer 1989): 3–18.

Huntington, Samuel P. *The Clash of Civilizations and the Remaking of World Order*. New York: Simon and Schuster, 1996. Translated by Suzuki Chikara as *Bunmei no shōtotsu* (Tokyo: Shueisha, 1998).

———. "The Clash of Civilizations?" *Foreign Affairs* 72, no. 3 (Summer 1993): 22–49.

Ikenberry, G. John. *Liberal Order and Imperial Ambition: Essays on American Power and International Order*. Cambridge: Polity Press, 2006. Translated in 2 vols. by Hosoya Yūichi as *Riberaruna chitsujo ka teikoku ka: Amerika to sekai seiji no yukue* (Tokyo: Keisō Shobō, 2012).

Jervis, Robert. *System Effects: Complexity in Political and Social Life*. New Jersey: Princeton University Press, 1997.

Nagai Yōnosuke, and Tsuchiyama Jitsuo, eds. *Chitsujo to konton (kaosu): Reisengo no sekai* [Order and Chaos: The Post–Cold War World]. Tokyo: Ningen no Kagaku-sha, 1993.

Phillips, Kevin. *Arrogant Capital: Washington, Wall Street, and the Frustration of American Politics*. Boston: Back Bay Books, 1995. Translated by Ina Hisayoshi as *Amerika de "kakumei" ga okiru: Washinton kaitai o semaru shin popyurizumu* (Tokyo: Nikkei Business Publications, 1995).

Taleb, Nassim Nicholas. *The Black Swan: The Impact of the Highly Improbable*. New York: Random House, 2007. Translated in 2 vols. by Mochizuki Mamoru as *Burakku suwan: Fukakujitsusei to risuku no honshitsu* (Tokyo: Diamond, 2009).

Wilson, Dominic, and Roopa Purushothaman. "Dreaming with BRICs: The Path to 2050." *Global Economics*, Paper no. 99 (October 2003). https://www.goldmansachs.com/insights/archive/archive-pdfs/brics-dream.pdf.

Zakaria, Fareed. *The Post-American World*. New York: W.W. Norton, 2008. Translated by Nirei Kōichi as *Amerika-go no sekai* (Tokyo: Tokuma Shoten, 2008).

III-(14) Vision for a Free and Open Indo-Pacific

Kitaoka Shinichi

ABSTRACT Japan's strategy (later renamed as a vision) for a Free and Open Indo-Pacific (FOIP) was first enunciated by Prime Minister Abe in Nairobi in August 2016. Though widely seen as an effort to counter China's Belt and Road Initiative (BRI), the FOIP concept is more accurately an effort to extend Japan's economic development to Southeast Asia and South Asia and to gradually strengthen Japan's involvement in regional security. As such, it is intended to sustain the order that China's BRI challenges. This paper reassesses the significance of the FOIP vision in this light and thinks about what Japan can do to strengthen institutions to this end.

A "Vision" Rather Than a "Strategy"

First, the "Free and Open Indo-Pacific" vision is not a strategy. A strategy is a method employed to realize higher-level objectives and is a policy-based system. Rather, a "free and open Indo-Pacific" is the primary vision or guiding principle for other policies. Recently, the government has come to refer to a free and open Indo-Pacific as a "vision," though some suggest this is to eliminate the military implications attached to the term strategy. However, I believe the use of the term vision is accurate.

A free and open Indo-Pacific is absolutely necessary for Japan's survival and development. China, Russia, and the United States will survive even if the Indo-Pacific does not become free or open. It is the same for Great Britain, France, and Germany because they are far away from this area. For Japan, however, it is a vitally important task.

It is not necessary to reiterate how important the Pacific Ocean is to Japan. Japan even went to war with the United States over it; although it lost, Japan secured freedom in the Pacific by uniting with the United States after the war.

The sea route from India to the Middle East has also been important since the Meiji era. Japan's merchant ships and trading companies have been involved in business in India and Pakistan for quite a long time. The Japan-UK alliance also served as a means by which Japan could secure an open Indian Ocean. After the war, the overwhelming strength of the United States came to maintain the freedom of the Indian Ocean.

During the 1973 oil crisis, anxiety surrounded the supply from the Middle East of crude oil, which was of vital importance to Japan. The issue was settled in a relatively short period, but from then on, Japan has been obliged to recognize the problem surrounding the Middle East as one of the major issues of diplomacy. Later, although Japan was greatly affected by abandoning its oil interests and the withdrawal of Japanese residents during the Iranian Revolution (1978–79) and the Iran-Iraq War (1980–88), it did not do much to address these problems. The possibility of dispatching minesweepers was considered during the Iran-Iraq War but did not occur (while then prime minister Nakasone Yasuhiro showed interest, it is said that Chief Cabinet Secretary Gotoda Masaharu was strongly opposed to the move).

However, during the Persian Gulf crisis and War of 1990–91, there was intense debate over the kind of contributions Japan should make toward restoring order. Ultimately, Japan contributed a significant sum of US$13 billion, though this was under-recognized by the international community. In May 1991, after the war had ended, Japan dispatched minesweepers, which was more widely recognized.

Ten years later, on 11 September 2001, terrorist attacks were perpetrated in coordinated strikes in the United States. When the United States launched its attack on Afghanistan's Al-Qaeda, Japan enacted the Anti-Terrorism Special Measures Law and dispatched ships to conduct refueling of US and other countries' ships in the Indian Ocean (which continued until 2010). Furthermore, in 2003, after the United States had begun its attack on Iraq, Japan dispatched its Self-Defense Forces to Iraq for the purpose of supporting the country's reconstruction. In addition, when pirates became active in the waters off the coast of Somalia, Japan dispatched Maritime Self-Defense Force ships and established a base in Djibouti in 2009. In fact, as the need for stability in the oceans from the Middle East to the Indian Ocean continued, Japan gradually began to expand its activities.

India: An Important Presence

One of the most important changes to have occurred in the region of the Indian Ocean has been the emergence of India. At the time of the Cold War, India, which was essentially socialist and not open to other countries, began liberalizing. However, due to nuclear tests conducted in India and Japan's sanctions against such testing, the strengthening of Japan-India relations was slow to proceed. Under the Mori Yoshirō cabinet, the Japan-India Eminent Persons' Group met in 2001. While the author was able to participate, the magnitude of expectations of both countries and the deviation from reality turned out to be significant.

In 2005, Japan, along with India, Brazil, and Germany, developed an intense campaign aimed at reforming the United Nations Security Council. While Japan proceeded to submit a resolution that included increasing the number of permanent members (in May), the campaign suffered a setback in August. One of the remarkable changes that resulted from this movement was the change in the American position from accepting Japan as the only new permanent member to the position that India should also be admitted.

Since that time, the number of symposia and research groups that have included Japan, India, the United States, and sometimes Australia has increased. The quantity of published articles emphasizing the connectivity of the two oceans has also increased.

When the G20 Summit was founded in 2008, it was joined by the former Group of Seven (G7), which was the meeting attended by heads of state of leading countries—the European Union and 12 new countries, among which were four countries that front on the Indian Ocean: Indonesia, Australia, India, and South Africa. Furthermore, Saudi Arabia is also located nearby (the other seven countries were Russia, China, South Korea, Brazil, Argentina, Mexico, and Turkey). The composition of the G20 Summit alone indicated the worldwide significance of the Indian Ocean.

The China Threat

However, a threat to a free and open Indo-Pacific has also emerged. That threat is China. It was in May 2007 that a Chinese People's Liberation Army officer commented that the Pacific Ocean was wide enough for the United States of America to take responsibility for the East and China for the West. Furthermore, in the South China Sea, where there are territorial disputes, including those involving the Philippines, Vietnam, and Malaysia, China claimed the "nine-dash line" and proceeded with construction of landfills and military bases on many islands. In response to these actions, in 2013 the Philippines appealed to a court of arbitration for the invalidation of the nine-dash line, but China refused to participate in the trial. Moreover, in 2016, when the court recognized the Philippines' appeal and judged China's nine-dash line claim to be unfounded, China claimed the judgment was merely a piece of paper and not only ignored it but also applied pressure on neighboring countries. Countries afraid of China often avoided reference to this ruling.

The ruling itself is powerless unless supported by force. Only the United States is capable of such a display of power against China. However, the

United States did not make immediate protests. In response to remarks from Chinese navy officials, it should have declared immediately that the Pacific is an open sea, its freedom is guaranteed by law, and that no particular country, including the United States, should have any special responsibilities or rights pertaining to it. To be silent in the face of a country's problematic behavior is to be complicit. While the Obama administration touted a "pivot to Asia," the policy did not yield actual results.

The Emergence of the "Belt and Road Initiative"

China also began to expand its influence through the development of infrastructure in regional areas, an effort which came to be known as the "Belt and Road Initiative."

Xi Jinping laid out the initiative in his 2013 speeches at Nazarbayev University in Kazakhstan and before the Indonesian Parliament. The "Silk Road Economic Belt" component runs from west China to Europe through Central Asia, and the "One Road" component refers to "the twenty-first century maritime silk road" sea route connecting Southeast Asia, Sri Lanka, and the coastal part of the Arabian Peninsula to the east coast of Africa; the initiative includes plans to promote infrastructure development, trade, and investment. Soon they were integrated into one concept, the Belt and Road Initiative.

It is certain that the demand for infrastructure is strong in various parts of the world. However, the Belt and Road Initiative, rather than being an overall vision, seemed to support China's goals in particular, namely, the intention to expand China's political influence, the motivation for Chinese companies to invest, the willingness of Chinese financial institutions to invest and loan, and the willingness of Chinese enterprises to export excess products such as iron and to secure necessary resources from abroad. We ought to consider the circumstances surrounding each project rationally, without overestimating or underestimating China's motives.

In May 2015, the Abe cabinet launched the "Partnership for Quality Infrastructure" in Japan. Japan has a long history of experience in infrastructure development in Southeast Asia through official development assistance (ODA) and has tried to advance cooperation with the Asian Development Bank further. Japan thus began publicizing its high-quality infrastructure all over the world, especially in Asia: it may seem expensive at first, but it is easy to use, long lasting, environmentally friendly, part of disaster preparation, and economical in the long term.

The War of Infrastructure Bids between Japan and China

Around that time, there was a plan to build a high-speed railway between Jakarta and Bandung in Indonesia. Japan and China fought hard during the bidding process. In the summer of 2015, China's bid won, shocking a number of Japanese officials involved in the process.

Although I was not yet president of Japan International Cooperation Agency (JICA), I watched the proceedings of this high-speed rail project rather coolly. The most efficient high-speed railways are 500 kilometers long and run through areas with a large affluent populations. Indeed, with respect to Japan's high-speed Shinkansen train, the line that extends from Tokyo through Nagoya to Osaka, along which 40 million people live, is in a class of its own. Almost as efficient as this line are some sections of lines in China. If the line is shorter, however, the reduction in time is small in relation to the cost of construction and operation. If the line is longer, airplane travel is more appropriate. From Jakarta to Bandung is about 170 kilometers, too short a distance for high-speed rail.

In October 2015, I became the president of JICA, and after that, as well, infrastructure remained a major issue. In December 2015, Japan decided to bid on the high-speed rail project running between Mumbai and Ahmedabad in India. This project was expected to cost about ¥1.8 trillion, with a 0.1% interest rate to be paid back over 50 years, with no payment required for the first 15 years. As an Independent Administrative Agency, JICA's activities have to align with the policies of the government (cabinet minister in charge).

Japan and China also competed for the high-speed railway linking Malaysia's Kuala Lumpur and Singapore, with Japan attempting to rebound from what it saw as China's predominance. Competition between Japan and China over the construction of a high-speed railway was also seen in Thailand.

Putting Japan's bid proposals into context, the Japanese companies' infrastructure construction technology tends to be high spec/high precision/high functionality, often exceeding local needs, and as a result, the cost tends to be high. According to the rules of the Development Assistance Committee of the Organization for Economic Cooperation and Development (OECD), Japan's loans must be, in principle, "untied" (no strings attached) unless highly concessional financing terms (low interest/long term) are stipulated.

In other words, even if Japan finances a project, the contractor for the project must be selected by international competitive bidding, and there may be a case in which Chinese companies can be selected to use Japanese loans and would be thanked by the people of that country. In addition, DAC member countries have to pay careful attention to environmental and social considerations in accordance with international standards. As a result, it takes time to confirm a project's impact on the environment and society; during that time, the costs related to the project also increase.

On the other hand, "tied" loans are possible for non-DAC member countries (as is the case with China) and bringing the companies within their own country is unrestricted. Currently, it cannot be said that sufficient consideration has been given to environmental and social concerns, and the period of time for a project can therefore be shortened, and the rise in the cost can be suppressed accordingly (however, it seems that China has recently begun to develop guidelines with regard to environmental and social considerations). In reality, while there are few difficulties associated with land expropriation within China, the acquisition of land in foreign countries is not easy, and China is struggling; the Jakarta-Bandung high-speed railway has also been stalled due to land acquisition issues.

As already mentioned, China's Belt and Road Initiative is a combination of infrastructure construction projects in neighboring countries and is linked to China's expansion of influence. As with the loan for the Port of Hambantota (Magampura Mahinda Rajapaksa Port) in Sri Lanka, it was decided that if funds are loaned and cannot be repaid, the port operational rights may be leased to China for a period of 99 years. Ironically, this move was reminiscent of the nineteenth- to twentieth-century imperialist diplomacy developed by the Western powers and Japan against China. However, opposition from the local people occurred, and China responded by making concessions, dividing the company, and weakening exclusivity.

While the interest rate on China's loans cannot be generalized because there are various cases, with regard to project financing in Sri Lanka, Indian strategic researcher Brahma Chellaney told China's *Global Times* that "Japan's project interest rate is only 0.5%, while China's is 6.3%."

In any case, if Japan wants other nations to use Japanese products, technologies, and standards, we should arrange low-interest loans that are favorable to recipient countries. However, it must be acknowledged that a side effect of democracy includes the fact that prime ministers and presidents often want a project finished during their term in office, ignoring realistic construction timelines. Yet, if low-quality materials are chosen as a result, the project may suffer from bad infrastructure or cumulative debt later on. That being said, it is certain that China's technology is steadily improving.

JICA's Four Principles of Infrastructure

In 2016, I instructed JICA to establish and emphasize the four principles of infrastructure investment. These four principles stipulate that a project should: first, contribute to the development of the country; second, help strengthen the relationship between the country and Japan; third, benefit the Japanese economy and business; and fourth, not be an excessive burden on JICA's financial capacity. It seemed that, with these principles in mind, there might be some issues that could prove problematic with regard to the four aforementioned high-speed rail projects.

In 2017, some of the shares of Sihanoukville Port in Cambodia, a project on which JICA cooperated, were released. Although these were part of the public stock offering, more shares would be released in the future. There was information that China was interested in the operating rights to the port. Were China to hold the operating rights, the possibility might also arise of it holding exclusive management in the future. JICA decided to purchase those shares in order to prevent such a possibility. It would enhance the enterprise value of the port and contribute to the economic revitalization and improved connectivity of Cambodia and the Mekong region. Japan has already invested in the port through overseas investments and loans. Through JICA's contribution, the deep knowledge of the port management industry that Japan possesses will be utilized for future operations. This was in June 2017.

In the same discourse in June 2017, Prime Minister Abe presented four conditions necessary for Japan to cooperate on individual projects included in the Belt and Road Initiative. The conditions were: infrastructure be open to use by all; it be developed through procurement that is transparent and fair; the project be economically viable; and it be financed by debt that can be repaid without harming the recipient country's financial health. I believe the principles I had established within JICA are consistent with these, and I believed them to be sufficient. It just so happened that, at the time, I was sitting next to the Chinese ambassador to Japan, Cheng Yonghua; he, too, had a favorable reaction. Because China also self-identifies as a great civilization, there should be no reason for opposition.

In September 2017, I traveled to New York to participate in the United Nations General Assembly and met with a senior US government official. He wanted to meet with me to prepare for President Trump's planned visit to Asia (including Japan) in the autumn.

When I touched on China's loan policies at that time, mentioning Hambantota Port, he was completely unaware of the situation. In fact, he knew nothing of the OECD's untied rules or environmental or social considerations and was unaware that China was unrestrained by them

and thus was in a very advantageous position. Upon hearing my explanation, he agreed with my proposal to try to establish principles for countries providing assistance to developing countries, including China.

The US Is Increasing the Severity of Confrontation

In December 2017, the United States established a new national security strategy and laid out a tough policy with regard to China.

The United States began to criticize China's method of assisting developing countries, using the term "new imperialism." There must have been some other people who tried to persuade the US as I had. On 1 February 2018, prior to a visit to Latin America, Secretary of State Rex Tillerson gave a speech at a university in Texas criticizing China, stating that "Latin America does not need new imperial powers that seek only to benefit their own people."

On 30 July 2018, Secretary of State Mike Pompeo spoke at the Indo-Pacific Business Forum, sponsored by the United States Chamber of Commerce, emphasizing the importance of a free and open Indo-Pacific and accordingly announcing three fundraising initiatives.

On 3 October 2018, the US Congress passed a law to establish the United States International Development Finance Corporation (USIDFC). The Overseas Private Investment Corporation, which had been sluggish up to that point, was reorganized and then established a course for massive investments and loans in the open Indo-Pacific. In Pompeo's July address, only a small commitment of US$100 million was made; however, it was stated that the USIDFC had committed to tens of billions of dollars. Remarks by Vice President Mike Pence on 4 October have received much attention. In that speech, Pence stated that the engagement policy regarding China had been wrong, and he launched a policy of severe, all-out confrontation.

In December, the United States' criticism of China extended to its actions in Africa. The president's National Security Advisor John Bolton criticized China for driving Zambia and Djibouti into crisis with the use of excessive loans.

Such abrupt criticism of China by the Trump administration in recent years reminds me of the famous words of George Frost Kennan: "Democracy is peace-loving but fights in anger." Although the response was late in coming, the confrontational tone was severe.

Prime Minister Abe Shinzō's visit to China in October 2018 and the cooperative attitude shown there was in line with Abe's principles of July 2017; some say, however, that given the context of intense conflict between the United States and China, Japan should not engage too closely with China.

However, there are sometimes cases where the Japanese and US interests do not match. The US's severe criticism of China can be attributed to the words of the vice president, the secretary of state, or the presidential advisor; very few criticisms can be attributed to President Trump himself. President Trump comes from the business world. It is not implausible that he might suddenly join hands with China if it appears profitable. Japan must also prepare for such a possibility.

China is Japan's neighbor. In order to counter China's expansion, cooperation with the United States is absolutely necessary. However, it is desirable to avoid unnecessary confrontation. Conditional cooperation with the Belt and Road Initiative is also desirable, although under specific conditions. In order to neutralize the potential dangers of China's Belt and Road Initiative, China should also be guided to support the "Free and Open Indo-Pacific" vision.

Relationships Based on Mutual Trust, Freedom, and the Rule of Law

There are a number of interesting activities in support of the Free and Open Indo-Pacific vision.

One example is cooperation in the field of maritime security. JICA has invited maritime security staff from Indonesia, Malaysia, the Philippines, Vietnam, and others to Japan to spend one year studying at the National Graduate Institute for Policy Studies (GRIPS) in Tokyo, with continued studies carried out at the Japan Coast Guard Academy in Kure, Hiroshima Prefecture for another year.

The participants will come from island nations.

The Philippines has 7,000 islands and Indonesia has nearly 13,000. Without a coast guard, it is difficult to crack down on smuggling and piracy. Encouraging the sovereignty of these countries will also act as a deterrent against China.

Infrastructure construction should also support the development of friendly nations (my first principle); I believe countries must cooperate with each other even if they do not necessarily award bids to Japanese companies.

For many years, it has been known that Japan's approach to aid is different from that of Western countries. Japan does not assume a position of superiority but rather cooperates as a partner working together to decide what would benefit the developing country. As indicated by the name—Japan International Cooperation Agency—JICA has emphasized attitudes promoting cooperation over aid or assistance. It is mutual trust that underlies this approach. In July 2017, I chose the words "Leading the world with trust" as JICA's vision, because I wanted to remember this history and tradition.

The weakness of the Free and Open Indo-Pacific vision lies in its relationships with non-democratic countries in the region. For example, before the previous general election in Cambodia, the administration dissolved the opposition party and drove influential media out of business. Japan provided the necessary support and encouragement so that elections could be carried out in a manner that appropriately reflected the people's will, but Japan did not officially criticize Cambodia or reduce its aid. If Cambodia had been severely criticized over these issues, the country would have been more likely to accede to Chinese influence. While there was the possibility that trust in Japan would be damaged if no criticism took place, there was also the possibility that the pro-Japanese feelings of the Cambodian people might be harmed had it been criticized. Overall, cooperation has continued at roughly the same level, and the decision was made to wait for change over the long term.

The situation of the Rohingya people in Myanmar is more difficult. The problem is that the majority of the people in Myanmar are highly indifferent to the Rohingya population. It seemed likely that if pressure were put on the Aung San Suu Kyi regime, which was democratically elected, the regime might grow closer to China, or collapse and return to a military regime, or both. Therefore, Japan has been trying to assist the Rohingya refugees who escaped to Bangladesh and continued cooperation with Myanmar as usual, waiting for long-term change.

Related to the subject of mutual trust, it is interesting to note the recent beginnings of the JICA Development Studies Program. This program emerged due to the following factors.

Japan is the first and best example of modernization from a non-Western background. It is also the most successful country in ODA. East Asian countries with which Japan cooperated in the 1950s were at about the same economic level as sub-Saharan Africa; however, when compared with African countries supported by the West, East Asian countries have become remarkably developed. Accordingly, Japan should serve as a center for development studies. I hope that young people in developing countries will come to Japan and learn about Japanese modernization and development cooperation. To that end, the program will focus on English-language courses that incorporate the Japanese modernization experience, such as law, political science, economics, agriculture, disaster prevention, etc., accepting young people from many developing countries to universities focused on and enthusiastic about accepting foreign students from developing countries (in principle, to two-year master's programs). With the current interest of approximately 20 universities, the program began last year, in commemoration of the 150th anniversary of the Meiji Restoration. The program is continuing to expand and strengthen.

There is worldwide competition to invite young and capable people. Naturally, China is also focusing on attracting foreign students. However, there are things that cannot be learned in China. These include freedom and democracy and the rule of law. These are things that we want our young people in developing countries to learn. Their study alone is not enough; our society must also do better—not only for national security in the broad sense but also for the

interests of the nation. In that sense, the heart of the Free and Open Indo-Pacific vision is not only infrastructure, it is also the building of trusting relationships, development of human resources, and protection of individual freedom and the rule of law.

Kitaoka, Shinichi. "Vision for a Free and Open Indo-Pacific." *Asia-Pacific Review* 26:1 (2019), 7–17. © Nakasone Peace Institute reprinted by permission of Taylor & Francis Ltd, https://www.tandfonline.com on behalf of Nakasone Peace Institute.

Bibliography

Reuters. "Latin America Should not Rely on China: U.S. Secretary of State Tillerson." 2 February 2018. https://www.reuters.com/article/us-usa-diplomacy-latam-china-idUSKBN1FL6D5.

Chronology of the Heisei Era

	Date	Event	Prime Minister
1989	Jan. 7	Death of Emperor Shōwa. Crown Prince Akihito enthroned. New era named Heisei.	Takeshita Noboru
	Feb. 24	State funeral for Emperor Shōwa.	
	Apr. 1	Tax reform implemented, including adoption of 3% consumption tax.	
	Apr. 12	Chinese premier Li Peng visits Japan. Apr. 13: Premier Li granted audience with emperor.	
	Apr. 15	(China) Death of Hu Yaobang. Apr. 18: Start of mourning activities by students (pro-democracy movement). May 17: One million gather in Tiananmen Square. May 20: Martial law declared in Beijing.	
	Apr. 25	Prime Minister Takeshita Noboru announces resignation.	
	Jun. 2	Uno Sōsuke elected Liberal Democratic Party (LDP) president at joint plenary meeting of LDP Diet members from both houses. Takeshita cabinet resigns en masse. Jun. 3: Uno designated 75th prime minister and forms cabinet.	Uno Sōsuke
	Jun. 4	(China) From night of Jun. 3 until following morning, armed military units mobilize and forcibly remove students occupying Tiananmen Square, leaving many dead and injured (Second Tiananmen Square incident).	
	Jun. 23	Chinese Communist Party (CCP) holds fourth plenum. Zhao Ziyang stripped of all general secretary functions and replaced by Jiang Zemin. Nov. 9: Fifth plenum held. Deng Xiaoping resigns as chairman of Central Military Commission and replaced by Jiang.	
	Jul. 14	15th G7 Summit (Summit of the Arch) held in Paris, France.	
	Jul. 23	15th election for House of Councillors held. First reversal in ruling party since start of national elections. (Japan Socialist Party (JSP): 46; LDP: 36; Rengō no Kai: 11; Kōmeitō: 10; Japan Communist Party (JCP): 5; Democratic Socialist Party: 3; Various: 15.)	
	Jul. 24	Prime Minister Uno Sōsuke announces resignation.	
	Aug. 7	115th extraordinary session of Diet held (to Aug. 12). Aug. 8: Kaifu Toshiki elected LDP president by LDP Diet members from both houses. Aug. 10: Uno cabinet resigns en masse. House of Representatives elects LDP's Kaifu 76th prime minister. House of Councillors elects JSP's Doi Takako. Joint conference breaks down. Kaifu named prime minister under Article 67 of Constitution and forms cabinet.	Kaifu Toshiki
	Aug. 19	(East Germany) About 1,000 people cross border into Hungary and start exodus toward West. Sep. 10: (Hungary) Exit permits given to East Germans in residence. Sep. 11: Start of major migration toward West Germany. Nov. 4: Largest demonstration ever (one million people) in East Berlin. Nov. 9: Opening of border with West Germany. Fall of Berlin Wall (to Nov. 10). Dec. 1: Revision of Constitution. Dec. 3: Socialist Unity Party steps down.	
	Oct. 14	Former prime minister Tanaka Kakuei announces retirement from politics.	
	Nov. 6	Asia Pacific Economic Cooperation (APEC) launched with Japan as one of 12 founding countries.	
	Dec. 2	Presidents George H.W. Bush and Mikhail Gorbachev hold summit in Malta. Dec. 3: Announcement of end of Cold War.	

	Date	Event	Prime Minister
1990	Feb. 18	39th general election for House of Representatives held. (LDP: 275; JSP: 136; Kōmeitō: 45; JCP: 16; Democratic Socialist: 14; Socialist Democratic Federation: 4; Progressive: 1; Independents: 21.)	
	Feb. 27	118th ordinary session of Diet held (to Jun. 26). Kaifu Toshiki tapped to form second cabinet.	
	Apr. 26	Election System Council submits plans for introduction of single-seat constituencies combined with proportional representation.	
	May 24	Korean president Roh Tae-woo visits Japan. Emperor expresses "deepest regret" for "sorrowful past."	
	Jun. 23	Kaifu Toshiki is first prime minister to participate in Okinawa Memorial Service for All War Dead.	
	Aug. 2	Iraqi Army invades and takes control of Kuwait, starting Gulf War. UN Security Council adopts resolution demanding immediate unconditional withdrawal.	
	Aug. 6	UN Security Council passes resolution sanctioning Iraq. Aug. 8: Iraq announces annexation of Kuwait. Aug. 25: United Nations authorizes military enforcement of economic sanctions.	
	Aug. 29	Government announces assistance measures for Middle East, including funding for multinational force.	
	Sep. 5	South Korea and North Korea hold first south-north talks in Seoul.	
	Sep. 9	Iran and Iraq restore diplomatic relations.	
	Sep. 14	Government provides additional US$1 billion to support multinational force and approves approximately US$2 billion in economic aid to neighboring countries.	
	Sep. 24	Former deputy prime minister Kanemaru Shin and JSP vice chairman Tanabe Makoto visit North Korea. Sep. 26: Meeting and discussion with Kim Il-sung. Sep. 28: LDP, JSP, and Korean Workers' Party issue joint announcement.	
	Oct. 3	(Germany) Reunification of Germany (East Germany absorbed by West Germany) under name Federal Republic of Germany and with Berlin as capital.	
	Oct. 10	Ozawa Ichirō and other LDP leaders visit North Korea and agree on rapid normalization of relations. Oct. 11: Captain and chief engineer of *Fujisan Maru 18*, held by North Korean authorities on suspicion of spying, returned home.	
	Nov. 12	Enthronement ceremonies for Emperor Akihito. Attended by approx. 2,200 people, including representatives from 158 countries, United Nations, and European Commission.	
	Nov. 21	Signing ceremony for Charter of Paris for a New Europe. Ratified by 34 participating countries of Conference on Security and Cooperation in Europe (CSCE) and officially marks end of Cold War.	
	Nov. 29	UN Security Council passes resolution approving military action if Iraq does not leave Kuwait by 15 Jan. 1991.	
	Dec. 29	Reshuffle of second Kaifu cabinet.	
1991		Japan's bubble economy bursts.	
	Jan. 14	Responding to United Nations request, government announces US$38 million in assistance for Gulf refugees. Jan. 24: Additional assistance of US$9 billion set for mainly US multinational force.	

	Date	Event	Prime Minister
1991	Jan. 17	Mainly US multinational force attacks Iraqi Army and installations in Kuwait, using fighter planes and missiles. Feb. 24: Multinational force launches ground attack. Feb. 26: Iraq announces withdrawal. Feb. 27: President Bush announces liberation of Kuwait and victory in war. Apr. 3: UN Security Council adopts a ceasefire resolution.	Kaifu Toshiki
	Apr. 16	Soviet president Gorbachev visits Japan for first time and publicly acknowledges existence of territorial issues (to Apr. 19).	
	Apr. 24	Cabinet decision made to dispatch Japan Maritime Self-Defense Force (JMSDF) minesweepers to Persian Gulf to remove underwater mines. Apr. 26: Minesweepers sail out.	
	Jun. 25	Croatia and Slovenia declare formal independence from Socialist Federal Republic of Yugoslavia. Jun. 27: Yugoslav Army intervenes in Slovenia but withdraws after 10 days, effectively confirming Slovenia's separation. Croatian War of Independence begins (1991–95).	
	Jul. 31	Strategic Arms Reduction Treaty (START I) signed at US-Soviet summit meeting in Moscow.	
	Aug. 10	Prime Minister Kaifu holds talks with Premier Li Peng in China, emphasizing total restoration of Japan-China relations and promising ¥130 billion loan.	
	Sep. 19	Government submits Act on Cooperation with United Nations Peacekeeping Operations and Other Operations (PKO Act) to House of Representatives.	
	Oct. 27	Miyazawa Kiichi elected LDP president.	
	Oct. 30	Arab countries and Israel sit at same table for first time at Middle East Peace Conference, sponsored by United States and Soviet Union.	
	Nov. 5	122nd extraordinary session of Diet held (to Dec. 21). Kaifu cabinet resigns en masse, Miyazawa Kiichi designated 78th prime minister and forms cabinet.	Miyazawa Kiichi
	Nov. 27	Special PKO Committee in House of Representatives forces passage of PKO Act. Dec. 3: House of Representatives approves amended PKO Act. Dec. 20: Act fails to pass in House of Councillors.	
	Dec. 6	Korean victims of Asia-Pacific War, including former comfort women, file suit in Tokyo District Court seeking reparations from Japanese government.	
	Dec. 8	Russia, Ukraine, and Belarus seal agreement to set up Commonwealth of Independent States (CIS), heralding end of Soviet Union.	
	Dec. 21	Heads of 11 republics sign CIS protocol and Union of Soviet Socialist Republics ceases to exist. Dec. 25: Gorbachev resigns as president. Soviet Union dissolved.	
1992	Jan. 1	Japan starts two-year term as nonpermanent member on UN Security Council.	
	Jan. 7	President George H.W. Bush visits Japan. Jan. 9: Tokyo Declaration announced pledging global cooperation.	
	Jan. 9	Akashi Yasushi, UN under-secretary-general, named special representative of the secretary-general of United Nations Transitional Authority in Cambodia (UNTAC).	
	Jan. 17	Prime Minister Miyazawa makes public apology regarding comfort women issue.	
	Jan. 18	Deng Xiaoping tours Southern China (to Feb. 21), promoting "reform and opening" and economic growth.	

Date	Event	Prime Minister
Jan. 27	Government recognizes Russia as successor to Soviet Union.	
Feb. 7	12 EC countries sign Maastricht Treaty (Treaty on the European Union).	
Feb. 21	United Nations dispatches PKO troops to European country (Yugoslavia) for first time.	
Feb. 25	China adopts Territorial Sea Law, declaring Senkaku, Spratly, Parcel, and other islands Chinese territory.	
May 7	Former governor of Kumamoto prefecture Hosokawa Morihiro forms new party. May 22: New party name announced as "Japan New Party."	
Jun. 15	Act on Cooperation with United Nations PKO Act adopted.	
Jun. 16	United States and Russia agree on large-scale limitation of strategic arms.	
Jul. 1	Government announces intervention and investigation regarding Imperial Japanese Army involvement in recruiting comfort women. Jul. 6: Chief Cabinet Secretary Katō Kōichi apologizes to South Korea and other Asian countries but denies coercion.	
Jul. 22	ASEAN adopts Declaration on the South China Sea, stressing peaceful resolution of territorial disputes.	
Jul. 26	16th election for House of Councillors held. LDP recovers, complete defeat for alliance. Lowest voter turnout in history. (LDP: 68; JSP: 22; Kōmeitō: 14; JCP: 6; Democratic Socialist Party: 4; Japan New Party: 4; Independents: 9.)	
Aug. 22	Kanemaru Shin, chairman of LDP Takeshita faction, exposed as having taken ¥500 million from former Tokyo Sagawa Express president Watanabe Hiroyasu. Sep. 25: Kanemaru provides written statement to Tokyo District Public Prosecutor's Office, acknowledging donation. Sep. 28: Kanemaru receives summary indictment and fined ¥200,000. Oct. 21: Kanemaru resigns from Diet.	
Sep. 2	United Nations officially requests Japanese government join PKO in Cambodia. Sep. 8: Cabinet formulates implementation plan. Sep. 17: First Japan Ground, Air, and Maritime SDF contingent (423 people) departs for Cambodia.	
Sep. 16	PKO Act invoked for first time with dispatch of observers for elections in Angola.	
Oct. 23	Emperor and empress visit China for first time (to Oct. 28).	
Nov. 3	Bill Clinton wins US presidential election.	
Dec. 10	Split in LDP Takeshita faction. Former secretary-general Ozawa Ichirō sets up Hata faction.	
Dec. 12	Miyazawa reshuffles cabinet.	
1993 Jan. 1	Official start of EC's single European market (giant economic area with 12 participating countries, population of 340 million, and GNP of US$6 trillion).	
Jan. 3	US and Russian presidents sign Strategic Arms Reduction Treaty (START II) in Moscow.	
Jan. 10	(Iraq) Forces inside Kuwaiti territory attacked, numerous missiles and weapons seized. Jan. 13–18: Air strikes by US, British, and French air forces on missile sites in southern Iraq. Military facilities bombarded. Jan. 19: Iraq announces unilateral ceasefire.	

Date	Event	Prime Minister
1993 Feb. 9	(North Korea) International Atomic Energy Agency (IAEA) requests special inspection of two suspicious waste sites. Feb. 20: North Korea refuses inspection.	Miyazawa Kiichi
Feb. 25	Kim Yong-sam takes office as president of South Korea.	
Mar. 6	LDP vice president Kanemaru Shin arrested on tax evasion charges.	
Mar. 15	(China) 8th National People's Congress opens. Jiang Zemin elected president and pursues path of higher growth.	
Mar. 26	Japanese government decides to send Japan Self-Defence Force (JSDF) to Mozambique for PKO (from May 11–15).	
Jun. 18	JSP, Kōmeitō, Democratic Socialist Party, and 39 members of LDP Hata faction submit no confidence motion, passing in House of Representatives with 225 votes in favor. House of Representatives dissolved. Ten people, including Takemura Masayoshi, quit LDP. Jun. 21: "New Party Sakigake" formed.	
Jun. 22	44 Hata faction Diet members quit LDP. Jun. 23: Shinseitō Renewal Party formed.	
Jul. 18	40th general election for House of Representatives held. LDP loses majority, JSP crushed, and new parties make great strides. (LDP: 223; JSP: 70; Shinseitō: 55; Kōmeitō: 51; Japan New Party: 35; Democratic Socialist Party: 15; JCP: 15; Sakigake: 13; Socialist Democratic Federation: 4; Independents: 30.)	
Jul. 30	Kōno Yōhei elected LDP president.	
Aug. 3	Coalition of eight parties asks former JSP leader Doi Takako to become speaker of House of Representatives. Aug. 6: Doi becomes first female speaker in history of Japan's Constitutional government.	
Aug. 5	127th extraordinary session of Diet held (to Aug. 28). Aug. 6: Prime Minister Miyazawa Kiichi announces resignation. Japan New Party leader Hosokawa Morihiro elected 79th prime minister. LDP in opposition for first time since founded in 1955. Aug. 9: Miyazawa cabinet resigns en masse. Hosokawa coalition cabinet formed.	Hosokawa Morihiro
Aug. 23	Prime Minister Hosokawa makes general policy speech, mentioning political reform and expressing deep regret and apologies concerning war responsibility.	
Sep. 20	Murayama Tomiichi elected JSP chairman.	
Oct. 5	First Tokyo International Conference on African Development (TICAD I) held in Tokyo.	
	China conducts underground nuclear tests, drawing international protests.	
Oct. 11	[Russia] President Boris Yeltsin visits Japan. Oct. 13: Japan-Russia Tokyo declaration on economic matters announced.	
Nov. 1	Maastricht Treaty comes into effect, marking start of European Union (EU).	
Dec. 15	GATT Uruguay Round adopted. Agreement on World Trade Organization (WTO) starts.	
1994 Jan. 1	North-American Free Trade Agreement (NAFTA) comes into effect. European Economic Area (EEA), combining 12 EU member states and 3 EEA European Free Trade Association (EFTA) states into single market.	
Jan. 29	House of Representatives passes political reform bill without date of coming into effect. Mar. 4: Single-seat constituency bill approved.	

Date		Event	Prime Minister
1999	Jan. 1	Euro adopted as single European currency.	Obuchi Keizō
		First reshuffle of Obuchi cabinet.	
	Jan. 14	LDP and Liberal Party (led by Ozawa Ichiro) form coalition government.	
	May 28	Law Concerning Measures to Ensure the Peace and Security of Japan in Situations in the Area Surrounding Japan enacted and Self-Defense Forces Act partially revised.	
	Aug. 30	(Indonesia) Independence Party wins overwhelming victory in East Timor election. Oct. 19: People's Consultative Assembly declares 1978 annexation of East Timor invalid and approves independence.	
	Sep. 17	(United States) Economic sanctions against North Korea relaxed for first time since Korean War.	
	Sep. 21	Obuchi Keizō reelected LDP president.	
	Oct. 5	Kōmeitō (New Kōmeitō) joins coalition government with LDP and Liberal Party, giving coalition majority in House of Representatives. Second reshuffle of Obuchi cabinet with establishment of coalition.	
	Nov. 28	Prime Minister Obuchi meets with President Kim Dae-jung of South Korea and Premier Zhu Rongji of China in Manila in first summit meeting between three countries.	
	Dec. 20	Portugal returns Macau to China, marking end of western colonial rule in Asia.	
	Dec. 31	United States returns Panama Canal to Panama, closes military bases, and withdraws completely.	
		(Russia) President Yeltsin announces resignation and designates Prime Minister Vladimir Putin as successor.	
2000	Mar. 18	(Taiwan) Chen Shui-bian of Democratic Progressive Party wins presidential election.	
	Mar. 26	(Russia) Putin elected president.	
	Apr. 2	Prime Minister Obuchi suffers stroke and falls into coma. Apr. 3: Aoki Mikio becomes acting prime minister. Apr. 5: Obuchi cabinet resigns en masse. General meeting of LDP members from both houses elects Mori Yoshirō 85th prime minister. Mori cabinet formed in coalition with Kōmeitō and Conservative Party.	Mori Yoshirō
	May 14	Death of Prime Minister Obuchi.	
	Jun. 13	President Kim Dae-jung of South Korea visits North Korea for first north-south summit meeting with General Secretary Kim Jong-il.	
	Jun. 25	42nd general election held. Despite LDP setbacks, Kōmeitō and Conservative Party maintain coalition majority. (LDP: 233; DPJ: 127; Kōmeitō: 31; Liberal Party: 22; JCP: 20; SDP Japan: 19; Conservative Party: 7; Various and Independents: 21.)	
	Jul. 4	Prime Minister Mori forms second cabinet.	
	Jul. 21	26th G8 Summit (Kyushu-Okinawa Summit) held in Nago, Okinawa. Joint "Okinawa 2000" declaration signed.	
	Sep. 3	Russian president Putin visits Japan.	
	Dec. 5	Prime Minister Mori reshuffles second cabinet.	
2001	Jan. 6	In central government shake-up, 22 ministries reduced to 12 ministries. Prime Minister Mori reorganizes second Mori cabinet along with ministry reform.	
	Jan. 20	George W. Bush sworn in as 43rd president of US.	
	Mar. 2	(Afghanistan) Taliban destroys Buddhist statues at Bamyan.	

Date		Event	Prime Minister
	Apr. 8	Prime Minister Hosokawa Morihiro announces resignation.	
	Apr. 25	Members from five parties and parliamentary groups, including Japan Renewal Party, form new group, "Kaishin." Apr. 26: JSP leaves coalition in protest.	
	Apr. 28	Hosokawa cabinet resigns en masse, Hata Tsutomu designated 80th prime minister and forms cabinet, first minority cabinet in 39 years.	Hata Tsutomu
	Jun. 10	Emperor and empress visit United States (to Jun. 26).	
		China conducts nuclear weapons test. Oct. 7: China conducts another nuclear weapons test.	
	Jun. 17	Former US president Jimmy Carter visits North Korea and negotiates nuclear program with General Secretary Kim Il-sung.	
	Jun. 25	Prime Minister Hata Tsutomu announces resignation.	
	Jun. 29	House of Representatives votes to designate new prime minister. Murayama Tomiichi, backed by LDP, JSP, and Sakigake, beats Kaifu Toshiki, supported by old ruling coalition.	
	Jun. 30	Hata cabinet resigns en masse and Murayama Tomiichi designated 81st prime minister. Coalition cabinet formed with LDP's Kōno Yōhei as deputy prime minister and foreign minister and Sakigake's Takemura Masayoshi as minister of finance.	Murayama Tomiichi
	Jul. 8	Death of Kim Il-sung, president of North Korea. Jul. 17: Funeral following ten-day nationwide mourning period underpinning Kim Il-sung system.	
	Jul. 20	Prime Minister Murayama accepts JSDF as constitutional.	
	Jul. 25	ASEAN Regional Forum (ARF) established.	
	Dec. 8	Nine opposition parties (JCP excepted) form New Frontier Party. Kaifu Toshiki elected party leader, Ozawa Ichirō secretary-general. Dec. 10: Official establishment of New Frontier Party.	
	Dec. 15	Resolution introduced by Japan entitled "Nuclear disarmament with a view to the ultimate elimination of nuclear weapons" adopted by United Nations General Assembly as resolution 49/75H. China and Russia vote in favour, US, UK, and France abstain.	
1995	Jan. 1	WTO launched.	
	Jan. 17	Great Hanshin-Awaji Earthquake strikes Japan, leaving 6,434 dead or injured.	
	Mar. 19	Korean Peninsula Energy Development Organization (KEDO) established, based on October 1994 Agreed Framework between US and North Korea. Japan participates as executive board member. 31 May 2006: KEDO decides to terminate light-water reactor project in response to North Korea's continued non-compliance with agreed procedures.	
	May 15	China conducts nuclear weapons test. Aug. 17: Further nuclear weapons test.	
	May 30	Japanese Official Development Assistance (ODA) up 17.4% year on year in 1994, to US$13,469 million, topping world rankings for fourth consecutive year (Japan remaining top for total ten consecutive years from 1991–2000).	
	Jun. 9	House of Representatives adopts Resolution to Renew the Determination for Peace on the Basis of Lessons Learned from History on occasion of 50th anniversary of end of World War II.	
	Jul. 19	Murayama cabinet establishes Asian Women's Fund. 31 March 2007: Fund dissolved.	
	Jul. 20	Agreement reached in Japan-US civil aviation talks.	

Date		Event	Prime Minister
1995	Jul. 21	China conducts first of series of missile tests in waters near Taiwan, initiating 1995–96 Taiwan Strait Crisis.	Murayama Tomiichi
	Jul. 23	17th election for House of Councillors held. New Frontier Party makes strong showing, ruling parties barely get more than half of votes, and voter turnout lowest ever at 44.52%. (LDP: 46; New Frontier Party: 40; JSP: 16; JCP: 8; Sakigake: 3; Democratic Reform League: 2; Various: 1; Independents: 10.)	
	Aug. 4	133rd extraordinary session of Diet held (to Aug. 8). Both houses unanimously approve parliamentary resolution against resumption of French and Chinese nuclear tests.	
	Aug. 8	Murayama reshuffles cabinet.	
	Aug. 15	Murayama cabinet decides on official statement "On the occasion of the 50th anniversary of the war's end." Expresses deep remorse and heartfelt apologies for war of aggression.	
	Sep. 4	Group of US servicemen kidnap and rape 12-year-old Okinawan schoolgirl. Sep. 19: Governor Ōta Masahide lodges protest with US Ambassador Walter Mondale and US forces. Sep. 29: Indictments by Naha District Public Prosecutors Office. 8 Sep. 1996: Okinawa Prefectural Assembly holds referendum on consolidating US military bases and shrinking US presence in Okinawa. Majority endorse base consolidation.	
	Sep. 12	Prime Minister Murayama tours Middle East. Sep. 14: Announces dispatch of JSDF troops to Golan Heights. Sep. 17: Visits Israel for first time.	
	Sep. 22	Hashimoto Ryūtarō elected LDP president.	
	Dec. 11	United Nations General Assembly decides on removal of "enemy state" clause from UN Charter and deletion of "former enemy states" clause.	
1996	Jan. 5	Prime Minister Murayama Tomiichi announces resignation.	
	Jan. 11	135th extraordinary session of Diet held (to Jan. 13). Murayama cabinet resigns en masse, Hashimoto Ryūtarō elected 82nd prime minister and forms cabinet.	Hashimoto Ryūtarō
	Feb. 23	Prime Minister Hashimoto visits United States. Reaches agreement with US president Clinton to move forward in dealing with and shrinking US military bases in Okinawa.	
	Apr. 12	Japan-US agreement on complete return of US Marine Corps Air Station Futenma.	
	Apr. 16	US president Clinton visits Japan. Apr. 17: Summit meeting to discuss Far East tensions. Japan-US Joint Declaration on Security issued.	
	Apr. 18	Prime Minister Hashimoto visits Russia and meets with President Yeltsin.	
	Aug. 15	Prime Minister Hashimoto expresses "profound remorse and condolence" toward many countries, particularly those of Southeast Asia, for damage inflicted.	
	Sep. 9	Minister of Health and Welfare Kan Naoto and Hatoyama Yukio agree to form new party. Sep. 10: Democratic Party of Japan (DPJ) chosen as new party's name. Sep. 17: Sakigake Party and Social Democratic Party (SDP Japan) members part ways. Sep. 28: Hatoyama and Kan elected DPJ leaders in founding meeting. (Participation of 52 members from House of Representatives and 5 from House of Councillors, making it third most powerful party in House of Representatives.)	

Date		Event	Prime Minister
	Oct. 20	41st general election for House of Representatives held. First election with single-seat constituencies and proportional representation. LDP recovers and SDP Japan crushed. (LDP: 239; New Frontier Party: 156; DPJ: 52; JCP: 26; SDP Japan: 15; Sakigake Party: 2; Various: 1; Independents: 9.)	
	Nov. 5	(United States) President Bill Clinton reelected.	
	Nov. 7	138th special session of Diet held (to Nov. 12). Second Hashimoto cabinet formed. SDP Japan and Sakigake Party agree to cooperate with government from outside cabinet—first purely LDP cabinet in three years and three months.	
	Dec. 2	Japan and US agree on addressing and reducing US military presence in Okinawa and launch Special Action Committee on Okinawa (SACO) process to reduce burden on Okinawans and strengthen Japan-US alliance.	
1997	Jan. 1	Japan starts term as nonpermanent member on UN Security Council.	
	Apr. 1	Consumption tax raised to 5%, of which 1% designated local consumption tax.	
	Jul. 1	UK returns Hong Kong to China.	
	Jul. 2	Bank of Thailand unpegs Thai baht from US dollar and adopts floating exchange rate, leading to currency collapse and triggering Asian financial crisis.	
	Sep. 8	Hashimoto Ryūtarō reelected LDP president. Sep. 11: Reshuffles second cabinet.	
	Sep. 18	Kan Naoto elected DPJ president, with Hatoyama Yukio secretary-general.	
	Sep. 23	Revised Guidelines for Japan-US Defense Cooperation approved at Japan-US Security Consultative Committee meeting.	
	Oct. 8	(North Korea) Kim Jong-il elected general secretary of Workers' Party of Korea.	
	Dec. 3	Administrative Reform Council recommends restructuring with Cabinet Office and 12 ministries.	
	Dec. 17	1st ASEAN+3 Summit held in Kuala Lumpur, Malaysia. Japan, China, and South Korea invited.	
	Dec. 18	(South Korea) Kim Dae-jung elected president.	
1998	Jul. 12	18th election for House of Councillors held. SDP Japan defeated and JCP picks up seats. (LDP: 44; Democratic Party: 27; JCP: 15; Kōmeitō: 9; Liberal Party: 6; SDP Japan: 5; Independents: 20.)	
	Jul. 24	Hashimoto resigns as LDP president. Obuchi Keizō elected successor.	
	Jul. 30	143rd special session of Diet held (to Oct. 16). Second Hashimoto cabinet resigns en masse, Obuchi Keizō elected 84th prime minister and forms cabinet, calling it "economic revitalization cabinet."	Obuchi Keizō
	Aug. 31	North Korea fires first missile (Daepodong-1) over Japan. US military forces in Japan track landing to waters off Sanriku coast. Sep. 4: North Korea announces launch of first artificial satellite.	
	Oct. 7	South Korean president Kim Dae-jung visits Japan. Emperor expresses "deep sorrow" at past rule over Korean Peninsula. Oct. 8: Japan and South Korea declare New Japan–Republic of Korea Partnership towards the Twenty-first Century.	
	Oct. 19	Second Tokyo International Conference on African Development (TICAD II) held in Tokyo.	
	Nov. 11	Prime Minister Obuchi visits Russia. Nov. 13: Leaders of both countries sign Moscow Declaration.	
	Nov. 26	Japan-China Joint Declaration on Building a Partnership of Friendship and Cooperation for Peace and Development issued.	

Date	Event	Prime Minister
Mar. 5	Vote of no confidence in Mori cabinet fails in House of Representatives. Former LDP secretary-general Katō Kōichi and others abstain (Katō rebellion).	
Mar. 16	Government acknowledges first deflation since end of World War II.	
Apr. 18	Prime Minister Mori Yoshirō announces resignation.	
Apr. 24	Koizumi Junichirō elected LDP's 20th president. Apr. 26: Mori cabinet resigns en masse, Koizumi elected 87th prime minister and forms cabinet in coalition with Kōmeitō and Conservative Party.	Koizumi Junichirō
Jul. 29	19th election for House of Councillors held. Ruling coalition maintains majority. (LDP: 64; DPJ: 26; Kōmeitō: 13; Liberal Party: 6; JCP: 5; SDP Japan: 3; New Conservative Party: 1; Independents: 3.)	
Aug. 10	Koizumi reelected LDP president at general meeting of party members from both houses.	
Aug. 13	Prime Minister Koizumi visits Yasukuni Shrine, drawing criticism and opposition both in Japan and overseas.	
Sep. 11	(United States) Simultaneous terrorist incidents, including World Trade Center towers being hit by hijacked planes, leading to 3,000 deaths, including 24 Japanese nationals. Sep. 15: US government attributes attack to Al-Qaeda, Muslim fundamentalist terrorist organization run by Osama Bin Laden under Afghan Taliban protection.	
Sep. 19	Government decides to dispatch JSDF to provide support for reprisal attacks by US military. Nov. 27: Approved by Diet.	
Oct. 7	US, British, and other forces launch offensive in Afghanistan in retaliation for Sep. 11 terrorist attacks. Nov. 13: Taliban forces defeated. Dec. 22: Provisional Karzai government inaugurated.	
Oct. 8	Prime Minister Koizumi meets with Premier Zhu Rongji and President Jiang Zemin in Beijing and expresses heartfelt apology and regrets to all Chinese victims of Japan's invasion. Oct. 21: Koizumi visits Shanghai to participate in APEC summit meeting and meets with President Jiang Zemin again.	
Oct. 15	Prime Minister Koizumi visits South Korea, meets with President Kim Dae-jung. Prime minister expresses for first time "regret and apologies for Japanese colonial rule."	
Oct. 20	Prime Minister Koizumi meets with President Bush in Shanghai. Japan to be given prominent role in Afghan reconstruction.	
Oct. 29	Anti-Terrorism Special Measures Law adopted, making it possible to provide logistics support to US military operations in a major shift in Japan's national security policy. Nov. 2: Promulgated and enters into force. Nov. 9: JMSDF ship sets sail, heading for Indian Ocean to provide logistics support to US military. Ratification of International Convention for the Suppression of Terrorist Bombings, with seven related laws adopted.	
Dec. 7	PKO Act amended to lift ban on participation in core peacekeeping force operations.	
Dec. 11	China joins WTO.	
2002 Jan. 1	Euro comes into circulation as single currency for 12 European countries.	
Jan. 21	International Conference on Reconstruction Assistance to Afghanistan opens in Tokyo, with US$4.5 billion in aid pledged.	
Mar. 2	Japan Ground Self-Defence Force (JGSDF) advance party leaves for PKO duties in East Timor (total 680 people dispatched).	

	Date	Event	Prime Minister
2002	May 13	Japan loses top place in ODA rankings.	Koizumi Junichirō
	May 21	Act on Promotion of Global Warming Countermeasures revised.	
	Jun. 4	Cabinet decision on ratifying Kyoto Protocol to prevent global warming. Jun. 5: Ratification documents deposited with United Nations.	
	Jun. 5	Terrorist Financing Act adopted, along with three laws relating to financing of terrorism. Jun. 11: Ratification of 12 terrorism-related conventions.	
	Aug. 26	United Nations holds World Summit on Sustainable Development (to Sep. 4).	
	Sep. 17	Prime Minister Koizumi becomes first Japanese prime minister to visit North Korea, holding historic Japan-North Korea summit meeting with General Secretary Kim Jong-il, and signing Japan-DPRK Pyongyang Declaration. North Korea acknowledges abduction of Japanese citizens.	
	Sep. 30	Reshuffle of Koizumi cabinet.	
	Nov. 4	China and ASEAN sign Framework Agreement on ASEAN-China Economic Cooperation and Joint Declaration on Cooperation in the Field of Nontraditional Security Issues, also signing Declaration on the Conduct of Parties in the South China Sea.	
	Dec. 16	JMSDF Aegis class cruiser *Kirishima* sails for Indian Ocean to provide logistics support to US and British forces, in line with Anti-Terrorism Special Measures Law.	
	Dec. 25	Dissolution of Conservative Party and establishment of New Conservative Party (including five defectors from DPJ). Dec. 26: LDP, Kōmeitō, and New Conservative Party coalition formed.	
2003	Jan. 10	North Korea announces withdrawal from Nuclear Nonproliferation Treaty (NPT), citing US hostility as security threat. First firm suspicions of North Korean nuclear weapons development.	
	Mar. 15	(China) CCP secretary-general Hu Jintao becomes president of People's Republic of China. Mar. 16: Wen Jiabao becomes premier of state council of People's Republic of China.	
	Mar. 20	Start of Iraq War. US Army invades Iraq based on suspicions it is developing of weapons of mass destruction. Apr. 14: Hussain dictatorship crushed and US assumes control of whole country. May 1: Announcement of end of main military conflict. Jul. 13: Iraqi Governing Council (IGC) inaugurated. Dec. 13: President Hussain apprehended.	
	Apr. 1	Japan Post Public Corporation takes over from Postal Services Agency and starts operations. Prohibition on private sector involvement relaxed.	
	Jun. 6	Three laws relating to war contingency, including Armed Attack Situation Response Law, adopted. Jun. 13: Promulgated and come into effect. Japan's security legislation in place.	
	Jun. 27	Cabinet decides on Basic Policies for Economic and Fiscal Management and Structural Reform 2003 in three-part package (Trinity Reforms) reducing national government subsidies, capping total amount of local allocation tax, and using transfer of tax revenue sources for local government finances.	
	Jul. 26	Iraqi Reconstruction Special Measures Law adopted. Aug. 1: Promulgated and comes into effect. Possible to send JSDF to Iraq to provide logistics support for US and British forces for humanitarian and reconstruction activities based on UN Security Council Resolution. Dec. 26: First round of Iraq reconstruction support. First JSDF mission sent.	

Date	Event	Prime Minister
Sep. 20	Koizumi reelected LDP president. Sep. 21: Abe Shinzō becomes secretary-general. Sep. 22: Second reshuffle of Koizumi cabinet.	
Sep. 29	Third Tokyo International Conference on African Development (TICAD III) held in Tokyo.	
Oct. 10	House of Representatives dissolved. Nov. 9: 43rd general election held. Three ruling parties maintaining strong majority, crushing defeat for New Conservative Party in opposition, major gains by DPJ, and major losses for JCP and SDP Japan. (LDP: 237; DPJ: 177; Kōmeitō: 34; JCP: 9; SDP Japan: 6; New Conservative Party: 4; Assembly of Independents: 1; Liberal League: 1; Independents: 11.) 5 single-seat constituency seats moved to reflect population changes. LDP sets age limit of 73 on proportional representation candidates. Former prime ministers Nakasone Yasuhiro and Miyazawa Kiichi retire.	
Nov. 19	158th special session of Diet held (to Nov. 27). LDP's Kōno Yōhei becomes speaker of House of Representatives. Second Koizumi cabinet formed.	
Nov. 29	Three people, including two Japanese diplomats, shot dead in Iraq.	
2004 Jan. 16	First JGSDF deployment based on Iraqi Reconstruction Special Measures Law.	
Jan. 31	JSDF deployment approved by House of Representatives. Feb. 9: Approved by House of Councillors.	
Apr. 8	(Iraq) Armed group Sarayaal-Mujahideen announces capture of three Japanese citizens and demands withdrawal of JSDF.	
Apr. 27	LDP decides on draft for amending Constitution.	
May 22	Prime Minister Koizumi visits North Korea and holds talks with General Secretary Kim Jong-il.	
May 27	Two Japanese hostages executed in Iraq.	
Jun. 1	(Iraq) Interim government installed, with multinational forces remaining in country.	
Jun. 2	Laws relating to privatization of four highway public corporations adopted. Japan Highway Public Corporation and others to be privatized in fiscal year 2005.	
Jun. 18	Cabinet approves JSDF participation in Iraq multinational force. Jun. 28: JSDF (approx. 600 people) participates in multinational force in Iraq for first time.	
Jul. 11	20th election for House of Councillors held. DPJ gains and JCP loses heavily. (DPJ: 50; LDP: 49; Kōmeitō: 11; JCP: 4; SDP Japan: 2; Independents: 5.) 1:5.13 disparity in number of voters per seat.	
Sep. 17	Japan-Mexico Free Trade Agreement signed.	
Sep. 21	Japan, Brazil, Germany, and India launch G4 group and release press statement on United Nations and UN Security Council reform.	
Sep. 27	Second Koizumi cabinet reshuffled. Non-politician Takenaka Heizō appointed minister for postal system privatization.	
Oct. 27	Armed insurgents in Iraq capture and kill Japanese nationals.	
Nov. 2	(United States) President Bush reelected.	
Dec. 26	Major earthquake off coast of Sumatra and large tsunami in Indian Ocean, resulting in over 230,000 dead or missing, including 42 Japanese nationals.	

	Date	Event	Prime Minister
2005	Jan. 1	Japan starts term as nonpermanent member on UN Security Council.	Koizumi Junichirō
	Jan. 7	JMSDF dispatched to site of Indian Ocean earthquake and tsunami.	
	Feb. 16	Start of Kyoto Protocol to prevent global warming.	
	Mar. 8	(China) Jiang Zemin resigns as president of National Central Military Commission and retires completely. Mar. 13: Hu Jintao inherits all posts.	
	Apr. 9	Violent anti-Japanese protests in China.	
	Apr. 22	Prime Minister Koizumi expresses regret and apologizes for colonial rule and aggression at leaders' summit on 50th anniversary of Bandung Conference. Apr. 23: Koizumi meets Chinese president Hu Jintao.	
	May 16	Amended Immigration Control Act comes into effect. Refugee Examination Counselors System initiated and counselors announced.	
	Jul. 5	Six bills related to privatization of postal service pass in House of Representatives. 51 LDP members break ranks (37 voting against, 14 abstaining).	
	Jul. 6	G4 (Japan, Brazil, Germany, and India) submit Draft Resolution on Security Council Reform to UN Security Council, calling for UN Security Council to be enlarged to 25 members, including six additional permanent seats. Proposal not put to vote.	
	Aug. 2	House of Representatives adopts Parliamentary Resolution on 60th anniversary of end of World War II, affirming commitment to contribute to international peace.	
	Aug. 8	Six bills for postal service privatization rejected by House of Councillors (30 LDP members voting against) and killed. House of Representatives dissolved. Shimamura Yoshinobu, minister of agriculture, forestry and fisheries, opposes dissolution and dismissed. Aug. 11: Shimamura succeeded by Iwanaga Mineichi.	
	Sep. 11	44th general election held. LDP wins working majority for first time in 15 years. Kōmeitō, JCP, and SDP Japan hold on to Diet seats. New parties acquire Diet seats. DPJ crushed. (LDP: 296; DPJ: 113; Kōmeitō: 31; JCP: 9; SDP Japan: 7; People's New Party: 4; New Party Nippon: 1; Independents: 19, of which 13 opposed to postal service privatization.)	
	Sep. 21	163rd special session of Diet held (to Nov. 11). Koizumi Junichirō reelected prime minister. Third Koizumi cabinet inaugurated, with all cabinet posts hold-overs.	
	Oct. 14	Six bills relating to privatization of postal service adopted.	
	Oct. 24	United Nations celebrates 60th anniversary of establishment.	
	Oct. 31	Third Koizumi cabinet reshuffled. Major turn-over in cabinet posts. Abe Shinzō becomes chief cabinet secretary.	
	Nov. 22	LDP celebrates 50th anniversary since creation and announces draft for amending Constitution.	
2006	May 1	Decision on restructuring US forces in Japan to expand and strengthen cooperation between JSDF and US military, while reducing of burden on Okinawa.	
	Jun. 20	Order given to withdraw JGSDF troops from reconstruction effort in Iraq. Japan Air Self-Defence Force (JASDF) to continue activities and widen scope.	
	Jul. 15	UN Security Council passes resolutions regarding North Korean missile launches.	
	Aug. 15	Prime Minister Koizumi visits Yasukuni Shrine for first time on anniversary of end of war.	

Date	Event	Prime Minister
Sep. 26	165th extraordinary session of Diet held (to Dec. 19). Koizumi cabinet resigns en masse, Abe Shinzō elected 90th prime minister and forms LDP-Kōmeitō coalition cabinet.	Abe Shinzō
Oct. 8	Prime Minister Abe meets with Chinese and South Korean leaders in Beijing and Seoul, using first foreign visits to improve relations.	
Oct. 9	(North Korea) Underground nuclear test conducted. Oct. 13: Additional sanctions imposed by Japan. Oct. 14: UN Security Council Resolution.	
Nov. 18	Abe meets with President Hu Jintao at APEC meeting in Hanoi.	
Dec. 26	Japan-China Joint History Research Committee holds first meeting in Beijing (to Dec. 27).	

Date	Event	Prime Minister
2007 Jan. 9	Ministry of Defense starts operation. Jun. 1: Amended Act for Establishment of the Ministry of Defense adopted. Sep. 1: Comes into effect. Defense Facilities Administration Agency abolished and folded into Ministry of Defense.	
Jan. 14	2nd East Asia Summit (EAS), 10th ASEAN Summit, 10th ASEAN+3 Summit, and 7th Summit meeting among Japan, China, and South Korea held in Cebu, Philippines (to Jan. 15). Abe meets with Chinese premier Wen Jiabao on margin of ASEAN+3 Summit.	
Mar. 13	Prime Ministers Abe and Howard issue first Japan-Australia Joint Declaration on Security Cooperation.	
Apr. 11	Chinese premier Wen Jiabao visits Japan. Acknowledges numerous past apologies and expressions of remorse made by Japanese leaders and shows appreciation for Japan's economic assistance.	
Apr. 25	China passes US as Japan's largest trading partner in fiscal year 2006.	
May 14	National Referendum Law adopted pursuant to Article 96 of Constitution. May 18: Promulgated, putting in place legal structure for amending Constitution. Effective 18 May 2010.	
Jul. 29	21st election for House of Councillors held. LDP suffers major losses and LDP-Kōmeitō majority overturned, leaving two houses controlled by different parties. (DPJ: 60; LDP: 37; Kōmeitō: 9; JCP: 3; SDP Japan: 2; People's New Party: 2; New Party Nippon: 1; Independents: 7.) Voters-per-seat disparity at 4.86.	
Aug. 7	167th special Diet session (to Aug. 10). DPJ's Eda Satsuki elected speaker of House of Councillors (quits party to be non-partisan).	
Aug. 10	Agreement between the Government of Japan and the Government of the United States of America Concerning Security Measures for the Protection of Classified Military Information, or the Japan-US General Security of Military Information Agreement (GSOMIA), concluded and implemented.	
Aug. 27	Abe cabinet reshuffled.	
Sep. 25	Abe cabinet resigns en masse, LDP President Fukuda Yasuo becomes 91st prime minister. Sep. 26: Fukuda cabinet formed.	Fukuda Yasuo
Oct. 1	Japan Post split up and privatized, leading to creation of Japan Post Group and end of government-owned postal monopoly.	
Nov. 2	Anti-Terrorism Special Measures Law lapses. JMSDF Indian Ocean refueling activities stopped.	
Nov. 20	ASEAN+3 Summit held in Singapore and Second Joint Statement on East Asia Cooperation released.	

	Date	Event	Prime Minister
2008	Jan. 11	Replenishment Support Special Measures Law rejected by House of Councillors but adopted after passing House of Representatives second time. Jan. 16: Promulgated and comes into effect. Feb. 21: Maritime SDF resumes refueling activities in Indian Ocean. Dec. 12: Activity period extended after revised law enacted.	Fukuda Yasuo
	Jan. 30	Contaminated dumplings imported from China by JT Foods poison several families in Japan, prompting government probe into food security.	
	Mar. 2	(Russia) Dmitry Medvedev elected president. May 7: Medvedev takes office. May 12: Putin (ex-president) cabinet formed.	
	May 6	President Hu Jintao visits Japan, leading to Joint Statement between the Government of Japan and the Government of the People's Republic of China on the Comprehensive Promotion of a "Mutually Beneficial Relationship Based on Common Strategic Interests."	
	May 12	Great Sichuan Earthquake occurs, leaving 69,180 dead, 18,498 missing, and 374,176 injured.	
	May 28	Fourth Tokyo International Conference on African Development (TICAD IV) held in Yokohama.	
	Jun. 18	Japan and China release press statement on Cooperation between Japan and China in the East China Sea. Both countries agree to consult further.	
	Jul. 7	34th G8 Summit (Hokkaido Tōyako Summit) held (to Jul. 9).	
	Aug. 2	Fukuda cabinet reshuffled.	
	Aug. 8	(China) 2008 Summer Olympics opening ceremony in Beijing.	
	Sep. 1	Prime Minister Fukuda Yasuo announces resignation.	
	Sep. 15	(United States) Lehman Brothers records largest ever bankruptcy. Sep. 16: AIG Insurance bailed out by government. Sep. 25: Washington Mutual records largest bank failure in history. Sep. 29: Government's US$700 billion financial bailout plan, Proposal for Emergency Economic Stabilization Act, defeated and Dow Jones average has worst ever single-day loss, plummeting US$777.68. Oct. 3: Emergency Economic Stabilization Act enacted.	
	Sep. 16	Lehman Brothers Japan files for civil rehabilitation proceedings.	
	Sep. 18	Bank of Japan reaches swap agreement with United States and injects dollars into market for first time.	
	Sep. 22	Election held for LDP presidency. Asō Tarō wins. Sep. 24: Fukuda cabinet resigns en masse. LDP cabinet holds majority in House of Representatives and Asō cabinet formed.	Asō Tarō
	Sep. 25	Former prime minister Koizumi Junichirō announces intention to retire from political life.	
		United States nuclear-powered aircraft carrier USS *George Washington* docks at Yokosuka Naval Base.	
	Oct. 1	Japan International Cooperation Agency (JICA) reborn after merger with Japan Bank for International Cooperation's (JBIC) Overseas Economic Cooperation Operations.	
	Oct. 11	US removes North Korea from list of terrorist countries.	
	Nov. 14	Debut G20 Summit held in Washington, DC, as response to 2007–08 financial crisis and in recognition of need for greater global cooperation.	
	Nov. 28	JASDF ordered to withdraw from Iraq. Dec. 23: Return to Japan complete, excepting wrap-up personnel.	
	Dec. 8	Two Chinese government vessels trespass into Japanese waters around Senkaku Islands for first time.	

	Date	Event	Prime Minister
2009	Jan. 1	Japan starts 10th term as nonpermanent member on UN Security Council.	
	Jan. 20	(United States) Barack Obama inaugurated as president.	
	Feb. 14	Last JSDF troops repatriated from Iraq.	
	Feb. 18	Prime Minister Asō visits Sakhalin, Russia and meets with President Medvedev. First visit to Sakhalin by Japanese prime minister since World War II.	
	Mar. 30	JMSDF begins first overseas maritime security operation as part of effort to counter piracy in seas off Somalia. Facilities set up in Djibouti to support local activity.	
	Apr. 5	(United States) President Obama visits Prague and expresses "America's commitment to seek the peace and security of a world without nuclear weapons."	
	Aug. 30	45th general election held. DPJ wins decisively, with LDP suffering historic defeat and losing hold on government. (DPJ: 308; LDP: 119; Kōmeitō: 21; JCP: 9; SDP Japan: 7; Your Party: 5; People's New Party: 3; New Party Nippon: 1; Reform Club: 0; New Party Daichi: 1; Independents: 6.) Overseas ballots accepted even in single-seat constituencies. Koizumi Junichirō and Kōno Yōhei retire. LDP's Kaifu Toshiki and Kōmeitō president Ōta Akihiro lose their seats.	
	Sep. 16	172nd special session of Diet held (to Sep. 19). Yokomichi Takahiro of DPJ named speaker of House of Representatives. Asō cabinet resigns en masse, Hatoyama Yukio elected 93rd prime minister and forms coalition cabinet with SDP Japan and People's New Party.	Hatoyama Yukio
	Oct. 10	Prime Minister Hatoyama visits Beijing and releases Joint Statement on the 10th Anniversary of Trilateral Cooperation with China and South Korea. Hatoyama stresses importance of Japan-US relationship while pursuing Asia policy.	
	Nov. 13	US president Obama visits Japan (to Nov. 14).	
	Dec. 1	EU Lisbon Treaty comes into force. Herman van Rompuy becomes new EU president. 1 Jan. 2010: van Rompuy takes office.	
	Dec. 10	DPJ secretary-general Ozawa Ichiro visits China and holds talks with President Hu Jintao. Accompanied by delegation of 632 people, including 143 DPJ Diet members.	
	Dec. 24	Japan-China Joint History Research Committee concludes work and issues report.	
2010	Jan. 15	End of refueling foreign vessels in Indian Ocean as part of anti-terrorism effort.	
	Jan. 20	China overtakes Japan as second-largest economy (GNP) in world.	
	Mar. 31	Heisei wave of great municipal mergers ends. Number of municipalities almost halved to little over 1700.	
	Apr. 8	16th ASEAN Summit held in Hanoi, Vietnam.	
	Apr. 12	Prime Minister Hatoyama visits US to attend Nuclear Security Summit and meet with world leaders (to Apr. 13).	
	May 18	National Referendum Law passed requiring majority of votes to amend Constitution.	
	May 28	SDP Japan's Fukushima Mizuho dismissed as minister of state for consumer affairs and food safety due to disagreement over policy for relocating US Marine Corps Air Station Futenma. May 31: SDP Japan leaves coalition.	
	Jun. 4	Hatoyama cabinet resigns en masse. Kan Naoto elected DPJ leader and designated 94th prime minister by Diet. Jun. 8: Kan cabinet formed in coalition with People's New Party.	Kan Naoto

	Date	Event	Prime Minister
2010	Jul. 11	22nd election for House of Councillors held. (LDP: 51; DPJ: 44; Your Party: 10; Kōmeitō: 9; JCP: 3; SDP Japan: 2; Sunrise Party of Japan: 1; New Renaissance Party: 1; People's New Party: 0, Various and Independents: 0.) DPJ wins less than half of seats, leading to two houses being controlled by different parties.	Kan Naoto
	Aug. 10	Government moves ahead with discourse by Prime Minister Kan including "deep regret" on colonial past in run-up to centenary of Japan's annexation of Korea.	
	Sep. 7	Chinese trawler operating within Japan's territorial waters collides with Japanese Coast Guard patrol boats off Okinawa's Senkaku Islands. Sep. 8: Captain of trawler arrested. Sep. 25: Captain released without indictment. Nov. 4: Video of collision released on YouTube.	
	Sep. 17	First reshuffle of Kan cabinet.	
	Sep. 28	(North Korea) General Secretary Kim Jong-il's third son, Kim Jong-un, officially designated as successor.	
	Oct. 30	5th EAS held in Hanoi. Russia and US invited as special guests. Prime Minister Kan holds talks with Premier Wen Jiabao. Nov. 13: Kan meets with President Hu Jintao during APEC conference in Yokohama to confirm return to strategic mutually beneficial relationship.	
	Nov. 13	Asia-Pacific Economic Cooperation (APEC) meeting held in Yokohama (to Nov. 14). Prime Minister Kan meets with President Obama, President Hu Jintao, and President Medvedev.	
	Dec. 3	Diet Member Salary Law amended to calculate Diet members' allowances on per-diem basis.	
	Dec. 15	UN Security Council moves to end sanctions against Iraq.	
	Dec. 20	Japan and Korea sign agreement for Cooperation in the Peaceful Uses of Nuclear Energy.	
2011	Jan. 14	Second reshuffle of Kan cabinet.	
	Jan. 31	DPJ's Ozawa Ichirō becomes first Diet member ever to be indicted for violating Political Funds Control Law.	
	Feb. 5	United States and Russia launch Strategic Arms Reduction Treaty (New START).	
	Mar. 11	Great East Japan Earthquake occurs, followed by devastating tsunami, leaving 19,747 dead and 2,556 missing (as of 1 Mar. 2021), approx. 470,000 immediate evacuees, and triggering meltdown at Tokyo Electric Power's Fukushima Daiichi Nuclear Plant. Headquarters for Emergency Disaster Response set up and nuclear emergency announced.	
	Mar. 15	(Syria) Attacks on Syrian opposition become fiercer, nearing civil war.	
	May 2	United States assassinates Al-Qaeda leader Osama Bin Laden in Pakistan.	
	May 31	Japan-Peru Economic Partnership Agreement signed. Dec. 9: Approved by Diet. Effective 1 Mar. 2012.	
	Jul. 15	US forces begin withdrawal from Afghanistan.	
	Aug. 19	Kan cabinet decides on 4th Science and Technology Basic Plan which cites "strengthening national security and key technology" as R&D priority.	
	Aug. 29	Noda Yoshihiko becomes DPJ president. Aug. 30: Kan cabinet resigns en masse. Sep. 2: Noda Yoshihiko designated 95th prime minister and forms cabinet in coalition with People's New Party.	Noda Yoshihiko
	Nov. 12	Prime Minister Noda attends APEC leaders' meeting in Hawaii (to Nov. 13). Meets with President Obama and announces participation in negotiations for Trans-Pacific Partnership (TPP).	

Date	Event	Prime Minister
Dec. 14	US announces end of Iraq War.	
Dec. 17	(North Korea) Death of General Secretary Kim Jong-il.	
Dec. 20	Cabinet decides to dispatch PKO personnel to Republic of South Sudan, starting Jan. 2012.	
Dec. 27	Noda cabinet reviews and announces relaxation of Three Principles on Transfer of Defense Equipment and Technology at NSC.	
2012 Jan. 13	First reshuffle of Noda cabinet.	
Feb. 10	Reconstruction Agency starts operation following reorganization of East Japan Earthquake Reconstruction Headquarters.	
Mar. 4	(Russia) Putin elected president.	
Apr. 16	Tokyo governor Ishihara Shintarō in Washington, DC announces intention to purchase Senkaku Islands from private Japanese owner.	
Apr. 27	Act for Partial Revision of the Postal Service Privatization Act and others passed and enacted. May 8: Promulgated. Oct. 1: Japan Post Network Company and Japan Post Service Company merge to become Japan Post.	
May 5	All of Japan's nuclear power plants down. Jul. 1: Kansai Electric Power's Ōi Nuclear Power Station restarts reactors.	
May 7	(Russia) Third inauguration of Putin as president. May 8: Former president Medvedev appointed prime minister.	
Jun. 4	Second reshuffle of Noda cabinet.	
Jul. 31	Tokyo Electric Power receives ¥1 trillion from Nuclear Damage Compensation and Decommissioning Facilitation Corporation, effectively becoming nationalized.	
Sep. 11	Uotsuri shima, Kita Kojima, and Minami Kojima in Senkaku Islands nationalized. Security assured by Japan Coast Guard.	
Sep. 21	Noda Yoshihiko reelected as DPJ president.	
Sep. 26	Abe Shinzō elected LDP president.	
Oct. 1	Third reshuffle of Noda cabinet.	
Nov. 7	(United States) Obama wins reelection as president.	
Nov. 11	(Syria) Opposition parties unite to form National Coalition for Syrian Revolutionary and Opposition Forces. Recognized worldwide as legitimate representative.	
Nov. 15	Japan and North Korea open talks at Ministry of Foreign Affairs level (to Nov. 16).	
	(China) Xi Jinping becomes CCP general secretary.	
Nov. 16	Prime Minister Noda dissolves House of Representatives.	
Dec. 16	46th general election held. Major defeat for DPJ, win for LDP, and government hand-over. (LDP: 294; DPJ: 57; Japan Restoration Party: 54; Kōmeitō: 31; Your Party: 18; Tomorrow Party of Japan: 9; JCP: 8; SDP Japan: 2; People's New Party: 1; New Party Daichi: 1; New Party Nippon: 0; Independents: 5.) Dec. 25: LDP and Kōmeitō agree to form coalition. Both houses controlled by different parties.	
Dec. 26	182nd special session of Diet held (to Dec. 28). Ibuki Bunmei elected speaker of House of Representatives with Akamatsu Hirotaka vice-speaker. Noda cabinet resigns en masse, Abe Shinzō designated 96th prime minister and forms second Abe cabinet in coalition with Kōmeitō. First come-back prime minister in 64 years.	Abe Shinzō

	Date	Event	Prime Minister
2013	Jan. 22	Philippines institutes arbitral proceedings against China contesting validity of "nine-dash line" demarcating China's territorial claims in South China Sea.	Abe Shinzō
	Jan. 30	Prime Minister Abe makes first reference to revising Constitution in Diet, with relaxation of Article 96 rules as starting point.	
	Feb. 12	(North Korea) Third underground nuclear test. First test under Kim Jong-un. Mar. 7: UN Security Council sanctions North Korea.	
	Feb. 25	(South Korea) Park Geun-hye inaugurated as president.	
	Mar. 14	(China) Xi Jinping elected president at National People's Congress. Mar. 17: In first speech in office, promises "Chinese dream" of national rejuvenation. Sep. 7: Proposes early version of Belt and Road Initiative (BRI; formerly One Belt One Road, or OBOR).	
	Mar. 15	Prime Minister Abe officially announces participation in TPP negotiations.	
	Apr. 5	Japan and US reach agreement on return of land south of Kadena used by US military, premised on relocation of US Marine Corps Air Station Futenma to Nago vicinity in "fiscal year 2022 or later."	
	Apr. 29	Prime Minister Abe visits Russia and meets with President Putin, reaching agreement on speeding up talks concerning Northern Territories.	
	May 24	Bill related to instituting single ID number system for all residents (My Number) approved and adopted. Effective Jan. 2016.	
	Jun. 1	Fifth Tokyo International Conference on African Development (TICAD V) held in Yokohama.	
	Jun. 7	US president Barack Obama and Chinese president Xi Jinping meet in California (to Jun. 8).	
	Jul. 21	23rd election for House of Councillors. Resounding victory for LDP, winning 65 seats out of total of 121 and holding majority including Kōmeitō's 11 seats. Both houses brought under control by same party.	
	Jul. 23	Japan takes part in TPP negotiations for first time.	
	Sep. 7	Tokyo selected to host 2020 Olympic and Paralympic Games.	
	Nov. 27	Bill to establish National Security Council to manage government's foreign and national security policies approved by House of Councillors and adopted.	
	Dec. 4	National Security Council (NSC) established.	
	Dec. 6	Act on Protection of Specially Designated Secrets adopted.	
	Dec. 17	Government makes first decisions on National Security Strategy and lays out National Defense Program Guidelines for FY 2014 and Beyond and Medium-Term Defense Program (MTDP) for FY2014 to FY2018.	
	Dec. 26	Prime Minister Abe Shinzō visits Yasukuni Shrine one year after taking office in first visit as prime minister. China and South Korea declare strong opposition and US expresses "disappointment" in rare statement.	

Date	Event	Prime Minister
2014 Jan. 7	National Security Secretariat, operational arm of National Security Council, starts operating. Vice-Minister of Foreign Affairs Yachi Shōtarō appointed first head of agency.	
Jan. 27	Prime Minister Abe visits Republic of India, holds summit meeting with Prime Minister Manmohan Singh, and signs joint statement Intensifying the Strategic and Global Partnership.	
Apr. 1	Cabinet adopts The Three Principles on Transfer of Defense Equipment and Technology, replacing The Three Principles on Arms Exports and Their Related Policy Guidelines.	
	Consumption tax increased to 8% (was 5%). First increase in consumption tax in 17 years.	
Apr. 23	President Obama makes state visit to Japan. Apr. 24: Holds meeting with Prime Minister Abe. At joint press conference following meeting, president states that Senkaku Islands fall within Article 5 defense obligations under Treaty of Mutual Cooperation and Security between Japan and United States.	
May 15	Commission on Article 9 organized by Prime Minister Abe declares exercise of collective self-defense and participation in UN collective-security activities permissible under current Constitution. May 27: Ruling coalition parties discuss right of collective self-defense. Government puts forward 15 examples and one reference case. Jul. 1: At special cabinet meeting, government reverses previous cabinets' interpretation of Constitution and approves exercise of right of collective self-defense. Says necessary minimum use of military force permitted if conditions pose existential threat to nation.	
May 27	Ruling coalition parties discuss right of collective self-defense. Government puts forward 15 examples and a reference case.	
Jun. 13	National Referendum Law amended, with minimum voting age set at 18 years old.	
Jun. 29	Iraq Syria Islamic State (ISIS) declares own state in region of northern Iraq. Changes name to Islamic State (IS).	
Aug. 8	US and other members of coalition of willing start aerial attacks on IS bases within Iraq.	
Sep. 3	Second Abe cabinet reshuffled. Twelve changes among 18 cabinet members. Largest number of women ever, with 5 female cabinet members.	
Sep. 6	Prime Minister Abe visits Bangladesh and holds summit meeting with H.E. Sheikh Hasina, prime minister of People's Republic of Bangladesh. Sep. 7: Abe holds summit meeting with President Mahinda Rajapaksa in Sri Lanka and releases Joint Statement between Sri Lanka and Japan.	
Sep. 21	Japan Innovation Party formed with merger of Japan Restoration Party and Unity Party. Hashimoto Tōru and Eda Kenji elected as joint leaders.	
Sep. 26	(Hong Kong) Students opposing pro-democracy candidates not being allowed to take part in election for Hong Kong chief executive start demonstrations and roadblocks (Umbrella Revolution) (to Dec. 15).	
Oct. 8	Interim Report on the Revision of the Guidelines for Japan-US Defense Cooperation released by Japanese and US governments.	
Dec. 10	Act on the Protection of Specially Designated Secrets (SDS Act) comes into effect.	
Dec. 14	47th general election held. LDP and Kōmeitō gain seats for total of 326, more than two-thirds (317) of total.	
Dec. 24	188th special session of Diet held (to Dec. 26). Third Abe coalition cabinet inaugurated.	

	Date	Event	Prime Minister
2015	Jan. 24	IS releases video footage of execution of hostage Yukawa Haruna. Feb. 1: Video footage of execution of Gotō Kenji released.	Abe Shinzō
	Feb. 10	Cabinet decides on Development Cooperation Charter	
	Mar. 28	China issues official outline for BRI.	
	Apr. 29	Prime Minister Abe addresses US Congress, expressing regret over World War II and committing to maintaining security treaty.	
	May 14	At special cabinet meeting, government decides on proposal for Legislation for Peace and Security, enabling limited exercise of right of collective self-defense. May 26: Explanation of bills in House of Representatives and start of deliberations.	
	May 17	Referendum conducted on abolishing city of Osaka and dividing it into five special wards (Osaka Metropolis Plan) defeated by narrow margin and rejected. Dec. 18: Osaka Mayor Hashimoto Tōru announces retirement from politics effective as of end of term.	
	Jun. 4	House of Representatives holds meeting of Commission on the Constitution. All three invited Constitutional scholars declare Legislation for Peace and Security unconstitutional.	
	Jun. 29	Signing ceremony for Chinese-initiated Asian Infrastructure Investment Bank (AIIB) held in Beijing. Dec. 25: Articles of Agreement come into effect.	
	Jul. 20	US and Cuba re-establish diplomatic relations after 54-year hiatus and open embassies in each other's capitals.	
	Aug. 14	At special cabinet meeting, government settles on Prime Minister Abe's remarks on 70th anniversary of end of World War II. Prime Minister Abe expresses "deep regret and heartfelt apologies" for World War II.	
	Sep. 8	Election held for LDP presidency. Prime Minister Abe reelected without vote.	
	Sep. 19	Legislation for Peace and Security passes House of Representatives and adopted. Conditions placed on exercise of right of collective self-defense and limits placed on logistics support by JSDF. Vote takes three continuous days (Dawn Diet). Sep. 30: Laws relating to maintenance of security promulgated.	
	Sep. 25	2030 Agenda for Sustainable Development (SDGs) adopted at United Nations General Assembly in New York.	
	Oct. 5	Joint meeting of 12 countries considering joining TPP yields statement of agreement on major elements.	
	Oct. 7	Third Abe cabinet reshuffled. Major ministers remain unchanged. Nine new cabinet members appointed.	
	Oct. 27	United States Aegis destroyer sails within 12 nautical mile limit of man-made islands built by China in South China Sea as part of operation Freedom of Navigation.	
	Nov. 7	China's president Xi Jinping and Taiwan's President Ma Ying-jeou meet in Singapore, marking first cross-strait heads of state meeting since 1949 split.	
	Dec. 12	21st session of Conference of the Parties (COP21) to the United Nations Framework Convention on Climate Change, Paris Agreement, signed.	
	Dec. 28	Japanese and Korean foreign ministers meet in Seoul, reaching agreement (final and irreversible resolution) on comfort women issue. Japan acknowledges involvement of Imperial Japanese Army and responsibility of Japanese government and will contribute ¥1 billion to fund set up by Korea.	
2016	Jan. 1	Japan starts term as nonpermanent member on UN Security Council.	

Date	Event	Prime Minister
Jan. 16	(Taiwan) Presidential election held. Democratic Progressive Party's Tsai Ing-wen elected as Taiwan's first female president.	
	US, UK, Germany, France, Russia, and China announce lifting of sanctions against Iran following Iran Nuclear Deal.	
	AIIB declared open for business.	
Feb. 4	12 participating countries reach agreement and sign TPP Agreement.	
May 9	International Consortium of Investigative Journalists analyzes "Panama Papers," finds over 210,000 corporations in tax havens located in 21 jurisdictions, and releases list of corporations and people involved, including 400 Japanese companies and individuals.	
May 21	Prime Minister Abe announces Partnership for Quality Infrastructure at 21st International Conference on the Future of Asia in Tokyo. Japan agrees to provide approx. US$110 billion in Asia in collaboration with Asian Development Bank (ADB) over following five years.	
May 26	G7 Summit held in Ise-Shima, Mie Prefecture. May 27: Leaders issue declaration on avoiding global economic crisis.	
May 27	President Obama makes first-ever visit to Hiroshima, site of first atomic bombing, in official capacity as US president and lays wreath at memorial cenotaph for atomic bomb victims.	
Jun. 23	(United Kingdom) Brexit referendum on leaving EU passes with 52% voting to leave. Jun. 24: Prime Minister David Cameron announces his resignation. Jul. 13: Theresa May becomes prime minister.	
Jul. 1	Twenty hostages, including seven Japanese, killed in terrorist attack in Dhaka, Bangladesh.	
Jul. 8	Civil war erupts in South Sudan.	
Jul. 10	24th election for House of Councillors held. Pro-Constitutional reform LDP and Kōmeitō secure two thirds in both houses. Candidates jointly backed by opposition parties win 11 single-seat constituencies.	
Jul. 12	In suit filed against People's Republic of China at Permanent Court of Arbitration in The Hague, court rules for Philippines, rejecting China's claim to territorial waters in South China Sea as having "no legal foundation."	
Aug. 3	Second reshuffle of third Abe cabinet.	
Aug. 8	In video message to people, emperor expresses wish to abdicate, stating that age may make it difficult "to carry out [his] duties as the symbol of the State."	
Aug. 27	Sixth Tokyo International Conference on African Development (TICAD VI) held in Nairobi, Kenya (to Aug. 28). Prime Minister Abe announces Free and Open Indo-Pacific strategy (later "vision").	
Nov. 9	(United States) Donald Trump officially declared winner of presidential election.	
Nov. 15	Cabinet decision to assign JGSDF personnel taking part in PKO activities in South Sudan new duties (rush to rescue) in line with national security-related laws.	
Dec. 9	TPP and related legislation approved in House of Councillors.	
Dec. 13	Osprey aircraft from US Marine Corps Air Station Futenma crashes off Nago coast, causing serious injuries.	
Dec. 20	Supreme Court rejects appeal by Okinawa Governor Onaga Takashi against government lawsuit on overturning approval for landfill work in Henoko in preparation for relocation of US Marine Corps Air Station Futenma.	
Dec. 27	On visit to Hawaii Prime Minister Abe visits USS *Arizona* memorial to victims of attack on Pearl Harbor with President Obama.	

	Date	Event	Prime Minister
2017	Jan. 23	(United States) President Trump sign executive order to withdraw from TPP Agreement.	Abe Shinzō
	Mar. 5	LDP extends terms for party president to three consecutive three-year terms.	
	Mar. 10	Government decides to withdraw JGSDF personnel posted to South Sudan as part of PKO. May 27: Withdrawal complete.	
	Mar. 29	(United Kingdom) Government makes official announcement of withdrawal from EU.	
	Apr. 25	Government starts landfill work in Henoko, Okinawa, in preparation for relocation of US Marine Corps Air Station Futenma.	
	May 3	On 70th anniversary of Constitution, Prime Minister Abe announces target date of 2020 for enactment of amendments.	
	May 9	(South Korea) Moon Jae-in of Democratic Party, largest left-leaning opposition party, wins presidential election (to May 10).	
	May 14	Summit meeting in Beijing on BRI to create Chinese-influenced economic sphere (to May 15).	
	May 27	JSDF withdraws from PKO in South Sudan.	
	Jun. 1	(United States) President Trump announces withdrawal from Paris Agreement on measures to counter global warming. Other countries confirm determination to adhere to agreement.	
	Jul. 4	(North Korea) Hwasong-14 Intercontinental Ballistic Missile (ICBM) fired. Hawaii and Alaska within range. Jul. 28: Successful second firing of Hwasong-14.	
	Aug. 3	Third reshuffle of third Abe cabinet.	
	Oct. 22	48th general election for House of Representatives held. Major victory for LDP which, together with Kōmeitō, retains two thirds of seats.	
	Nov. 1	195th special Diet session held (to Dec. 9). Abe Shinzō elected 98th prime minister and forms fourth Abe cabinet (all ministers remaining unchanged).	
	Nov. 9	(China) President Trump visits China and meets with Premier Xi Jinping. Conclusion of trade negotiations worth about US$250 billion announced.	
	Nov. 11	11 TPP countries (12 minus United States) agree on outline of new Comprehensive and Progressive Agreement for Trans-Pacific Partnership (CPTPP, or TPP11 Agreement). 8 Mar. 2018: TPP11 Agreement signed by 11 nations. 30 Dec. 2018: TPP11 Agreement enters into force.	
	Nov. 20	(United States) President Trump returns North Korea to list of state sponsors of terrorism for first time since 2008.	
	Dec. 19	US National Security Strategy released, condemning China and Russia as threats to national security.	
2018	Jan. 4	(South Korea) President Moon Jae-in says "Japan-Korea agreement on comfort women was mistake."	
	Mar. 18	(Russia) Presidential election held. Putin reelected for fourth term with 76% of vote.	
	Apr. 27	North-South Korea summit meeting at Panmunjom between South Korean president Moon Jae-in and North Korean Workers' Party general secretary Kim Jong-un.	
	May 8	President Trump announces withdrawal from six country Joint Comprehensive Plan of Action (JCPOA) concluded in 2015 to curb Iran's nuclear activities and resumes sanctions.	

Date	Event	Prime Minister
Jun. 12	President Trump and General Secretary Kim Jong-un meet in Singapore in historic first US-North Korea summit meeting. Joint communiqué specifies complete denuclearization of Korean Peninsula and commits US to provide "security guarantees."	
Jun. 29	Laws relating to workplace reform, including high-level professional system and upper limit regulation penalizing excess overtime, adopted.	
Jul. 17	Japan and EU leaders sign Economic Partnership Agreement (EPA). Effective Feb. 2019.	
Sep. 20	Election held for LDP presidency. Abe Shinzō wins third term, defeating Ishiba Shigeru. Abe gains 553 votes against Ishiba's 254, but Ishiba remains popular in provinces.	
Oct. 2	Fourth Abe cabinet reshuffled, with 13 new members.	
Oct. 4	(United States) Vice President Mike Pence delivers critical speech about China during address on administration's policy at Hudson Institute.	
2019 Feb. 1	Start of Japan-EU EPA. Birth of major trading area accounting for one third of global GDP and 40% of world trade.	
	(United States) President Trump makes official announcement of complete withdrawal from Intermediate-Range Nuclear Forces (INF) Treaty with Russia. Collapse of INF Treaty.	
Apr. 30	Emperor Akihito abdicates, becoming emperor emeritus.	
May 1	Emperor Naruhito accedes to throne. Era name changes from Heisei to Reiwa.	

About the Authors

Kitaoka Shinichi

President, Japan International Cooperation Agency (JICA)
Professor Emeritus, University of Tokyo

Dr. Kitaoka is president of the Japan International Cooperation Agency (JICA) and professor emeritus of the University of Tokyo and Rikkyo University. He studied at the University of Tokyo specializing in modern Japanese politics and diplomacy (B.A. in 1971, Ph.D. in 1976). He taught at Rikkyo University (1976–97) and his alma mater (1997–2004, 2006–12), while serving as ambassador extraordinary and plenipotentiary to the United Nations (2004–06). He later became president of the International University of Japan (IUJ, 2012–15). He has been on the advisory panels for many prime ministers and foreign ministers. He was the acting chair of the Advisory Panel on Reconstruction of the Legal Basis for Security (2007–08, 2013–14), of the Advisory Panel on the History of the 20th Century and on Japan's Role and the World Order in the 21st Century (2015), and of the Advisory Panel on Security and Defense Capabilities (2018). He received the Imperial Medal with Purple Ribbon in 2011.

Kokubun Ryosei

Former President, National Defense Academy (NDA) of Japan

Kokubun served as president of the National Defense Academy (NDA) of Japan from 2012 to 2021 and has been professor emeritus at Keio University since 2019. After completing his undergraduate and graduate degrees at Keio University, he began teaching there as an assistant professor in 1981. Kokubun became an associate professor in 1985 and a professor in 1992 going on to serve as director of Keio's Institute of East Asian Studies from 1999 to 2007 and dean of the university's Faculty of Law and Politics from 2007 to 2011. He has been a visiting scholar at Harvard University, the University of Michigan, Fudan University, Beijing University, and National Taiwan University. Kokubun's research interests encompass Chinese politics and international relations in East Asia. He is a former president of the Japan Association of International Relations and the Japan Association for Asian Studies, he has published and edited numerous English publications as well as Japanese, including *Japan-China Relations through the Lens of Chinese Politics* (Japan Publishing Industry Foundation for Culture, 2021) and *Japan-China Relations in the Modern Era* (Routledge, 2017). He was awarded the Asia-Pacific Prize (The Mainichi Shimbun) in 1997, the Suntory Prize for Social Sciences and Humanities (Suntory Foundation) in 2004, and the Kashiyama Prize (Kashiyama Foundation) in 2017.

Nakanishi Hiroshi

Professor, Kyoto University

Nakanishi is professor of International Politics in the Law Department at Kyoto University. He served as dean of the School of Government of Kyoto University from 2016 to 2018. He studied at the Graduate School of Law of Kyoto University and Department of History of the University of Chicago. He became an associate professor at Kyoto University in 1991 and professor in 2002. His major interests include the historical development of international relations in the Asia-Pacific in the twentieth century, historical development of international relations theories, and Japanese foreign and security policy. He served as president of the Japan Association of International Relations from 2014 to 2016. His major publications include *Kokusaiseiji towa nanika* [What Is International Politics?] (Chūōkōron-Shinsha, 2003, Yomiuri Yoshino Sakuzo Prize winner), *Kokusaiseijigaku* [International Politics] (Yūhikaku, 2013, co-written with Ishida Atsushi and Tadokoro Masayuki), and *Kōsaka Masataka to sengo Nihon* [Kōsaka Masataka and Postwar Japan] (Chūōkōron-Shinsha, 2016, co-edited with Iokibe Makoto).

Shiraishi Takashi
Chancellor, Prefectural University of Kumamoto

Shiraishi majored in international relations at the University of Tokyo in 1972 and obtained his Ph.D. in history from Cornell University in 1986. Shiraishi has lectured at the University of Tokyo (1979–87), Cornell University (1987–98), Kyoto University (1996–2005), and the National Graduate Institute for Policy Studies (GRIPS, 2005–09). He served as an executive member of the Council for Science and Technology Policy (CSTP), Cabinet Office (2009–12), and president of GRIPS (2011–17). In 2007, he received the Imperial Medal with Purple Ribbon. Shiraishi has published many books, including three award-winning books: *An Age in Motion* (Cornell University Press, 1990); *Indoneshia: Kokka to seiji* [Government and Politics in Indonesia] (Libroport Co., 1990); and *Umi no teikoku: Ajia o dou kangaeru ka* (Chūōkōron-Shinsha, 2000), a recipient of the Yomiuri Yoshino Sakuzo Prize, translated as *Empire of the Seas* by Japan Publishing Industry Foundation for Culture in 2021. His other works include *Chūgoku wa Higashi-Ajia o dou kaeruka* [How Is China Changing East Asia?] (co-authored with Caroline Sy Hau, Chūōkōron-Shinsha, 2012), and *Kaiyō Ajia vs. tairiku Ajia* (Minerva Shobō, 2016), translated as *Maritime Asia vs. Continental Asia* by Lynne Rienner Publishers in 2021.

Tanaka Akihiko
President, National Graduate Institute for Policy Studies (GRIPS)

Tanaka is president of the National Graduate Institute for Policy Studies (GRIPS). He served as president of the Japan International Cooperation Agency (JICA) from 2012 to 2015. Tanaka was also executive vice president of the University of Tokyo (2009–11). He is chairman of the board, Japan, for UNHCR, and a distinguished fellow at the JICA Ogata Research Institute. He obtained his bachelor's degree in international relations at the University of Tokyo in 1977 and Ph.D. in political science at the Massachusetts Institute of Technology in 1981. He has numerous books and articles on world politics and security issues in Japanese and English including *The New Middle Ages. The World System in the 21st Century* (The International House of Japan, 2002) and *Japan in Asia: Post-Cold-War Diplomacy* (Japan Publishing Industry Foundation for Culture, 2017). He received the Imperial Medal with Purple Ribbon in 2012.

（英文版）論文集 平成日本を振り返る　第一巻 外交、安全保障
Examining Heisei Japan: Diplomacy and Security, Vol. I

2021 年 8 月 31 日　第 1 刷発行

監修・著者　北岡伸一

著　者　国分良成、白石 隆、田中明彦、中西 寛

企　画　公益財団法人日本国際問題研究所

発 行 所　一般財団法人出版文化産業振興財団
　　　　　〒101-0051 東京都千代田区神田神保町2-2-30
　　　　　電話　03-5211-7283
　　　　　ホームページ　https://www.jpic.or.jp/

印刷・製本所　大日本印刷株式会社

English text © Kitaoka Shinichi, Kokubun Ryosei, Nakanishi Hiroshi, Shiraishi Takashi, Tanaka Akihiko
Printed in Japan
ISBN 978-4-86658-116-3